THE LOVING BOND:

Companion Animals In The Helping Professions

THE LOVING BOND:

Companion Animals In The Helping Professions

Phil Arkow, Editor
for the Latham Foundation

R & E Publishers, Inc.
P.O. Box 2008
Saratoga, CA 95070

Phil Arkow is Education and Publicity Director for the Humane Society of the Pikes Peak Region, in Colorado Springs, Colo., where he has maintained a personal and professional interest in the unique bond between people and pets and the therapeutic applications of this linkage since pioneering the "Petmobile" program in 1973. A native of Philadelphia, Pa., he earned a B.A. in English literature from the University of Pennsylvania and was a professional newspaper journalist for a number of years before entering the animal care and control field. He was a co-founder and served as Executive Secretary of the National Animal Control Association and has been active in numerous state and national animal welfare organizations. He lectures frequently at human/companion animal bond conferences and at training seminars for animal shelter personnel. He is the author of "Pet Therapy": A Study and Resource Guide to the Use of Companion Animals in Selected Therapies. *His writings have appeared in numerous professional and mass-market publications.*

Published by R&E Publishers, P.O. Box 2008, Saratoga, CA 95070, (408) 866-6303. Printed in the United States of America.

ISBN # 0-88247-763-3 LC # 86-62713

Cover photo: John Morgan

Table of Contents

Preface

Since this book was first published in 1984 as *Dynamic Relationships in Practice: Animals in the Helping Professions,* there has developed an even more widespread interest in and acceptance of pet-facilitated therapy (PFT). There has emerged a tremendous proliferation of local human/animal bond committees and community programs, of service agencies and regional councils. Both scientific and applied interests are actively exploring the interdisciplinary aspects of what happens when people and animals come together.

Today, the public is sensitized to the concept that pets may be therapeutic for people, an idea which was somewhat strange when it was advanced little more than a decade ago. Today, colleges offer courses in the human/animal bond and applied therapy, veterinary students learn the ethical and emotional aspects they will use with future clients, and PFT specialists secure legislation to assist people with special needs who benefit from animals in their environments. Prisons are implementing vocational training programs for inmates in dog or horse training. New books, research papers and published proceedings of scholarly conferences are continually being added to the corpus of knowledge of this new field.

That PFT has emerged as its own specialization is remarkable — particularly in the light that any holistic concept could gain support in a high-tech age of specialization. Its interdisciplinary nature is bringing together doctors, veterinarians, recreational therapists, social workers, psychologists, chaplains, humane organizations, and dozens of others, all with a common goal: to improve the welfare of people and pets with special needs in practical programs. The documentation for their work is being conducted in an ever-widening circle of academic interest comprised of disciplines from anthropology to zoology, at hundreds of universities around the world. And we've only just begun to scratch the surface of man's special symbiosis with the companion animals that share our homes, our lives and our planet.

When the idea for this book was conceived by the Latham Foundation, it was envisioned as a "compendium" — a brief and concise guidebook of useful, practical information for the student or applied practitioner engaged in a PFT program. The first edition was neither as concise nor as brief as initially planned, due to the remarkable proliferation of information and applications. But it was practical, and quickly became a standard reference in this new field. This second edition, which contains much of the original text and noteworthy updates to keep pace with the growth of the field, is anticipated to continue in the same tradition to an even more widespread readership.

Like its predecessor, *The Loving Bond* attempts to bridge the gap which sometimes exists between the scientists, with their need for documented experimentation and published papers, and the program specialists, with their need for workable ideas. Consequently, we have sought a middle ground: the authors are all widely-recognized and often scholarly authorities in their areas of expertise, but the writing is aimed at practical applications. As with any new specialization, the scientific foundation is still questionable and data and documentation, though becoming more available, are still inadequate. Boris Levinson, often considered PFT's "founding father", considered this dilemma:

> *"On the one hand, this discipline touches upon problems that might well be investigated by rigorous, scientific experimentation. On the other hand, it involves enquiry where measurement cannot bring answers and intuition must reign — a path of study used by artists, as well as by generations of ordinary people. Both approaches are, in my opinion, equally valid and equally worthwhile."*

The Loving Bond begins with a unique Foreword by Levinson — believed to be his last published writing before his death. Section I deals with the historical and contemporary overviews of man's symbioses with animals. Section II explores human psychology, animal behavior, the ethical and symbolic impacts of animals in our midst, grief management, and some basic legal issues confronting PFT specialists.

With Section III, we look at PFT programs in action: applications for the visually-impaired, the physically-limited, the home-based elderly, the institutionalized, as well as farm-based and equestrian therapy programs. In Section IV, we explore programs from some of the many disciplines involved: veterinarians, nursing homes, humane societies, and state regulatory agencies.

Section V provides the PFT specialist with ideas for initiating programs, through publicity, volunteer management and long-range planning and development. Section VI is a reference guide, listing resource organizations, publications, and major areas of academic research to stimulate further study.

Readers will note an absence of footnotes in these pages. As this is not a scholarly journal, and since the corpus of written material about PFT is still so limited, the publishers felt the reader seeking details about an author's statements could obtain this information from other means. Consequently, each chapter contains a list of Suggested Readings, most of which provided the substantiation for each article. The Resource Reading List in Section VI contains most of the basic books on the subject, many of which include scholarly footnotes.

For the reader seeking still more clarification, the authors in *The Loving Bond* have graciously consented to be available for questions. Readers are invited to write for information at the following addresses:

R.K Anderson
CENSHARE, School of Public Health, Univ. of Minnesota,
515 Delaware St. S.E., Minneapolis, MN 55455
Phil Arkow, Humane Society of the Pikes Peak Region,
P.O. Box 187, Colorado Springs, CO 80901
Jennifer Bassing, Guide Dogs for the Blind,
P.O. Box 1200, San Rafael, CA 94915
Bonita Bergin, Canine Companions for Independence,
P.O. Box 446, Santa Rosa, CA 95402
Carol Browning, 6182 South 2855 East, Ogden, UT 84403
Stanley L. Diesch, College of Veterinary Medicine
University of Minnesota, Minneapolis, MN 55455
Ian Dunbar, Center for Applied Animal Behavior
2000 Center St. #1406, Berkeley, CA 94704
James Harris, Montclair Veterinary Hospital,
1961 Mountain Blvd., Oakland, CA 94611
William Kay, Carole Fudin and Susan Cohen, Animal Medical Center,
510 E. 62nd St., New York, NY 10021
Aline & Robert Kidd, Mills College/VA Medical Center,
203 Vallecito Lane, Walnut Creek, CA 94596
Dan Lago and Barbara Knight, Gerontology Center,
S-110 Henderson Human Development Bldg.,
Pennsylvania State University, University Park, PA 16802
David Lee, Oakwood Forensic Center,
3200 N. West St., Lima, OH 45801
Juana Lyon, Companion Animal Association of Arizona,
1050 W. Laguna Azul Ave., Mesa, AZ 85202

Lida McCowan, The Cheff Center, P.O. Box 171, Augusta, MI 49012
Cappy McLeod, 313 N. Tejon St., #14, Colorado Springs, CO 80903
Joseph W. Meeker,
Route 2, Box 256A, Vashon Island, WA 98070
Clarice Seufert, Health Resources Div., Minnesota Dept. of Health, P.O. Box 9441, Minneapolis, MN 55440
Hugh Tebault, The Latham Foundation,
Clement & Schiller Streets, Alameda CA 94501
Robert ten Bensel, School of Public Health, Univ. of Minnesota, 1360 Mayo Memorial Bldg.,Box 197, 420 Delaware St. S.E., Minneapolis, MN 55455
Sally O. Walshaw, Michigan State University,
A-136 East Fee Hall, East Lansing, MI 48824

Numerous concerns still confront the PFT specialist. Though no one seriously involved with PFT considers it a panacea, the popular press has dramatized successful programs to the point where program failures are often overlooked. Research into PFT among institutionalized populations often obscures the need to investigate the roles of animals in the lives of the vast majority of the public who live happily and healthily at home with animals. There is still a semantic debate as to whether what enthusiastic, albeit untrained, specialists call "therapy" is therapeutic in the strictist sense of the word. Debates are heard regarding the need for certification and standardization of program guidelines. The recent crisis in the insurance industry hit many programs hard. The scientific community is still seeking accurate methodologies and measurement instruments to detect and measure the effects of pets. Animal rights advocates warn against degrading the animals in PFT programs as mere tools or objects of scientific inquiry, or as what philosopher Bernard Rollin called "disposable psychological fixes, even for people in need."

PFT is today's variation on an old and inexplicable theme: our attempt to deal with the wonders of nature and the realities of man in nature, with the paradox of our fond admiration and not-so-kind use of animals, with the respect and fear inherent in confronting those that are like us — and not quite like us.

PFT has a long way to grow and I am thankful for the opportunity The Latham Foundation has given me to be a part of it. The growth is stimulating. In his remarkable Foreword, Levinson notes how, a mere 20 years ago, he predicted that pets could be "co-therapists" and how 10 years ago he argued that veterinarians would become instrumental in human mental health. Both predictions have already come true. In this, his last published writing before his death, he suggests that one day, pets will accompany us beyond the bounds of this planet we call Earth to relieve the loneliness of interstellar travel.

While we await what Levinson calls "a quiet revolution," there is much work and documentation to be done. In her closing chapter, Carol Browning writes, "Even without the proof of quantitative research we believe that diverse groups working together with a positive attitude can help create a world that respects the dignity and worth of all life."

I want to acknowledge the people and animals that helped this book, like its predecessor, become a reality: Hugh Tebault and The Latham Foundation, for their foresight and direction; the Humane Society of the Pikes Peak Region, for initiating the Petmobile programs and for their indulgence in supporting this work; my wife, Melody, for her understanding; and our dog, "Millard," for reminding me every day, in his own quiet way, of what it's all about.

Phil Arkow
Colorado Springs, Colo.

Foreword

Boris Levinson

"...a quiet revolution..."

Introduction

During the last fifty years a quiet revolution has occurred in our understanding of and our relationship with the animal kingdom.

It has become quite apparent that our relationship with the animal kingdom contains the nexus of our relationship with nature and human beings. A new understanding has arisen that we are responsible for all life, animals as well as human; that our survival depends on preserving animals and seeing them as our friends and equals. We have come to see that flora and fauna, including man, exist in an indissoluble bond in nature which we destroy at our peril.

We have come to some realizations about our world that leave us feeling alone in an inhospitable universe. We no longer see our planet as the centerpiece but as a mere speck in the whirling dynamics of the expanding universe. We know that the earth is evolving like a living being and that the only constant in this universe is change. We realize that we are not even a small pebble on the beach. As individuals we are not very important and our lives are only a second in the stretch of eternity. We feel lonely. We need companions, friends, allies.

Our natural allies are animals, our fellow sojourners on earth. Without

Generally recognized as one of the "founding fathers" of the human/companion animal bond movement, Boris M. Levinson, Ph.D., pioneered the use of animals in psychotherapy with his "co-therapist" dog, "Jingles." He was the author of numerous books and articles on pets and their roles in human development and child psychotherapy. Prior to his death in 1984, he was Professor Emeritus of psychology at Yeshiva University in New York and a fellow in numerous professional societies.

them we would perish. We must therefore be responsible for animals, learn to understand them and cooperate with them. We must make life happier, more desirable for them and thus, in turn, for ourselves.

Animals are witnesses to an unwritten compact between us and nature. Their survival is a guarantee that human life will also continue on this planet.

Some of us have stopped thinking of animals as inferior beings, but rather as sentient creatures belonging to a different species; not like us in many ways but not inferior to us.

Some people have concluded that our relationship with the animal kingdom has to change. They believe that we must find means of stopping the slaughter of animals for food, that animal experimentation should be stopped, that laws have to be passed forbidding the sale of animals in pet shops, that the acquisition and disposal of animals must be regulated.

We may ask why this interest in animal companions has arisen at this point in our history and why when we are so concerned about the future of mankind on earth, do we tie its survival to the future of animal life. Of course, such interest does not arise full blown as from the head of Athena, but stems from currents, cleavages, changes in our social climate.

If we were to study the history of art, religion and literature (both oral and written) in diverse societies, whether these be pastoral, hunting, tribal, or industrialized and technological, looking also at the different ethnic cultures within these societies, we might be able to trace how man has tried to come to terms with himself as a "reasoning animal." We might then be able to determine what has happened to human social relationships and the human stewardship of natural resources when animals have been either elevated or denigrated in relation to man.

History of the relationship between man and animal

Like humans, many animals high on the evolutionary scale love, hate, grieve, support each other, have a sense of guilt, compassion, feelings of elation and depression and even emotional problems. There is not a widespread acknowledgment of this fact in our industrialized urbanized technological society where animals are viewed more as nonsentient property than as fellow creatures, much as human slaves have been viewed over the centuries. Pet owners who are attuned to their animals often know otherwise (just as slave owners must have known of the human feelings of their "property" while simultaneously denying their existence). Yet even some of these owners, pressured by a paucity of living space, geographic mobility and the antipathy of a society which views companion animals as a nuisance, choose to regard the animals in their charge more as toys or furniture, to be discarded or ignored when inconvenient, than as responsive organisms much like themselves.

This has not always been the case. Animals were an integral part of primitive man's universe. Early cultures regarded them as equals and partners, or even as superiors. The Dobu Islanders of the Western Pacific stress the solidarity between man and dog. The dog is more important than human acquaintances and occasionally even more important than a wife. Among some primitive tribes even today there is little difference between animal young and human young in that animal puppies and human babies are indiscriminately suckled at the breast of the nursing mothers of the tribe. This is seen in Australia, New Guinea and the Guaharabi of the Amazon forests. A counterpart to this practice is described in legends of animals suckling human infants, e.g. the wolf which fed Romulus and Remus, the founders of Rome. Early cultures attributed to animals the same characteristics they attributed to the human soul, namely, life and death, will and judgment. In various Indian cultures humans were considered "primus inter pares" rather than superiors in relation to animals. Anthropologists have described savages who talked quite seriously to animals, whether alive or dead, just as they would to men, alive or dead, offering them homage and asking their pardon when it was their painful duty to hunt and kill them. Many primitive tribes believed that animals had souls, so that they killed animals to have them accompany a dead person to the netherworld. Some Eskimo tribes would slay a dog when a child died and put the dog's head in the child's grave so it could lead the child's soul to the land of the dead. Some primitive peoples believed, and still believe, that humans originally descended from specific animals. The presumed animal ancestor is designated as the tribe's totem and viewed as its tutelary spirit and protector. The members of the totem are under a sacred obligation not to destroy their totem and to abstain from eating its meat or deriving any other enjoyment from it.

In the ancient world, animals were viewed as rational beings and partners. The sacred dogs of China had a special place in the Emperor's court. They also helped form the Emperor's bodyguard. In ancient Egypt, cats were held in great esteem. Since it was believed that the cat was immortal, a special effort was made to preserve the body so that the soul could have a place to return to. The cat was embalmed, placed in a coffin and buried in a sacred vault in a stretch of land along the banks of the Nile reserved as the burial place for cats. The cat's "family" members would shave their eyebrows as a sign of mourning. The Hittites believed that God had a dog and one of their kings addressed the Sun god in his prayers as "the lord who daily sits in judgment upon man, dog and pig."

Early Judeo-Christian tradition emphasized the fact that animals had feelings and could grieve and reason. They were believed to pray to God, obey His commandments and be responsible for their actions. Among the Hebrews, an ox which killed a human being was subject to the death penalty by stoning. In the Jewish tradition rules were set down regarding the treatment of animals: an overloaded animal must be relieved of its burden; the feelings of mother animals had to be respected; a young animal must not be slaughtered during the first week of life; an adult and its young might not be killed on the same day. The rabbis discouraged hunting as causing acute grief among animals, encouraging vegetarianism instead. Animals were recognized to differ from each other in their behavior. Thus, the ravens fed Elijah, the lions did not eat Daniel, but the whale swallowed Jonah. Animals owned by Jews were covered by Jewish religious customs: for example, resting on the Sabbath.

The following story from the Talmud illustrates this:

> "Once upon a time an Israelite who owned a ploughing-heifer became poor and sold her to a pagan. He took her and ploughed with her during the weekdays. On the Sabbath, he brought her out, as before, to plough, but she lay down under the yoke. Though he beat the heifer, she would not budge. Seeing this, he went to the Israelite who had sold the heifer and said, 'Come and take your heifer, perhaps she is grieving for her former owner, for though I beat her, she will not move.' The Israelite understood that the reason why the heifer would not plough was because it was the Sabbath day, on which she was accustomed to rest, so he said to the pagan, 'I will come and raise her.' When he came he whispered into her ear, 'Heifer, heifer, you know well that when you were mine you ploughed all the week and you rested on the Sabbath, but now, through my sins, you have passed to a pagan master. I beseech you, rise and plough.' The heifer did so at once."

The Catholic attitude was that man's duty to respect the divine design in creation included the moral obligation to regard animals as sentient beings entrusted to his reasonable dominion. In this view animals were wards rather than partners of their human companions. St. Francis of Assisi saw the animal world as a training ground for human moral behavior. He said, "If you have men who will exclude any of God's creatures from the shelter of pity and compassion, you will have men who will likewise deal with their neighbors."

In the medieval world people viewed animals as rational beings accountable for their deeds. Animals were entitled to the same legal protection as human beings. Domestic animals were tried in the ordinary criminal courts while wild, noxious animals such as rats were tried by the ecclesiastical courts. Animals were sometimes admitted as court witnesses. Both courts could impose the death penalty. The ecclesiastical court also had the power to excommunicate. Incidentally, the same treatment was accorded to very young children.

Emotional love and care among higher animals

Prior to the complete dualism between matter and consciousness introduced into philosophical thinking by Rene Descartes in the 17th century, many of the foremost philosophers included animals within the same realm as that occupied by humans. Thus, Spinoza spoke of animals as having feelings, Montaigne stated that animals had a language of their own and Leibnitz claimed that the only difference between animal and human souls was one of quantity, not quality. The implication of these views was that animals had rights and claims on man as valid as man's rights and claims on animals.

Ethologists, in their close observation of animal behavior, have pointed to the evidence of sympathy and a capacity for altruism in various species. Thus, adult pelicans will support each other and crippled pelicans for several years, if necessary. Wolves have been known to help other wolves build their den and to provide for their young. Wolves can transmit their emotions by the way they howl. Dolphins help unconscious companions who are in danger of drowning. Wolves and dolphins can form friendships among their own kind. Elephants have shown themselves to be capable of affection. Porpoises will feed injured members of their species. They will also help man even at risk to themselves. Dolphins can develop ulcers from grief. Vervet monkeys have a rudimentary language.

Animals have the capacity to become strongly attached both to members of their own and other animal species and to help their human owners. Thus, their reactions to separation and reunion very much resemble human reactions.

The special quality of an animal's feeling for its master was likened to religious devotion by Charles Darwin in his *Descent of Man:*

> "The feeling of religious devotion is a highly complex one, consisting of love, complete submission to an exalted and mysterious superior, a strong sense of dependence, fear, reverence, gratitude, hope for the future and perhaps other elements. No being could experience so complete an emotion until advanced in his intellectual and moral faculties to at least a moderately high level. Nevertheless, we see some distant approach to this state of mind in the deep love of a dog for his master, associated with complete submission, some fear and perhaps other feelings. The behavior of a dog when returning to his master after an absence . . . is widely different from that toward his fellows. In the latter case the transports of joy appear to be somewhat less and the sense of equality shown in every action."

A fruitful area of research would be to discover how owners of companion animals and those animals communicate with each other.

Alienation and modern society

Today, more than ever, human beings are feeling the effects of alienation from the natural world that they impose upon themselves or that is imposed upon them by society. This problem, which has existed as long as man has been on this earth, has become more acute since humans now have more time for leisure and for contemplation of themselves and their works.

Alienation is not new to the human being; it has existed in various forms throughout the centuries. The Biblical myth of Adam and Eve being expelled from Eden is an acknowledgement of the alienation of the human being from his natural habitat back when the human race was in its childhood.

Today, alienation of the individual has become the focal theme of our literature, art, music and social sciences. (To compound the difficulty, the various environments which the individual inhabits work at cross purposes with each other.)

Changes have occured in our post-industrial society which make it necessary to have an agent or agents to bring people closer together. Families have become smaller; family members live at great distances from each other. Even though surrounded by people, a person may be without intimate relationships to sustain him. He may feel lonesome and look for companionship, closeness, warmth. Sometimes he finds this in pets.

Pets are therefore playing a more important role than they did when the extended family provided more companionship and learning experiences and when life, particularly in rural areas, provided more opportunities for daily contact with animals.

But why pets? Why are we attached to them? The answers are both psychological and physiological.

Man is by nature part animal and for that reason he feels a kinship with animals. Working with animals unconsciously reminds him of his long distant past when he was emerging from "animalhood." Contact with animals brings him closer to nature and Mother Earth. Contact with pets provides experiences of touching and being touched, the contact comfort first experienced in infancy.

Human need for touch and contact comfort

Touch

Prior to birth, the fetus receives touch stimulation from the amniotic fluid which transmits its mother's movements. During the birth process, it receives major stimulation when it goes through the birth canal.

At birth, the neonate begins to interact with his environment in a manner which lays the groundwork for later good or poor mental health. At this time the neonate is already equipped with some skills by which to affect his world. He is not as helpless as many a parent thinks. His cries, smiles and touch elicit responses from his caretakers that satisfy his needs. He is sensitive to the activities of his mother (if she is the caretaker) and of other persons in his environment and responds positively or negatively to what they do with him. The neonate has an innate need, strengthened by experience, for touch stimulation which gives it pleasure and relief from anxiety. Later on, touch demonstrates caring and affectionate closeness and becomes an important component of love.

As the child begins to explore his world, the haptic (touch) modality is the first sense modality to be utilized for exploring the environment. The child will try to explore the world using this modality and he will begin to differentiate between inner reality and outer world by means of haptic manipulation, only later turning to vision as the primary source of information.

The child orients himself toward his mother so as to be stimulated and fed by her. There is thus an ongoing, active reaching out and body communication between child and mother. This communication is concrete and physical, truly a language of the body, the "silent language". Thus, physical communications appear to be necessary and present from the very first contacts between child and mother soon after birth.

During the first six months of a child's life, the infant is completely dependent upon his mother for food, comfort and contact sensations. If there is enough pleasurable contact comfort, the child will eventually experience himself as an individual separate from his mother and will develop an adequate body image. Later on, as the child grows older, other individuals will satisfy this need for physical contact. This mode of communication will remain with him throughout his lifetime. He will be able to express his most intimate thoughts and feelings most effectively and satisfyingly through physical contact rather than through words.

As the infant begins to feed, the mother nourishes him and supplies him with the warmth, cuddling and softness that the child associates with love and security. He touches his mother. She is soft and seems to be yielding, succorant and comforting. The infant begins to associate soft, pleasing touch sensations with the availability of security. The desire for this contact with a soft mother appears to be unlearned.

This contact releases endorphins in the nervous system which alleviate anxiety and this sense of relief forms the foundation for social attachment. The internalized sense of security made possible by the social attachment permits the child to separate from the caretaker for longer and longer periods without overwhelming anxiety. Research has indicated that opiates (chemically comparable to the internally-produced endorphins) alleviate separation anxiety in puppies.

Soft contact begins to evoke experiences of being loved and secure. Soft touch and stroking sensations reduce tension and produce relaxation. Soft contact brings about the blocking of the "opiate receptors" in the limbic system, corpus striatum and hypothalamus through the production of endorphins (a by-product of complex biochemical reactions in the brain which are not yet well understood. They act the way morphine does, by creating euphoria).

The bond between humans and animals works both ways. "King" was an early recipient of the American Humane Association's William O. Stillman award for saving the life of a child about to be run over by a car. People need pets—and pets need people.

Attachment behavior

Both animal and human companionship (which entail a psychologically-based set of behaviors) are initiated by attachment behavior, which is a biologically-based set of actions. A child must become attached to a person or animal before either can become its companion.

Attachment can also be experienced toward an inanimate object which provides contact comfort. The pleasant feelings aroused by touch are evoked, through conditioning, by any soft objects such as a familiar blanket, which becomes for the child a "transitional object" between his caretaker figures and his own self as a source of security and comfort. A "security blanket" is just that for a child who has become attached to it. It promotes adaptive behavior by enabling the child to draw on his inner resources when he is separated from his usual attachment figures (the mother or other caretakers). It has been suggested that a security blanket is as effective in helping pre-schoolers adjust to novel environments as was the mother and that mothers and blankets have persisting positive effects even after they have gone.

By extension from the transitional object (a blanket or soft toy), secure, euphoric feelings can be derived from a real animal, familiar, soft and furry, such as a dog. The kind of companionship which can evolve between child and animal can be made use of, not only in daily life but in psychotherapy as well, whether with children or adults, since this need for comfort never disappears.

Young children very readily identify with animals. Clinical observations made during pet therapy sessions reveal that some children unconsciously believe they may be transformed into animals and that animals may become children. Children also often assume that their pet understands their speech, is responsive to their moods, sympathizes with their feelings and is of their religious persuasion.

Children, as they grow, face certain developmental tasks. Depending on their previous history, some children experience these as challenges while others experience them as threats. An animal can enhance the adventure for the former and serve as a protector for the latter. The child plays an active role in influencing his pet and the latter, in turn, influences the child. They are encompassed in a dynamic and ever-changing relationship which is less complex and ambivalent than the relationship with the human caretakers.

Love is the priceless ingredient with which our pets enrich our lives. Through the experience of being loved by a pet, a child may develop the feeling that he is a good individual, since he is unconditionally loved by the animal. The child begins to feel good about himself and his uniqueness and recognizes that he is a person in his own right and that he counts. Psychoanalytically speaking, this feeling leads to the development of a strong ego.

Children have a particular need for the kind of nonverbal learning and emotional interaction that comes from living with a pet. Children learn primarily through sensorimotor give and take with their environment. Even when they have language at their disposal for acquiring and storing information, they derive their understanding of how the world—human and nonhuman—functions by direct experiencing of what things and people do to them and what they, in turn, do to things and people. Words codify a knowledge that is gained through the body. Pets are a wonderful medium of such nonverbal, body-mediated interaction.

The acquisition of autonomy requires taking control of one's own behavior, the mastery of one's impulses and the development of self-discipline. The ability to delay gratification, to exercise patience, to carry out responsibilities and to recognize and defer to the needs of others on occasion are all part of a self-directed human being. A child who is responsible for the well-being and training of a pet has to exhibit all these capacities. Moreover, the child is trying to inculcate some of these same abilities in his pet, who must wait to be fed or walked, will not always be played with on demand, must learn not to damage furnishings, etc. Of course, the more self-mastery the child has acquired, the better he can train his pet, but the very act of trying to train the pet successfully will reinforce self-control in the child.

Not only children, but adolescents, adults and the aged as well, secure comfort from the touch and attachment behavior involved in a relationship with a companion animal. At each stage of life the companion animal has different meanings and plays a different role in the individual's emotional and physical economy.

Research into the relationships between humans and their companion animals should provide us with information about the effects of these relationships on many aspects of personal and social life and development. For example:

Do animal companions have a different role in the personality development of boys and girls?

Do owners treat their pets differently when they see the latter as similar to or different from them in personality traits?

Do children who have companion animals acquire empathy for fellow humans more quickly than those without pets? Do adults who had pets as children show more empathy toward others than those who did not?

Do owners who have experienced the death of an animal companion handle human bereavement more effectively than non-owners or owners who have not experienced the death of a pet?

Are pet owners more comfortable with their own sexuality than non-owners?

How are animals used as child substitutes? Do childless people feed zoo animals more frequently than those with children? Why is it so prevalent to feed zoo animals?

What influence, if any, does owning a family pet have on the incidence of child and spouse battering, divorce, desertion, or criminal actions by family members? Does the presence of an animal companion reduce or increase parental stress? Does animal companionship significantly reduce the stress of divorce or widowhood and help in the effective management of these situations?

How do companion animals affect those with health problems? It would be valuable, for example, to investigate the effect of animal companionship on people with terminal illnesses, such as cancer. Is there a difference in survival rates between owners and non-owners of animal companions? What of those with chronic illnesses, such as diabetes, muscular dystrophy, arthritis, cardiovascular diseases, etc.?

Is there a different incidence of mental illness—such as severe depression, schizophrenia—between animal owners and non-owners?

History of the use of companion animals as psychotherapeutic aides

As I survey the field of human/companion animal therapy which is growing at an exponential rate, it reminds me of the time in my youth when I lived in East New York, on the outskirts of New York City. Ours was the last house within the city limits and only a hundred yards away there was a dairy farm where we could purchase milk. When I last visited that old neighborhood, I found that the farm had disappeared and that the entire area, as far as the eye could see, had been built up. The same is true for human/companion animal therapy; developments in the field are proliferating so rapidly that it is difficult to keep track of what is going on, even for one who is immersed in the subject.

The use of animals as an aid to mental hygiene has a long history. The primitive men who first adopted animals as companions had already discovered their value. The ancient Greeks used dogs as therapeutic agents at the great shrine dedicated to Asclepius at Epidaurus.

In more recent times, animals were used as part of the therapeutic environment by the York Retreat in England (1792), and in Bethel in Bielefeld, Germany (1867). In 1940, dogs were brought in as companion animals for convalescent airmen at the Air Force Convalescent Hospital in Pawling, New York.

My own research, beginning in 1961, and that of Samuel and Elizabeth Corson, since 1975, made dogs an integral part of psychotherapeutic programs.

Today, as subsequent chapters in this book will show, companion animals are making vital contributions to mental health at every stage in the individual's life cycle. They do so by providing love, affection, understanding, touch and contact comfort, encouraging even very old persons to engage with them in relaxing and stimulating play behavior.

Companion animals are also employed in direct psychotherapeutic work with persons of all ages, cultures and educational backgrounds, displaying a variety of physical or emotional problems whether these people live in their own homes, hospitals, nursing facilities, camps or prisons.

I see human/companion animal therapy as comprising a process in which contact comfort and the opportunity for attachment behavior are either present or easily available.

There are various ways in which the companion animal may be used.

The companion animal as a psychotherapeutic adjunct

When companion animals are used as psychotherapeutic adjuncts, they frequently decrease the initial shock incidental to encountering a therapist or beginning a new therapeutic experience. Petting the companion animal during a session distracts the individual's attention from himself. The companion animal, by permitting itself to be petted, gives the individual a relaxed and accepted feeling, as if he were with a friend, which unconsciously may be equated with being comforted by one's own mother in an anxiety-provoking situation. When it is the therapist's animal which is making the patient feel accepted, the patient may experience the therapist as accepting him, too.

What is most important when companion animals are used as adjuncts is the establishment of a relationship between patient and therapist, and not the specific approach used by the latter. Once the therapist has secured the confidence of the patient with the aid of the animal adjunct, he may begin to use whatever techniques he is most comfortable with. Children in psychotherapy will often express to a doll or puppet what they cannot bring themselves to say directly to the therapist, who carries the aura of authority. Adults too, can use an animal for the same purpose, testing out in this way how much the therapist understands and how well he tolerates what he understands of the patient's secrets.

The companion animal as sole therapist

When a companion animal is the sole therapeutic agent, the nature and intensity of the owner's relationship with the animal will determine its therapeutic effect.

When we have a companion animal functioning as sole therapist, we assume that the individual has self-directing capacities which can emerge through interacting with the animal companion and that there is meaningful communication taking place between master and pet. The animal companion can help the individual express himself, release his emotions and overcome his inhibitions, so that an effective therapeutic change can occur. The companion animal provides the individual with a chance to change at his own pace, exerting no coercion or pressure, having no expectations to be complied with or rebelled against.

The relaxation which the owner feels when talking to, petting, playing with, perhaps literally leaning on his companion animal, permits him to get in touch with his emotions, with the inner self that he may not have felt safe enough to confront before. Whatever insights he obtains in this way are due entirely to his own inner activity. He need feel neither gratitude, dependency, nor humiliation, as he might if the insights had been the result of a human therapist's interpretations.

An owner who has a close relationship with his companion animal feels that the animal understands him, accepts him with all his foibles and hang-ups, cares about him and will defend him. The master also feels the companion animal is communicating his regard for his owner by his affectionate behavior and has the same emotions as his master. This nonverbal communication of "unconditional positive regard", which he may never have recieved from a human being, can bring about a positive change in the master.

Companion animals as catalysts

In discussing companion animals as catalysts for increased socialization and self-disclosure, we must consider the radical change that has occured in the way we construe therapeutic services today. We no longer think that one must be a professional psychotherapist to be able to help a fellow human being in distress. Anyone can help in certain ways. We now emphasize that paraprofessionals, peer groups and self-help groups all have much to contribute. The use of animal companions in addition to the above provides another focus for mutual social support. For example, many humane societies have volunteers who bring dogs, cats and other animals to nursing homes, homes for the aged, hospitals, schools and residential settings for emotionally and physically handicapped children on a weekly or monthly basis. As a result of their contact with the animals, the patients may feel free to disclose and to discuss with the volunteers many of their deepest concerns.

Man's need for companionship and a friendly ear is sometimes met by a professional therapist, sometimes by a familiar pet. Sometimes they're one and the same, as this child and dog, re-enacting a scene from the "Peanuts" cartoons, demonstrate quite vividly. *(Photo by Phil Arkow)*

Many sincere, honest, well-meaning individuals have selected themselves as providers of companion animals who serve as catalytic agents for self-revelation and social interaction. We would be correct in assuming, I believe, that the vast majority of these volunteers have a positive regard for others and care about them. The fact that they have volunteered to serve others must indicate some empathic understanding of how other people feel and what they need in their predicaments.

However, although they can offer a sympathetic ear and friendly understanding along with the valuable animal contacts, these volunteers cannot function in the same way as trained therapists. They may not recognize the severity of the emotional problems in some of the old people or children who turn to them. They may not realize that the feelings which have been tapped by the contacts with the animals need to be dealt with on another level besides that which can be provided by a concerned and caring listener. These volunteers must be helped to know when the recipients of their services need professional guidance and how such guidance can be suggested and made available.

I would therefore suggest that volunteers who bring animals into institutional settings and find themselves lending a human ear to distressed residents be given an intensive course of training which will help them spot signs of emotional distress requiring further attention. It will enable them to make use of the trust which people have in them and the companion animals they bring to visit.

Companion animals as a means of communing with nature

Due to the kaleidoscopic changes which have occurred in the past few decades in our social norms and cultural climate, we find ourselves at a crossroads. We are uneasy, sick of soul and estranged from life. We feel anxious and powerless. In our attempts to be scientific, we have suppressed our fantasies and our unconscious strivings. We are not free to feel, but instead must think and evaluate.

We have no standards to uphold, nothing to fight for, nothing we can hold on to and call sacred. We are rootless, vainly seeking a haven where we can gain some surcease and peace of soul. Our estrangement from life is compounded by the fact that we have alienated ourselves not only from our inner beings but also from nature and our natural allies, the animals.

Searching our memories for the time when we were at peace with ourselves and the world, we usually find that it was in our earliest childhood, when mother was providing touch comfort, love and acceptance. Reviewing what is known of the history of our species, we find that it was animals who, from primeval times, provided our ancestors with the same priceless gifts.

Since that uncomplicated, unconditional kind of love and comfort can no longer be had from mother or anyone else now that we are adults (otherwise we would not be feeling such a sense of deprivation), we turn to our friends, the animals, who can still provide it.

When some of us walk in the forest, meander at the seashore or climb a mountain, accompanied by our companion animal whom we caress, we become euphoric. We can afford to let down our guard against bombardment from external stimuli in our normally hectic world. We feel secure, are more sensitive to minimal stimuli and become aware of our innermost feelings. We are at one with the universe.

Opportunites for study

Research is wide open in the area of the therapeutic use of animal companions, whether in formal psychotherapy or as a therapeutic element in the daily environment.

The first broad area involves amassing data about the animals themselves. We must establish criteria for the selection and breeding of animals which are suitable for work with children, the aged, the retarded and the physically and emotionally handicapped. Animals used as co-therapists in an office setting may need different selection characteristics from those used in prisons, nursing homes, hospices for the dying, or schools for the mentally retarded, etc. We might experiment with the use of a wide variety of animals, exploring for each one its particular contribution to therapeutic work. We must also learn how to train the animal companion to further the goals of therapy or therapeutic living and determine the best manner for introducing animals into various settings.

Another area of investigation involves the human therapist/animal co-therapist relationship. What, for example, is the difference in personality between those therapists who can effectively use animals and those who cannot or do not wish to? How can we train people to use animals as co-therapists? How does the use of an animal affect the therapist's attitude toward his or her patient, e.g., if the patient dislikes or mistreats the animal which is so important to the therapist? How does a patient's relating to the animal affect the therapist's self-image and sense of competence? Is the animal experienced as a rival by the human therapist?

Companion animals have proven particularly useful in psychotherapy with children. Here many questions suggest themselves. For example:

What problems best lend themselves to being worked out with the aid of a pet in play therapy? With what types of children, from what types of family? How do the personalities of child, therapist and animal interact? How does the animal help the child achieve insight and increased maturity? How can a pet at home augment, or even substitute for, the activity of a therapist? How does the child identify with the animal? How does the therapist make use of the child's nonverbal behavior with the animal? What is the difference between children who can and cannot make use of animals in their treatment? Is the relationship between the animal and the child similar to the one between the animal and the therapist? What limits should be set on a child in relation to the animal and how does this affect the treatment? When is the use of an animal co-therapist inadvisable?

Finally, we may explore the nature of therapy itself, especially with therapists who use animals with some patients and not with others. What does the animal introduce into the situation which is therapeutic or, in some cases, not therapeutic? What is a therapist who uses an animal co-therapist conveying to his patient by this action? Do animals make more of a contribution at some stages of therapy than at others? Are there phases of therapy during which the presence of an animal would detract from the therapeutic work?

There are other interesting research problems. How does companion animal therapy compare with other current therapies in terms of changing and strengthening the patient's ego? Does the use of an animal promote better integration and more autonomy? Do transference and counter-transference differ in companion animal-treated cases and conventional psychotherapeutic approaches? Are specific types of companion animals helpful to people with specific types of problems?

Pets in space

In a 1962 article I made the following observation: "Only a few general aspects of the role of the veterinarian as a mental hygienist have been spelled out. The specific ways in which veterinarians can exercise their mental hygiene function will have to be spelled out by members of the profession.... As members of the veterinary profession pursue and develop this new phase of their practice, beneficial results should accrue for all of society."

In 1974 I predicted that, "In the year 2000, the training and functioning of veterinarians will have changed radically. The veterinarian will become involved in the emotional life of the family whose pet he treats. He will become aware of the meaning of the pet to its owner. The veterinarian will become an accepted and honored member of the mental hygiene team." Events have moved much faster than I then thought possible. What I projected as a thing of the distant future is a reality today.

I am now predicting that animal companions will soon be travelling in space. Veterinarians should become aware of this opportunity in aviation medicine and act accordingly.

We are now planning to organize multinational space crews composed of men and women of different cultural backgrounds, levels of education, technical skills, etc. Many problems will have to be resolved once a decision is made to engage in missions of long duration. The spaceship will be a microcosm reflecting the usual problems incidental to overcrowding, isolation and danger. Added to these will be the stress of knowing that in an emergency, unlike situations on earth, no help from the mother planet can be forthcoming.

There will be problems in selecting the crews and helping them adjust to life in space over prolonged periods. In the absence of privacy, tensions will arise which may decrease efficiency and create hostility that can be highly dangerous under such conditions.

Tensions will be compounded by loneliness. The need to caress, to give and receive comfort and love will be strongly felt at such times.

It will become imperative to introduce pets as participants in these missions. Veterinarians will have to learn to select animal astronauts suitable for training to accompany human astronauts on long space missions. Such animals will be in situations unlike any they have ever experienced, and for which their genetic heritage has not adapted them.

Research problems

Much research will be needed to answer the questions raised by the potential travel of companion animals in space. What kinds of pets should be selected? How should they be treated to prepare them for the mission? What criteria should be employed to evaluate the emotional stability of these pets? What kind of space would such animals need on board? What kind of food? How would they communicate with their owners and with the other members of the crew? How would the animals respond to weightlessness? Would the pet's circadian clock change in space? Would the pets be able to adapt, survive and be of service? How would the pet adapt to the comparative isolation of life in a capsule? Would it become bored? aggressive? antagonistic? show spatial disorientation? Would pets develope the same symptoms as their human companions, such as insomnia or anorexia?

What emotional problems might arise between crew members and their pets? How could these be prevented?

Many other questions would suggest themselves as selection and training programs got under way.

Companion animals and the future

Finally, how do I see the future of animal-human relationships?

Let me fantasize about a utopian situation in which there will be peace between man and beast because there is peace between man and man. In a world at peace we no longer have racial, ethnic, or national strife. War has been abolished and nuclear weapons sent to the sun to be destroyed.

In this peaceful world man is no longer a menace to wildlife or to nature. He has stopped worshipping progress and science. He has achieved the age-long dream of inter-species communication. He has arrived at a universal respect for animals and has the conviction that their preservation insures his own.

Exploitation of man by man no longer exists. Man is no longer carnivorous but herbivorous. This eliminates the ambivalent relationship which exists between man and animal when man is both shepherd and predator. The former predators will now eat synthetic protein food. Through gene-splitting we will have animals to fit every need other than food.

Man and beast will be brothers. No longer will there be any need for zoos. Certain planetoids will be reserved for animals where they can live and die undisturbed. There will also be extensive wilderness areas in every country. All animals will have been studied to permit them to follow their natural bent in mating and raising their young. Since these animals will live in their natural environment, they will no longer be bored with life or have the emotional problems so evident in current pictures of animals in modern zoos.

Perhaps this vision is too fantastic. But what does our current world offer as an alternative?

This is the eleventh hour for our existence on this planet. We have robbed and despoiled the earth. We have spread toxins and poisons throughout the globe. We have reduced wildlife almost to the vanishing point. Soon we won't be able to commune with nature; there will be no nature left.

We are destroying our soil, the basis of our life. We are destroying the animals and the bacteria which live on our soil, are dependent on the soil and maintain the soil.

We have taken literally the Biblical statement that God gave man dominion over the earth. We have neglected to heed the accompanying injunction to save and protect the animals under our dominion. We have failed to see the animal as friend, partner and equal.

We have failed to realize that there is an ever-changing tree of life. The higher one is on the tree, the more disposable one may become, while the lower one is in that hierarchy, the more important one may be. In fact, it is when we finally get to the roots of the tree that life becomes important. Without algae which release oxygen, the world as we know it could not exist.

In our "scientific" attempt to classify, to order, to fit everything into neat formulas, we have deluded ourselves into believing that technology will save the world. We have as a result reduced the world to dust. Spirit has escaped us, possibly never to return. We have failed to realize that humans are an integral part of the universe, that we are all a link in the chain of life. When one small link is broken, no matter how insignificant it may appear, the entire structure eventually perishes.

At this point we leave our reader, who alone can decide what he or she can do to protect this planet which is our home.

Suggested reading:

Levinson, Boris "The Future of Research into Relationships Between People and Their Animal Companions." *International Journal for the Study of Animal Problems,* 1982, 9(4), 283-294.

Levinson, Boris *Pet-Oriented Child Psychotherapy.* Springfield, Ill.: Charles C. Thomas, 1969.

Levinson, Boris *Pets and Human Development.* Springfield, Ill.: Charles C. Thomas, 1972.

Section I - Introduction to the Human-Animal Bond

1

Historical Perspectives: Human Values for Animals and Vulnerable People

Robert W. ten Bensel

"...a broadening awareness of vulnerability..."

Nature attains perfection, but man never does. There is a perfect ant, a perfect bee, but man is perpetually unfinished. He is both an unfinished animal and an unfinished man. It is this incurable unfinishedness which sets man apart from other living things. For, in the attempt to finish himself, man becomes a creator. Moreover, the incurable unfinishedness keeps man perpetually immature, perpetually capable of learning and growing.

- Eric Hoffer (1903-1983)
Reflection on the Human Condition, **1973**

The welfare of animals depends on understanding of animal suffering, and one does not get this understanding intuitively.

- Peter Medawar (Nobel Laureate)

Human relationship to animals in antiquity

How have we, as human beings, perceived ourselves in relationship with animals? Our writings indicate a changing, but often ambiguous relationship. On the one hand, we have viewed ourselves as having "dominion" over animals (Genesis 1:26), with resultant exploitation of animals. On the other hand, animals have served as symbols of human and divine values, with their virtues and vices. In antiquity, animals in the everyday world were viewed as

Robert W. ten Bensel, M.D., M.P.H., is professor in the School of Public Health and Pediatrics at the University of Minnesota, where he is a faculty member in the Maternal and Child Health major. He has been active in animal and child abuse studies for many years. This chapter is adapted from programs he presented at the Conferences on the Human-Animal Bond at the University of Minnesota and the University of California-Irvine in June, 1983.

utilitarian for food and sport. Yet we have used animal metaphors, myths, and symbols in order to understand the meaning of life. Over the centuries, we have extended to animals and vulnerable people the full protection of society's resources.

Perhaps the best known example of an animal symbol in the human family is the totem. Totemistic symbols offer protection of the spirits to those humans living within a tribal or family structure. Sigmund Freud, in his book, *Totem and Taboo,* writes, "What is a totem? It is as a rule an animal . . . which stands in peculiar relationship to the whole clan. In the first place, the totem is the common ancestor to the clan; at the same time it is a guardian spirit and helper, which sends in oracles and, if dangerous to others, recognizes and spares its own children."

We have moved away from what was once a very close (even ancestral) relationship to animals and nature. By a long struggle, we have sought to liberate ourselves from our animal nature. Ernest Becker writes in *Escape From Evil,* "Once man got enough power over the world to forego the totemistic ritual identifications, he became more and more eager to explain away any relationships with animals." Thus, wc, who once had shared a common world with animals, separated ourselves intellectually and emotionally from them. Is this why we have some ambiguity in the ways we view and treat animals in our culture? Do we seek clarification of this ambiguity by examining the meaning of animals? Or do we look at what it means to be human?

The dictionary distinguishes human beings from lower animals because they are of the "earth" (*humus*), because they are "earthlings" and, therefore, "mortal." "Animal" is defined by its attributes relative to humans. Terms referring to the same level as, or including, humans and animals are "animal", which reflects the sensual and physical nature, as opposed to the spiritual or intellectual nature of humans; "brute" which is used to describe the fundamental powers possessed by all creatures, yet implies courseness and roughness; and "creature" which means any living being, especially animals and humans. Degrading terms are "beast" which places the animal beneath humans in a very disagreeable position; and "bestial" which refers to the vileness of moral degradation of human's sexual perversions (paraphilia). Thus our choice of words makes judgments about our degree of being human or animal.

Words attempt to communicate our values of "good" and "evil," thus reflecting our ethical beliefs. Since we use words, we become the human center for communication to animals and nature, similar to the situation that existed when the earth was the center of the solar system. As humans, we are of the earth, somewhere between animal and the divine. This is the philosophical position well stated in Plotinus (A.D. 205-270) in *Third Ennead:* "Humanity is poised midway between gods and beasts and inclines to the one order, now to the other; some men grow like to the divine, others to the brute, the greatest numbers stand central..." Does this explain why we seek to identify human characteristics in animals? Do we move to protect animals because we see them as extensions of ourselves? Do animals who are perceived as having negative traits, that is, as being less than human, become exploited and destroyed by humans?

Over many thousands of years, animals have become, through domestication, part of the human family. Carson, in *Men, Beasts and Gods,* estimates that the dog became part of the human family 35 to 60 thousand years ago. In ancient Egypt, the cat ate at the same table as did humans and was deified. The ancient Egyptians were also responsible for the first conservation laws. Though the pharaohs enjoyed hunting, they set up

Anatomical mixings of man and animal have occurred throughout history—from mythological centaurs and satyrs to comic characters who symbolize a message. In this case, "Sparky" encourages residents of Lincoln, Neb., to buy their dog licenses.

game preserves to protect wild beasts and issued hunting licenses to limit the slaughter of waterfowl. Through the long process of domestication of animals, we became increas-ingly symbiotic with them. Certain animals ceased to be our enemies and, in fact, became extensions of ourselves and were given the human society's full measure of protection.

Animals also were used as symbols in other ways. For instance, the Egyptian god Horus (c. 1250 B.C.) is usually shown in groups of four with animals. The number four is considered a religious symbol indicating the spiritual perfection of humans. Carl Jung, in *Man and His Symbols,* notes that the four apostles were often depicted as animals. In addition, All Soul's Day is symbolized by four doves.

When animals were mixed anatomically with humans, they almost universally represented demons of disease and evil. Lion-headed, eagle-footed Assyrian Babylonian demons represented violence and usually held the mace of wounding and the dagger of killing. It was felt that the gods were often disguised as beasts when they approached women. Zeus approached Europa as a bull, Leda as a swan, Persephone as a serpent, and from such unions issued many half-man, half-beast denizens of the mythological woods: satyrs (half-goat), centaurs (half-horse), and minotaurs (half-bull). The centaur was the only animal of antiquity considered by the ancients as having any good traits. They were too fond of the horse to consider the union of this nature with humans as forming a very degraded compound.

Religious thought has greatly influenced our moral views. In Judeo-Christian heritage, Adam and Eve were the first humans. Artwork depicts Adam and Eve eating the apple from the Tree of Knowledge of Good and Evil. This symbolizes the origin of the moral confusion (or moral ambiguity) that men and women have in perceiving a right from a wrong. Adam and Eve covered their genitals and were driven from the Garden of Eden, thus symbolizing human beings moving away from nature, away from their "Peaceable Kingdom," to search for their meaning in the world.

In England, public awareness of cruelty to animals began during the latter half of the 18th century. The rise in consumption of gin, the lack of social controls, an increase in violence, and a concern for the welfare of children spawned the beginning of the "infant child welfare movement" and of a humane ethic to prevent cruelty to animals and to innocent and vulnerable children. An influential person of the period was William Hogarth (1697-1764). Hogarth was best known for his satire on the social scene in London. He demonstrated his close affinity with animals by placing his dog "Trump" prominently in the foreground of his self-portrait. Many of his drawings and engravings portray the cruelty of cockfighting, bear baiting, and setting animals on animals. He depicts a society that was cruel to animals, children, and adults. Hogarth emerged as the first truly modern artist. By the 1730s, Hogarth had begun to depict the vices and follies of his age. The energies of his productive career focused on the poor, and he turned more and more to depicting the problems of his time, including the impact of the gin epidemic.

Sir Henry Fielding's *Inquiry into the Case of the Late Increase in Robbers* (1751) also addressed similar issues. Both Fielding and Hogarth portrayed the problems of alcohol, poverty, and cruelty in hopes of reaching the lower classes and reforming "some reigning vices peculiar" to them. In 1751, Hogarth made available to the general public low-cost engravings on *Gin Lane* and *Beer Street* portraying the evils of gin and the benefits of beer. His four *Stages of Cruelty* show the progression of Tom Nero torturing animals as a child, beating a disabled horse as a young man, and, finally, killing a woman. In the second *Stage of Cruelty,* he shows the impact of cruelty to animals spreading to children as a boy is being run over by a cart in the streets of London. In *Cruelty in Perfection,* he murders a woman, and in the *Rewards of Cruelty,* after he has been publically hanged, his corpse is publically dissected by the Barbers-Surgeons' Company. In the final scene, Tom is now the victim, and the dog is licking Tom's heart.

Not only did Hogarth directly attack the custom of baiting badgers, bulls, and bears and of the "drawing up" of dogs with fireworks, but also he linked the depicted cruelties with the practices of the day which had official and public support. John Houghton (1694) writes that bear baiting is "a sport the English much delight in, and not only the baser sort, but the greatest ladies." Hogarth had made an early attack on the baitings which was printed in the *Craftsman,* July 1, 1738. He writes, "I am a professional Enemy to Persecution of all Kinds, whether against Man or Beast."

Hogarth's impact on English attitudes was enormous by creating greater awareness in all classes of people and by donating his artistic talents to the Foundling Hospital of London. Hogarth's Epitaph was written by David Garrick (1717-1779):

Farewell great Painter of Mankind!
Who reach'd the noblest point of Art
Whose pictur'd Morals charm the Mind,
And through the Eye correct the Heart.

If Genius fire thee, Reader, stay:
If Nature touch thee, drop a tear:
If neither move thee, turn away,
For Hogarth's honour'd dust lies here.

The Old Testament and the Talmud deal with the human-animal relationship. For example, the story of Abraham and Isaac (Genesis 22) is important in symbolic relationships between humans and animals. "God tested Abraham, 'Take your only son Isaac, whom you love . . . offer him to Me as a burnt offering.'" The angel of the Lord stopped the sacrifice and a ram was offered instead of Isaac. Symbolically, this story moves humans away from the practice of human sacrifice by the substitution of an animal. The word "victim" means sacrificial human or animal. In Leviticus 18:23, the Lord says to Moses, "and you shall be with no animal and defile yourself with it; neither shall a woman stand before an animal to commit lewdness with it; it is a perversion." The Talmud says, "You say that flies, fleas, mosquitoes are superfluous, but they have their purpose in creation as a means of final outcome." Proverbs 12:30 states, "A righteous man has regards for the life of his beast." Other religious writers and philosophers noted the ethical issue of animal suffering and the human response to it. Buddha (c. 566-480 B.C.) said, "When a man has pity on all living creatures, then only is he noble."

Similar views were expressed in the secular world of antiquity. Aristotle (384-322 B.C.) and other philosophers viewed animals as having qualities of humans. Aristotle declared that human beings and animals share a common "sensitive soul." In ancient Greece, there is recorded both humanity and cruelty to animals. History reveals that bears were forced to dance, dogs were set on cats, and Asiatic cockfights were incorporated into the Greek culture. At the same time, some animals, such as pigeons, were considered good companions. According to Roman law, animals were private property and were regarded as things to be used at their owner's discretion. "Cattle" and "chattel" have the same root word; chattel included movable, private property or capital and included children and slaves under Roman law. In Roman times, dogs were often executed along with their criminal masters. Also, dogs were crucified for failing to warn towns about approaching invaders.

Cruelty to animals

The earliest writing that cruelty by humans towards animals could spread to other human beings is from Ovid (Publius Ovidus Naso, 43 B.C. - A.D. 17). The Roman poet writes, "T'was slaughter of wild beasts, me thinks, that makes man first with blood to stain his cool blade." The word "cruelty," itself, has early Latin origins (*credelis*) meaning bloody and raw. As currently used, cruetly refers to the infliction of pain or suffering by someone morally unfeeling. The Romans used animals for sport and killing in the Coliseum. Later, humans were used for sport and persecution in other arenas.

Philosophers and theologians had generally adopted Aristotle's conclusion that there is no future life for animals. Thus, animals were killed, or tortured, or exploited as accepted or approved by the people of the time. Saint Thomas Aquinas (1225-1274), following Roman law, had to deny that animals can have rights to protection. Even today, French laws and some U.S. laws adhere to this precedent and punish acts of cruelty to animals only when it occurs in public, so as to scandalize human observers. However, Aquinas also made two arguments against cruelty to animals: "Holy scriptures seem to forbid us to be cruel to brute animals . . . that is either . . . through being cruel to animals one becomes cruel to human beings or because injury to an animal leads to the temporal hurt of man."

There was little, if any, writing to document that animals suffered mental agony and needed protection because of this suffering until the late 18th century. Apparently, empathy and a feeling of suffering for animals were absent in the 16th, 17th and early 18th centuries. The one notable exception was Montaigne (1533-1592).

Montaigne heightened society's awareness to cruelty, suffering, and the pain of animals. His *Essay on Cruelty* bridged the earlier Roman writings to the 16th century. "At Rome after the people had become accustomed to the slaughter of animals, they proceeded to that of men and gladiators . . . Men of bloodthirsty nature where animals are concerned display a natural propensity to cruelty." A sensitive person, Montaigne stated boldly, "I cruelly hate cruelty, both by nature and reason, as the worst of all vices. I am so soft in this that I cannot see a chicken's neck wrung without distress, and cannot bear to hear the squealing of a hare between the teeth of my hounds, although the chase is a vehement pleasure."

In contrast, Rene Descartes (1595-1650) viewed animals as machines, with no feelings. Immanuel Kant (1724-1804) recommended avoiding cruelty to animals lest it might spread to humans. He argued that although such behavior was not intrinsically wrong, it might predispose the perpetrator to behave in a sadistic fashion towards humans as well.

The public's increasing awareness of the impact of science and the rising impersonal, mechanical world of the Industrial Revolution started to raise the questions of cruelty to animals in the latter half of the 18th century. Edward Jenner (1749-1823) is considered the discoverer of the vaccination principle; he inoculated a boy, James Phipps, with cowpox matter taken from the dairymaid, Sara Melmes, in 1794. Variolation, using infected cow's lymph, came under vigorous attack from the press, the sciences and the clergy; the clergy were said to have thundered against the inequity of transferring diseases from beasts of the field to man. Those concerned about taking infected matter from a sick cow induced early vaccinators to adopt an arm-to-arm technique between an infected human with cowpox to the nonaffected person whenever possible. By 1801, over 100,000 people had been vaccinated in Britain. There was concern that other diseases would be transmitted from animals to man. Antivaccination and antivivisection groups merged to combat the misuse of animals. Protests appeared that expressed concern that humans would turn into cows. Animals were considered separate from human beings and needed to be kept separate for humans' protection.

This was only part of a growing stream of writing. The first mention of the "rights of animals" appeared in 1749. Philosophical essays appeared on the moral treatment of lower creatures, while protests about particular forms of animal cruelty and edifying tracts, published in the 1780s, were designed to excite in children a "benevolent conduct to the brute creation."

Jeremy Bentham (1748-1832), famous English philosopher and jurist, posed the ethical issue in 1780 as, "The question is not, can they *reason?* Nor, can they *talk?* But can they *suffer?*" The treatment of domestic as well as wild animals was lamented in the late 18th century in England. The unhappiest

The cat: in ancient Egypt it was deified, in the Middle Ages in Europe it was a sign of the devil. Today, nationally-known figures like Morris represent the resurgence in popularity of our finicky feline friends.

animals were seen to be those of the Latin countries in southern Europe, because it was there that the old Catholic doctrine, that animals had no souls, was still maintained.

James Turner, in his excellent book *Reckoning with the Beast,* deals with problems of animals, pain and humanity, and the Victorian mind. Aside from the rising scientific data on animals that was learned from experimentation, certain individuals had an awareness that animals had "feelings" and a "degree of reason."

The late 18th and early 19th centuries brought a change in attitude toward slavery, the desire for freedom, and the rights of humans. The concept of human rights which had been acquired began to expand toward a concept of the rights of animals. People's sense of what was justifiable treatment of animals was based on their own self-interest, not on the interest of the animals. "Those rare souls who gathered to notice maltreatment of animals felt uneasy only because the habit might expand to abusing human beings. Pity was reserved for people," writes Turner.

Towards the end of the 19th century, others grounded their arguments solely on the rights of animals, that cruelty to animals was morally wrong because it caused pain and suffering to the animals—independent of the consequence to humans. Therefore, the concept of a "spirit" or "soul" in animals was introduced as an issue in the debate over animals' place in nature and with human beings. "We have to decide, not whether the practice of fox hunting, for example, is more, or less, cruel than vivisection, but whether *all* practices which inflict unnecessary pain on sentient beings are not incompatible with the high instincts of humanity," writes Henry Salt. The feeling of moral outrage is well described in a line from *Auguries of Innocence* by William Blake (1757-1827): "A robin redbreast in a cage puts all heaven in a rage."

Protection for animals

The first attempt at humane legislation was made in England in 1800 when Sir W. Pulteney introduced a bill to outlaw bull-baiting, but the bill was defeated. In 1809, Lord Thomas Erskine presented a bill to prevent "malicious and wanton cruelty to domestic animals, horses, oxen, sheep and pigs." In 1822, Richard "Humanity" Martin introduced legislation to protect the rights of beasts. Martin's bill, which passed, was referred to as "The Animal Magna Carta." Protection was extended to horses, mares, mules, asses, cows, heifers, steers, oxen, sheep, and other cattle. This laid the groundwork for the Society for the Prevention of Cruelty to Animals in 1824. Controversy again arose as to whether the state had a legal basis to govern the care of animals. Thomas Hood (1799-1845) captured this controversy in his *Ode to Richard Martin:*

Drovers may curse thee,*
*Knackers** asperse thee,*
And sly M.P.s bestow their cruel wipes;
But the old horse neighs thee,
And zebras praise thee,
Asses, I mean—they have as many stripes!

With Queen Victoria's rising to the throne of England in 1837 and her intense interest in animals, the Society became known as the Royal Society for the Prevention of Cruelty to Animals (RSPCA). Queen Victoria commented in her Jubilee Address (1887), "Among other marks of the spread of enlightenment amongst my subjects . . . (I have noted) with real pleasure, the growth of more humane feelings towards the lower animals." During this period of time, other anticruelty laws were passed: all baiting was outlawed in 1835; dog fights were outlawed in 1839 and 1854; and cockfighting was outlawed in 1849. These laws were consolidated under the "Protection of Animals Act" in 1911.

In 1859, Charles Darwin's publication of the *Origin of the Species* reawakened the discussion of "the animal in man and the animal humanized." This discussion emphasized that having compassion for animals meant nature had sympathy and love and that kindness to animals was a *sine qua non* of civilization. England has had a long-standing history of concern, compassion, and debate regarding the relationships between humans and animals. England is the first country that moved toward awareness and action for the protection of animals.

Two factors intensified the discussion about the need to control exploitation and to reduce the suffering of animals in industry, science, and society. One factor was the appreciation that humans were not supernatural but related to or descendent from animals. The other factor was the rising esteem for science as the key to the future of the human race.

Kenneth Clark, in his book *Civilisation,* states that the Anglo-American culture was born of the romantic era and that is what give us hope. During the 19th century, animals were depicted in romantic settings, especially with children. Artists are sensitive to the changes and direction society takes. Ezra Pound said, "Artists are the antennae of the race." The growing romantic idealization of the animal and child in art reflected the innocence of animals and children, which led subsequently to the protection of children and to other vulnerable persons. This extension, however, took place in America rather than in England.

**Drover - a driver of cattle or sheep*
***Knacker - a person who buys useless or worn-out livestock and sells the meat or hides.*

England provided much of the philosophical and legal base that came to America. The *Body of Liberties of the Massachusetts Bay Colony* (1641-1692) stated, "no man shall exercise any tyranny or cruelty toward any brute creatures which are usually kept for man's use." In Boston in 1790, a horse beater was characterized as having "unlawful rage and cruel inclination." He was punished for the common law offense ofbeing a public nuisance. In 1816, a New York court warned it would punish anyone showing "cruelty towards animals." Local ordinances were passed in 1828, setting standards for the care of horses, cattle, and sheep in New York City.

The ultimate story of how concern for animals led to a system of protective services for children centers around Henry Bergh (1813-1888), who founded the New York Society for Prevention of Cruelty to Animals. He was the son of a rich New York shipbuilder and Jacksonian Democrat. Well-educated and a man of leisure, Bergh was appointed by President Lincoln in 1863 as the Secretary of the American Legation in St. Petersburg, Russia. He was horrified by the Russians' barbarous treatment of animals, especially the whipping of horses, and resigned his post in October, 1864. During his return trip to America, he stopped in London and visited a meeting of the Royal Society for the Prevention of Cruelty to Animals during the spring of 1865. Upon his return to New York, Bergh enlisted the support of New York's elite for an anticruelty society. Actively publicizing the effects of cruelty to animals, he delivered a paper in February, 1866, on *Statistics Relating to the Cruelties Practiced on Animals.* He petitioned the New York Legislature for an act of incorporation, and it was granted on April 10, 1866. On April 22, 1866, the American Society for the Prevention of Cruelty to Animals was formally organized in New York.

Bergh went on to devote himself to improving the welfare of animals. He

By fostering kindness to animals and children, people would be kinder to their fellow humans and build a humane society. More than a century later, humane groups like The American Humane Association promote kindness toward all living things.

invented the horse ambulance before ambulances were used by human hospitals. He brought legislation to bear upon the overworking of animals used in pulling trolley cars; as many as 25,000 horses a year were dying as a result of mistreatment by carrying heavy loads in New York City.

Humane education spread to the common people through the work of George Angell. Angell, born in Massachusetts, was greatly influenced by Hyram Powers' advice to him 1870: "Educate the hearts of the people and the heads will take care of themselves." His efforts brought an organized, humane approach to education of the ordinary citizen.

The bridging of protection for humans as well as for animals directly resulted from the "Mary Ellen" case of 1874. Jacob Riis recounts the story in his 1905 book *The Children of the Poor:*

> In the summer of 1874 a poor woman lay dying in the last stages of consumption in a miserable little room on the top floor of a big tenement in this city. A Methodist missionary, visiting among the poor, found her there and asked what she could do to soothe her suffering. "My time is short," said the sick woman, "But I cannot die in peace while the miserable little girl whom they call Mary Ellen is being beaten day and night by her stepmother next to my room!" Prompted by the natural instinct of humanity, the missionary sought the aid of the police, but she was told that it was necessary to furnish evidence before an arrest could be made. "Unless you can prove that an offense has been committed, we cannot interfere, and all you know is hearsay!. . .[Then the missionary said] "There is one man in this city . . . who has spent his life . . . for the benefit of unoffending animals. I will go to Henry Bergh." She went, and the great friend of the dumb brute found a way. "The child is an animal," he said, "There is no justice for it as a human being; it shall have the rights of the stray cur in the street. It shall not be abused."

Henry Bergh acquired a lawyer, Elbridge T. Gerry, and the case was taken to court. Mary Ellen testified, "My mother and father are both dead . . . I don't know how old I am . . . I have never been allowed to go out of the room . . . I have never been allowed to play with children . . . Mama has been in the habit of whipping and beating me almost every day . . . I don't know for what I was whipped. Mama never said anything." Police reporter Jacob Riis wrote in his report, "I saw a child brought in carried in a horse blanket, at the sight of which men wept aloud, and I heard the story of little Mary Ellen told again that stirred the soul of the city and roused the conscience of the people that had forgotten. And as I looked, I knew I was where the first chapter of the children's rights was being written."

As a result of the "Little Mary Ellen Case," the New York Society for the Prevention of Cruelty to Children was established in 1875. By 1877, there were 271 local humane agencies from New Hampshire to California, and on October 9, 1877, 22 delegates from 10 states met in Cleveland to form the American Humane Association.

Thus, there has been a continued progression to higher levels of ethical action by society. We have moved from cruelty toward compassion for animals as well as for humans. Pity and empathy have become regulators of nonviolent behavior by our realizing that all creatures suffer. We must learn this lesson in each generation, for we do not have a group memory.

The social ethic of protection is a value of public health. It is moving us toward a broadening awareness of the vulnerability of not only children, but also other humans who are in need of protection. Public attention to "battered children" occured only in 1962. "Battered wives" were identified in 1969 as a social problem after a century of silence. The abuse of the elderly surfaced to public attention in 1978. Institutional abuse became a concern in 1976, and some states established public policies to protect all vulnerable children and adults from neglect and physical and sexual abuse as late as 1980. This protection requires reporting, investigating, and establishing procedures and services to correct the situations leading to the abuse and neglect. Prevention programs have been available only for several years and have focused upon educating people about the needs and rights of humans, support groups, crisis intervention, and social and health services.

Humane education started as one of the few socially acceptable outlets for feelings of compassion in the 19th century. It brought "peace with the new ideas, the new factories, the new masses of the Victorian Age, by insisting that kindness also become a part of the new way of life," writes Turner, Compassion for the suffering of humans and animals in the 20th century is still in the early stages of becoming a dominant value in our culture. Humans and animals are connected to each other just as we are connected by all nature.

Compassion is the basis of all morality.
Arthur Schopenhauer (1788-1860)

Man can no longer live for himself alone. We must realize that all life is available and that we are united to all life. From this knowledge comes our spiritual relationship with the universe.
- Albert Schweitzer (1875-1965)

Suggested Reading

Carson, Gerald *Men, Beasts and Gods: A History of Cruelty and Kindness to Animals.* New York: Charles Scribner's Sons, 1972.

Clark, Kenneth *Animals and Men.* New York: William Morrow and Co., Inc., 1977.

Clark, Kenneth *Civilisation.* London: BBC and John Murray, 1969.

Leavitt, Emily *Animals and their Legal Rights: A Survey of American*

Laws, 1641-1978. Washington: Animal Welfare Institute, 1978.
Salt, H. *Animal rights: considered in relation to social progress.* Clarks Summit, Pa.: Society for Animal Rights, Inc., 1980.

2

Contemporary Perspectives on Pets and People

Sally O. Walshaw

"...the bond is receiving greater respect..."

What is man without the beasts? If all the beasts were gone, man would die from great loneliness of spirit, for whatever happens to the beasts also happens to man. All things are connected.

Chief Seatlh, 1855

The bond between animals and human beings has existed for thousands of years, probably since man first began to domesticate animals. Presumably this bond developed as an adaptive response to environmental factors. Thus it was to the advantage of primitive man, a poorly armed hunter, to form a close association with the ancestral dog. Numerous examples are found in the writings and art of ancient peoples, indicating that animals were frequently kept as pets in many cultures.

The human-animal bond has endured through the ages despite some negative aspects of human-animal encounters, such as animal behavior problems, diseases transmissible from animals to man, and the allergic responses of some individuals to animals. Animals with which people may form bonds are members of many different species (Table 1).

The bond between an animal and a human being has been considered by some to be a sign of eccentricity in a person. However, for a number of reasons, this bond is currently receiving greater respect and attention. Some of these reasons are:

(1) psychologists and others have demonstrated the therapeutic value of using animals to help depressed people;

Sally O. Walshaw, M.A., VMD, is associate professor in the Veterinary Program at Michigan State University, East Lansing, Mich. A founder and current secretary of the MSU Committee on the Human/Animal Bond, she and her family participate weekly in the Visiting Pet Program at a local nursing home. *This chapter originally appeared in Kal Kan Forum, Vol. 2, No. 1, Winter, 1983. Reproduced by permission.*

(2) therapists have found animals very useful in physical therapy programs for the handicapped; and

(3) studies have revealed that pet ownership has positive effects on human health.

The value of dogs for the blind has been well documented. This chapter describes some of the ways in which animals can enrich the lives of human beings.

Defining the bond

The dictionary defines *bond* as "a uniting or binding element or force; a tie." Many questions about one of the most extensively studied bonding behaviors—that which occurs between a human mother and her child—remain unanswered. Serious studies of the bond between man and animals have only recently been undertaken.

One theory regarding the development of the bond between a person and an animal is based on the importance of the sense of touch. Touch is the earliest functional sense in a human infant and it persists in an elderly person even after other senses, such as vision and hearing, have become diminished. Of course, not all human-animal bonds can be explained by this principle. For certain species of animals that do not tolerate handling, e.g., fish and certain birds, the bond may result from appreciation of the animal's beauty or from companionship provided by the animal. The formation of a bond between a person and a dog is facilitated somewhat by the innate social behavior of dogs. "Dogs love company and suffer without it. Such company may be either canine or human," according to psychiatrist Alasdair MacDonald.

Table I. Animals with Which People May Form Bonds

General Group	Examples
Traditional companion animals	Dog, cat, horse, pet bird
Laboratory animals	Rabbit, mouse, gerbil, hamster, guinea pig, rat
Nondomestic animals	Snake, turtle, fish
Farm animals	Cow, pig, sheep, goat, chicken, duck, goose

The importance of pet animals

Pets and child development

A child psychologist, Dr. Boris M. Levinson, has suggested a number of ways in which pet animals can help to foster normal child development.

His conclusions have been at least partially verified by a study conducted in the United Kingdom, but additional investigation is needed in this field. Dr. Levinson's views regarding the role of a companion animal in child development may be summarized as follows:

For a child less than two years of age, touching a pet may be a very pleasurable experience; the child discovers the texture of fur, feathers, or scales. A pet animal in the home may stimulate a young child to crawl or walk as he attempts to follow it about the home.

By the age of approximately two years, the child becomes subject to increasing demands by his parents regarding acceptable social behavior, e.g., using the toilet, controlling aggression. From this point onward, throughout childhood and adolescence, the pet can serve a very important role as a nonjudgmental companion and love object.

Between the ages of approximately two and seven years, children have a need to fantasize, and this activity will often involve a pet. The pet also serves to help children differentiate between their magical fantasy worlds and reality. A child who is angry at his pet may wish that it would go away or disappear. Because the pet does not disappear, the child learns "that a wish does not imply a deed and that one can exercise some assertiveness and even hostility without necessarily incurring punishment," Levinson writes.

A child can be encouraged to assume responsibility for aspects of pet care appropriate to the child's age and level of development. Through such tasks as feeding, exercising, and training a pet, a child can begin to develop self-esteem, improved social skills with peers and adults, and nurturing attitudes. Moreover, a pet can aid in development of a child's learning ability because the child may actively seek more information about care of the pet. A child who has the opportunity to train a pet, especially a dog, will observe that time and patience are essential to the learning process. A child who owns a responsive pet can learn, by observing his pet's behavior, that one receives affection when one gives affection.

A number of potentially stressful events in a child's life may be eased by the presence of a companion animal. Examples include the arrival of a new baby brother or sister, serious illness or death of a family member, and starting school.

It is important to mention certain negative aspects of child-pet relationships that can arise. Some children have withdrawn completely from normal social interactions with other human beings into a fantasy world that involves a pet. Such children, and those who exhibit repeated or extreme cruelty toward animals, should be examined by a health professional skilled in dealing with psychological problems of children.

Some concerns about children and pets

A pet animal can injure a child, and indeed, large numbers of children are bitten by dogs every year in the United States. Parental supervision of child-animal interactions is important in minimizing the possibility of injury. The choice of an appropriate companion animal for a household with children requires some knowledge of animal behavior, including behavioral characteristics of specific breeds. Breeders, animal behaviorists, and veterinarians can serve the community by advising prospective pet owners on these matters. Obedience training can help a dog accept the dominant position of the human beings in the household.

A number of diseases are transmissible from animals to humans of all ages. However, children may be somewhat more likely than adults to contract some of these diseases for several reasons:

(1) many young children will eat dirt or suck on their fingers after playing in dirt;

(2) children often seek very close contact with their pet animals; and

(3) children may not bother to wash their hands after playing in dirt or with animals.

Nevertheless, a pediatrician, H.A. Carithers, after listing in a medical journal the diseases that pets can transmit, stated, "most non- allergic children should be allowed to have pets despite the fact they may at times transmit disease. The advantages far outweigh the risk, which is not great."

A pet animal's place in the life of an adult

Pet animals can improve the quality of an adult's life in a number of ways. Pets enable those who enjoy exhibiting their pets at animal shows to participate in this recreational activity. Such pets can be a source of considerable pride, thus contributing to the owner's self-esteem. The benefits of vigorous outdoor recreation as well as the satisfaction resulting from dog-human teamwork are enjoyed by owners of dogs used for hunting or obedience work.

For adults who are childless, a pet may be a child substitute, allowing them to express their nurturing attitudes. In some cases, owning a pet may help prepare an adult for parenthood.

One of the most important roles a pet can fulfill is that of a companion. The nonjudgmental, "no strings attached" affection displayed by certain species of animals toward their owners is as important for adults as for children. This companionship can be especially important for adults living alone because it provides them with a sense of being needed, a feeling of being useful. In fact, there is statistical evidence that chronic loneliness can predispose one to serious disease and even premature death, as James

J. Lynch has written in *The Broken Heart - The Medical Consequences of Loneliness.*

The question is sometimes raised as to whether pet owners tend to have less affection for other human beings than do nonpet owners. Several researchers have shown that the opposite is true in most cases.

Certain pet animal species (dogs, cats, some pet birds) actively seek and enjoy caressing, stroking attention from their owners. Other species of pet animals that are usually confined to cages within the home (e.g., guinea pigs, rabbits, snakes) also seem to respond to gentle handling and petting by their owners. Petting an animal constitutes one of the very few acceptable outlets for an adult to utilize his sense of touch in an affectionate, relaxing way.

Depending on the species of pet, a pet owner may be compelled to exercise. The form of exercise ranges from strenuous for the horse owner to very mild for the tropical fish owner. For a physically handicapped or elderly person, however, simply moving about the home to feed the fish or pet a bird may be useful exercise.

A companion animal, especially a dog or cat, provides its owner with the opportunity to engage in play. Such opportunities for unstructured play are relatively rare in the lives of adults and are obviously beneficial in our stressful society.

There is evidence that pets can exert beneficial effects on the health of adult human beings. A study of patients who had been hospitalized for coronary heart disease, conducted by Erika Friedmann and others, revealed a significant improvement in one-year survival rates if the patients owned pets. The type of pet was immaterial and included dogs, cats, and birds. The beneficial effects of pets on survival were seen in both unmarried and married individuals. These findings suggest that pets provide a unique relationship that is important for human beings irrespective of their human associations.

The higher survival rate of coronary disease patients who own pets may be partially explained by the pet's possible effect on the person's blood pressure. It has been demonstrated experimentally that a person's heart rate and blood pressure decrease while the person is petting a dog. Similarly, a decrease in blood pressure has been observed in the following animal species while they were being petted: dogs, guinea pigs, rats, rabbits, cats, and pet horses.

An additional benefit of companion animals is that they can help adults feel more a part of the natural world. This is certainly desirable in a highly technological society, especially for city dwellers.

Animals and elderly people

A pet may be even more important for an elderly individual than for a young adult or child. The opportunities to give and receive affection are

Touch is the earliest functional sense in infants and persists long after senses have dimmed in the elderly. Dog's innate social behavior makes them prime candidates for human/companion animal bond programs.

often quite limited for elderly people. An aged person may benefit greatly from having a pet that depends on him for food, affection, and shelter: the owner must get out of bed even if just to feed his bird or fish.

For elderly persons living in cities, pet dogs may help decrease their anxieties about being robbed or assaulted. Even a small dog will bark a warning if someone is approaching the home. In addition, the sensitive hearing ability of the average dog probably will exceed that of its elderly owner.

A study conducted in England with a group of elderly persons living alone revealed that one of the major functions of a pet animal may be to serve as a "social lubricant," that is, "a focal point for communication with friends, family and neighbors." Budgerigars (parakeets) were provided to a group of retired persons, who were then visited monthly by a social worker. The effects of the birds on the lives of these elderly persons were assessed by means of a questionnaire given before and five months after the birds were placed in their homes. The presence of the birds correlated with significant improvement in the subjects' attitudes and mental health, according to researchers R.A. Mugford and J.G. M'Comisky.

Elderly persons in nursing homes can derive special pleasure from touching and petting an animal. The social isolation and lack of sensory experiences in the authoritarian atmosphere of such institutions can hasten the deterioration of the residents. The introduction of pets into nursing homes, either as visiting pets brought on a regular basis by volunteers or as resident pets, has brought much joy into the lives of many nursing home residents. Guidelines for the introduction of pets into nursing homes have been published. (*See Chapter 16*).

Pet loss and human emotion

Pets fulfill many needs in the lives of people of all ages. It is understandable, therefore, that pet death usually results in grief for the owners. The grief experienced by bereaved pet owners seems to follow a similar pattern to grief at the death of a person and includes denial (shock, disbelief), anger (developing awareness), depression (guilt, restlessness, withdrawal) and, finally, acceptance. Some signs of normal grieving are weeping, pain, anger, loss of appetite, insomnia, depression, withdrawal, preoccupation with the memory of the lost one, and feelings of guilt or loneliness.

Observations of many owners' reactions over a number of years have led one veterinarian, G.D. Whitney, to conclude that persons 60 years of age and older experience the most profound grief at a pet's death. This same author also stated that children up to 19 years of age usually adjust fairly quickly to the death of a pet. Explanations for an age-related effect on grief are based on the relationship of the animal to the owner. An elderly person living alone whose sole companion is a pet animal would be expected to grieve more at the pet's death than would an active 10-year-old child surrounded by the distractions of school and home life.

At the time of a pet's death or euthanasia, parents are often concerned about possible adverse emotional effects on their children. However, the opportunity for a child to experience and express grief at such a time within the framework of a loving family is a valuable preparation for coping with loss throughout life.

Children need to know four basic things about death, although the manner and depth of explanation depend on a child's age and level of maturity. Children need:

Pets are non-judgmental, non-threatening, love objects and play significant roles in child development. *(Photo by Phil Arkow)*

(1) a definition of death (e.g., lack of movement, cessation of breathing and eating);

(2) to know the cause of the death, if known, so that death does not seem so arbitrary;

(3) a description of normal feelings associated with loss (e.g., pain, anger); and

(4) a philosophical framework within which to place death (e.g., heaven, natural cycles).

It is important to be honest with the child about the animal's death, although certain details, e.g., the killing of a baby animal by its mother, might be too upsetting to reveal to a child.

Grief in children is characterized by a shorter span of sadness (although children may return to the subject again and again), a stronger need for denial, the tendency to suppress all questions if the adults seem disturbed by the issue, and reactivation of the subject as the child progresses into different developmental stages.

One of the main problems facing a bereaved pet owner is the fact that in Western society there is no culturally acceptable way of mourning a pet. At worst, friends and acquaintances, on learning of a pet's death, may make callous remarks such as "Well, at least you can be thankful that it was only a dog and not one of your children." At best, few people, if any, will acknowledge the pet's death to be a significant loss for the owner.

Grieving children and adults may derive some comfort through such measures as the burial of the pet, a contribution made in the pet's name to an animal charity, or the production of a scrapbook of pictures, stories and poems about the animal. There are several excellent books that can help children and adults cope with a pet's death. Certainly compassion for our fellow man should lead us to extend comforting measures to bereaved pet owners as we would to other bereaved persons. *(See Chapter 6)*

Animals as therapeutic aids

Animals have been used as adjuncts in the therapy of people with physical handicaps, mental retardation, psychological disorders, and criminal tendencies (Table II). Some terms used to describe therapy that utilizes animals are *animal-facilitated therapy, pet-facilitated therapy, pet therapy, animal-assisted therapy, pet-mediated therapy, pet-facilitated psychotherapy,* and *pet-oriented psychotherapy*. The term *animal-facilatated therapy* will be used here because it encompasses pet and farm animal species and physical as well as psychotherapy.

Many individual success stories about animal-facilitated therapy have been reported, but few carefully controlled, statistically valid scientific investigations have been conducted in this area. Well-designed research studies could lead to improvement of existing animal-facilitated therapy programs and establishment of new ones.

Animal-facilitated therapy for the handicapped

One of the best known and long-established uses for animals in modern society is that of guide dogs for blind persons. In most cases, such dogs are permitted on public vehicles, in restaurants, and in other areas where dogs are not generally allowed. Society recognizes the valuable function that these dogs perform. A study conducted in England revealed higher levels of self-esteem in guide dog owners than in sightless non-owners even if the non-owners were quite mobile and independent. *(See Chapter 8).*

TABLE II. Animals as Therapetuic Aids

Human Problem	Animal(s) Used
Physical handicaps	
Blindness	Dog, horse
Deafness	Dog
Neuromuscular disorders	Horse, monkey
Mental retardation	Dog, cat, rabbit, horse, farm animals
Psychological or emotional disturbances	Dog, cat, horse, farm animals, bird, fish, pet rodents (gerbil, guinea pig, etc.)
Criminal offenses	Cat, bird, fish, pet rodents, farm animals
Disabilities associated with aging	Dog, cat, bird, rabbit, pet rodents, farm animals

In the 1970s, several programs were established to train dogs to help people with hearing impairments. Dogs with this training alert their owners to various sounds, e.g., baby crying, telephone ringing, smoke alarm buzzing, and doorbell ringing. *(See Chapter 9).*

Horseback riding for the handicapped was reported as long ago as 1875 and is conducted in several countries, including the United States. A handicapped rider is assisted, if necessary, by volunteers walking on both sides of the horse, and the rider is protected by safety harnesses and a helmet. The riders do exercises on horseback and participate in various games designed to improve balance, coordination, and muscular strength.

Important social and psychological benefits have been observed, which include improved self-esteem and motivation. For someone ordinarily confined to a wheelchair, it is a uniquely pleasurable experience to sit on a horse and communicate with others without having to look upward. An excellent film on horseback riding for the handicapped was photographed at the Cheff Center for the Handicapped in Augusta, Michigan. This film is entitled *Ability, Not Disability* and is available from the Latham Foundation. *(See Chapter 12).*

Still in the experimental stage is a program in which Capuchin monkeys are trained to assist quadriplegic individuals in a variety of ways. In a segment of the CBS television show *60 Minutes*, a monkey was seen feeding and getting a drink for a paralyzed person, turning on a tape recorder, and operating a small vacuum cleaner on command.

Another recent development is the training of dogs to assist people with impaired neuromuscular function. The dogs are being taught various tasks such as opening doors and retrieving specific household objects.

Animal-facilitated therapy for mentally retarded persons

Some schools for mentally retarded children in the United States utilize animals in their teaching programs. The children enjoy the physical activity associated with the animals, including farm animals. Through helping with animal care tasks, the children can learn cooperation and certain concepts, such as right and left, push and pull.

Many mentally handicapped individuals feel inferior and unloved and consequently may become more and more withdrawn and helpless. Animals, as nonjudgmental, affectionate companions, can add a special dimension to the lives of mentally retarded children and adults. There are reports of success in teaching animal care duties to mentally retarded adults using dogs and, in one center, a rabbit.

Pet-facilitated psychotherapy

The use of pet animals as adjuncts to therapy for people with psychological disorders was reported as long ago as the eighteenth century. For the most part, the animal has served as an agent by which the therapist can begin to gain the trust of the patient. This has been the case especially with withdrawn, hostile, or fearful patients. The patient (whether child or adult) may address all his remarks or attention to the animal for the first few sessions, then he begins to talk to the therapist about the animal, and finally he begins to talk to the therapist about himself.

Although much of the literature on using pets for psychotherapy consists of case reports rather than rigorous scientific studies, these reports indicate that this approach is very promising. One such report by Levinson describes an eight-year-old adopted child who had convinced himself that being surrendered for adoption meant that he was bad. Through conversations with the therapist about the therapist's cat adopted from an animal shelter, the boy ultimately came to believe that he was lovable and, in fact, loved by his adoptive parents. "Skeezer," a mixed-breed dog that lived for a number of years in the Children's Psychiatric Hospital at the University of Michigan, was credited by the staff with being extremely valuable in reaching troubled children.

One of the few scientific studies of pet-facilitated psychotherapy was conducted by Samuel and Elizabeth Corson at Ohio State University using what they term "feeling heart" dogs. They found improvement in the patients' responsiveness to questions after dogs were introduced into the therapy program: patients' verbal responses occurred more quickly after the questions were asked and the patients used a greater number of words in their answers.

A study, conducted by Michael McCulloch, a psychiatrist in Portland, Oregon, investigated the importance of pets in the lives of individuals who suffered mental depression as a result of severe physical illness. Two-thirds of these patients indicated that their general mood was improved by the presence of their pets. Pets helped them to feel needed and to retain a sense of humor.

Animal-facilitated therapy in institutions for the elderly

The psychological problems of depression and withdrawal from social interaction are not uncommon among elderly persons confined to nursing homes and hospitals: In a study by the Corsons using dogs, the general morale of many of the nursing home residents improved and the willingness to exercise of a number of the residents increased. Cats have also been well received by geriatric residents of institutions. In a study using cats in a Veterans Administration Hospital geriatric ward, staff members noted improvements in the patients' overall responsiveness and sense of reality, as well as other benefits such as a more home-like atmosphere on the ward and pleasure associated with giving and receiving affection from the cats, Clark Brickel has reported.

A case history from the Corsons' work illustrates potential rewards of animal-facilitated therapy in institutions for the elderly:

> Jed was in his late seventies and had been a nursing home resident for 26 years. He was admitted to Castle Nursing Homes, Millersburg, Ohio,

Elderly residents in nursing homes can derive particular pleasure from petting animals. Pet visits can combat social isolation and the lack of sensory experiences in an institution. *(Photo by Susan Reardon)*

in 1949, after suffering brain damage in a fall from a tower. At the time of his admission he was believed to be deaf and mute as a result of his accident.

Through the ensuing years Jed was antisocial and often appeared to be unaware of those who cared for him. The staff used hand signals in attempting to communicate with him. Since Jed could read, the nurses would also write notes to him in order to try to ascertain his needs. Jed's only form of verbal communication was grunting and mumbling which was incoherent and not necessarily used to make his needs known. He spent most of his time sitting in silence, apparently deaf, with intermittent outbursts of mumbling to himself. In 1975, shortly after the arrival of the "feeling heart" dogs at the Castle Nursing Homes, the administrator, Donald DeHass, brought dog Whiskey (a German shepherd X husky) to visit Jed. Jed's reaction was immediate—he spoke his first words in 26 years: "You brought that dog." Jed was delighted and chuckled as he petted the dog.

With the introduction of the dog, the communication barrier was broken. Jed started talking to the staff about "his" dog. The nurses noted an improvement in Jed's disposition and in his interactions with the staff and other residents. Jed started drawing pictures of dogs and now has a large collection of canine drawings. This artwork is fairly sophisticated, and his collection contains various breeds of dogs. Many of the pictures exhibit well-drawn detail (such as teeth, whiskers, toenails, eyelashes, etc.) and interesting postures of the animals. Jed was later introduced to Fluff, an outgoing, active wire-haired fox terrier. Jed immediately made friends with the dog and told her, "I'll take care of you." This was the beginning of a continuing friendship. The staff and nurses have stated that they believe that pet-facilitated psychotherapy made Jed a happier person and more willing to interact with people. They also believe that his speech improved, particularly in clarity. Jed made a greater effort to be verbally understood, especially when he wanted to visit his canine friend or to inquire about the dog's welfare.

Animal-facilitated therapy in correctional institutions

There have been many reports of prison inmates adopting and lavishing affection on various animals, including dogs, cats, birds, mice, and rats. There are successful animal-facilitated therapy programs using cats in two California prisons. There have also been negative experiences in which unstructured and poorly supervised programs involving animals increased antagonism among prisoners.

Some institutions for disruptive or emotionally disturbed children who are criminal offenders use animals to aid in developing a sense of responsibility in the children. Both positive and negative results have been reported, the negative consisting primarily of instances of animal abuse by the children.

One of the most successful animal-facilitated therapy programs involving prisoners is located at Lima State Hospital for the Criminally Insane in Ohio. In this program, a patient is permitted a pet of his own if he proves himself reliable in caring for the ward animals (fish and gerbils). After acquiring his own pet, the patient must provide money for pet food out of his own personal allowance or by working in the hospital. Benefits of this program include a decrease in violent episodes, improvement of morale of staff as well as patients, and lower medication requirements. *(See Chapter 11)*.

Rehabilitation of individuals in prison is one of the most challenging tasks facing the staff of those institutions. For the safety of society, it is also one of the most important responsibilities of the correctional system. Animal-facilitated therapy may be of value in the rehabilitation process. To minimize risk to the animals and people, such programs should be carefully designed and well supervised.

The human-animal bond: a topic for research

There are many unanswered questions about the human-animal bond and its significance throughout the life of a human being. Animal-facilitated therapy is for the most part a new field and requires careful investigation so that maximum benefits can be realized.

At the present time, a number of research proposals are being prepared and studies are being conducted in many countries. Many universities have established centers or committees to study the human-animal bond. These groups are generally multidisciplinary in composition, their members being physicians, nurses, psychologists, social workers, veterinarians, and other interested individuals in the university and surrounding community. Several authors have raised intriguing research questions for workers and provided guidelines for conducting research in this field. *(See Appendix II)*

The human-animal bond: some possibilities for the future

Statistically sound research in this area is urgently needed. The nature of nonverbal communication is an important topic for investigation. The effects of animal-facilitated therapy must be documented so that such programs can be initiated and improved. This research is urgently needed because it is ethically questionable, regardless of good intentions, to subject people already suffering from physical and/or mental illness to an untested form of therapy. Study of the human-animal bond itself should yield information that could help an owner form a mutually enjoyable relationship with a pet.

The topic of the human-animal bond has been added to the curriculum of most veterinary schools. This subject should also be included in the training of physicians, nurses, psychologists, social workers, physical therapists, and teachers. Parents and members of the clergy also need to be informed about the human-animal bond. Continuing education and community education programs should address this topic. *(See Chapter 14).*

Research confirming the anecdotal reports of successful animal-facilitated therapy would probably result in the writing of "prescriptions for pets." A major stumbling block to implementing such a recommendation is the refusal of many landlords and institutions to allow pets. Legislation will be necessary to permit pet ownership while respecting environmental concerns and the rights of nonpet owners. There is no substitute for responsible pet ownership as an aid to changing public attitudes on this issue. One example of a positive institutional attitude toward the human-animal bond would be for hospital admissions clerks to inquire about any pets in the home. The hospital would notify friends or volunteers to care for the pet(s) during the person's hospitalization, if the patient is unable to do so.

Ethical responsibilities toward animals are as yet not completely defined. Animals used as adjuncts to therapy must be protected from maltreatment and their needs for rest as well as food and shelter must be met. A working animal's need for a "vacation" was recognized by the personnel at the University of Michigan; therefore, they arranged for Skeezer, their canine cotherapist, to spend an occasional weekend at a nearby rural home.

Best friends

Modern technology has liberated human beings from certain exhausting labors and from some devastating diseases. Urban and suburban living in a fast-paced society, however, take their toll in stress-related ailments and increasing alienation from the natural world. Animal companions may provide human beings with a link to that world and in so doing may help us preserve some of the better qualities of human nature. By helping people to relax, animals may provide some defense against stress. There are very few components of modern society that lower one's blood pressure as occurs when one pets an animal or observes an aquarium of fish.

The following statement by veterinarian and animal welfare advocate Michael Fox could perhaps be amended to extend to all the animals that enrich the lives of human beings: "**Although the dog is man's best friend, could it be that man will someday be man's best friend also? Perhaps being a dog's best friend is a start in the right direction.**"

Suggested reading:

Fogle, Bruce (ed). *Interrelations Between People and Pets.* Springfield, Ill.: Charles C. Thomas, 1981.

Levinson, Boris *Pets and Human Development.* Springfield, Ill.: Charles C. Thomas, 1979.

Corson, Samuel, and Corson, Elizabeth (eds). *Ethology and Nonverbal Communication in Mental Health.* Oxford: Pergamon Press, 1980.

Anderson, R.S. (ed). *Pet Animals and Society.* Baltimore: Williams & Wilkins, 1975.

Arkow, Phil *"Pet Therapy": A Study of the Use of Companion Animals in Selected Therapies.* Colorado Springs, Colo.: Humane Society of the Pikes Peak Region, 1983.

Bustad, Leo *Animals, Aging and the Aged.* Minneapolis: University of Minnesota Press, 1980

Neiburg, H. and Fischer, A. *Pet Loss - A Thoughtful Guide for Adults and Children.* New York: Harper and Row, 1982.

Viorst, J. *The Tenth Good Thing about Barney.* Hartford CT: Atheneum, 1971.

Cusack, Odean and Smith, Elaine. *Pets and the Elderly.* New York: The Haworth Press, 1984.

Grollman, Earl A. (ed.) *Explaining Death to Children.* Boston: Beacon Press, 1967.

Osterweis, Marian; Solomon, Fredric; and Green, Morris (eds.) *Bereavement: Reactions, Consequences, and Care.* Washington, D. C.: National Academy Press, 1984.

Quackenbush, Jamie and Voith, Victoria. The human-companion animal bond. *The Veterinary Clinics of North America,* Vol. 15, No. 2. Philadelphia: W. B. Saunders Company, March 1985.

Sussman, Marvin B. (ed.) *Pets and the Family.* New York: The Haworth Press, 1985.

Section II -

Understanding Both Sides of the Bond

3

Who Needs Animals?

Joseph W. Meeker

"Without animals, we cannot become ourselves..."

Since all life lives from other life, all of us animals need one another. But the obvious importance of evolutionary history and daily nourishment are not nearly enough to explain the fundamental bond that ties us to the animals with whom we share the planet. Our connections with animals span the depths of time, space, mind, and spirit. Without them, we cannot truly become ourselves.

Living with a pet seems a simple enough thing on the surface, but when you look fully at the implications of household pets, the complexities are vast. It is perhaps fortunate that some parents don't know what they are getting into when they buy a puppy or kitten for their toddler, or they might never take that first step (in some cases they shouldn't). One motive parents have for adding an animal to their household is to help their children "learn responsibility." Feeding and caring for an animal are supposed to teach the child to keep a regular schedule for meals and cleanup. Moms everywhere know that it often doesn't work that way, for they end up doing the daily chores while the child concentrates on what it most needs and wants from the pet: fuzzy love uncluttered by rules.

Children rarely need to be taught to love an animal, for that comes naturally. Why should it? The answer lies in several millions of years of close sharing that have passed between humans and other creatures. Whether wild or domesticated, animals have played a major role in shaping the emotional and mental lives of people as long as they have been around on the planet. Every culture is rich in animal stories for children, and these have grown from direct experiences and deep wisdom accumulated over trackless time. The animals in the best children's tales

Joseph W. Meeker, Ph.D., teaches graduate studies in Whole Systems Design at Antioch University in Seattle, Wash. His background includes comparative literature, philosophy, wildlife ecology, and post-doctoral studies in comparative animal and human behavior with Konrad Lorenz at the Max Planck Institute in Germany.

are not mere symbols for abstract ideas or moral rules; they are the bearers of truths which cannot be learned in any other way. When an American Indian child learns of the many ways of the coyote, he or she is learning how the world works.

Animal educators

A kitten or a coyote can teach any child much about the realities of the world. Love is one of those lessons, but only one among many. A growing child often has its first experience of illness, injury, or death through an animal it has known. Caring for a sick cat or grieving at the irreversibility of its death often shapes how a child will react to those experiences in mature life. How to handle feelings of aggression and fear are other lessons we often learn from animals. Birds teach music, and our minds learn to soar in imagination on their wings. Several dozen garden spiders in my childhood taught me the beauty and practicality of webs, and the structural principles which underlie good form and good engineering.

Human relationships with animals are usually reciprocal; when we perceive them, we are also being perceived by them. One wonders what animals may learn from us? Perhaps not much, for astonishingly few of them have chosen to sit at our feet. Of the millions of animal species on the planet, only a handful—less than fifty—have proved susceptible to domestication. The vast majority cannot (will not?) adapt their ways of living to the lifestyles of humans, and those which have done so often find good cause to regret it.

The process of domestication requires that we find ways to weaken or to compromise the basic integrity of an animal species, and to prevent it from attaining normal maturity. We feed it, so it loses its ability to earn its own living. We restrain its movement, so it becomes lethargic and sedentary. We regulate its normal social relations and sexual life, so it becomes neurotic or bizarre compared to its wild relatives. And our attempts at breeding and genetic engineering often distort its physical characteristics drastically. If domestic animals sometimes seem beastly, it is because humans have made them so.

Instead of teaching by example, as animals do for us, we prefer to train them to perform for our gain or pleasure. The applause when a dolphin or lion leaps through a hoop of flame has been earned by the trainer, and does not reflect our understanding of the marvels that those animals are, in and of themselves. Such displays perpetuate the myth that humans are in control of the natural world, and actually work against our need for better understanding of animal life. Zoos display caged and begging creatures, usually behaving abnormally. Yet even from these warped and wounded animals we can learn about ourselves and the world.

Marginal domestication

Some borderline animals live on the fringes of human influence, accepting and rejecting our ways as they see fit. Cats are like that. Whether we have domesticated cats, or they us, is a question cat owners and biologists can debate for hours. It was that way with the quarter-wolf malamute sled dogs I used to work with in Alaska. Their domestication was only skin deep, and they never let me indulge in the illusion that I was in control of their lives. If they did what I wished, it was clearly because they had decided to do so, and it told me that they had accepted me as a cooperating member of their group. Often that didn't work, and I did things their way. Efficiency is not among the characteristics of dog sledding.

Training animals to perform for our pleasure does not reflect our understanding of the marvels that these animals are. Such displays perpetuate the myth that humans are in control of the natural world. *(Photo by Phil Arkow)*

One of the strongest dogs, Joe, was a marvel of energy and a terror to try to manage. He was the team comedian, loving to play tricks, clown around, or pull surprises out of nowhere. Sometimes he was a bully, snarling at weaker dogs or at me over a scrap of food when I knew he was full fed and just wanted to display his power. I was ready for danger or buffoonery whenever I approached him, and he provided both. But when Joe was seriously injured in a fight with several dogs, and was gashed to the bone from his nose to the back of his head, he let me hold his head in my lap while he was sewed up with needle and thread and no anaesthetic. In his eyes I saw trust, affection, and gratitude, mingled with his fear and pain. In a couple of weeks, he was his normal crazy self again, but the bond between us was stronger. I count Joe among the better teachers I have known in my life.

Animal ethics

The ways in which humans relate to animals are based upon ethical

Animals are the Others, different from us but resembling us enough so that we can recognize important parts of ourselves in them. Sometimes this gets taken to an extreme, as this man and his dog (or dog and his man?), winners in an owner-pet look-alike contest, demonstrate. *(Photo by Phil Arkow)*

principles, stated or unstated. Every culture has a code of animal beliefs which governs the ways people think and feel about various animals, and all lay down laws about what can and cannot be done to or with them, which animals are to be feared, which hunted, which befriended, which worshipped, which exploited. It should come as no surprise to hear that the way we treat animals is usually parallel to the ways we treat our fellow human beings, for the ethics of both patterns rise from the same cultural roots. American settlers and frontiersmen brought with them attitudes which they applied to the animals and people they found in North America, and to those they brought here for their own purposes. Indians and buffaloes alike were seen as wild creatures to be exterminated from the plains. Black people were brought from Africa and used as domesticated animals to perform agricultural and domestic drudgery. Americans have lived according to a mythology of power which affirms the right of people to impose their will on any creature, human or animal, whose ways do not resemble their own.

Animals, Indians, and black people have not been the only victims of that philosophy. Another aspect of it is sexism, where males impose their will upon females and restrict their lives through the exercise of power. Part of that philosophy is the belief that the world consists of "resources" waiting to be used by anyone having the power to use them, and that it is a proper road to human glory to exercise that power in every way possible. Racism and sexism are among the results, to which we can now add "resourcism."

Education by totem

As a graduate student in wildlife ecology, I was told that wild animals are a "crop" to be managed like any other crop for maximum human benefit. I debated that as best I could using the puny powers available to students, but soon realized that I was up against an argument that was deeply imbedded in the culture and enforced by its institutions. Feeling the wrongness of that belief, but unable to get around it, I leaped when I was offered a job as ranger at Mt. McKinley (now Denali) National Park in Alaska. That began the most significant educational experience of my life, living for two years in the midst of one of the continent's last remaining wildlife concentrations, studying the animals, sharing a wilderness with them, and learning, as they must, how to cope with a very harsh environment.

Of the many animals I became close to, both scientifically and emotionally, the Alaskan moose *(Alces gigas)* strangely stood out as a creature of great importance to me. Something about its movement, color, shape, demeanor, and character spoke more deeply to me than other animals. It looked, and was, an ancient creature whose form had not changed for many millenia, and it carried its inherited antiquity with grace and dignity. I learned all I could about moose, studying in books and laboratories, and spending many hours watching, photographing, and drinking in mooseness with everything I had. Now and then I overstepped the boundaries, and was sent scurrying up a tree by bulls defending their space or by cows fearful that I might harm their calves. Even these encounters increased my awareness that the moose was a creature of spiritual importance to me: I had discovered my totem animal.

Years later, when I was studying animal behavior under Konrad Lorenz in Germany, I told him some of my moose stories. He laughed and said that earlier that day he and his wife, Gretl, had been watching me walk across a field, and had decided that I reminded them of a moose. Tall, with long legs, big nose, and a loose, stooped gait, my appearance brought the moose to their minds. That evening when Konrad gave me a copy of one of his books, he drew in the flyleaf a sketch of my relationship to the Alaskan moose.

Attentiveness to the wild animals who share our urban ecosystems leads to personal awareness of animals and planetary consciousness. We must learn to become better neighbors, lest the entire neighborhood deteriorate beyond recovery. *(Photo by Phil Arkow)*

With the very best regards to
my dear friend
Joe Meeker
who, allthough coming from a
very different side, is a
most helpful ally
Seewiesen Nov. 9/11/1971
Konrad

Totem animals (or plants, or mountains) have been an essential means of self-discovery for most of the people who have lived on earth. A totem is something separate from oneself, living by its own rules, not under human control, yet still expressive of one's personal spirit and meaning in life. It is at once an image of the Otherness of natural creation, and of the close connectedness which humans share with the natural world. Anyone who lacks a totem, I think, is living in a state of spiritual, emotional, and intellectual deprivation.

Otherness and usness

Clever people that we are, we create substitutes for totems because they are hard to find in urban or industrialized places. Teenagers who in saner times would have been embarking on vision quests in search of their totems, instead yearn for automobiles named for powerful animals: lynx, falcon, bobcat, cougar, or the sacred thunderbird. Their sports teams have names like tigers, lions, bears, eagles, or other fearsome wild creatures. A young person can get a semblance of identity from association with machines or groups of people named for wild animals, but that is a far cry from the real thing of knowing personally the genuine animal that links a person with the planet.

Wildness lies within us, the residuum of millions of years when people learned how to live by attending to the land and the creatures which surrounded them. Human domestication of those creatures is a recent phenomenon of only eight or ten thousand years, and our mechanized separation from nature is a short blip of a couple of centuries on the multi-million year time scale that has formed human consciousness. The deepest parts of people still nestle in a world populated by many different species of plants and animals which we know as companions in the processes of life. However much we may overlay that knowledge with illusions that we are the earth's centerpiece, our ties to other animals persist in leaking into modern life, subtly but persistently reminding us of their importance.

Humans are a unique species of animal, but then so are all the others. The interplay among species is a game of Usness and Otherness for all creatures who play it. From our point of view, animals are the Others, different from us in many ways but resembling us enough so that we can recognize important parts of ourselves in their forms, behavior, and relationships. It is difficult to guess what we might mean to another species, but there is no doubt that we have affected their lives in countless ways. Many animals might describe us as the Others who often disregard the rules of life. But the responsibility of all species is the same: to fulfill the potential that exists in every life form as fully as possible. I must try to become as complete a man as I can, just as a moose must try to become a complete moose.

Companion animals

The fulfillment of any given life cannot occur in isolation. Maturity grows from interactions at every stage of life. Although we may pretend that interactions with other people are the only essential contacts that will help us to grow, deep within us we know better. Reaching out to other animals is a normal and necessary part of every human life, and it is a rare or deformed person who does not do so in one way or another. There is a voice within us to say that we cannot completely be Us unless we somehow make contact with all that Otherness.

We do live in a rare and deformed time when, as never before, the separation between most people and animals is enormous. Even worse, the ways we are living in industrial society are causing or hastening the extinctions of many animal species which can never be replaced. Each species that is lost is a piece of the earth, and a piece of humanity, gone forever. How many pieces can we lose without destroying the game of life itself? No one knows the answer, but it may be the most important question there is.

The bond of companionship between humans and animals takes two major forms: personal and planetary. In order to salvage and sustain the natural heritage we share with animals, it will be necessary to re-align those two forms and to seek their unity. The task begins with ourselves, each of us individually examining and enhancing the roles that animals play in our lives, and our role in theirs.

Pets are the nearest animals to most American families. Even though many generations of domestication separate them from their wild ancestors, still they are parts of the Other. It is a mistake to think of a pet as a piece of owned property whose life is fully controlled by a human master. Love and mutual respect are the most important things to strive for in relationships with a household animal, and the idea of ownership impedes those feelings. Pets should be observed closely and listened to for what they have to teach us. Their approach to problems that must be solved, pains that must be relieved, and relationships that must be nurtured are different from ours, but instructive to us none the less. To regard a dog or cat as your teacher is an important first step toward discovering humility before life, and the rewards of taking more steps in that direction are very great.

Pets may be the most obvious animals in and around our homes, but they are not as abundant, nor as instructive, as the wild animals that live with us. Every home has its spiders, who have been known for many millenia as great teachers to humans. An hour spent now and then watching a spider build and maintain her web is well invested if it can teach the wonderful combination of calm patience, swift and purposeful action, and careful creativeness that spiders know so well. Near my desk I keep a diagram of the stages in the construction of a typical spider web to remind me of the step-at-a-time attentiveness that is necessary to create anything that will be both beautiful and practical. I also share my office with quite a few real spiders who daily add footnotes and appendices to the lifeless diagram on the wall. Other small creatures drop in from time to time bearing different lessons, like the wasps who fly in the window to hunt

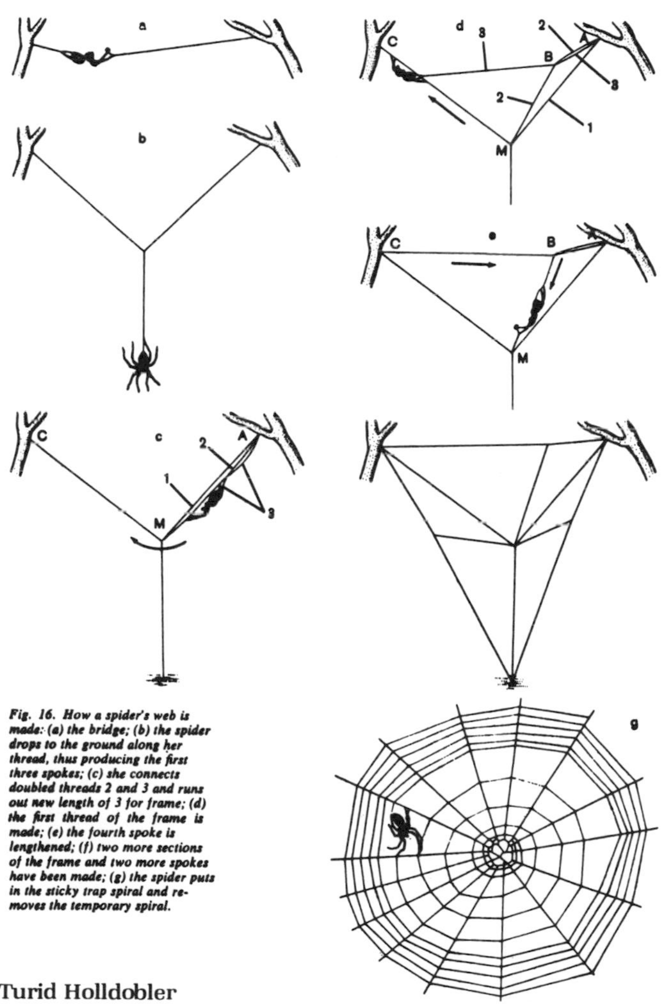

Fig. 16. How a spider's web is made: (a) the bridge; (b) the spider drops to the ground along her thread, thus producing the first three spokes; (c) she connects doubled threads 2 and 3 and runs out new length of 3 for frame; (d) the first thread of the frame is made; (e) the fourth spoke is lengthened; (f) two more sections of the frame and two more spokes have been made; (g) the spider puts in the sticky trap spiral and removes the temporary spiral.

spiders, or the squirrel who chatters news to me while digging for acorns in my potted plants.

Even in a city, it is possible to know many wild animals personally. Insects, rodents, and birds are everywhere among us that we have not poisoned to death. Most waters support fish, and there are aquariums that will bring their beauty and grace into our homes. Attentiveness to the animals nearby has always been a human habit, and it is one which can be easily developed into a learning experience that expands the human mind while leading it toward better health.

As personal awareness of animals grows, so does planetary conciousness. Once we appreciate the needs other animals have for the right to live their lives according to their own ways, it is easier to understand that human activities must be conducted in ways that will sustain all life forms. Power over nature is not the highest role humans can play on earth. Our attempts to control natural proceses have been disastrously successful in recent centuries, and the whole earth is groaning to pay the prices of our excesses. We must learn quickly to become better neighbors to the creatures with whom we share life, lest the whole neighborhood deteriorate beyond recovery.

Cooperation with life

Companionable participation, not power, is the best gift we can offer to life. Differences between human and non-human forms of life are abundant and wonderfully instructive. Every plant and animal demonstrates a different way of life, reminding us of the richness and diversity of styles that are possible in the processes of being. What we share with them, however, is at least as profound as our differences from them. Together, we are all participants in the planet's experiment in living. If we can understand what that means, then human self-interest and the preservation of other creatures become one cause and one connected experience.

Self-interest is inevitable, and is a normal part of the game of life. If elephants or salamanders felt that they were the most important and potent creatures on earth, and forgot that they were members of the living community, it is a safe bet that they would legislate in their own best interests much as people do. Perhaps the dinosaurs ruled the earth for their own benefit, and look how they turned out: extinct. We needn't follow their example.

Suggested reading:

Shepard, Paul *Thinking Animals.* New York: Viking Press, 1978.

Livingston, John *The Fallacy of Wildlife Conservation.* Toronto: McClelland & Stuart, 1981.

Lorenz, Konrad *Studies in Animal and Human Behavior.* (2 vols.) Cambridge: Harvard University Press, 1970.

Thomas, Lewis *The Lives of a Cell.* New York: Viking Press, 1974.

Meeker, Joseph *The Comedy of Survival.* Los Angeles: Guild of Tutors Press, 1980.

4

Pet Owner Psychology: The Human Side of the Bond

Aline H. Kidd and Robert M. Kidd

"similarity and complementarity"

An equestrian, paralyzed by polio in both legs, wins a silver medal in dressage at the 1952 Helsinki Olympics...

A number of patients with neurological damage and neuro-muscular disease are more physically relaxed, have improved circulation and get both sides of the body working more smoothly together after a series of riding lessons...

Some epileptics are taught to focus attention on equestrian techniques and so increase their ability to relax and reduce the number and severity of their seizures...

A handful of mentally retarded and emotionally disturbed individuals are taught to ride—and gain increased self-esteem, gain ability to concentrate on external stimuli, and show a better physical well being...

Several mute autistic children are introduced to ponies and porpoises and begin speaking to animals and then include people in their verbal communications...

Aline H. Kidd, Ph.D., is professor of psychology at Mills College, in Oakland, Calif. She is a prominent educator, a licensed clinician and experimental research scholar in human behavior and personality. Her husband, the Rev. Robert M. Kidd, chaplain, serves on the Animal and Human Research Subcommittees at the V.A. Medical Center in Martinez, Calif. They are collaborating on a long-term research project involving human personality and human/companion animal bonding.

Some women, institutionalized and bed-bound with tuberculosis, regain a sense of responsibility, a new focus of interest, and an interesting companionship from Chum, a live-in turtle...

Young and old, sick and healthy, outcast and comrade often get a real psychological lift from snakes after they discover that snakes are essentially helpless, are effectively deaf, have no limbs with which to flee or protect themselves, and that while very few have any ability to bite, most enjoy cuddling and touching...

Orman, a wing-damaged flightless pigeon, acquired a new career helping to reduce aggression and destructiveness, helping to teach responsibility and self-control among children at a playground near his companion-human's home...

Budgerigars helped improve physical and social well-being significantly in companion-humans in an elderly citizens community...

Small cage birds increased the need and desire to speak, lessened anxiety, taught responsibility, and gave patients in a state mental hospital living beings to which they could relate...

Human-animal bonding—dogs and cats, horses and turtles, reptiles, birds, and fish—household companion-animals of all shapes and sizes

Children can learn important educational messages from animals: empathy, the exchange of affection, mastery, and self-esteem. Humane societies regularly conduct education programs to focus on children's attitudes toward other living creatures. *(Photo by Phil Arkow)*

can help fill some human need for physical or psycho-social comfort, can help reduce stress and lower blood pressure, can help make life more worth living anywhere at home or abroad in the world today. The lonely and troubled, the introverted and withdrawn often learn laughter and living, frequently regain a sense of community and purpose, of reality and sanity when they acquire a companion-animal to take care of and which in a sense helps take care of them in return, when they take on a pet which can often help heal a body as well as a spirit through the medicine of laughter, acceptance, and love.

Human-animal bonding is usually dated to 12,000 B.C. and primarily came about for economic reasons. Archaeological evidence suggests that dogs were first domesticated and trained to help hunters trap and kill game for food by herding the larger grazing animals which ran at speeds faster than humans. However, a recent find in an ancient near-Eastern burial ground dating back 14,000 years contained a male skeleton with its arm around a dog's skeleton. This startling find suggests that human/companion animal bonding has been around at least as long as human/economic animal bonding. Of course the economic benefits of the human/animal bond have been extremely important historically, and remain significant today in that animals are still used for transportation, for guard and detective duty, for pest control, and for food—both as hunters and hunted. But during the course of human history, the economic aspects and attitudes toward the human/animal bond have changed and become less significant, while the companionship benefits have become more vitally important.

Companion animals clearly provide social, emotional and physical benefits to children and adults of all ages. These benefits are especially important to the physically and emotionally handicapped who, because of chronic conditions or age, are isolated by circumstances rather than by choice from normal or mainstream social interactions. Our current technologically mechanized society forces both children and adults to relate to machines. While verbal skill and intellect are usually needed as a bridge for human-human or human-machine interactions, animals relate non-verbally, make no demands for reasons and explanations, and respond to human needs at the feeling level. This is especially beneficial for children who often find it difficult to clarify feelings and needs verbally. Obviously only live animals can really fill the human need for responsive acceptance and loyalty because, having sensitivities, needs, and personalities of their own, only live animals can truly serve as companions, friends, confidants, playmates, and scapegoats. The right animal, if carefully chosen, will accept an owner completely: giving and receiving affection and love, sympathy and sensitive responsiveness, cuddling and meaningful companionship.

Companion animals serve important educational roles. Children and adults alike can learn genuine responsibility. They learn that pet care means giving up some selfish pleasures and handling such unpleasant tasks as cleaning up excrement and living quarters as well as grooming and otherwise caring for the needs of a being other than oneself. Children and adults alike can learn something about empathy and the exchange of affection without jealousy; can learn something about self-mastery and discipline as well as pet mastery, and so learn about increased self-esteem from success, and about handling sorrow and disappointment from failures, perhaps through the death of a beloved but short-lived pet or through comfort from a pet companion when a family crisis separates a child from a parent or a primary caretaker. Certainly children learn with increased interest and reduced truancy in schoolrooms where pets have added zest to educational work and play programs. Indeed, play is very important to all humans, and especially play with pets, because play with peers is a learned situation of tension where one person wins and another loses. Play with a pet is relaxing and satisfying because both human and animal win. There is no loser.

Negatively, of course, family pets are extra work for parents with small children for whom they have added the pet. Pets can track in dirt and may have diseases transmissible to humans. Pets may hurt small children who are sometimes cruel to animals because they are not yet aware of the differences between living and stuffed animals. Nevertheless, experiencing pets affects a person's entire life by teaching the happier and the more painful moments of life itself.

Furthermore, pets are even more important in the lives of the sick, disturbed, or handicapped. Horseback riding has improved the mental health and dramatically increased physical health and muscle tone in people with neuromusuclar problems. Brain-damaged children have demonstrated improved language ability and increased attention spans after being introduced to dolphins. Because pets do not criticize or correct human behavior, their companionship and invitations to play benefit children in depression and often entice them back to a reason for living. And since pets do not discriminate on a basis of intellect, race, or appearance, their unquestioning acceptance helps raise the lowered self-esteem of children who are isolated from peers and social interactions.

Emotionally disturbed and retarded persons who are unable to relate adequately to normal people often are able to relate to animals, probably because they have had happy past experiences with pets, or possibly because the type of unhappy interactions they had experienced with other humans was absent from the fun and games with animals. Pets are ever present twenty-four hours a day, ready to be friends, confidants, playmates, or scapegoats; ready to give subordinate, non-threatening unconditional love. They have no other obligation but to be there. They can reduce the need, if need there be, of a therapist to no more than a couple of hours a week.

Indeed, pets can be useful in the diagnosis of disturbed people in general. Disturbed children, especially, often react to their pets with behaviors echoing the treatment they get from their parents. Disturbed persons may treat animals cruelly because they are acting out on the animal the indignities they have received from others. Disturbed and battered children find it very difficult to describe the cruel, inhuman treatment they have suffered from their parents or other adults and, though the pet should be rescued or protected, the observation of such cruel behaviors can serve as clues to possible causes of their real problems. Such behaviors can also indicate peer interactions and suggest why some people are friendless. In therapy, a pet may serve as a topic of conversation, and the patient's questions or comments about pets often indicate questions about themselves or their relationships with other humans.

Institutionalized retarded or disturbed patients also can benefit from the presence of pets. Withdrawn patients are first stimulated to interact with the pet and then with peers and staff. The affection pets give increases feelings of self-worth, and the helping to care for a pet helps the patient to feel capable of giving to and caring for another living being and so increases self-esteem. Such patients often have trouble relaxing enough to sleep or frequently are awakened by nightmares or night terrors. Studies show that taking a pet to bed improves the sleep pattern and behavior.

One of the problems which will arise under these circumstances is that of protecting the pet from harm or cruelty. Close adult supervision can negate this difficulty, but initial choice of the best type of pet for the particular patient will also help avoid the problem. The disturbed or retarded and those with severe problems with authority who fear close personal relationships tend to relate best to cats. Those with a large number of fears and phobias tend to relate well to small caged animals such as hamsters or rabbits. The lonely and withdrawn seem to prefer small dogs. A pet which is poorly matched with a person's emotional situation will be of no benefit and may even add to psychological harm. A large, very friendly German shepherd puppy who knocks down a small child in order to lick its face may only frighten and increase that child's fears and uncertainties, and reduce the child's self-confidence.

Obviously, many of these benefits apply to people of all ages and conditions. For handicapped, retarded, or psychologically disturbed adults, whether institutionalized or not, pets help provide the same non-threatening, non-judgmental, reassuring non-verbal communication link with life that they offer to children. They help break the cycle of withdrawal, isolation, loneliness and helplessness which characterize the lives of so many of these people, and serve as re-socializers to increase the person's verbalization and interactions with family and neighbors, or with staff and other patients. By serving as semi-helpless creatures dependent on people, they can help pull such people out of a fantasy world and back into the real world. No one can remain in a fantasy world and take adequate care of a companion animal. In mental institutions, ward pets have demonstrably increased morale and *esprit de corps,* often by restoring a patient's sense of humor. As is proved daily—laughter is good medicine, and a sense of humor is extremely important for good mental health.

Of course there are certain difficulties in using pets with the mentally ill. Even though most patients bond in a healthy way to pets, some respond under severe stress by choosing to withdraw and to love and mother only a pet rather than interact appropriately with other people. There have been

Childhood experiences with pets may be an indicator of animal preferences in later life. *(Photo by Phil Arkow)*

reported instances where violent patients show extreme cruelty to pets and, if patients who are attached only to an animal are scratched or bitten by that animal, their psychopathology may be intensified rather than helped. For most mental patients, however, animals are perpetual infants—innocent, trusting, loving, and totally dependent, often reflecting the patient's own status and situation, and serving as living beings to which patients can relate while they are learning to relate in more acceptable and realistic terms to other humans.

But what particular *needs* can be filled through companion animals? For the elderly, they can be a less expensive answer to and salvation from the debilitating and deteriorating effects of loneliness and isolation, especially for the newly widowed, and retired, and the effects of convalescent homes. Companion animals become a goal, a purpose for going on living. They help their owners keep in touch with reality. The need for both animal and elderly owner to establish and maintain a daily care routine encourages an orientation to present reality and reduces the tendency of the elderly to slip into the past. Their loving presence helps maintain a retired human's sense of identity through the assurance that such owners are *needed* by another living being. They also serve as social lubricants or substitutes for human relationships by encouraging activity and helping serve as outlets for recreation and pleasure.

There is clear evidence that pet ownership is beneficial to adults with physical problems. Pets keep them busy and active and increase the amount of exercise in which the owner engages. Heart attack victims with pets have a significantly better survival rate than do heart attack victims who are not pet owners. Quietly watching fish swimming in a tank has been shown to lower blood pressure. Stroking and petting an animal with which one has bonded also lowers blood pressure, although blood pressure does not drop when one strokes an animal which is a stranger to one.

Animals perform a number of services for the handicapped. Seeing-eye dogs who guide the blind are well known. There are now, however, also reports on successful seeing-eye parrots, and the relatively new hearing-ear dogs, often called "signal" dogs because they alert their owners to ringing alarm clocks, fire alarms, doorbells, crying babies, telephones, and other distress signals to which they have been trained to respond. Service dogs can be trained in a number of useful ways: to carry packs or pull wheelchairs, to retrieve specific needed items, to turn switches off and on, and to perform rescue services in remote areas of various countries. Monkeys have also recently been trained to serve as hands for paralyzed owners. Truly, service animals do a great deal toward providing independence for owners who would otherwise have more limited lives or have to enter institutions. *(See Chapters 8 and 9).*

However, pets cannot benefit everyone. Both urban and suburban women are happier with pets than without them, for example, but rural women who own pets are less happy than rural women who do not, possibly because rural families have other economically productive animals, and pets merely increase the work. Similarly, people who are gainfully employed seem to benefit less from pet ownership than do those who feel themselves to be less usefully productive—the young, the old, the handicapped, the psychologically disturbed. People who are deeply involved in services to other humans may feel that pet care would take too much time away from time needed to serve people. Certainly pet problems can reduce benefits—pets shed hair or feathers, dirty a house, create neighborhood problems, need exercise, restrict their owners' activities, and cause guilt or grief if they are lost or die.

Pets are sometimes used as substitutes for normal human-human relationship by some less stable adults, and are often given more time and care than the children in a family. We recently witnessed a mother who refused to have her son's broken arm set one day because she had an appointment to have her poodle groomed. We have also noted couples mutually destructive to each other who are kept together because of love for a pet. Recent studies note that although pets are popular with college students, they seem to provide no benefits whatsoever. The studies show no physiological or psychological health differences between students who own pets at present, those who have owned, and those who have never owned them. Failure to bond may well be at fault here, but the fact remains that every year colleges report the presence of large numbers of abandoned pets during school year vacations and the beginning of summer vacations.

And the pets also suffer accordingly. After all, animals are inferior to their owners, are scapegoats and are objects over which the owner has power of life and death. Like slaves in past ages, some pets are tolerated for useful reasons and others are mutilated—ears are docked, tails are shortened, claws are removed, wings are clipped. For some, scraps are fed, comforts and necessities are neglected and, as the final indignity when pets become too inconvenient, they are abandoned. And all for a lack of proper bonding. Indeed, 150,000 animals are destroyed by pet shelters in the United States every week. Some of them are from families where they were acquired for such wrong reasons as "the children need a pet" or "I never had a pet, but my child is going to love one." Without previous owner experience, the expectations are usually wrong; the amount of care needed and the responsibilities of ownership are unknown factors. Some people are unwilling custodians of undesired pets given or bequeathed to them and so may keep the pet for a time out of respect for the previous owner, but they rarely bond to the animal. If one marriage partner has had pets previously and the other has not, the pet lover may demand a pet but the other will usually reject it. Some pet lovers collect large numbers of strays which move them emotionally, but then find themselves unable to provide adequately for any or all of them. Certain cultural groups are more concerned with animals as food than as pets. In Northern California recently, certain East Asians who normally eat dogs as food have angered their neighbors and humane organizations who do not understand such behavior toward pet animals.

Obviously, then, humans and animals have been bonding for many reasons since the dawn of history. And many humans will continue making careers of promoting the bonding process in order to help provide maximum benefits for everyone who needs or wants them. But an extreme-

The concept of snakes as companions needs more exploration. Was it the thrill of dangerous living, economic benefits, or scientific inquiry which led one man to keep 48 rattlesnakes in his back yard, until they were confiscated by officers?

(Photo by Phil Arkow)

ly important aspect of the human/companion animal bonding process is the choice of the right animal to fit the real need. If the wrong type of animal is selected, there will be no bond, and a good animal may be abandoned or destroyed through no fault of its own. Further, the humans will receive no benefits and may actually be harmed physically or psychosocially. There are harmful possibilities that an individual or members of a bond-seeking family may acquire a sense of guilt over the failure of the selected animal to meet their usually unrealistic expectations, or may build up resentment over the amount and kind of care, or even learn to fear the particular kind of animal chosen. We've all heard the wife who laments regularly, "I'm so terrifed of my husband's guard dog that I'm afraid to go home." Or the person who complains, "Cats just know I hate them, so they crawl all over me and give me the creeps." Or, "My son loves horses but I can't stand being within ten miles of one." And, while five million Americans may well be bonded to their snakes, millions of others nurse fears and deep-held prejudices against them.

The need to match the right human with the right companion animal, then, raises several pertinent questions, the first of which is why do people choose the companion animal they do? Over 70 years ago, G. Stanley Hall first offered the belief that a person's age determined the preference for a given type of pet. Children under five preferred cats because they were generally smaller, less demanding, and seemed more cuddly and touchable than the average available dog. Middle childhood shifted preferences to the more active, mobile, and dependably companionable dog. Adolescents usually shifted back to cats because the feline independent way of flouting rules and regulations and pursuing easy living seemed to echo and relate to the teenagers' way of dealing with the problem of authority.

Historically this was an inventive and entertaining theory, but it was not actually researched, and modern studies prove it to be highly inaccurate. Indeed, current research into adult preferences suggests that childhood experiences which influence learned responses to various animals and domestic situations may be a basic key to companion-animal preferences. Bonded adult owners of cats, dogs, horses, snakes, and turtles all report that as children they had owned and loved their current particularly preferred species of pet. A person who had bonded to a cat, dog, horse, snake, or turtle as a child probably owns and is dog-, cat-, horse-, snake-, or turtle-bonded as an adult. Persons who learned to fear or hate certain types of animals as children usually fear or hate those same types as adults and certainly rarely own or bond to those types in the here-and-now. The exception would be where a present spouse prefers and insists on owning such companion animals despite the mate's antipathy.

For that matter, certain animals may have a very particular cultural meaning for given individuals, families, peoples, or groups. Some groups within specific tribal organizations still believe that their group is related to or descended from a particular animal and so show their respect by prohibiting the use of that animal as food except on specific ritual ocasions, or by worshipping and deifying the animal. The hairy Ainu still essentially treat the bear in this manner. Some distant South Pacific islanders still treat the shark this way with respect to their fishing and pearl gathering. South American tribes, Cub and Boy Scout groups, high school, college and professional sports teams, and some male organizations today use certain animal types as titles and mascots, either real or unreal as modern expressions of preference for a particular companion animal and, occasionally, of bonding.

Some individuals and groups are fascinated by the very special characteristics of certain animal types even though a love-hate bonding relationship may be involved. Although feared and hated, yet respected and sometimes worshipped for cultural reasons, the concept of snakes as companions needs more exploration. Snakes are largely respected for their economic benefits: pest control, guardians for precious possessions, medicinal purposes and food. But emotionally, some snakes provide the thrills of dangerous living, or enliven a human's sense of beauty and aesthetics through cuddling and touching, or inspire scientific study and success in breeding and rearing exotic, endangered species in captivity. In his book, *Snakes as Pets,* Hobart Smith summed up the psychological benefits by noting that anyone "... can understand that snakes are essentially helpless except for the ability of some to bite. Many do not have that recourse and all are effectively deaf and have no limbs with which to flee or protect themselves. Snakes are nature's most spectacular success story under seemingly insurmountable odds and this can be of psychological benefit in many ways.... Children especially may identify with snakes."

Current research shows that individuals who are particularly attached to a specific type of animal usually have either similar or complementary personality characteristics with it and, of course, that there are significant differences between persons who strongly prefer one type of pet and those who prefer another.

Male dog and male horse lovers are assertive, dominant, and "masculine" along traditional stereotypical lines, are low in need to care for others, and usually prefer the larger, more aggressive types of male dogs and horses which match or complement their self-image. Female owners of show horses are similar to male horse lovers, but female horse lovers who have them as "pets" tend to display the traditional stereotypical "feminine" behaviors.

Cat persons of both sexes demonstrate a need to be, or at least to feel, independent and are low in need to care for others. Additionally, male owners of cats are low in aggressiveness.

Turtle owners are generally hard-working, reliable, considerate, tend to view the world as lawful, to believe in rational analysis for decision making, are steadily goal-oriented, and upwardly mobile because they are usually discontented with their present status.

On the other hand, snake owners are relaxed, informal, novelty-seeking, changeable, unconventional, somewhat unpredictable, and unable to tolerate routines. Animal owners with such personality characteristics might well be attracted to animal types generally considered as exotic and unusual. Certainly the evil or dangerous reputations of snakes in general, though undeserved, could well be attractive to unconventional, somewhat unpredictable personalities. The fact that this was the only owner group in which the persons also kept tarantulas and black widow spiders as pets supports the suggestion that some snake owners are risk takers, are stimulated by possible danger, or by the sensual pleasures of cuddling and touching.

Bird owners, however, are contented, courteous, expressive, nurturant and unpretentious. They seek to maintain numerous personal relationships, to sustain harmonious relations among others, and are protective of friends. Like male horse owners, female bird owners are high in dominance, but bird owners of both sexes are generally social and altruistic and usually attracted to birds which are expressive in song and speech, are physically attractive, and which express affection by nuzzling and cuddling.

Certainly the principles of similarity and complementarity offer a probable explanation of companion animal choice among humans. People tend to select their friends and mates on such bases. The similarity principle holds that "birds of a feather flock together" and the complementarity principle that "you have what I lack myself." The reality is that people who share attitudes, values, and behaviors are attracted to one another but also seek the complementary opposites of themselves in acquaintances, colleagues, and friends.

The personality of turtle owners shows a similarity to the behavior and philosophy of the tortoise in that traditional fable by Aesop. The expressiveness and protectionist characteristics of bird owners are echoes of the behavior patterns of their pets. Cats and their owners are primarily independent and somewhat aloof.

On the complementarity side, one notes that the handicapped who cannot walk benefit tremendously from a horse's "four great legs beneath them." Service animals see and hear and do what their owners cannot do for themselves. Many timid elderly women find the noisy aggressiveness of their guard dogs very comforting. Certainly understanding of the similarity and complementarity aspects which underlie the various bases of choice which people use in selecting their mates, their friends, and their companion animals will continue to increase.

It needs to be noted, however, that one-half of all animal owners are what is termed "pet lovers"—owners who are not devoted to just one type of companion animal. They are fond of animals in general and usually own three or four or more different types of animals. The males tend to be assertive, confident, dominant, and the females are nurturing and enjoy caring for others. The personality characteristics involving the principles of similarity and complementarity are probably influential in the choice of pet groups, too, though little or no research data are available to date. Several of their pets may be loved for their similarity, several for their complementarity, or all of them for both. A woman who is somewhat dependent, caring, and nurturing, for example, may love her female collie and her female standard poodle for their behaviorial similarity to hers; may equally love her male boxer for its tenderly aggressive guardian behavior; and love her

Male and female horse owners have different attitudes about their animals. Male owners are assertive, dominant and masculine along stereotypical lines, epitomized, perhaps, by the John Wayne image. Female horse lovers treat their pets with more feminine behaviors.

female cats for their ability to be aloof, independent, and yet to get along with her beloved and loving dogs.

Although people and animals have been bonding for 14,000 years, the first speculations on the whys and wherefores did not appear until 20 years ago. A widespread international interest in "the bond" and in practical applications for the benefit of many people has grown rapidly in just the past few years, but adequate research into the real problems of beneficial bonding and placement, of matching pets and people, has not caught up with the need as yet. There are no data at all on why some people fear or hate animals, in general and in particular, or why some persons reject all pets of any kind. There are very few data on what happens to the animal or to the person if the selection is wrong. The question of breeds comes into the picture at this point. Clearly, the contrasting behavioral characteristics of mynah birds and falcons, of Doberman and Shih-Tzu dogs, of Arabian and Morgan horses, of Persian and Siamese cats, of the notoriously irritable western diamondback rattlesnake and the more placid rosy boa or gartersnake suggest that breed choice as well as pet type choice needs much further study. There has been only one study in this area so far and the findings show merely that the Great Dane has become a symbol of masculine assertiveness and the Chihuahua has become a symbol of femininity, and that owners of these breeds may have been unconsciously influenced in their choice. If the vast choice of breeds within a given pet category is considered, the need for a great deal of future research becomes clear. Similarly, the relationship of childhood pet ownership to adult pet bonding is becoming clearer, but to understand the importance of childhood bonding, research is needed on how children at various ages feel about animals in general and their own pets in particular. Meanwhile, current studies have begun to provide some solid bases of evidence for the mental, emotional, and physical benefits to be gained from ownership when the choice of companion animal is right for the individual.

All of which suggests that there are some good candidates—both on the human side and on the animal side—for the bonding benefits, and some not. Research into personality types, which includes aspects of similarity and complementarity, certainly offers some practical suggestions for successful human/companion animal bonding. Therefore it may well be that future research will help point out fresh aspects of similarity and complementarity which underlie the various bases of choices people use in selecting their mates, their friends, and their companion animals. We confidently predict that, in the future, pets and people can be matched in ways which will provide the maximum benefit to both the human owner and the animal.

Suggested reading:

Anderson, R.S. (ed.) *Pet Animals and Society.* London: Balliere Tindall, 1974.

Arkow, Phil *"Pet Therapy" A Study of the Use of Companion Animals in Selected Therapies.* Colorado Springs, Colo.: Humane Society of the Pikes Peak Region, 1983.

Cusack, Odean *Pets in Clinical Psychotherapy.* New York: Haworth, 1986.

Fogle, Bruce (ed.) *Interrelations Between People and Pets.* Springfield, Ill.: Charles C. Thomas, 1981.

Katcher, A. and Beck, Alan. *New Perspectives on our Lives with Companion Animals.* Philadelphia: University of Pennsylvania Press, 1983.

Kidd, Aline H. & Kidd, Robert M. Animals: Best Friends and Good Medicine. *1985 Medical and Health Annual.* Chicago: Encyclopedia Britannica, 1984.

Levinson, Boris *Pet-Oriented Child Psychotherapy.* Springfield, Ill.: Charles C. Thomas, 1969.

Levinson, Boris *Pets and Human Development.* Springfield Ill.: Charles C. Thomas, 1972.

5

Animal Behavior: The Animal's Side of the Bond

Ian Dunbar

"...treat animals as animals"

Introduction

With the growing interest in the Human/Companion Animal Bond, animals are being employed in increasing capacities to benefit humans. However, without a better understanding of the behavior and needs of the animals involved, it is unlikely that many programs will achieve their full potential. Instead there is a real risk that participating animals may develop behavior problems which will tend to overshadow the intended benefits of the people-pet partnership.

There are a number of reasons why an understanding of animal behavior is important. First, it is essential for the selection and improvement of the natural abilities of participating animals. In addition, a knowledge of the behavior of animals will offer forewarning of the types of problems that we might expect. A further need for an understanding of animal behavior is to ensure the well-being of participating animals. This chapter will emphasize the notion of temperament training as it applies for the encouragement and refinement of the animal's good qualities and in terms of the reduction of its bad qualities, i.e., for the prevention and treatment of behavior problems.

Most people's understanding of animal behavior is ludicrously and pathetically shallow. To give a simple example: everyone knows that when a dog wags its tail it is friendly and happy, right? Wrong! Certainly, dogs do

Ian Dunbar, Ph.D., M.R.C.V.S., is an internationally recognized authority on dogs. He is the author of the book Dog Behavior *and a new series of 15 educational Behavior Booklets to solve common pet problems. He has been published in numerous scientific journals and popular magazines, and has lectured to veterinary colleges and associations in six countries. He is director of the Center for Applied Animal Behavior in Berkeley, Calif.*

usually wag their tails when they are happy: a high-frequency, high-amplitude wag. But not all friendly dogs will wag their tails and not all dogs that wag their tails are necessarily friendly. Dogs exhibit a variety of tail wags and they all express different emotions. An extremely high-frequency, low-amplitude vibration of the tip of the tail means that the dog is "on edge" and extremely tense; alternately, a low-frequency, high-amplitude tail swish means that the dog is mean—very mean, and that there is a good chance that it will attack. (This latter tail "wag" is similar to the way a cat will "wag" its tail when it is upset.) Thus, it may not always be a good idea to approach a dog with a waggy tail.

For the most part, the extent to which people make an attempt to understand animal behavior depends on their attitudes towards animals. In the book *Sirius*, by Olaf Stapledon, the main character, a Welsh sheepdog named Sirius, was born with the brain capacity of a human but the senses and physique of a dog. Sirius classified people with respect to their attitude towards dogs. There were those who were simply indifferent to dogs, "lacking sufficient imagination to enter into any reciprocal relationship with them." There were dog-detesters, "who were either too highbrow to descend to companionship with a dumb animal or too frightened of their own animal nature." There were the dog-lovers, whom Sirius detested. "These were folk who sentimentalized dogs, and really had no accurate awareness of them, exaggerating their intelligence and loveableness, mollycoddling them and overfeeding them.... For this sort, dogs were merely animate and pathetically human dolls." Finally, there were the dog-interested, "who combined a fairly accurate sense of the difference between a dog and a man with a disposition to respect a dog as a dog, as a rather remote but essentially like-minded relative." Sirius' classification might apply to the way that people feel about all types of animals.

One reason why some people do not make more of an effort to understand animal behavior is that they fall into the category of being indifferent towards them. (One worker researching the human/companion animal bond has even gone so far as to openly admit that he does not like animals.) There is an increasing tendency to treat companion animals as objects. Some people talk of companion animals as if they are disposable items: such as stuffed toys, or some kind of prescribable medication (a pet pill), that may be dished out to humans who might derive some benefit from their companionship. Researchers have referred to animals as "therapeutic agents," "social lubricants" and "bonding catalysts." If researchers treat animals as expendable objects, it is unlikely that they will ever make the effort to learn to understand them or appreciate them. As such, neither human/companion animal bonds nor the animals themselves will ever achieve their full potential.

Other people working with animals go to the opposite extreme and anthropomorphically treat them as furry (or feathery) humans. In this situation, it is also uncommon for animals to achieve their full potential, because most people are unaware of the animal's capabilities. It is unfortunate that many "animal lovers" who promote the use of companion animals have a disturbingly unrealistic view of animals and animal behavior. It is ironic that the attitude of many "animal lovers" fosters equivalent inhumanities. For example, an often-used quote by George Eliot states: "Animals are such agreeable friends; they ask no questions, pass no criticisms." Similarly, from a leaflet promoting the use of pets for the elderly: ". . . animals make good friends. They are devoted and unjudging, content to love and be loved." The above quotes extoll the virtues of animals as loving and devoted companions for humans (almost to the exclusion of similar relationships between people). Certainly, animals can make extremely good friends but this is not necessarily the case. Most animals ask many questions of their owners but usually these go unnoticed, which is why (in their animal way) they are forced to pass criticisms. There are some animals that are in no way devoted to their owners and indeed, have little reason to be. Many animals are surprisingly judgmental about their owner's behavior and some, unfortunately, are quick to pass sentence. And finally, no animal is content simply to love and be loved. Certainly love is an essential ingredient for any human/companion animal bond but for the animal, at least, it is in no way sufficient.

Many "animal lovers" make the mistake of assuming that animals understand more than they do (probably as an excuse not to have to try to understand their language and behavior and not to attempt to teach them ours). Consequently, many animals are compelled to take the initiative and improvise (or misbehave, as we humans usually interpret their behavior). However, when an animal develops behavior problems (usually because people have made little attempt to understand and communicate with it), it is invariably the animal that suffers.

Many faithful, trusting and devoted pets, living with equally devoted and well-meaning owners, are subjected to horrendous inappropriate punishment. Examples of this are legion and the worst do not necessarily involve physical abuse but rather perverse psychological punishment. For example, an owner sees a dog or cat misbehaving and calls the trusting critter, which approaches its owner in good faith, only to be greeted with a barrage of mental (and/or physical) abuse. Punishment alone does not teach the animal that the behavior is wrong; rather, the animal simply learns that it is unwise to misbehave *in the presence of its owner,* i.e., the problem has been exacerbated, and from now on the animal will tend to misbehave only in the owner's absence (and this can be a much trickier problem to resolve). More disturbing, however, is the fact that the owner called the animal and *then* punished it, i.e., he told the animal to do

A dog is not a miniature human in a furry little coat. It is a distinct entity, its own being, with its own behaviors, biological needs and predispositions, gene pool and training regimen. *(Photo by Phil Arkow)*

something and then punished it for doing it. Basically, the owner is effectively training the pet not to come when called, and sooner or later, he will call the animal and (understandably) it will not come. Then, no doubt, the owner will get angry because the animal will not obey. The poor pet can not win.

Even worse is when the owner chastises the animal long after the "crime" was committed. The animal does not associate the punishment with the crime but instead, tends to associate the punishment with the presence of the owner. The animal just does not understand what is going on. Some owners harass the dog long after the initial punishment, perhaps for example when the animal is hiding under the couch. Again this only punishes the animal for lying quietly (albeit miserably) and for allowing the owner to approach; indeed, a sad state of affairs.

The reasons why people frequently abuse their pets in this fashion are that in addition to touting animals as the epitome of many of the good qualities of humans, unfortunately many so-called "animal-lovers" are similarly anthropomorphic in their insistence that animals harbor many of our human foibles and negative qualities. They feel that the animal misbehaves out of spite, or perhaps that it perniciously plotted and premeditated the crime in their absence. The owner often feels cheated and hurt and may react like a child by withholding affection. To be effective, reprimands and/or punishments should be short and sharp and immediately follow the crime. However, because the owner has found it necessary to punish the animal for misbehaving (usually because it has not been sufficiently educated *vis a vis* appropriate domestic behavior), a minute or two later, the owner should call the pet and make up by being as sweet as pie, just as if the whole thing had never happened.

If people would only treat animals as animals and not as cute furry humans, it would be much easier to solve these problems and even to prevent them from developing in the first place.

Animals are not simply objects, nor for that matter are they sub-human or lesser organisms. In fact, in a number of ways their physical, sensory and mental attributes are far superior to those of humans and could even be considered *supra*-human. Animals are not necessarily inferior to humans; they are just different. On the other hand, an animal's qualities of love, devotion, affection, and companionship are not necessarily always superior to similar qualities in humans. Animals are not universally accepting, universally loving little humanoids in furry suits; they are animals, that feel differently, think differently, and act differently from humans. It is much more humane to recognize and respect animals as animals. Each species is different, having unique species-specific behaviors, languages, and customs, i.e., a dog is a dog, a cat is a cat and a horse is a horse (a blatantly obvious but often neglected fact).

Luckily, there are many people who are truly interested in animals and feel that it is well worthwhile making an attempt to understand their behavior. Recently, ethology has become a hot topic in veterinary schools and animal husbandry curricula and for other professionals who work with animals. Unfortunately, many people become disenchanted when they discover that a rudimentary understanding of ethology is not the panacea that it was thought to be. This raises the question of whether ethology is really what we need. Although an understanding of ethology is essential for any person working with animals, it is not sufficient by itself.

Ethology?

Recently, there has been a trend for people to use "ethology" almost as a buzzword. Many people simplistically assume that a passing familiarity with an animal's ethogram is all that is needed to cure "the heartache and the thousand natural shocks that flesh is heir to." Ethology is not necessarily a cure-all for behavioral problems.

Before we go any further it would be prudent to define what we mean by ethology. Normally, when we speak of ethology, we mean the study of the behavior of an animal in its natural environment, i.e., in the wild. However, since there is a (sometimes erroneous) tendency to equate ethology with animal behavior, much of our knowledge of the behavior of domestic animals has been extrapolated from the ethology of wild conterparts or related species. For example, many recommendations concerning the training and husbandry of domestic dogs is based upon a rather meager understanding of wolf behavior.

Certainly there are many general similarities between the behavior of domestic dogs and wolves (and other wild *Canidae).* Furthermore, being cognizant of an animal's ethogram, or behavioral repertoire, is useful in that it forewarns us how the dog might behave if it grew up entirely with other dogs in the wild. This is all very well, but the domestic dog does not grow up in the wild exclusively with members of its own species; instead it grows up in a domestic environment, usually within a human family. Consequently, if we talk about the ethology of the domestic dog, we must consider its behavior within its natural setting, i.e., the domestic environment.

The selective breeding of thousand of years of domestication has had a substantial effect upon behavior. Whereas the behavior of a domestic animal may resemble that of its wild counterpart or related species in a number of general (but species-specific) ways, it is different in many respects. Without a doubt the greatest difference lies in terms of the animal's interactions with humans. As such it is impossible to study the behavior of domestic animals without taking into account human behavior.

The effect of humans on animal behavior can not be overemphasized. For a domesticated animal (and especially a social animal like the domestic dog), humans constitute a major and crucially important facet of its everyday life. Obviously, this is especially important when we consider animals as pets and companion animals. Domestic animals are involved in a continual two-way interaction with their human companions, such that the behavior of humans continually affects the behavior of animals and animal behavior affects human behavior, which again in turn affects animal behavior and so on.

To fully comprehend what is going on with our faithful furry (or feathery) friends within a human/animal bond, even the combined theory of animal behavior and human psychology is still not sufficient. In addition, we must learn to apply this knowledge in an eclectic approach to unravel the sophisticated and intricate interactions that form the dynamic interface between humans and animals. Moreover, we must remember that it is not so much that we should study the interaction between human psychology and animal behavior, or the interactions between humans and animals, but rather, it is individual humans that interact with individual animals. Apart from dogs being dogs, cats being cats and horses being horses, they are all individuals; this is something that many people seem to forget. A dog is not just a dog but, as with humans, it is a particular individual dog that has its own unique individual behavioral characteristics and idiosyncracies. To acknowledge the individuality of participating humans and animals is essential for the understanding of interspecific interactive psychology.

Rather than extrapolating from our knowledge of the ethology of wild animals and compiling an overview of the behavior of the many different species of companion animals, this chapter will be more of an *underview* of animal behavior, analyzing it from the point of view of individual animals. There is not sufficient space to do the subject justice and we will just highlight some of the practical points that will hopefully help to make things easier and more enjoyable for both the animals and humans involved.

Maximizing the potential of individual programs

Animals have done some marvelous things to benefit human kind. Perhaps one of the most spectacular examples is that of guide dogs that help the blind. *(See Chapter 8)* However, it would seem that we have hardly scratched the surface in terms of what animals can offer. In terms of maximizing the potential of individual programs it is important to first select the best animals for the job and then specifically train them for that purpose. At present, program coordinators pay some attention to the selection of their animals. However, with the exception of animals with highly specialized and complicated functions, such as seeing-eye dogs, hearing-ear dogs, and primates and dogs that have been trained to aid the physically handicapped, few animals are specifically trained for their more general functions of companionship. For animals used as companions, there is a tendency to view them as furry objects or stuffed toys that are expected to do their best to look cute and be stroked.

Workers usually acknowledge that they require certain qualities from an animal, and whereas they will search for animals that approximate those qualities, they do little else to improve the animal's natural abilities. Essentially, it is folly to rely upon something as complicated and changeable as an animal's temperament for the beneficial effects within the bond. Thus, in addition to selecting an animal for temperament, it makes sense to incorporate some concept of temperament training that both maximizes the good points of the animal's personality and minimizes the bad points (or behavior problems). Modifying an animal's temperament is just as easy as the basic principles that underlie obedience training. For example, if a dog is required to be friendly, cute, and happy for placement in an orphanage, then not only should an attempt be made to choose a dog that appears to fit the bill but in addition, it would be advisable to try to stabilize this personality by regularly training the dog to be even friendlier, even cuter and even happier. Especially since it is likely that this dog will be incessantly stroked (particularly during the first few weeks), it should be prepared to accept and enjoy this onslaught of attention (not all of it pleasant).

Selection

There are two main considerations in selecting an animal as a companion for humans. The first is that the humans will be happy with the selection and the second is that the animal will be happy about being selected. A very obvious factor that has a direct bearing on the selection of animals is their ability to be good companions. This may sound simplistic, but it is often overlooked. People are individuals and so are animals. One person's idea of a good companion (whether animal or human) may not be another person's idea. Some people like cats, others like dogs, some like both and some like neither and instead, would rather have a budgie perch on their finger, or perhaps, talk to a goldfish in a bowl.

When dealing with individuals, it is an obvious precaution to ask them whether they like animals and if so, which ones in particular. Then, one should try and cater to their individual tastes. This is a much harder task when dealing with groups; rarely will they agree on the type of animal. Usually it is better for an outsider to select an animal for the group. In a visiting program the choice is not so critical because it is possible to take a variety of animals and vary them from week to week.

Selecting the species

The first thing to decide is what species to use. The general requirements are that the animal: is social and/or easily socialized towards people; is neither aggressive nor dangerous; is neither under stress nor fearful; is adaptable; and obviously that humans enjoy watching or interacting with the animal. In deciding what sort of animals would work best as companions, it is worthwhile considering which animals have adapted well to pethood.

When jointly considering popularity, adaptability, and the degree of interaction with humans, certainly cats and dogs have to be at the top of the list. Both species have more than weathered the test of time in terms of their ability to both give and receive affection and attention from humans. Some birds adapt quite well and interact fairly well with humans. Fish, too, are extremely popular.

The selection of a species depends very much upon its intended function: whether the animal is intended for a visiting or placement companion animal program; whether it is intended as a companion for an individual or for a group of people; and what types of people will be interacting with the animal.

When animals are required for placement usually more conventional pets are used and cats, dogs, fish and birds seem to be the favorites. There can be a little more latitude when selecting an animal for placement or visitation to an individual home. When dealing with individuals, it is much easier to describe how to appropriately handle the animal. When selecting an animal for an institution or a group of people, if it is an animal that will be freely interacting with a number of humans, it needs to have an extremely sound and hardy disposition to weather the onslaught of affection. Alternately, it may be an animal that is not regularly handled, such as a fish in a tank or a bird in a cage. Only in rare cases should undomesticated animals be used for companion animal programs. No matter how much socialization they have received they still tend to react badly to confinement, transportation, and handling.

With visiting programs, more usually the animal is taken to an individual's home or to some institution, although in some cases the human goes to visit the animal; for example, when an animal is used as a "co-therapist" by a psychologist or psychiatrist, or in horseback riding programs for the handicapped. Generally, there is more leeway when choosing an animal for a visiting program, since the visitors may be varied from week to week and also there is no need to instruct participants about long-term care of the animal. Consequently, many programs have utilized less common pets, such as rabbits and rodents, snakes, insects, tarantulas, goats, ferrets, etc. The major requirements for visiting animals are:

1. that they are easily transported and therefore fairly small;
2. that they adapt readily to new environments; and
3. that they are well socialized towards humans and readily accept strangers.

Selecting the individual animal

Normally, the main considerations are that the animal is sociable and will interact freely with humans. The domestic dog fits this description to a tee. It is a highly social animal that during its early development can be easily socialized towards humans. As a result, most dogs naturally form an intense and dynamic bond with humans. Domestic cats, on the other hand, lead a more solitary existence. That is not to say that they are necessarily independent creatures, as many people assume. In fact, it is thought that the foundation of their successful domestication is their dependence upon humans for food. Although most cats are more than well-equipped to hunt and fend for themselves, they will readily accept regular free meals from their owners. In fact, in adulthood, they display a fine example of behavioral neoteny in that they have retained the infantile food-soliciting gestures of kittenhood. An adult cat will rub against the ankles of its human companions in much the same way that kittens will rub against their mother's legs to induce her to lie down so that they can suckle. Characteristically, cats will display this rubbing behavior whenever their owners pass near the refrigerator, although in the domestic setting the infantile food-soliciting gesture has also been transformed into an affectionate greeting. Adult dogs employ similar puppy food-soliciting gestures, such as pawing and muzzle licking, as friendly and submissive greetings.

For the most part the animal is selected because humans like it; they think it is cute and they want to interact with the animal and give it affection, and much of this affection involves physical contact. Obviously, then, it makes sense to select an animal that likes interacting with humans and enjoys being stroked and petted. Some breeds of cat and dog thoroughly enjoy human proximity and contact; others can be stand-offish and touch-sensitive. Similarly, other species are totally unsuitable for even small amounts of petting and stroking. A simple test is to put a likely animal in a situation where it has a three-way choice to approach humans, approach others of its own species, or to remain on its own.

Normally, visiting and placement programs within large groups require exceedingly gregarious animals that enjoy a lot of human contact, because they are going to get a lot of human contact (and not all of it will be necessarily gentle). There may be exceptions to this general rule. Some groups may prefer an animal that is less sociable; they may not necessarily want to interact with an exuberant, overly friendly and boisterous animal but would prefer one that is more of a loner. For example, for extremely elderly or sick people it may be better to select a more independent and quiet cat, or an older dog, rather than a young puppy.

Whatever the choice there are obviously going to be some drawbacks. However, with a little applied psychology these drawbacks can sometimes be turned into plusses. For example, introducing a shy dog to an orphanage and explaining that this is a lonely and abused dog may help to draw some of the children out of themselves, getting them to show some care and affection for another living being. Similarly, a shy dog placed with a single person may be a good excuse to get the person out and about (to give the dog badly needed socialization).

Temperament testing

When considering animals as companions, obviously the first step is to try and select the best available individual for the job. A number of temperament tests have been devised for the selection of individual animals for a variety of purposes. The majority of tests are structured to investigate qualities such as socialization, activity levels, trainability, and aggressiveness. Most tests are excellent in terms of the actual testing and observation of the animals but unfortunately, there are severe constraints both in terms of their universal usage and in terms of the interpretation of the results.

Many people tend to rely on established tests rather than adapting them to suit a specific purpose. For example, the same standard test and hence the same criteria may be used to select guide-dogs for the blind and hearing-dogs for the deaf. Or, the same test may be used to select a dog for placement in an orphanage and a dog for placement with an eighty year old gentleman.

The interpretation of the tests often goes awry because many of the dog's characteristics are confused. For example, one puppy temperament test describes three types of approach behavior: pup #1, that charges out of its cage, jumps up and bites the tester on the hand; pup #2, that runs enthusiastically out of its cage, approaches with tail wagging and sits and licks the tester's hand; and pup #3, that would not come out of its cage. Pup #2 was described as the ideal pet for a family with children, highly socialized and trainable. Pup #1 was described as too aggressive and difficult to train for the average person and pup #3 was labelled as an unsuitable pet because it was insufficiently socialized. The denigration and disregard of pups 1 and 3 is extremely disturbing. Pup #3 may be the ideal companion for our eighty year-old gentleman, who lives alone in a small apartment. With pup #1, it is a little hasty to say that it would be difficult to train. On the contrary, it has just demonstrated a speedy and enthusiastic recall and, with only a little help from an understanding owner, it could be well on the way to becoming an extremely obedient canine citizen. Similarly, the assumption that it will be too aggressive is probably way off track. On the contrary, usually it is the pup that does *not* bite as a youngster that augurs ill for the future. When young pups bite excessively, the problem is immediately obvious to its owners, who feel that they must do something about it and indeed, the pup receives a hearty education in how to inhibit both the frequency and force of its bites. On the other hand, if, as a puppy, the dog never bit its owner, then it never has the opportunity to learn that biting humans is wrong. As such it does not develop a bite inhibition and so, when it bites as an adult, it does so forcefully and repeatedly.

In this instance, a simple socialization or visiting test is being used to draw complicated conclusions about trainability and aggression. If the desire is to learn something about trainability, then it makes sense to specifically test for that characteristic. And for training, the acid test is to go ahead and see what can be accomplished in five minutes of trying to get the pup to come, heel, sit, down and stay. And indeed most puppies will demonstrate that they have an infinite inclination and capability to learn, if only they are given appropriate opportunities to do so. Similarly, if we need to know about aggressiveness, then, test for aggressiveness: conduct hierarchy tests; handling tests (sensitive spots—ears, mouth, paws and scruff); "ouch tests" (skin scrunch, paw pinch and tail tug); restraint (hug, hold down, roll over, holding paws together) and judge the pup's reaction. However, with aggressiveness (or more specifically, biting behavior), it makes much more sense to assume that all dogs are potential biters and actively train all of them not to bite. We must remember that, from the dog's point of view, biting is a perfectly normal canine behavior.

In addition, we should bear in mind that the use of temperament tests to select animals for particular behavioral characteristics has another severe constraint. A temperament test only reflects the relative good and bad qualities of individual animals on the day that they were tested. Like humans, animals have good days and bad days. It may be that the animal had been isolated and/or confined for a long period immediately prior to testing and so appeared friendlier and more sociable than normal. Alternately, the animal may characteristically be extremely friendly but did not show this for some reason that was not apparent on the day of the test; perhaps it was too tired, too hot, had just had a disagreement with another animal (or person), or perhaps some silly human had stepped on its tail. For this reason, to get a reliable assessment of the animal's personality, it is a good idea to test it on several separate occasions; the greater the number of tests, the more reliable the picture of the animal's personality.

Even so, an animal's temperament changes with time, and it would be folly to assume that an animal's naturally good temperament will necessarily remain that way, particularly if it is participating in regular visitation programs, or if it is placed in a large group (especially with a group of children). Each person with whom the dog interacts will have an effect on the animal's temperament and children seem to have the knack of teaching animals bad habits quicker than anyone (and of course animals are more likely to try to get away with more when around young children). In time the dog's temperament is likely to drift. And of course, one of Murphy's Laws is that when things drift they always drift in the wrong direction.

We must not lose sight of the fact that all a temperament test helps us determine are the animal's good points and bad points on the days of the test. A series of temperament tests will no doubt give a fairly reliable picture of the animal's personality. However, the function of a temperament test is not solely to discover animals that have desirable qualities and sound temperaments and then once selected, to become presumptively audacious about our pet paragon with the "perfect personality" and consequently, to do nothing further to ensure that it remains "perfect." Neither does a temperament test give us cause to abandon animals that, on the day of the test, may have exhibited behavior problems or otherwise did not come up to "specs." An animal's temperament is extremely flexible and the younger the animal the more easily it may be modified, either intentionally or unintentionally. If we become *blasé* about an animal's "perfect personality" it will almost certainly deteriorate with time. No matter how sound an animal's temperament, it can still be made more sound. Similarly, the whole point of locating behavior problems is so that something may be done about them. Indeed, a secondary function of temperament tests should be as a learning exercise, so that each time the animal undergoes the test, its general behavior and temperament are gradually modified. Thus, our "untrainable" pup #1 will no longer jump and bite because after it comes like an obedient flash, it will be told to sit (and it cannot jump and bite and remain sitting at the same time). Similarly, with patience, the poor, wimpy, undersocialized and otherwise discarded, pup #3 can be coaxed out of its cage and enticed to approach and sit, so that after going through the test a number of times its behavior will come to approximate the original performance of "perfect" puppy #2 (although, by now of course, pup #2 will be better still).

Temperament training

The concept of temperament training is vital to any person working with animals. Rather than relying on the animal's natural inclinations to continue to behave in the manner that we would like, it is wise to implement a course of temperament training to assure that the animal's good qualities are continually reinforced and hence improved. Even when selecting an animal for a permanent placement, no matter how ideal its personality may seem, it could always be better and indeed, it is extremely easy to make it better. For example, no matter how friendly an animal may be, it can always be friendlier and no matter how calm it may be, it can always be calmer. Once placed, it is advisable to periodically check on the animal to ensure that temperament training is continued.

All animals will require basic *gentling and handling* exercises. Whereas this may be obvious with the larger domesticated animals, such as horses, many people tend to forget that dogs and cats are also animals and as such, they can hurt people. Obviously, all animals can hurt people when they are acting aggressively and they can act this way for a number of reasons; because they are mean, frightened or in pain, because they are protecting something... their food, toys, territory, themselves and their owners. I once met a cat that would attack anyone who shouted at its owners, which the owners interpreted as family protection (However, the cat also attacked people who shouted for any reason and for that matter, anyone who sat in its chair.) More usually though, animals hurt people by accident. A cat may unintentionally scratch when it jumps up into someone's lap, a dog may hurt people when it tries to say "Hello, I'm friendly" by pawing or jumping up. Also, both dogs and cats often bite and claw when they are playing, because no one has ever told them that this type of play is unacceptable with humans.

The handling exercises, which will prevent such intentional or accidental aggressive behavior from developing, are ridiculously straightforward and commonsensical, so much so that few people bother to do them regularly. In the course of routine husbandry and health care the animal will have to be regularly restrained, examined, and groomed. The sensitive areas are usually the ears, paws, and muzzle. Both dogs and cats may need their teeth and ears cleaned and dogs may need their nails trimmed. Care should be taken that animals do not mind this type of intervention. The animal must become accustomed to being regularly patted, petted, and hugged. This may seem silly but with most animals there comes a time when petting becomes irritating and hugging becomes restraining. In addition, animals must be prepared for the possibility of accidental pain (paw stepped on, tail caught in the door) and intentional abuse (paws pinched, tail tugged, hitting and kicking, etc.). Even though intentional animal abusers may deserve what they get, if a dog bites, for any reason, in effect it may be signing its death warrant and could eventually be euthanized. And no dog deserves that.

Most dogs and cats like being petted, patted, stroked and hugged but even the most affectionate of animals reaches a point when it has had enough: because the petting was too rough; because even fairly gentle petting was continued to the point of irritation; or because the animal was petted at a time when it wanted to be left alone.

Nonetheless, the animal must be prepared for an onslaught of "affection." Testing it with a five-or ten-minute period of gentle petting is not sufficient. Gradually and gently, the animal must be built up to accept the colossal levels of attention that it will receive during visiting programs or when initially placed with groups. Building up the animal's confidence with prolonged relaxing massage sessions, making sure that there are no especially sensitive spots and that the animal can be handled over all of its body, is especially important. It is essential that the animal will accept this kind of handling, that it learns to enjoy it, that it is not stressed, and that under no circumstances would it react adversely.

Patting probably deserves special attention because most people assume that animals find it inherently pleasurable. This is not necessarily the case. I am reminded of an anecdote told by an animal psychologist working at a zoo. The psychologist temporarily had a sloth hanging in his closet. In time, he thought he understood the sloth's behavior and was delighted to find that when he patted the animal on the head, it would, in its own inimitable indolent fashion, slowly and gently exhale, making a soft, contented hissing sound. The psychologist eagerly demonstrated this to all his visitors in much the same way that dog owners have to show how they have taught their dog to shake hands. Many years later, the psychologist met a zoologist who was a sloth expert. In passing conversation the sloth expert volunteered the information that the truth of the matter was that there was very little that was known about sloth behavior with the notable exception that, when sloths are vehemently displeased, they make a slow, soft hissing sound. Patting may similarly

Behavior modification and other training techniques can create an animal's "tricks"—in reality, hyperdevelopment of the animal's natural skills, such as catching a Frisbee or discriminating between blocks in an obedience test.

(Photo by Phil Arkow)

aggravate dogs and cats. Cats actively dislike it and some dogs do, too. Other dogs will tolerate patting but would seem to prefer other forms of physical petting. Whatever our individual interpretation of an animal's feelings about patting, it is an inappropriate way to greet an animal.

When meeting animals children often pat them on the head or shoulders. Touching a strange dog on the withers is not a good idea: in canine language the person is saying that he or she is dominant. Unless the dog has been taught that it is not meant to be threatening when humans touch it in this spot, the dog may disagree. In addition, the act of repeatedly touching the dog by quickly moving the hand towards and away from the dog often gets the dog very excited. If the dog is in any way hand-shy it may view the rapid contact as a threat. However, more usually it is the act of pulling the hand away that tends to excite the dog and may incite it to bite. Usually the dog is only biting in play, but it hurts all the same.

Children must be educated to first let the dog investigate them before they even try to touch it; then, offer a hand for a sniff, and after slowly making contact, to keep the hand on the dog, scratching and rubbing so the dog gets used to the contact. In addition, the dogs (and cats too) must be trained to accept inappropriate greetings and affection.

Nonetheless, no matter how well we educate animals and their human companions, there are still cases where the animal is treated inhumanely and is physically or psychologically abused. This may be either an intentional or an unintentional act on the part of the person. With overexuberant petting there is often a fine line separating genuine affection and unintentional abuse. Numerous times I have seen children have a tug-of-war over a four-month-old puppy, arguing about whose "turn" it is to pet it. (I have even seen adults squabble in a similar manner.) At this stage the petting usually ceases to become enjoyable for the dog. Sometimes, there is little difference between hugging and physical restraint. Dogs and cats must learn to accept both. Many children have been seriously injured by an animal's escape reactions precipitated by an overzealous hugging spell. Also, many children seem to have the unfortunate habit of doing silly things with animals: dogs receive unsolicited (and in some cases, unwanted) pats, they have tails pulled and paws pinched; cats usually get their tails tugged and are dropped out of windows to see if they land on their feet. This type of abuse is usually unintentional because the children do not know any better. Adults should make it their business to teach children how to know better.

It seems sad that we have had to talk about training an animal to accept affection from humans but unfortunately, some people's view of affection may not be consonant with the animal's view. And usually if the animal protests in any way the human invariably blames the animal as being aggressive, overly protective or sensitive, perhaps a fear-biter or uncontrollable and ultimately, the poor animal suffers. People must be taught to be gentle and understanding and that even animals need little quiet moments too, while on the other hand, cats and dogs especially must be taught that they must not react adversely to any kind of abuse. The animal must be taught that there is never any reason of any proportion that warrants biting a human. In addition to handling and gentling exercises, emphasis should be placed on other anti-aggressiveness exercises, specifically training young animals to inhibit their biting, scratching, clawing, kicking, and pecking. It is much easier and more effective to prevent the development of these behaviors than it is to attempt to cure them once established in adult animals.

Obedience training

In addition to training and preparing animals to accept large amounts of affection, it is useful to train them to solicit affection. It is not unusual for animals to visit a number of people yet for some reason refuse to visit others. The last thing we would want in a therapy program is for people to become upset just because a doggy or kitty will not come up and say hello. Basically, the training involves teaching the animal to come when called and stay close to the person and perhaps perform some attention-soliciting gesture, such as a lateral rub for cats, to jump in their lap for cats and puppies, or to sit, shake hands and wag its tail for a dog.

It is extremely easy to teach virtually any animal to come when called. It is useful with animals like cats, dogs, and birds to get them to approach people but also it is an essential safety precaution for all animals in case they escape. There is nothing worse than having to catch a horse that will not come in from the pasture for riding lessons, an untrained cat that runs out to the street, a bird that flies out the window, let alone more exotic animals that have been used in visiting programs, such as ferrets or tarantulas. Whereas many people realize the necessity to train domestic dogs, very few people attempt to train other animals. If we force animals to live in a domestic setting, it is only fair that we try and understand their behavior and languages, and in addition, it is common sense that we try to teach them some of our language. This latter process is known as training. It is a means to facilitate communication. By tapping on the side of the tank as a signal it is even possible (and a lot of fun) to train fish to come and eat food held in our fingers, or to get a spider to come for a tasty morsel of fly fricassee. By using different tap frequencies it is possible to get the fish to go to different parts of its tank for food.

The process is simple and most animals will get the idea in only a couple of days. First choose a suitable signal—either the request "come here," other words such as *"venez ici,"* other sounds like a whistle or handclap, or handsignals. (Animals that use a lot of body language will learn hand-signals much quicker than verbal commands.) First give the signal and then immediately offer the animal a food treat. Repeat this several times standing right in front of the animal so that it gets the idea that this is an enjoyable game. Then step back and call the animal again and reward it if it comes. Once the animal begins to respond reliably, two people can use the same signal and call the animal back and forth. Once the animal has learnt the meaning of the signal it should be used before all pleasureable activities, such as mealtimes, walks and play periods etc. It should be noted here that on no account should people call the animal and then punish it. This is a frequent error that is made with cats and dogs.

Once the animal will come when called, it is time to train it to stick around. When training a dog to stay, it helps to first tell it to sit or lie down. With a cat it is simple to tell it to jump up into someone's lap. Alternately, cats may be trained like dogs. Most people are enthralled when they see a dog sit, beg, lie down, roll over and play dead, let alone a cat, yet it is just as easy to train a cat. By using a food lure, as the animal approaches, give the command to sit and raise the food just a little, moving it backwards over the animal's head. As the animal's head goes up and backwards to follow the food, its rear end will go down. If the animal jumps up, the food is held too high. If the animal backs up, try it in a corner. As soon as the animal sits, give it the food. To get it to lie down, quickly lower the food between its forepaws and slowly draw it out away from the animal. If the animal keeps standing up, the food is being pulled away too quickly. An alternative method is to hold a piece of food under a coffee table that is just a little lower than the animal's back; as the animal approaches pull the food away so that the animal has to lie down to creep under the table. As soon as the animal lies down give it the food.

Once the animal will come and sit and/or lie down it is time to teach it to stay. The method is simple. Before giving the animal any food for sitting down, count to three. Once it has been rewarded for staying for three seconds, then next time try waiting five or 10 seconds before giving it a reward. Gradually, the length of the stay is built up as training progresses. It is possible to teach an animal all sorts of things using a system of food lures and food rewards.

Now that the cat or dog will approach and stay around, we may as well train it to look as if it is having a good time. Training a cat to purr or a dog to wag its tail is equally as easy. We think of a command and keep repeating it until the animal performs the behavior that we want and then immediately say good dog (or good kitty) and give it a food reward. Most dog owners have taught their dogs to wag their tails on command but do not even realize it. Training a cat to purr will take a little more patience and may require a good many strokes and ear scratches to get its motor started but as long as it is rewarded immediately, the cat will soon get the idea.

If for some reason an animal is reluctant to approach some person (which sometimes is the case when people are sick), there is no need to let the person know that we are commanding the animal to come and stay and shake hands and wag its tail, or perhaps jump in the person's lap. The "command" for this may be something quite natural like "Say hello" or "Be friendly".

Training can be a lot of fun both for the animals and the people concerned. If people feel that training is a chore, that it is restrictive or regimental for the animal, or that either they or their pets are not having a good time, then they would do well to revise the uneasy, unenjoyable, inefficient and probably ineffective methods that they are employing.

Behavior problems

In addition to maximizing an animal's good qualities, the techniques of behavior modification and temperament training are useful to help minimize the animal's bad habits. The types of problems that we experience when working with animals are hardly surprising. Animals have been exhibiting the same old problems for years and years. Since these problems occur with such regularity and consistency, we should consider that existing methods of treatment are limited in their effectiveness. In fact, the current philosophy for dealing with behavioral problems is still somewhere in the Stone Age and often quite inhumane and barbaric. Basically it consists of ignoring the animal while it is relatively well-behaved and then punishing it (usually hopelessly inappropriately) when it misbehaves. This method has proven itself to be remarkably laborious and notably ineffective. The poor animal has to learn what not to do by a process of trial and error. Moreover the entire "learning process" is further confounded by the fact that it is impossible for most people to punish an animal at the appropriate time. Usually the punishment comes long after the crime: as such its intended effect is minimal. Instead the delayed punishment only confuses the animal because it cannot work out why it is being psychologically and in some cases physically abused at the whim of some human, (whom previously it trusted).

There are a myriad of examples of this particular abuse. The poor cat that sometime during the day added a few decorative striations to the walnut veneer of a nice bit of Chippendale excitedly runs to greet its owners when they return home and for its trouble is met (at the best) with a string of abuse. In the eyes of the cat, the owner is punishing the cat's greeting behavior, not the scratching problem. No wonder so many cats are "independent" and hide in closets; they have just had enough of living with silly and unthinking owners. Similarly, the dog that runs off in the park and is punished when it returns to its owner: as far as the dog knows, the owner is punishing the dog for returning, nor for running away. The dog is unlikely to hurry back the next time. Usually all the animal learns is to keep well clear of humans.

Even if the human catches the animal in the act of misbehaving and punishes it immediately, the animal may not learn that the behavior is wrong. Many animals simply learn that it is inadvisable to misbehave in the onwer's presence. And so the tomcat still sprays urine at night and the dog still barks incessantly when left alone all day. I once had the pleasure to meet one dog that would sit on the owner's lap watching television, then calmly jump down, walk behind the sofa and defecate (this was discovered later) and then return to settle down in the owner's lap for the rest of the movie. This especially annoyed the owner because he was certain that the dog knew that it was wrong to defecate in the house because on several occasions he had beaten it within an inch of its life whenever he caught it in the act. No wonder the dog would hide behind the sofa when it defecated. When asked if he ever took the time and trouble to explain to the dog where he would like it to place its feces he replied that the dog would never defecate when he took it outside. Of course it wouldn't; the poor critter was afraid of having its brains battered. All he had taught the dog was never to defecate in the owner's presence.

Using only punishment to treat behavior problems is ineffective and usually exacerbates the existing problem and often creates new problems. For example, if the animal is confused by inappropriate punishments it will likely become stressed and of course two of the cardinal signs of stress are diarrhea and increased urination. If it ever becomes necessary to remprimand or punish an animal for misbehaving we should be absolutely certain that beforehand we have taught the animal how to behave appropriately.

Since for so long we have been getting unsuitable answers to the question of how to treat behavior problems, perhaps it is time to consider that we are asking the wrong question. Rather than asking "How can we treat behavior problems in animals?" perhaps we should consider, "How can we *prevent* the development of behavior problems?" It is much easier and certainly more prudent to prevent problems from developing than it is to attempt to cure them once they have become firmly entrenched as habits. This makes particular sense because, for any animal, the specific types of problems come as no great surprise. With only a rudimentary familiarity of the behavior of the particular species, with special considerations of the breed stereotype and a knowledge of the domestic setting, we can predict with surprising accuracy the behavioral problems that will develop. For example a dog will most likely bark, growl, snap, bite, dig, chew, urinate, defecate, roam, and chase. A cat will most likely scratch and bite, claw furniture, urinate and defecate, and "go crazy" late in the evenings. With horses, aspects of their urination and defecation behavior are not so important because they are seldom in areas where this would cause a problem. Instead horses bite, buck, bolt, kick and develop a variety of stable vices, such as wind sucking and crib biting.

It should be obvious to most that, from the animal's point of view, all of the behavioral problems listed above are normal and natural behaviors. In fact, some of these are necessary physiological functions. It is not the behaviors in themselves that are abnormal, but rather that they occur inappropriately (from a human point of view), i.e., that they occur at inappropriate times, in inappropriate places, or directed towards inappropriate stimuli. There is nothing wrong with dogs barking, but barking for excessive amounts of time would be inappropriate. There is nothing wrong with cats becoming hyperactive and climbing the walls, but this can be somewhat tiresome at 2:00 a.m. There is nothing wrong with cats and dogs urinating and/or defecating, but humans consider these behaviors inappropriate indoors unless performed on newspapers or in litter-boxes. There is nothing abnormal about cats scratching or dogs and horses chewing, but humans consider these behaviors inappropriate when directed towards household furniture or fittings. With our supposedly superior cerebrums, it should be relatively simple for us to teach animals to redirect these normal and natural behaviors to appropriate outlets and thus prevent them from becoming bothersome. This would make things so much easier for both the human and animal moieties of the bond—both in therapeutic programs and in daily living.

Conclusion

Much of this book and parts of this chapter have been devoted to the discussion of the numerous uses of companion animals for the mentally and physically handicapped, and the young and the elderly. In addition, there is discussion of how to handle the grief following the death of a pet. *(See Chapter 6.)* Practical programs and research in these areas have proven to be of immense value to all concerned. However, there is one major aspect of the human/companion animal bond that has received little attention: that of animals sharing life with "average normal healthy people." Hopefully, more researchers and educators will devote time to this area because so much can be done to improve the quality of the bond for the millions of people and pets in the world today.

In terms of animal behavior, I only hope that anyone working with animals will try to spend a little more time trying to understand their animal companions, if only in gratitude for the hours and lifetimes that those "therapeutic, socially lubricating, catalytically bonding," charming, delightful, and lovable little critters have spent trying to understand the many whimsical idiosyncracies and fickle foibles of their human companions.

Suggested reading:

Behavior

Hafez, E.S.E. *The Behavior of Domestic Animals.* Baltimore: William & Wilkins, 1969.

Dunbar, Ian *Dog Behavior.* Neptune, N.J.: TFH Publications, 1979.

Houpt, Katherine and Wolski, Thomas *Domestic Animal Behavior for Veterinarians and Animal Scientists.* Ames, Iowa: Iowa State University Press.

Beaver, Bonnie *Veterinary Aspects of Feline Bahavior.* Mosby, 1980.

Berman, M. and Dunbar, I. "The Social Behavior of Free-Ranging Suburban Dogs." *Appl. Anim. Ethol.* (10), 1983, 3-17

Dunbar, Ian "A Strategy for Dog Owner Education." *International Journal for the Study of Animal Problems, 2(1): 13-15, (1981).*

Dunbar, Ian and Bohnenkamp, Gwen: Behavior Booklets. Center for Applied Animal Behavior, 2000 Center St. #1406, Berkeley, CA 94704.

Training

The Monks of New Skete *How To Be Your Dog's Best Friend.* Boston: Little, Brown & Co., 1978.

Burnham, Gail *Playtraining Your Dog.* New York: St. Martin's Press, 1980.

Volhard, Joacquim and Fisher, Gail *Training Your Dog: The Step By Step Manual.* New York: Howell Books. 1983.

Whitney, Leon: *Dog Psychology: The Basis of Dog Training.* New York: Howell Book House, 1972.

Tucker, Michael: *Dog Training Made Easy.* New York: Rigby Publishers Ltd., 1980.

6

Thanatology: Death of a Pet

William Kay, Carole Fudin, and Susan Cohen

"... a need for understanding the feelings of loss and grief..."

Introduction

Few aspects of pet ownership have been less understood, studied, and formally documented than pet death. Yet attachment to pets in the western world suggests a need for understanding the feelings of loss and grief that many owners experience when pets die. Recently, health care scientists and veterinary practitioners have begun to study the nature of peoples' reaction to pet loss—conferences have been held and articles and books have been written to describe the phenomenon and to report the findings of those who have studied it under different circumstances.

Veterinarians, especially companion animal veterinarians, have for centuries had euthanasia as a therapeutic alternative to pain, suffering, old

William Kay, D.V.M., is Chief of Staff of the Animal Medical Center in New York City. He is a graduate of Michigan State University, is widely published and has done many presentations at veterinary conferences. The Animal Medical Center has established several programs to deal with the emotions surrounding pet loss. Carole Fudin, Ph.D., M.S.W., is a consulting psychotherapist to the Animal Medical Center and is director of Pet/People Problems: Education Therapy Service. Susan Cohen, M.S., is director of counseling and is chairperson of the AMC Institute for the Human/Companion Animal Bond.

age, and disease. Euthanasia is an important aspect of veterinary practice, and most veterinarians have observed the emotional upsets associated with euthanasia and death; however, some veterinarians have not developed the communication skills necessary to deal appropriately and successfully with clients who are suffering emotionally over the loss of a pet.

This chapter will cover several aspects of thanatology (pet death) including human and animal mortality, the American way of death, euthanasia, the need for anticipating an owner's reaction to loss of his pet prior to death, and the effect of pet death on the veterinarian, the staff of an animal hospital or shelter, and the clients.

The American way of death

For some people, concern about the death of a pet and its impact on the human companions may seem like a frivolous subject. This attitude may stem in part from never having lived with an animal, or, having done so, never forming a deep emotional attachment to one. Another reason for dismissing this topic may be the fact that discussing death and its impact on those left behind makes many of us uncomfortable and is something we would rather not consider.

It appears that within the past 10 years, in the United States and other western societies, discussions of death have increased greatly. Such discussions have been stimulated by the writings of social scientists such as Kubler-Ross and Becker, whose publications brought them to popular attention. Discussions of death also have been triggered by medical controversy regarding advances that have changed the nature of dying, making it hard to distinguish between life and death. Heightened death awareness is also associated with social disorganization and isolation, and with concern about the future of the world under the shadow of the nuclear bomb.

Despite the increased amount of discussion about death, western society still approaches death and dying with much trepidation. Discomfort with death stems from the fact that many people no longer maintain deep religious values which offer hope of death transcendence. In addition, one must incorporate an awareness of personal death into an impersonal technology that has fragmented family, friend, and kinship systems. In man's early history, death was part of everyday life. In modern times, however, death has been removed from common experience. Few people die at home among loved ones. People no longer live in communities with aunts, uncles, grandparents, siblings, etc.; therefore, when death touches them, they do not have the social and emotional support needed to help them through the experience of loss. It is relatively rare for most people to see an untreated dead person. The dead, whether human or animal, are whisked quickly away from view. Recent concerns about exploitive funerary practices have brought about a trend to deritualize the mourning period. The consequences of this trend have been to dispense with funeral rituals that guided people as they attempted to integrate loss into their lives.

Kastenbaum and Aisenberg have noted that in our society there is a preoccupation with the occurrence of accidental death. Deaths caused by airplane and automobile accidents and fires are given extensive media coverage. Surprisingly, however, only 5% of all deaths in the U.S. are caused by accident. The other 95% are caused by some biological process. It has been suggested that our obsession with accidental death affords us a way not to think about death being inevitable. It is easier to repress awareness of our mortality by concentrating on those who die in "unlucky" accidents, for deep down we believe that it is really an "accident" to be stricken by age or illness.

Given the fearful emotional climate attendant to death awareness in this society, it is relatively easy to understand why many bereaved pet owners receive little emotional support for the loss of "just an animal." In fact, some pet owners are perceived as bizarre. If the trend towards social disorganization and technologically induced isolation continues, however, there will be greater numbers of bereaved pet owners needing support and attention. Fogle has noted that as familial and communal structures have been lost, pets have increasingly filled the emotional void left behind. Pets provide the love, attention, and uncritical companionship that every human being needs. They can also travel with their owners, relocate with them, and provide a consistent link to something familiar which provides support through numerous life changes. But like us, pets do die, and generally their life spans are shorter than those of humans. Sadly, many pets die in accidents, but many also die of old age. They provide a vivid picture of life's natural processes. We can watch little beings develop from kittens and puppies through adolescence, adulthood, geriatric years, and then death. Their death symbolizes the inevitable end of human life, and perhaps this too makes people uncomfortable, reinforcing their desire to avoid recognizing the significance of pet loss.

For devoted pet owners, the death of one's animal can constitute a severe blow. Fogle has noted that many people feel biologic and emotional attachments to their pets. Pet animals become distinct personalities and are considered friends or family members. Therefore, when a pet dies, the human companion's grief can be the same in form and intensity as the grief which is felt when a human friend or relative dies. Wilbur, in a 1976 survey, asked bereaved pet owners if they would get another pet, and 15% said that they would not because the emotional strain was too great. It is not uncommon to hear pet owners share feelings in the early stages of their grief that they would be disloyal to their last pet if they obtained another. It is a feeling not unlike that of new widows or widowers who feel they would betray a lost spouse if they were to date or remarry.

Human and animal mortality

Since most people outlive their pets, the death of a pet is an event that a great majority of animal owners must face one day. While it can be extremely painful, Levinson suggests that it also can be an important part of human development. For children, the death of a pet can provide a very important life experience from which they can learn. As part of growing up, it is important to recognize that painful things happen in life, and not everything can be made better. It is also essential to feel unpleasant feelings in their full intensity, and to see that one can emerge from these feelings intact, stronger, and able to go on with life.

Adults too can grow and develop strength from coping with the death of a pet. The loss can be significant and meaningful in symbolic ways. It may stimulate the adult to think about the loss of other close relationships—past, present, and future. If the pet was aged, it reminds the adult of impending old age and generates thought about the quality of life one may wish to attain before life is over.

Therefore, the death of a pet has an impact both real and symbolic. The thoughts and emotions attendant to this loss are powerful and meaningful and worthy of support. The following is a summary of the normal grief reactions felt by pet owners when a pet dies.

Typical grief reactions

There are many emotional and physical reactions typical of a person who has lost a significant life relationship. Physically one may feel exhausted or may experience drastic alterations in eating and sleeping patterns. He or she may feel very nervous and irritable, experience difficulty breathing, and sigh a great deal. Nightmares and hallucinations of the deceased are not uncommon. In addition to these problems, many newly bereaved pet owners report seeing their pet or hearing the familiar sound of their pet's paws clicking on the floor. Grieving owners are often preoccupied with the image of the pet or objects associated with it. They may ruminate about the many things they loved about the animal—special mannerisms, tricks, and idiosyncracies become very important.

Emotionally, bereaved owners cry a great deal. They feel unable to concentrate, and they lose interest in people and the things that normally matter. There is an overall sense of depression which is frequently underscored by a deep feeling of guilt. If the pet's death was caused by an accident, it is common for the bereft owner to berate him or herself over and over for not having predicted the event and therefore prevented it. If the pet died naturally or was euthanized because of a chronically debilitating disease or old age, the owner may feel guilty, reasonably or unreasonably, for not having taken better care of the pet.

Bereaved owners may also feel very angry. Anger may be directed at the veterinarian for not performing a miracle, or it may be at the pet for abandoning his owner and upsetting a comfortable routine. Owners may resent people who have healthy animals or those who do not recognize the pet's significance. The physical and emotional symptoms are identical to those that were first described by Lindemann when he studied the surviving relatives of people who died in the Cocoanut Grove fire in Boston.

The intensity of bereaved owner reactions is different for each person and depends on the depth of attachment to the pet, the way the pet died (an anticipated or unexpected death), the way losses have been coped with

For devoted pet owners, the impending euthanasia of their beloved pet can constitute a severe emotional blow. Pets become distinct personalities and are considered as friends or family members. *(Photo by Phil Arkow)*

in the past, and other life events coinciding with the time of the pet's death. For most people, intense grief feelings begin within a few hours or days after the loss and reach a peak of severity within 14 days. After that time, they become less frequent, less severe, and eventually subside.

Stages of grief and mourning

Grief reactions are characterized by individual variation; however, a general pattern of stages has been identified. Pet owners may not experience all of these stages, or in the order presented, but everyone will feel some aspects of this grieving process.

First Stage: Numbness and Denial — At the time a pet dies, most people feel a sense of unreality and shock. It does not necessarily matter if the death was sudden or anticipated. It is typical for a pet owner to say, "No, it can't be true, not my pet." Numbness and denial are protective psychological defenses against feeling the full impact of loss. Owners may experience these feelings when given a catastrophic diagnosis by a veterinarian, and may go through many of the following stages prior to the animal's death. This is called anticipatory grief, which can ease somewhat the impact of the actual loss. When death occurs, owners may feel a sense of peace, or they may experience all the feelings and stages again to a lesser degree. Numb or denying owners may look and feel dazed. At the time of death, questions may be asked regarding the animal's condition which reflect the owner's feeling that the animal is still alive.

Second Stage: Painful Feelings — After shock and denial wear away, owners may feel anger. They may be angry at the pet for dying. It is not uncommon for them to feel angry at the veterinarian for not saving the animal. If the pet was killed accidentally, bereaved owners may feel like killing anyone who contributed to the accident. In time, the owners can recognize that the primary cause of their anger is that the pet left them behind. When this is integrated into the mourning process, anger begins to subside.

Owners may turn their anger against themselves and feel it as guilt. They feel responsible for the pet's death and blame themselves for not having done more to save the animal's life. In some cases, this may be justified; however, for most people this is not true.

Prolonged self-directed anger can turn into depression. Depressed owners generally have low self-esteem and punish themselves for being too inadequate to save their pets. Common symptoms of depression are feelings of helplessness, hopelessness, eating and sleeping disturbances, and a lack of interest in everyday things. Depressed owners may feel as though they are in a fog or trying to bear up under a great weight. For most people, depression goes away in a few days or weeks; if it lasts for several months or longer, professional help may be necessary.

Before continuing with the final stage of acceptance, some attention must be given to pathologic grief reactions. The grief reactions described thus far are normal, can be experienced by anyone, and tend to dissipate in a few days, weeks, or months. Some pet owners, however, experience a prolonged or exaggerated grief that can go on for an unspecified amount of time. This type of grief reaction stems from an inability to let go emotionally of the lost pet because the need for the animal's presence is so intense. McCulloch has described a case of a middle-class teenager, who, prior to the death of his dog, was a high achiever academically. Within one month after the death of his pet, he underwent severe personality changes and his school performance plummeted. Psychiatric consultation was sought and it brought out that the boy's transformation stemmed from his deep feelings of shame at grieving so deeply for "only a dog."

Pathologic mourning also may occur when the pet has functioned in a quasi-human role for the owner. This type of reliance on a pet usually undermines meaningful human relationships. Keddie suggests that the severence of this type of bond by death places the owner at greater risk to suffer an emotionally damaging type of reaction.

Grief for the death of a pet may be complicated when it triggers unresolved or suppressed grief associated with the death of a relative or friend. In such instances one death is linked symbolically to the other and a double mourning results.

In all the pathologic situations mentioned, the normal mourning process has been interrupted. Such individuals need professional help because it is unlikely that they can work through such complicated grief on their own. In therapy, bereaved owners can sort out their feelings, deal with what the pet means for them symbolically and realistically, and begin to view the loss in healthier ways.

Last Stage: Acceptance — When given enough time and allowed or helped to feel and work through the painful feelings described previously, bereaved owners reach a stage when there is no more anger, guilt, or intense pain about the pet's death. Thoughts about the deceased animal are no longer accompanied by "grief pangs." It is possible to reminisce, see the pet's belongings, see other animals which look like the lost pet, and not feel much pain. Owners may miss having a pet and consider obtaining a new one. A sign of acceptance is when the owner can clearly evaluate the appropriateness of obtaining a new pet. Will the present life style lend itself to responsible ownership? Can the owner give love to a new and different furry friend and appreciate its unique personality and characteristics?

In summary, it is important to know that mourning a lost pet is normal, natural, and nothing to be ashamed of. There also are certain things that owners can do to help themselves get through their grief. First, they must give themselves permission to have it. Second, it is helpful to reminisce about the good and bad times shared with the pet. Looking at pictures, visiting places frequented with the pet, holding toys, leashes, etc., are helpful in working through mourning.

Another helpful way to facilitate the grieving process is to have some kind of memorial for the pet. A memorial is beneficial whether the pet is buried by the owner on personal property or in a cemetery, or cremated privately or as part of a communal cremation. The memorial creates a sense of closure to the event of the pet's death and offers a chance to recognize and share one's feelings with others. The memorial can be a eulogy in the form of a poem, a letter, or a quotation borrowed from an admired literary figure. It also can be an impromptu service, a goodbye shared with supportive friends and family. This is a time to reach out to others and share feelings. Understanding friends, family, and other pet owners can be of great help in providing support to help the bereaved emerge from their grief intact, strengthened, and able to continue sharing their love with human and animal companions.

Need for anticipation of owner's reactions prior to death of the pet

Inasmuch as death is a major part of veterinary practice, it behooves us to anticipate owner reaction to pet death *before* the pet dies. Good practice management demands it. Veterinarians and animal health organizations compete for fees, donations, and public goodwill. Any who fail to recognize the emotional impact of pet loss on owners will lose out to those who handle it well.

Dealing with clients' reactions is more than a dollars issue. Given the increasing importance of pets in the lives of America's urbanized, mobile people, one can no longer ignore the social and mental health effects of pet loss. In contemporary America, a pet can serve as companion, workmate, protector, social lubricant, therapist to the isolated, greeter of latchkey children, and organizer of the elderly. To anticipate client reactions one must learn not only the stages of bereavement but the life circumstances of individual clients.

What does this pet mean to this client? In a community practice a veterinarian may have known both pet and owner for years. The staff may shop at the owner's supermarket, may have heard of the owner's recent widowing, or may know that the children live far away. Based on long-term knowledge of personality, finances, and living situation the veterinarian and staff can assess a familiar client's likely response to pet loss.

Individual practitioners may know something of the particular bond between a specific owner and his pet, but an owner may change veterinarians in the final stages of his pet's disease. Searching for a second opinion or a last chance, he may take his dying pet to an unfamiliar veterinarian. How can the veterinarian and his staff predict the response of an unfamiliar client?

Judicious questioning is the key to assessing client response. While some owners tolerate loss with apparent ease, others, whether or not they display their upset, suffer. Clinical experience suggests several life situations which seem to be connected with significant grief: 1) being elderly; 2) living alone; 3) suffering other recent loss; 4) identifying strongly with the pet; 5) having rescued the pet and nursed it through serious illness; 6) having lived with the pet through significant life changes. These categories are not exclusive. Nevertheless, if a client fits into even one, the veterinary health team can anticipate possible upset and provide the extra attention that will smooth interactions, prevent unpleasantness, and give the best care to both patient and owner.

The effect of pet death on the veterinary health team

How a member of the veterinary health team responds to pet death depends on the circumstances of the death, and the member's role and personal philosophy. There is a marked difference, for example, between losing, after heroic effort, the loved, elderly pet of a client-friend and the euthanasia of shelter animals. Both situations evoke feelings of sadness, but in the former the worker may feel proud that he participated in a gallant struggle, while in the latter situation there is no such element to alleviate the harsh reality.

Veterinarians, paraprofessionals, and lay staff report similar feelings when death brings an end to suffering. As one animal health technician explained, "If it's an old pet, I feel good giving it rest. Also, if we worked hard but still couldn't help the pet, we feel good because we tried." Stress enters for the team when a pet dies unexpectedly following lengthy treatment or when the owner is well known. Some feel badly for an elderly client, a young pet, or the family who has shared many years with their finned, feathered, or four-footed companion.

Confronting death can force confrontation of one's own spiritual belief and sense of mortality. People who have never believed in a personal afterlife yearn for a Garden of Eden for pets. Those formerly opposed to euthanasia come to see it as a blessing. A few relive other deaths or their own near misses. A 63-year-old veterinarian described his feelings as follows: "Ever since my heart attack, the line between life and death has seemed very fragile. Now when I push that plunger, I think 'This could be me.' "

Disappointment and powerlessness can set members of the veterinary team against the client, each other or society. When forced to choose between optimal therapy and money, many clients rail against professionals who do not donate services. Experienced staff deride the judgment of newcomers. Excellent surgeons who perform miracles routinely, tally up every loss as a failure; the longer they practice, the more failures they bear. Veterinarians or staff members may blame owners who wait too long to bring in their pet, too late for miracles.

Just as there are many responses to pet death, some ways of coping are more effective than others. Some professionals and assistants change specialties or employers. Some delegate responsibility, appointing one colleague to perform all euthanasias or sending junior staff to sit with grieving owners. Many veterinarians try to shield themselves from growing awareness of their own responsibility for the outcome of pet care and the emotional aftermath of the owners by hiding behind false professionalism—what one veterinary nurse calls "the robot approach."

Those members of the veterinary health team who cope effectively look squarely at death, confront their feelings about it, and embrace life. One veterinary assistant described her thoughts regarding the care of animals scheduled for euthanasia in the following way: "Sometimes an owner will tell us to put a pet to sleep at a time when we're very busy. The doctor might have to wait a half hour or so to do it. Sometimes I'd be in the back cleaning up, and I'd look in that cage and think, 'Maybe I shouldn't bother with this one—in another half hour it won't matter.' But then I'd think, 'Why shouldn't I make him as clean and comfortable as I can? He'll feel better, and so will I.' So I always fix up the cage and talk to the pet, stroke it, give it special attention. Since the owner isn't here, I do it." While the assistant can not alter the manner of death, she can take charge of her role as caregiver. In comforting a dying animal, she celebrates the highest professional and personal standard and gives herself the gift of closure in the relationship.

Euthanasia

Euthanasia, derived from the Greek word *euthanatos,* signifies an easy or painless death, i.e., a "good death." Of all features distinguishing veterinary and human medical practice, none is more dramatic and profound than the practice of euthanasia. Within the context of pet death, euthanasia is a major consideration. When its use is perceived as correct and appropriate, it is a blessing and a godsend to pet owners. When euthanasia is perceived as incorrect, it is the ultimate form of heartlessness, incompetence, and lack of caring.

In a sense, the ability and authority to practice euthanasia has been the ultimate bench mark of veterinary practice. It is a limiting device in that veterinary medical advances must be made alongside the fact that euthanasia is used in the treatment of a majority of pet animals, shortening the course of disease and therapy.

Euthanasia can be the simplest of events with little technical competence required, little psychosocial involvement, and little repercussion in the people involved. For others, euthanasia can be a vastly different experience. In the context of this chapter, the definition of euthanasia is the putting to death of an individual pet animal by a veterinarian after receiving permission by an owner or owner surrogate. Within this context, the results of euthanasia can be emotional or unemotional.

Several components are involved in the practice of euthanasia which must be considered by the veterinarian and his or her staff:

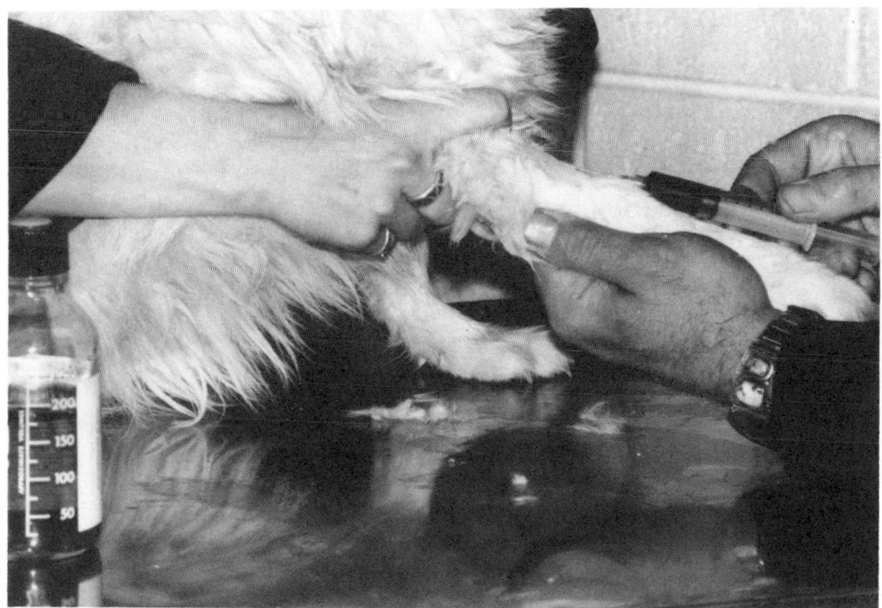

The stress of taking another animal's life can be profound among members of veterinary and shelter care teams. In shelters, where sheer volume and the lack of personal involvement with individual animals are routine, there are no feelings of heroic efforts to alleviate the harsh reality of mass, hand-held, death.

1. Timing
2. Decision making
3. Choosing an agent for euthanasia
4. Actual performance of the act of euthanasia
5. Handling the body
6. Burial and cremation
7. Communication with the owner
8. Post-euthanasia grief
9. Consideration of replacement pet
10. Handling money issues

Timing — No other aspect of pet euthanasia is as fraught with difficulty and ambivalence as selecting the correct time to perform it. Many features must be considered if owner satisfaction is to be achieved. Disease, injury, old age, and behavioral problems are untimely, and owners often ride a roller coaster of ambivalence in reaching a final decision. Therefore, it is nearly impossible to create a time to perform euthanasia that is considered ideal by everyone involved. Veterinarians and pet owners must accept this inherent imperfection and recognize the fact that there is no perfect time to euthanize a pet.

Decision making — Everyone involved, veterinarian, family, and friends, should participate in making the decision to euthanize a pet, but the final decision is ultimately made by the owner. The decision-making process is hampered by the fact that pet owners do not fully understand the process of aging, course of disease, or outcome of treatment. Family and friends may not know the depth of feeling on the part of the owner, or the owner's economic status or relationship with the pet. On their part, some veterinarians avoid the psychosocial dynamics of pet owners, considering this role to be outside their domain of knowledge, experience, influence, or responsibility. Veterinarians may not take the time to ask important questions regarding the needs and desires of their clients. Because veterinarians are seldom involved emotionally with the pet, they do not experience the owner's feelings. When an owner chooses euthanasia, the veterinarian should provide support.

The following guidelines are useful to veterinarians in helping owners to make a decision regarding euthanasia:

1. Do not assume that the owner grasps the full significance of the disease, injury, age, or behavioral problem of the pet.
2. Do not assume that the pet is "just a pet"; it might be something much more, such as a child substitute, a link to the past, or a link to another person.
3. Look at the pet from the owner's standpoint, not your own.

4. Do not impose your belief system on the owner.
5. Do not be in a hurry. An owner must reach a decision in his or her own time frame, not yours. Veterinarians who hurry may seem unconcerned.
6. Support any reasonable decision reached by the owner.
7. If the owner expresses a wish to watch and hold the pet during euthanasia, support this decision.
8. Support the decision for home burial, cremation, pet cemetery or other form of body disposition.

Choosing an agent — The agents available to veterinarians and shelters include barbiturate solutions, special euthanizing solutions (e.g., T-61, American Hoechst Corporation, Somerville, NJ), decompression chambers, and other anesthetics. For single pet euthanasia one should choose a non-narcotic agent that is readily available, easy to administer intravenously, effective in small doses, rapid acting, and without significant side effects such as gasping, twitching, cyanosis, stiffening and crying or other vocalization. Several agents are commercially available that meet the above criteria. Many veterinarians mix an ultrashort, active barbiturate with a standard euthanasia solution that contains a superconcentrated barbiturate or T-61. Care must be taken to follow the written label instructions. Also, veterinarians must know the proper amount of euthanizing solution to use and rate of administration. Improperly administered euthanasia solutions resulting in an improperly performed euthanasia can create serious upset, and undermine an otherwise excellent professional relationship.

Performance of Euthanasia — The seriousness of euthanasia makes it mandatory for the veterinarian and the staff to respond with concern. Some guidelines include:

1. Do not allow interruption by other clients, telephones, or staff during the procedure.
2. Have a clear understanding of the client's decision and desire to watch, touch and hold the pet during and after the procedure.
3. Have adequate support personnel to hold the pet and assist the owner.
4. Use a euthanizing agent that is familiar and works quickly, efficiently, and painlessly.
5. Explain the significance of body movements, urinating, defecating, etc., during euthanasia to the owner and any other observers.
6. Reserve enough space and time for the client to be with the pet's body following euthanasia and to speak with you following euthanasia.
7. Prepare a vein to insure a quick intravenous injection (the use of a preplaced intravenous catheter prior to euthanasia is often helpful).

Handling the Body — Handle the body with care, concern, and respect.

Some guidelines include:

1. If possible, do not remove the body until the owner leaves.
2. Close the eyes and place the tongue in mouth; clean the body carefully by removing blood, saliva, fluid, urine, feces, etc.
3. Wrap the body and place it in a box or other appropriate container. Tell the owner how it looks and how it will be wrapped if they choose to remove or view the body prior to burial, cremation, etc. Surprises are generally unpleasant.
4. Inform the owner about rigor mortis.

Burial and cremation — Support and assist pet owners with the burial/cremation/deposition process. Allow them time to choose. Tell them the cost and logistics of these options. Inform the pet cemetery as completely as possible about the pet and the owner. Tell the owners what to expect if they wish a final viewing. If a distraught pet owner asks about caskets, burial vaults, etc., use care in delivering your personal view.

Communication with the owner — Take the time to visit, telephone, or write the owner after his pet has been euthanized. This is satisfying to pet owner, friends, and the veterinarian. Most pet owners appreciate and sincerely acknowledge the support that such communication conveys.

Post-euthanasia grief — Grief is an important component of pet loss. When involved in supporting a person having recently lost a pet one should be able to recognize the symtoms of grief. Support for such grief is discussed elsewhere in this chapter.

Consideration of replacement pet — Just as people vary widely in their response to pet loss, they also vary widely in their response to the idea of a replacement pet. A good rule of thumb is to raise the question of a replacement without pushing or making a value judgment as to the appropriateness of a replacement.

Handling money issues associated with euthanasia — The majority of pets are euthanized. Among the important and frequent reasons is the cost of treatment and its impact on the owner and his family life. The true role of the pet is sometimes focused when the issue of money is raised, especially since many people willingly spend money for the treatment of a beloved pet as long as the outcome of treatment is clear. The pet's condition frequently determines how much money will be needed, for how long, and with what result. These things are frequently vague, however, making it difficult to predict the costs, which in turn makes it more difficult for pet owners to decide about treatment when money is a concern.

In summary, euthanasia is a complex issue. For veterinarians and other people working with pet animals it is an issue dealt with on a daily basis.

Everyone involved must recognize that the depth and range of emotional responses vary widely among people: euthanasia is a profound emotional issue for some pet owners and not a problem for others. Given the wide range of standards and beliefs within American society, it is an issue that must be handled case by case.

Since most euthanasias are performed individually by a veterinarian in an animal hospital or home setting, knowledge of the dynamics can make a complex and potentially traumatic experience easier. Despite evidence to the contrary, one of the most critical of issues between veterinarian and owner is still handled as if the skills necessary for handling it were natural and automatic. Euthanasia, as is true of other components of veterinary practice, requires the use of learned skills in the arena of communication as well as technique in order to be performed properly. It is the responsibility of the veterinarian to acquire these skills.

Some veterinarians use euthanasia as a way of avoiding the time and energy it takes to try new modes of therapy, continue treatment, or in other ways increase clinical competence. Euthanasia also may be used as an effective way of avoiding referral. Mistakes can be concealed. Pet owners should be made to understand that all treatment options have not necessarily been exhausted, all opportunities for referrals taken advantage of, or enough time elapsed to accurately determine the nature and cause of the disease, injury, or age-related or behavioral problem before euthanasia becomes an alternative.

Veterinarians are frequently suspected unjustly of motives at odds with pet owners, especially if the veterinarian is not familiar with the owner or the pet. This is especially true if a new or different veterinarian is involved in treating a serious disease or injury and is not readily available for in-depth discussion or consultation. The intensity of this type of situation is heightened when, because of the seriousness of the disease or injury, treatment is expensive and must begin immediately, as in emergency situations. Problems of this kind may be exacerbated when the veterinarian's practice is a great distance from the pet owner, as in the case of distant referrals. Under these and other anxiety-provoking circumstances, the veterinarian and owner may reach a decision to euthanize amidst dissatisfaction and misunderstanding. In addition, pet owners frequently change their minds when confronted with options. The factors are usually three: 1) the evolutionary nature of disease; 2) The various sequelae of treatment; and 3) the cost of pursuit. The pet owner and veterinarian must have as clear an understanding of these three factors as possible under the circumstances by keeping the lines of communication open. Only then can the act of euthanasia be performed in an atmosphere conducive to the acceptance, and the knowledge that the decision was the right one for pet and owner.

Suggested reading:

Becker, E.: *The Denial of Death.* New York, The Free Press, 1973.

Feifel, H.: *New Meanings of Death.* New York, McGraw-Hill Book Company, 1977.

Fogle, B. (ed.): *Interrelations Between People and Pets.* Springfield, Ill.; Charles C. Thomas Publishing Company, 1981.

Fulton, R., (ed.): *Death and Identity.* Bowie, Md., Charles Press Publishers, Inc., 1976.

Kastenbaum, R. and Aisenberg, R.: *The Psychology of Death.* New York, Spring Publishing Company, 1972.

Keddie, K.: Pathological mourning after death of a domestic pet. *Br J Psych* 131:21-215, 1977.

Kubler-Ross, E.: *On Death and Dying.* New York, Macmillan Publishing Company, 1969.

Levinson, B.M.: *Pets and Human Development.* Springfield, Ill., Charles C. Thomas Publishing Company, 1972.

Lindemann, E.: Symptomatology and management of acute grief. *Am J Psych* 101, 1944.

McCulloch, M.: *Proceedings,* Meeting of a Group for the Study of the Human-Companion Animal Bond. Dundee, Scotland, March 23-25, 1979.

Neiburg, H. and Fischer, A.: *Pet Loss: A Thoughtful Guide for Adults and Children.* New York, Harper and Row, 1982.

Wilbur, R.: *Pets, Pet Ownership and Animal Control. Social and Psychological Attitudes.* Proceedings, the National Conference on Dog and Cat Control. American Humane Association, Denver, Colo., 1976.

Kay, W., Neiburg, H., Kutscher, A., Grey, R., and Fudin, C.: *Pet Loss and Human Bereavement.* Ames: Iowa State University Press, 1984.

Quackenbush, J. and Graveline, D.: *When Your Pet Dies.* New York: Simon and Schuster, 1985.

7

Pets in Nursing Homes — A Comparison Between 1981 and 1986

Robert K. Anderson,

Each year since 1981, information regarding laws and regulations for pets in health care facilities has been collected to establish a reference library at the University of Minnesota's Center to Study Human/Animal Relationships and Environments (CEN/SHARE). The Center is serving as a research and reference resource to share these data throughout the U.S. As part of this research, we analyzed the data in several categories based on laws, regulations or written guidelines as reported by officials in each state.

These studies reveal significant changes in laws and regulations governing companion animals in nursing homes. In 1981 eight states prohibited all animals from nursing homes but in 1986 all states allowed pets in nursing homes even though four states still require special permission. The number of states developing specific regulations regarding pets in nursing homes has increased from 14 to 28 states. Those requiring a healthy animal increased from 10 to 16 states while those asking for appropriate behavior increased from 4 states

Robert K. Anderson, D.V.M., M.P.H. is Director of CEN/SHARE — the Center to Study Human/Animal Relationships and Environments — and is Professor of Epidemiology at the University of Minnesota. He is an editor of The Pet Connection, a book of proceedings from the 1983 Minnesota-California Conferences on the Human-Animal Bond and has authored more than 75 publications. He teaches a university course entitled Perspectives: Human-Animal Relationships in Society Today and with his colleagues in CEN/SHARE has produced video-tapes of 38 of these classes. CEN/SHARE has also produced 6 video-tapes on how to start pet programs in nursing homes. All of these video-tapes are available for rent or sale from Media Distribution, University of Minnesota, Box 734 Mayo Bldg., W-42 Centennial Hall, Minneapolis, MN 55455.

in 1981 to 12 states in 1986. It is noteworthy that only 6 states prohibit wild animals and 3 states, domestic turtles and 47 States allow birds even though 3 states specifically prohibit birds. And finally we found that 22 states allowed animals as desired by nursing home administrators except in food preparation or service areas since they have no regulations except the general food and safety laws.

These data reveal a wide range of difference in restriction among the states, but it is provocative to note that none of the state health officials in the years 1981 to 1986, reported any significant problems of injuries or illness associated with pets in nursing homes.

Additional supportive evidence of the lack of risk associated with pets in nursing homes is provided by a study conducted by the Center to Study Human-Animal Relationships and Environments, University of Minnesota. Their 12 month study of infections, injuries and allergies associated with visiting or live-in animals in 280 nursing homes showed that it is very safe to have pets and that people and environmental factors are 500 times more likely to be associated with adverse incidents.

An analysis of the laws and regulations restricting the presence of animals in skilled nursing homes and intermediate care facilities reveals great differences among the 50 states and challenges the need for the kind of restrictions imposed by many of the states. This chapter makes recommendations and emphasizes the need for developing outcome criteria based on sound epidemiologic evidence.

However, as we studied nursing homes, with and without animals, talked with residents, staff, administrators, provided consultation and reviewed the literature, we found several major concerns which must be considered and appropriately addressed whenever the presence of animals in health and long-term care facilities is considered. These concerns include:

1. the need for rational precautions to protect the health, safety and desires of:

   (a) residents and staff who wish to be away from animals because of dislike, fear, and potential problems of behavior, nuisance, odor, hair, urine, feces, disease, infection, allergies, bites, falls, etc.;

   (b) residents and staff who wish to have the companionship of visiting or resident animals to offer attention, affection, stimulation, touch, talk, motivation, responsiveness, and to facilitate socialization, self-esteem, self-confidence, reminiscence, physical and mental wellness;

2. the need for appropriate definition of purposes/objectives for the presence of visiting and/or resident pets, including one-owner pets;
3. the need to consider appropriate choices of visiting/resident pets based on normal species behavior, health maintenance, and the environmental needs of the animals;
4. the need to consider flexibility and many individualized ways to utilize animals in accord with the desires and constraints of residents and staff at different times and in different areas in different facilities; and
5. the need for states and long-term care facilities to adopt policies and regulations to encourage individualized plans that recognize the great differences among facilities, staff and residents.

Methodology

To obtain the most accurate and current information regarding laws and regulations restricting the presence of companion animals in licensed health care facilities in the U.S., we contacted the responsible agency in each of the 50 states each year. We asked agencies to provide current information for laws and regulations governing pets in long-term facilities (nursing homes) in each state.

Along with the covering letter we sent a special form requesting a copy of the appropriate sections or paragraphs of laws and regulations, and narrative information explaining any guidelines or interpretation for enforcement of the legal standards.

To reduce the problem of comparability among the states this chapter is limited to analysis of data pertaining to facilities designated by the states as nursing homes, or intermediate care facilities. This generally excludes any facilities such as hospitals, supervised living facilities, and board and care homes. It was interesting to note that laws and regulations for hospitals in many states do not mention pets or animals as prohibited or permitted.

In 1986, we sent our most recent data to each state and asked them to provide any changes or additions in the laws and regulations concerning presence of animals in nursing homes. Through follow-up letters and telephone calls, data were received from all 50 states in the U.S. providing a 100% response with data for analysis in this 1986 report.

Results and discussion

Results of analysis of the data are presented in Tables 1 through 4.

Table 1 shows that the number of states developing specific regulations governing pets in nursing homes between 1981 and 1986 has increased from 14 to 28 states. We interpret this as part of the trend to increased recognition of pet programs in nursing homes. All 50 states have laws and regulations governing food preparation and service in any public establishment which may be applied to long-term care facilities. All 50 states also have general laws and regulations relating to health and safety of people and/or animals in nursing homes. For example Alaska Administrative Code 5AAC81.130(c) (7) requires a permit for possession of live game and under that regulation the licensing agency issues regulations with restrictions for permitting or prohibiting dogs, cats, birds, etc., in nursing homes.

TABLE 1
Types of Legal Authority Used by States to Regulate Animals in U.S. Nursing Homes

	States			
	Number		*Percent*	
Types of Regulations	*1981*	*1986*	*1981*	*1986*
General food prep and service reg.	50	50	100	100
General for health and safety reg.	50	50	100	100
Specific regulations concerning animals	14	28	28	56

Data in Table 2 compares the number of states that prohibit animals in food areas (100%) and those at specifically prohibit animals in other areas such as medication rooms, linen and storage areas, and resident's rooms. Forty-five states now allow pets in residents rooms as compared to only 39 in 1981. Why do 5 states still prohibit pets in residents rooms?

Should these rigid prohibitions be questioned? Are they consistent? Are there animals that could be permitted in medication and treatment rooms? Should all animals be excluded from rooms of all residents? Are there valid epidemiologic data for some states to prohibit animals in these specific areas? There appear to be no reports of any significant differences in health or safety problems between the 5 states that prohibit animals in these specific areas and the 45 states which do not prohibit animals in these areas. Certainly the University of Minnesota study found no significant health or safety problems associated with animals in residents rooms.

TABLE 2
Areas Where Animals Are Not Allowed

	States			
	Number		Percent	
Prohibited Areas	*1981*	*1986*	*1981*	*1986*
Food preparation areas	50	50	100	100
Food service areas	50	50	100	100
Medication and treatment	16	13	32	26
Linen and storage areas	16	14	32	28
Residents/patients' rooms	11	5	22	10
Other areas	10	9	20	18

Data from Table 3 further emphasize the difference in the regulations among the states in prohibiting all animals (decrease from 4 states to none in 1986).

It is noteworthy that only 6 states prohibit wild animals, 3 states prohibit domestic turtles and 3 specifically prohibit birds although 47 states allow birds. Why do such a small percent of states have these prohibitions? What is the epidemiologic basis for such prohibitions? Have these prohibitions been evaluated? Why do 64% of the states (Table 2) allow animals in nursing homes without specific restrictions except in food preparation and service areas? Several of the states which generally permit animals stated that they had no reported safety and health problems with pets. Others said that the agency intervenes only upon complaint or an observed problem during a periodic inspection by the agency. It appears that 44% of the states depend upon the responsibility and accountability of individual nursing home administrators to regulate the presence of pets as judged by outcome measures, rather than by "how to" regulations.

TABLE 3
Types of Animals Specifically Prohibited in Nursing Homes

	States			
	Number		Percent	
Prohibited Animals	*1981*	*1986*	*1981*	*1986*
Birds	1	3	2	6
Domestic Turtles	1	3	2	6
Wild animals	4	6	8	12
All animals except fish	4	0	8	0
Resident animals (allow visiting animals)	*	5	*	10

*data for 1981 not available

These same principals of individualized planning and evaluation can be applied to assure reasonable health behavioral characteristics of an animal if a veterinarian is appropriately involved. This veterinarian should be involved in selection of appropriate animals and developing an individualized health maintenance and care plan for each animal with methods for continuous monitoring of the animal's health by staff and residents. The number of states that require immunizations of animals has increased from 13 to 16 but this is only one criteria for a healthy animal. Those states that mention animal "behavior", which most people judge to be very important in animal-human relationships, increased from 4 to 12 between 1981 and 1986. It is appropriate to note that six states require "health certificates" issued by a veterinarian which may give a false sense of security.

Most "health certificates" do not detect important zoonotic infections which may be in the incubation period or which may be carried and shed by the animal without clinical signs of disease. For example rabies, psittocosis, toxoplasmosis, leptospirosis, or salmonellosis may be transmitted to people with subsequent infection and illness in effectively exposed residents, staff, and visitors. To take the place of the inadequate and misleading "health certificate", animals should be permitted in nursing homes under individual health maintenance and care plans developed by a veterinarian with methods for continual monitoring of health by residents and staff.

TABLE 4
Health and Behavior Requirements for Animals Prior to Entering Nursing Homes

Pre-entrance Requirements	*States*			
	Number		*Percent*	
	1981	*1986*	*1981*	*1986*
Immunizations	13	16	26	32
Healthy animal	10	16	20	32
Health certificate	6	6	12	12
Appropriate Behavior	4	12	8	16

There appear to be no reported differences in disadvantages or problems occurring in nursing homes with and without animals, regardless of wide variations among the 50 states in legal authority and enforcement procedures to restrict or prohibit pets in nursing homes. This interpretation applies regardless of whether states prohibit pets, require special permission, restrict visiting or resident pets, have rules for people or pets, specify whether pets may be inside or outside, or have laws or guidelines or have only general outcome regulations rather than a specific "how to" regulations. These interpretations are supported by data from epidemiologic studies conducted by CEN/SHARE, University of Minnesota and the Minnesota Department of Health, which provide additional evidence that having pets in nursing homes is one of the safest and least hazardous activities.

The Human-Animal Bond Committee of the American Veterinary Medical Association has issued recommendations for veterinarians to consider as guidelines in consulting with nursing homes which desire visiting or resident pets. (See Chapter 14). These guidelines emphasize an individual plan to be developed for each nursing home as recommended here.

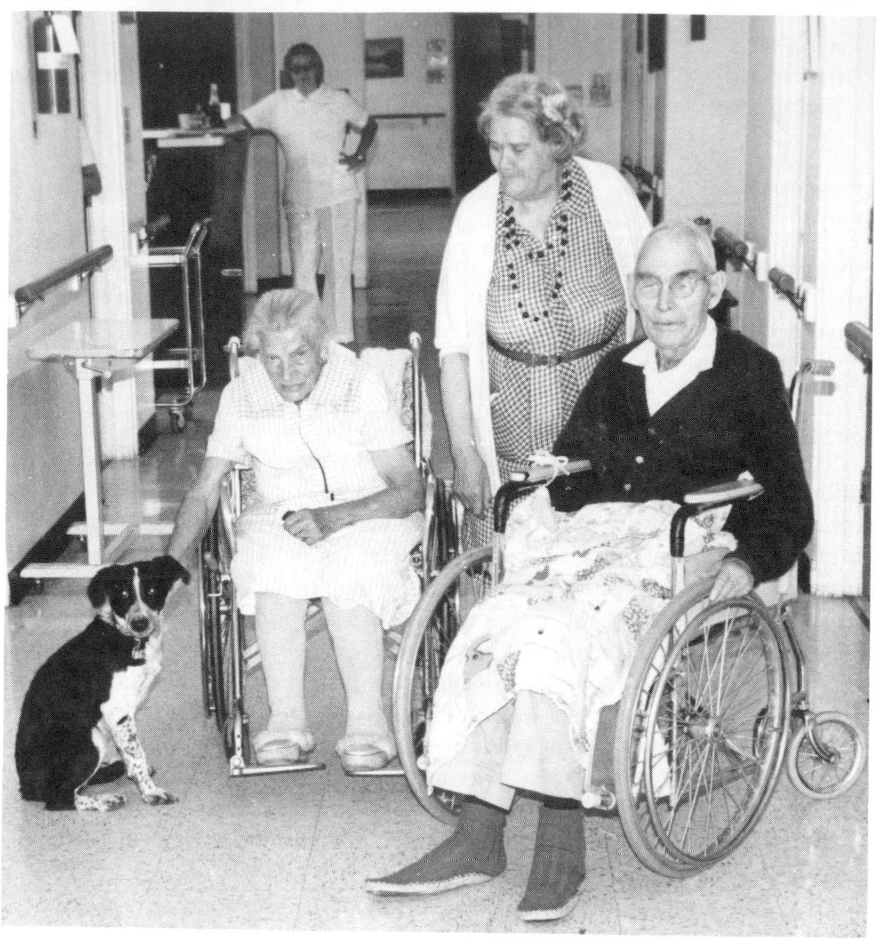

Since 1986 all states allow pets in nursing homes. *(Photo by Phil Arkow)*

SUMMARY AND RECOMMENDATIONS

1. This study challenges the value of and need for many of the present regulations specifying apparently ineffective and burdensome requirements and restrictions for animals as applied to all nursing homes in a given state.
2. It emphasizes that no one state-wide method, procedure, or regulation is appropriate or of value in all nursing homes.
3. It emphasizes the need for each nursing home to develop an individual plan with defined purposes and objectives:
   (a) to permit animals based on sound epidemiologic data and outcome criteria; and
   (b) to provide rational precautions for health and safety of people without unduly limiting the benefits of animals (as judged by the responsible administrator with consultation from veterinarians, physicians and others).
4. It is recommended that:
   (a) residents, staff, and appropriate consultants be involved in developing any plan for animals in a facility as well as in implementation and evaluation of such plans;
   (b) such plans consider the desires of residents and staff who wish to be away from animals as well as those who wish to have the companionship of visiting or resident animals; and
   (c) such plans consider the choice of animals based on normal species and breed behavior, health needs of the animals, and the purposes and objectives for the presence of animals.
5. Evaluation should involve outcomes and accountability — not "how to" regulations — and encourage more flexible, innovative methods that most effectively achieve the objectives of the facility.
6. Veterinarians should provide leadership in developing a plan for admitting and monitoring the health and behavior of visiting animals.
7. Veterinarians should be advisors in selecting appropriate animals and provide leadership in developing a plan for promoting and monitoring the health and behavior of resident animals as a continuing health maintenance program.

Summary of laws and regulations of the 50 states governing pets in nursing homes*

ALASKA

Alaska Administration Code 5 AAC 81. 130 (c) (7) states: No permit may be issued under (a) of this section for possesion, import or export of live game (live game definition covers everything from cats, dogs, reindeer, mice, to canaries, peafowls, pigeons &, turkeys) unless the Commissioner determines the animal will not present a public nuisance, health hazard or threat to public safety..."

Therefore, under that regulation the licensing agency requires (1) the animal may not "live in" or "sleep" in the immediate nursing home—only scheduled visiting animals for patient therapy; (2) a valid certificate from a veterinarian, when the agency permits animals in long-term care facilities for patient therapy, only for specified periods of time; (3) a dog or cat to have a health certificate by a qualified veterinarian stating that the animal is properly vaccinated and free from disease; (4) the agency does not permit birds in nursing homes or hospitals.

ALABAMA

Alabama currently has no statutes or regulations which stop the presence of animals in health care facilities except for regulations barring animals from food preparation and service areas.

The state Health Department and state Veterinary Medical Association have adopted protocols, not regulations, for visiting pet programs only. The program does not recognize permanent (resident) pet placement or mascots within nursing homes.

Visiting program protocols were established in 1981. As of October, 1982, there were fewer than 10 requests for information and no official notification of any facility starting a program.

Protocols provide specific requirements for nursing homes, for veterinarians and for pet owners. These include approval by each patient and each patient's physician. Also, the pet must be vaccinated and certified for health and temperament by a veterinarian. The protocol provides detailed guidelines.

ARIZONA

Arizona is allowing dogs and other pets in most areas of nursing homes except food areas, dining areas and treatment areas. Nursing homes are required to establish "Pet Policies" for the individual facility.

*Readers are cautioned that state laws, rules and regulations are constantly being revised. Though this summary reflects the most up-to-date information available at time of publication, readers should inquire locally regarding newer regulations in their particular state.

ARKANSAS

According to Arkansas Rules and Regulations for Nursing Homes, page 12, birds, cats, dogs and other animals are not permitted in nursing homes. The state has issued waivers in the past year to permit pets in nursing homes when scheduled as an organized activity. Local humane societies and animal control agencies have been responsible for bringing the pets into the nursing home. The pet program has been added to regulations effective January 1, 1984.

CALIFORNIA

There are currently no state health facility laws or regulations prohibiting pets in health facilities. The Department of Health Services would intervene only in the event of a complaint that the pet presented a hazard to the health and safety of the patients or the sanitation of the health facility. Evaluations of patients' conditions and their environment are routinely made during surveys of all health facilities which are conducted at least biennially in acute care hospitals and annually in long-term care facilities.

COLORADO

There are no specific references in these regulations regarding the possession of pet animals. The Office of Medical Care Regulation and Development has been consistently encouraged to allow pet animals in health care facilites as long as they meet the following criteria:

1. They are not kept in or allowed access to food handling and eating areas.
2. That birds and mammals are acquired and possessed in compliance with existing Colorado laws pertaining to pet animals. This means that psittacine birds must be leg-banded and must come from approved sources, and that dogs and cats must be currently vaccinated against rabies in compliance with local regulations.
3. That the animals do not interfere with the health and rights of other individuals in the facility. Factors affecting this requirement would include noise, odor, and allergies possibly caused by animal proteins.

The Colorado Department of Health recognizes and encourages the use of pet animals for their therapeutic value in long-term care facilities. The Department's Zoonoses Control group consults with all interested parties when individual decisions about the use of pet animals need to be made.

CONNECTICUT

The Public Health Code of the State of Connecticut does not prohibit the presence of pets in health care facilities. The following statute and regulations make reference to the limitations on animals in these facilities.

1. Public Health Code Section 19-13-B42 (p) (1) prohibits live birds or animals in food storage, preparation or servicing areas.
2. Public Health Code Section 19-13-A25 addresses psittacine birds and banding requirements.

In March, 1982, representatives from the Connecticut Humane Society, the Connecticut Veterinary Medical Society, the Connecticut Association of Health

Care Facilities (nursing homes), and the Department of Health Services formed a task force to develop guidelines for pet visitation programs which are also applied to resident pets in health care facilities.

Currently in the State of Connecticut there are a number of health care facilities (primarily skilled nursing and intermediate care facilities) which have resident dogs or cats, and many others which participate in an organized pet visitation program sponsored by the Humane Society or other community-based groups.

DELAWARE

The regulations governing these facilities have as an adopted requirement the provisions of the "Food Service Sanitation Manual," a publication of the Food and Drug Administration. This publication governs the dietary area and in reference to animals states: "7-806 Animals. Live animals, including birds and turtles, shall be excluded from within the food service operational premises and from adjacent areas under the control of the permit holder. This exclusion does not apply to edible fish, crustacea, shellfish or to fish in aquariums. Patrol dogs accompanying security or police officers, or guide dogs accompanying blind persons, shall be permitted in dining areas."

Other than this quoted section there are no regulations dealing specifically with the presence of animals in health care facilities.

Historically pets are found in and about the following facilities under the listed conditions:

Intermediate and Skilled Nursing Homes — occasionally found; usually pet brought in by staff, visit from SPCA representative, or "facility" pet maintained by employee. Excluded from dietary-dining areas.

FLORIDA

There are no restrictions on a statewide basis regarding the presence of animals in health care facilities. There are some restrictions in individual hospitals and health care facilities.

GEORGIA

Presently there are no laws or regulations in Georgia that specifically regulate animals or pets in long-term care facilities. Areas in the regulations do address residents' rights and development of administrative policies that consider safety, infection control, and sanitation.

The Department reports an increasing number of questions concerning this subject from nursing homes that desire a pet program and has established a committee to look into the pros and cons of pets in the nursing home environment.

HAWAII

The Hospital & Medical Facilities Branch, Department of Health, State of Hawaii, does not have regulations governing the presence of animals in hospitals or other health care facilities, and has not found this to be a problem.

IDAHO

The state licensing laws and regulations for hospitals, skilled nursing facilities and intermediate care facilities do not address the issue of animals in the facility.

The department reports that interest in animal-human relationships in long-term care facilities in Idaho is growing and the licensing agency in the absence of any regulations, has issued guidelines to facilities wishing to initiate a pet program.

ILLINOIS

The Department's Minimum Standards, Rules and Regulations for Long-Term Care Facilities do not prohibit the presence of animals except as referenced in the Department's Rules and Regulations for Food Service Sanitation, 77 Illinois Administrative Case 750, Section 750.1400.

There is available a guideline that the Department has utilized regarding Pets in Long-Term Care Facilities. The Illinois Department of Public Health has recognized that pets can be a valuable asset in long-term care facilities if managed properly.

INDIANA

The Indiana Health Facilities Rules, Title 410 IAC 16.22-2-6(i) and (j), regarding pets states:

"(i) Each facility shall have a policy concerning pets. Pets may be permitted in a facility but shall not be allowed to create a nuisance or a safety hazard.

(j) Any pet in a facility shall have periodic veterinary examinations and required immunizations."

IOWA

There shall be no animals or birds in the food preparation area of a nursing home. (III)

No animals shall be allowed within the facility (nursing homes) except with written approval of the Department and under controlled conditions. (III)

KANSAS

Kansas Administrative Regulations governing the operation of adult care homes are silent concerning animals or pets in the facility.

In the survey of a facility that allows animals, the department inspects to assure that the health, safety and comfort needs of residents are met.

It is expected that the facility have a policy and procedure written and implemented which includes, at a minimum: provisions for care of the animal; areas designated off-limits to the animal; and consideration made to assure residents their rights of choice regarding involvement with the animals.

KENTUCKY

The deparment has recently revised most of the licensure regulations for health facilites including those for hospitals, hospices, and long-term care facilities. Although the subject of pets in licensed facilities did come up during discussions of the long-term care regulations, none of these regulations include any requirements or prohibitions on this subject.

LOUISIANA

Historically, Louisiana has denied pets in health care facilities on the basis of a portion of the Sanitary Code regulating food service which excludes live animals from within food service operational premises and from adjacent areas. None of the licensing laws specifically address the item. Some nursing homes have aquariums with small fish.

In the last year or two, Pet Therapy groups have begun to bring pets. This is permissable, and the new standards for payment for nursing homes will address this issue, giving permission for supervised pets in nursing homes.

MAINE

At the present time there are no laws, rules or regulations that govern the presence of animals, i.e., dogs, cats, fish and birds, in health and long-term care facilities licensed or regulated.

MARYLAND

While Maryland law doesn't prohibit pets from being allowed into Health Department licensed or certified health care facilities, sanitarians have frowned on such practices. Currently, standards are being pilot-tested to allow limited access of pets into facilities under Department jurisdiction. This testing commenced on September 20, 1982. When finally approved, standards will be reflected in state-wide Health Department Regulations.

MASSACHUSETTS

The Department of Public Health licenses hospitals, clinics, nursing and rest homes, clinical laboratories and ambulance services. Only the regulations for the licensure of nursing homes (called Level I, II, or III care in the regulation) address the presence of animals in a health care facility. The regulation is part of housekeeping and maintenance standards and is printed in its entirety below:

(f) Pets.

(1) Pets or other types of animals shall not be allowed in any of the following areas: patient areas in facilities that provide Level I, II, or III care; kitchen and areas used for preparation, serving or storage of food; laundries or restorative services units.

(2) No commercial breeding of pets shall be allowed.

(3) All pets shall be adequately fed, sheltered and maintained in a sanitary manner.

MICHIGAN

The State of Michigan has not to date developed any regulatory program that specifically addresses the issue of pet introduction into regulated health care facilities. The Department receives inquiries in this matter and in all cases refers the question to the governing body of the particular health facility and suggests that their determination should prevail and such a determination should be based upon consultation with the infection control committee and practitioners serving the facility.

MINNESOTA

Rules as Adopted June 8, 1983

7 MCAR S 1.042 Pet animals in health care facilities

A. Definition. As used in 7 MCAR S 1.042, "health care facility" means a hospital, nursing home, boarding care home, or supervised living facility licensed by the Minnesota Department of Health under Minnesota Statutes, sections 144.50 to 144.56 or Minnesota Statutes, section 144A.01 to 144A.17.

B. Written policy.

1. Every health care facility shall establish a written policy specifying whether or not pet animals will be allowed on the facility's premises.

2. If pet animals are allowed on the premises, the policy must specify whether or not individual patients or residents will be permitted to keep pets.

3. This policy must be developed only after consultation with facility staff and with patients or residents, as appropriate.

C. Conditions. If pet animals other than fish are allowed on the premises, the following requirements must be met:

1. Written policies and procedures must be developed and implemented which specify the conditions for allowing pet animals on the premises.

2. The policies and procedures must:

a. describe the types of pet animals allowed on the facility's premises. This policy must be developed in consultation with a veterinarian and a physician.

b. describe the procedures for maintaining and monitoring the health and behavior of animals kept on the facility's premises. These procedures must be in accordance with a veterinarian's recommendations. A copy of these recommendations must be maintained in the facility; and

c. identify those areas in the facility, in addition to those areas described in 6., where pet animals shall not be permitted.

3. Regardless of the ownership of any pet, the health care facility shall assume overall responsibility for any pets within or on the premises of the facility.

4. The health care facility shall ensure that no pet jeopardizes the health, safety, comfort, treatment, or well-being of the patients, residents, or staff.

5. A facility employee shall be designated, in writing, as being responsible for monitoring or providing the care to all pet animals and for ensuring the cleanliness and maintenance of facilities used to house pets. This rule does not preclude residents, patients, or other individuals from providing care to pet animals.

6. Except for guide dogs accompanying a blind or deaf individual and except in supervised living facilities with a licensed bed capacity of 15 beds or less, pet animals shall not be permitted in kitchen areas, in medication storage and administration areas or in clean or sterile supply storage areas. *(See also Chapter 17).*

MISSISSIPPI

At the present time Mississippi has only a regulation prohibiting the presence of live fowls or animals in the food service area of long-term care facilities and personal care homes. There are no regulations governing the presence of animals in hospital or other health facilities. The unofficial policy regarding animals in health care facilities is to evaluate each situation on an individual basis. If the presence of an animal or fowl represents a threat to the health and safety of the patients, then the facility is prohibited from allowing the animal or fowl in the facility.

MISSOURI

On page 69 of the intermediate care/skilled nursing facility regulations, paragraph 10, the Division of Aging requires that live animals shall be excluded from within the food storage, service and preparation areas and provides that pets may be in the dining area when food is not being prepared. The Division of Aging does not prohibit pets from being present in the nursing home. The Division of Aging does state, however, that all such animals should be restricted to specified areas of the facility so as not to contaminate food, medical supplies, etc. In addition, it is important that each pet be healthy and trained adequately not to harm or injure residents of the facility. The Division notes that it has been shown that many people respond extremely well to pets; and, if they should fill a void and provide any small or large measure of joy to the residents of a facility licensed by the Division of Aging, they believe that it is very much worthwhile.

MONTANA

At the present Montana has no specific regulations prohibiting or allowing animals in long-term care facilities or hospitals. The only reference is in food preparation and service areas.

NEBRASKA

The only regulation which addresses animals is the Food Service Code of Nebraska. This code is very specific in stating that live animals, including birds and turtles, shall be excluded from within the food service operational premises and from adjacent areas.

NEVADA

The State of Nevada does not have any laws, regulations or rules pertaining to the presence of animals in health care facilities.

NEW HAMPSHIRE

New Hampshire has no regulations for pets in licensed facilities except as written into the Sanitary Food Code (State of New Hampshire, Department of Health and Human Services, Division of Public Health Services.)

NEW JERSEY

Nursing home regulations now permit pets within the building under conditions approved by the Department of Health. (June 1983)

NEW MEXICO

Pets of any type are not permitted in hospitals, and not permitted in food areas, medical/nursing supply areas, or treatment areas in skilled nursing homes. All other types of facilities are required to comply with the food service regulations of the state. Guide dogs for the blind and police patrol dogs may be permitted in dining areas.

NEW YORK

414.7 Animals. (a) No birds, turtles, dogs, cats or other animals, exclusive of those required for laboratory purposes, shall be allowed in a medical facility, except in a residential health care facility pet therapy program as permitted in this section. Guide dogs may accompany sightless persons.

(b) A residential health care facility may board one dog or cat provided: (1) the health, safety, welfare and rights of all patients/residents are assured; (2) a staff member has been designated to be responsible for the care and management of the animal; (3) the animal is free from disease and has received all immunizations as recommended by a licensed veterinarian; (4) the animal shall not be allowed in laundry, utensil storage or food preparation areas; and (5) the animal will at all times be accompanied by a person familiar with and capable of controlling the animal's behavior.

NORTH CAROLINA

There are currently no regulations on the subject of pets in any level health care facility. Owners or administrators generally establish their own policy on this subject. Regulations are currently being considered that would specifically allow pets in nursing homes, both skilled and intermediate.

NORTH DAKOTA

The governing body of the nursing home is responsible for the institution; acting for the governing body, the administrator must make a judgment concerning the practicality of permitting pets on the premises. The following points should be considered in making this judgment:

1. The rights of residents who object strongly to animals in their presence, whether for physical or psychological reasons.

2. The appropriateness of an animal in the home, for sanitary and esthetic reasons.

At the discretion of the administrator, the nursing home may admit pets on the premises, either on a temporary, visiting basis, or as permanent pets. There are however, the following restrictions:

1. No pets are permitted in dietary areas at any time, including food preparation, food storage, and dining areas.

2. No pets of any kind are permitted in acute care facilities.

3. Pets are restricted to domestic animals, as opposed to those which have been trained to become pets, such as skunks or raccoons. This prohibition recognizes the overwhelming preponderance of laboratory-confirmed rabies in wild animals.

Any nursing home which permits pets on the premises is required to have a policy in writing outlining their practice and restrictions.

OHIO

To the best of the Department's knowledge there are no state laws or rules concerning the health care of pets so far as infections and diseases are concerned. The laws pertaining to these matters would be under local jurisdiction. Nursing and rest home law and rules allow for the use of animals as pets simply by omission.

The only contra-indication appears in the *Food Service Operation Law, Rules and Interpretive Guide,* Rule 3701-21-04-L, which restricts animals from food service areas. Environmental Surveyors further discourage allowing the pets into loading and waste collection areas.

OKLAHOMA

The Oklahoma State Department of Health licenses and/or regulates hospitals (both general and/or specialty); nursing homes, skilled and intermediate; and room and board homes.

None of the laws, rules or regulations applied to these facilities address this subject. It has been Department policy to regulate this matter on an individual case-by-case basis using as guidelines other laws, rules or regulations dealing with sanitation, infection control, etc.

To the best of the Department's knowledge and belief, there are no animals in any of the facilities regulated by the agency.

OREGON

The Health Division encourages the use of pet therapy, provided that appropriate precautions are implemented to reduce the risks to patients of exposure to disease. Household pets (dogs, cats, birds, fish, hamsters, etc.) may be allowed in health care facilities under the following conditions:

1. Pets must be clean and disease-free.
2. The immediate environment of pets must be kept clean.
3. Small pets (e.g., birds, hamsters) must be kept in appropriate enclosures.
4. Pets must be hand-held, under leash control, or under voice control (if so trained).
5. Pets should not be allowed in food preparation or storage areas. Pets should not be permitted in any area if their presence would create significant risks to patients, staff, or others.
6. The administrator or his/her designee will determine which pets may be brought into the facility. Family members may bring residents' pets to visit them provided they have approval from the administrator and offer reasonable assurance that the pets are clean, disease-free, and vaccinated as appropriate.
7. Pets that are kept at the facility (or are frequent visitors) should have current vaccinations as recommended by a designated licensed veterinarian (including, but not limited to, rabies).
8. Facilities with pets that are kept overnight should have written policies and procedures for the care, feeding and housing of such pets, and for the proper storage of pet food and supplies. Facilities with birds should have procedures which protect patients, staff and visitors from potential problems with psittacosis (parrot fever). Procedures should provide for minimum handling of droppings which should be carefully placed in a plastic bag for disposal. A person who does not have patient care or food-handling responsibilities should care for the bird (i.e., janitor, housekeeper).
9. Exotic pets (i.e., iguanas, snakes, other reptiles, monkeys, ferrets) should not be kept at the facility because there is a high potential for direct injury from bites, exposure to salmonella and shigella and, in the case of monkeys, tuberculosis. If exotic pets are brought in for a visit (i.e., Wildlife Safari, etc.) they should be attended at all times by their owners. The owners should offer reasonable assurance that the animals are clean, disease-free and vaccinated as appropriate. Skunks, foxes, and raccoons are prohibited by state statute.

PENNSYLVANIA

In Pennsylvania, there are no laws or regulations which specifically prohibit animals from being taken into health care facilities, although the practice has generally been that animals are not permitted. This practice is one which is enforced by the providers themselves. In recent years, more and more facilities are beginning to utilize pets in therapy programs. This is encouraged by the state. There is a revision to the long-term care regulations which has not as yet been proposed publicly but would specifically permit the presence of animals in skilled and intermediate care facilities and provide guidelines which must be followed in order to protect the rights and the health and safety of the nursing home patients.

When pet therapy is utilized, the following standards apply:

1. Animals shall not be permitted in the kitchen or other food service areas, dining room, nursing station, utility rooms, and rooms of patients that do not like animals.

2. There shall be a careful selection of types of animals so they are not harmful or annoying to patients.

3. The number and types of pets should be restricted according to the layout of the building, type of patients, staff, and animals.

4. Pets shall be carefully selected to meet the needs of the patients involved in the pet therapy program.

5. The facility shall have written procedures established which will address the physical and health needs of the animals. Rabies shots shall be given to all animals who are potential victims of the disease. Care of the pets should not be imposed on anyone who does not wish to be involved.

6. Pets and places where they reside shall be kept clean and sanitary.

RHODE ISLAND

The Rules and Regulations pertaining to food establishments in Rhode Island prohibit the presence of animals in areas where food is prepared, served, etc. Otherwise, there are not legal restrictions on the presence of animals in health facilities. As a matter of practice, perhaps reflected in institutional bylaws or manuals of procedure, there are restrictions varying from liberal rules in some facilities to total exclusion from others.

TENNESSEE

In the Tennessee health statutes and regulations concerning pets in health care facilities, only the statutes pertaining to nursing homes and homes for the aged specifically prohibit pets (Tennessee Official Compilation of Rules and Regulations 1200-8-6-. 02(c).)

TEXAS

Texas has no laws or regulations covering health care facilities directly on this subject. There are general requirements on sanitation and prohibiting activities undesirable to the health and safety of patients/residents. "Guidelines" exist designed to maintain good health, safety and sanitation standards, however.

UTAH

Pets shall not be kept in the nursing home unless specific arrangements for their care are made. At no time shall pets be allowed in areas where food is prepared,

stored, or served, or where sterile techniques are observed.
Current interpretation by the Department: Current Utah nursing home rules and regulations do allow for pets in nursing homes, they are not allowed in food service areas nor in sterile patient care areas. Each facility would have to make a determination based upon their individual policies in this area.

VERMONT

Nursing home regulations prohibit animals in kitchen areas as follows: "Animals and birds are prohibited in food storage and preparation areas, except in the living quarters of the owner or administrator, or by special permission of the licensing agency." One state official commented, "Many of our nursing homes have dogs and cats, even ducks. The patients' response is very positive."

VIRGINIA

State health facility licensure regulations do not address this question except as requiring conformance with restaurant law.

Any animals that a health care facility may desire to keep on the premises for the residents' enjoyment must have current proof of freedom from disease, and of proper vaccinations.

The facility must also adhere to the above-referenced restaurant interpretations.

WASHINGTON

RCW 18.51.320 Contact with animals — Rules. (1) A nursing home licensee shall give each patient a reasonable opportunity to have regular contact with animals. The licensee may permit appropriate animals to live in the facilities and may permit appropriate animals to visit if the animals are properly supervised. (2) The Department shall adopt rules for the care, type, and maintenance of animals in nursing home facilities.

WAC 248-14-570 Pets. (1) Each patient shall have a reasonable opportunity to have regular contact with animals as they desire.

(2) The nursing home administrator shall consider the recommendations and preferences of nursing home patients, resident councils, and staff, and shall: (a) Determine the method or methods of providing residents access to animals. (b) Determine the type and number of animals to be available. Such animals may include, but are not limited to dog, cat, fish, mouse, gerbil, hamster, guinea pig, chinchilla and bird, providing a veterinarian shall verify psittacine birds have met USDA quarantine procedures and are certified free of psittacosis or other diseases transmittable to humans. Wild or exotic animals such as turtles, primates, skunks, and raccoons are not allowed. (c) Ensure the rights, preferences, and medical needs of individual patients are not compromised by the presence of animals. Arrangements shall be made so patients with allergies, fears, or phobias do not come near or in contact with those animals. (d) Ensure any animals visiting or living on the premises have a suitable temperament, are healthy, and of such a size their presence poses no significant health or safety risks to patients, staff or visitors. (e) Ensure the available space and floor plan of the facility are adequate to accommodate the

presence of selected animals. (f) Establish and implement written policies and procedures for animals visiting the facility and for the care and maintenance of animals living in the facility. (g) Designate specific nonnursing staff to be responsible for the care and maintenance and use of animals living in the facility.

(3) Animals except for fish in aquariums, shall not be permitted in: (a) Any areas where food is stored or prepared. (b) Any areas during times food is being served and consumed in group settings, except seeing eye, hearing ear, and assistance dogs are permitted in dining areas as needed. (c) Any area where dishes or cooking/eating utensils are cleaned or stored. (d) Any area where linens are laundered or stored. (e) Any drug or sterile supply storage areas. (f) A patient's room when the patient's condition contraindicates the presence of the animal.

(4) Animals living on the premises: (a) Shall be housebroken or trained to use a litter box or housed in cages or tanks cleaned at regular intervals appropriate for the animal's characteristics. (b) Shall have regularly scheduled examinations and immunizations by a veterinarian, as appropriate for the species. A record of examination and immunizations shall be maintained on the premises. (c) Shall be kept clean and free of external parasites such as fleas and ticks. (d) Shall be properly fed and groomed. (e) Shall be protected from mistreatment.

(5) Animals brought to the nursing home to visit: (a) Shall be properly supervised. (b) Shall be clean and free of external parasites such as fleas and ticks. (c) Shall have current and appropriate immunizations.

WEST VIRGINIA

Regulation - West Virginia adopted new nursing home licensure regulations, effective June, 1983, that permit animals in nursing homes for therapeutic purposes under specific conditions and controlled circumstances.

WISCONSIN

The rules do not prohibit pets from entering or being retained by the nursing home, but do state that animals shall not be allowed where food is prepared, served or stored or where food utensils are washed or stored. It may be necessary to have pets removed to correct a sanitation or safety problem. The nursing homes may also adopt and enforce policies that may be more stringent than state regulations.

WYOMING

Animals, birds, reptiles and similar pets shall not be permitted to be kept in the facility. Aquariums are excluded from this requirement providing they are properly secured, protected to prevent spillage or breakage and maintained in an approved sanitary manner. There are some exceptions for dogs, cats or birds in nursing homes. They must be from approved sources and be properly vaccinated.

The Federal pets-in housing law

On November 30, 1983, President Ronald Reagan signed into law, P.L. 98-181, "Pet Ownership in Assisted Rental Housing for the Elderly or Handicapped." The act, based upon bills sponsored by Congressman Mario Biaggi and Senator William Proxmire, provides for the right of pet ownership in federally subsidized housing. The law took effect November 30, 1983, and the Department of Housing and Urban Development (HUD) and the U.S. Department of Agriculture (USDA) had until November 30, 1984, to publish regulations under which the owner or manager of a covered project may write reasonable rules for the keeping of pets by tenants.

The law, written as Sec. 227(a) of the Supplementary Appropriations Bill H.R. 3959, (Housing and Urban-Rural Recovery Act of 1983) reads:

An Act: P.L. 98-181

Pet Ownership In Assisted Rental Housing For The Elderly or Handicapped

Sec. 227. (a) No owner or manager of any federally assisted rental housing for the elderly or handicapped may—

(1) as a condition of tenancy or otherwise, prohibit or prevent any tenant in such housing from owning common household pets or having common household pets living in the dwelling accommodations of such tenant in such housing; or

(2) restrict or discriminate against any person in connection with admission to, or continued occupancy of, such housing by reason of the ownership of such pets by, or the presence of such pets in the dwelling accommodations of, such person.

(b)(1) Not later than the expiration of the twelve-month period following the date of the enactment of this Act, the Secretary of Housing and Urban Development and the Secretary of Agriculture shall each issue such regulations as may be necessary to ensure (A) compliance with the provisions of subsection (a) with respect to any program of assistance referred to in subsection (d) that is administered by such Secretary; and (B) attaining the goal of providing decent, safe, and sanitary housing for the elderly or handicapped.

(2) Such regulations shall establish guidelines under which the owner or manager of any federally assisted rental housing for the elderly or

handicapped (A) may prescribe reasonable rules for the keeping of pets by tenants in such housing; and (B) shall consult with the tenants of such housing in prescribing such rules. Such rules may consider factors such as density of tenants, pet size, types of pets, potential financial obligations of tenants, and standards of pet care.

(c) Nothing in this section may be construed to prohibit any owner or manager of federally assisted rental housing for the elderly or handicapped, or any local housing authority or other appropriate authority of the community where such housing is located, from requiring the removal from any such housing of any pet whose conduct or condition is duly determined to constitute a nuisance or a threat to the health or safety of the other occupants of such housing or of other persons in the community where such housing is located.

(d) For purposes of this section, the term "federally assisted rental housing for the elderly or handicapped" means any rental housing project that—

(1) is assisted under section 202 of the Housing Act of 1959; or

(2) is assisted under the United States Housing Act of 1937, the National Housing Act, or title V of the Housing Act of 1949, and is designated for occupancy by elderly or handicapped families, as such term is defined in section 202(d)(4) of the Housing Act of 1959.

According to HUD (Official HUD Notice H-84-10, Feb. 28, 1984), the law applies to rental housing projects built exclusively for occupancy by the elderly and handicapped and assisted and/or insured under the following programs:

1. Low-income public and Indian housing
2. Section 8 New Construction, Substantial Rehabilitation, and Loan Management
3. Section 202
4. Section 221(d) (3)
5. Section 236
6. Section 221(d) (4)
7. Section 231.

The statute refers to projects "assisted" under the National Housing Act. While this terminology normally refers to subsidy and does not encompass projects which are insured without subsidy, HUD believes that Congress intended a broader coverage in the case of this particular enactment. Accordingly, elderly projects indicated in programs 6 and 7 (above) are included notwithstanding that they may be unsubsidized.

According to the Humane Society of the United States, USDA tenants covered by the law are "those residing in rural rental housing (RRH) or rural cooperative housing (RCH) housing projects designated for occupancy by senior citizens or handicapped persons. For purposes of this law, provisions applying to senior citizens apply also to handicapped persons. Tenants may inquire of their housing owner or manager as to whether their project is designated as described above and if so, the law will apply to them."

As this book was going to press, it was unclear whether HUD would interpret its definition of projects covered as those *"designated"* (in the law) or *"built exclusively"* (in the Notice) for occupancy by the elderly or handicapped. Certain projects built for other purposes and converted to elderly or handicapped usage, and projects containing a mix of elderly/handicapped and non-elderly/non-handicapped tenants would not be covered under the "exclusive" interpretation. Pending passage of the regulations, HUD authorized managers who found it necessary to adopt reasonable rules limiting pets on an interim basis. - *Ed.*

Legal rights of dog guides for the deaf

With the growing awareness, availability, and popularity of dog guides for the hearing-impaired, many states and the federal government have enacted laws granting legal rights and tax deductions for these animals and their owners similar to statutes enacted previously for guide dogs for the blind. The first such laws were enacted in Colorado in 1968; subsequently, the Internal Revenue Service implemented guidelines for maintenance tax deductions.

Today, in many places, dogs assisting the hearing-impaired are welcome in public accommodations, on public conveyances, and in public places, following living proof that these valuable animals, which enable their owners to lead more full and productive lives, do not complicate the functioning of these facilities. However, many deaf persons are still confronted with misinformation and a lack of awareness regarding the dog; consequently, many states have reinforced, through the legislative process, the rights of the hearing-impaired to be accompanied by guide dogs.

The following state-by-state summary of legal rights of dog guides for the deaf was compiled by the American Humane Association, based in Denver, Colorado. American Humane is national coordinator of the Hearing Dog program. *(See Chapter 9)*. Project Coordinator Cindi Osieczanek notes the list includes specialized legal rights guaranteed by statute. Many of the broad human rights statutes created to protect minorities against discrimination may also be applicable to the rights of dog guide users. Legal interpretation or legal action should involve an attorney. Unabridged copies of relevant statutes are available from individual state legislative libraries. - *Ed.*

ALABAMA

Act 869, Alabama Statutes of 1975, Sections 21-7-1 through 21-7-10, Chapter 7

Alabama statutory law guarantees a deaf person the legal right to be accompanied by a specially trained dog guide in all public accommodations and conveyances. No additional charge can be levied because of the presence of the dog, but the dog guide user is liable for any property damage attributable to the dog.

Public accommodations, for the purpose of this statute, include such places as hotels, restaurants, stores, public buildings, places of amusement and recreation and any other facilities to which the public is invited. (21-7-2, 21-7-3)

Conveyances include airplanes, motor vehicles, railroad trains, motor buses, streetcars, boats or any other transportation services offered for public use.(21-7-3)

Commercial housing, except for rented rooms in a private dwelling, cannot be denied to a dog guide user either because of his or her deafness or because he or she has a dog guide. The landlord, however, is not responsible for modifying the premises in any way. (21-7-9)

Violation: Any person, firm, or corporation or agent thereof who violates the above enumerated rights is guilty of a misdemeanor and subject to appropriate penalty. (21-7-5)

ALASKA

The state of Alaska has no legal provisions for a hearing impaired person to be accompanied by a dog guide.

ARIZONA

Arizona Revised Statutes, Title 24, Section 411

Arizona statutory law guarantees a deaf person the legal right to be accompanied by a dog guide in any place to which the public is invited. The same right exists in regard to common carriers. No extra charge can be levied because of the dog's presence, but the dog guide user is liable for any damages caused by the dog to the premises. The deaf person accompanied by a specially trained dog guide may first be required to identify the dog guide by exhibiting the dog's laminated identification card.

Public places include restaurants, cafes, hotels, motels, stores, places of amusement and all other facilities open to the public. (24-411A) A zoo may prohibit dog guides, but shall provide without cost, adequate facilities for the temporary confinement of dog guides. (24-411D)

Common carriers include trains, buses, taxis, airplanes, etc. (24-411A)

Violation: Any person, firm, association, corporation or agent thereof who interferes with the above enumerated rights is guilty of a petty offense. (24-411E)

ARKANSAS

Arkansas Statutes Annotated, Section 82-2901 through 82-2907 (Supp. 1983)

Arkansas statutory law guarantees a deaf person the legal right to equal opportunity in the areas of housing, employment, and the use of public accommodations and public carriers. It further guarantees the right of a deaf person to be accompanied by a specially trained dog guide in the enjoyment of these rights and privileges. The dog guide user cannot be charged an extra fee because of the dog's presence, but the dog guide user is liable for any damage the dog might cause to the premises.

The right to "equal accommodation" extends to all commercial housing, except for private single family dwellings, a portion of which is made available for rent. The landlord is not required to modify the accommodations or to assume a higher standard of care. (82-2903, 82-2904, 82-2905)

Public accommodations for the purpose of this Chapter, include hotels, places of resort and recreation, public buildings, restaurants, and all other places to which the public is invited. (82-2901, 82-2902, 89-2903, 82-2904)

Common carriers and conveyances include all modes of transportation open to public use, whether by air, land or water. (82-2901, 82-2903, 82-2904)

Violation: Any person, firm, corporation or agent thereof who violates the above rights is guilty of a misdemeanor. (82-2906)

CALIFORNIA

California Annotated Civil Code (West 1982), Sections 54 through 55.1, California Revenue and Taxation Code, Section 17253; 17253.5 repealed by Chapter 488, 1983 California Statutes

California law guarantees a deaf person the legal right to be accompanied by a specially trained dog guide in all public accommodations and on all public transportation. Also guaranteed is the right of a dog guide user to equal availability to commercial housing, but the landlord is not required to modify the premises or to maintain a higher standard of care than they provide other tenants. No extra charge can be levied by a public accommodation, common carrier or landlord because of the dog guide's presence, and the dog guide user is liable for any property damage caused by the dog. For purposes of California state income tax, all costs for the maintenance of the dog guide are deductible as medical expenses.

Public accommodations include hotels, motels, restaurants, stores, places of resort and recreation, and all other places to which the public is invited. Zoos are the only exception, but if a zoo excludes dog guides, the facility must provide an adequate kennel area for housing the dog guides. (Chapter 293, Section 54. la; Chapter 525, Section 1-54.7)

Common carriers or public transportation include airplanes, motor vehicles, railroad trains, motorbuses, streetcars, boats and all other forms of transportation offered for public use. (Chapter 293. Section 54. la)

Commercial housing includes all property offered for rent or use, except private single family dwellings of no more than one room for rent. (Chapter 293, Section 54.1)

Violation: Any person, firm or corporation who interferes with the above enumerated rights is liable for the actual damages as may be determined by a jury, up to a maximum of three times the amount of actual damages but in no case less than $250.

COLORADO

Colorado Revised Statutes, 18-13-107, 24-34-801 and 24-34-802

Colorado law guarantees a deaf person the legal right to be accompanied by a specially trained dog in all public accommodations and on all common carriers. No extra charge can be levied because of the dog's presence, but the dog guide user is liable for any damage the dog might cause to the premises.

No person shall interfere with a dog guide on a leash which is blaze orange in color. (18-13-107)

Public accommodations include hotels, motels, lodging places, restaurants, grocery stores, places of resort and amusement, and any other place to which the public is invited. (24-34-801d)

Common carriers include airplanes, motor vehicles, railroad trains, motor buses, streetcars, boats and any other conveyances offered for public use. (24-34-80ld)

Violation: Any person, firm, corporation or agent thereof who interferes with the above enumerated rights is guilty of a misdemeanor and punishable by a fine not to exceed $100, or confinement in jail for not more than sixty days, or both. (24-34-802)

CONNECTICUT

Connecticut General Statutes, Section 22-345, 22-346 and Section 46a-64

Connecticut statutes guarantee a deaf person the legal right to be accompanied by a specially trained dog guide in all public accommodations and on all forms of public transportation. The dog must be in harness and in the direct custody of the individual. Also, a dog guide user has a legal right of access to all commercial housing and public and commercial buildings, and cannot be discriminated against because of his or her dog in renting or purchasing housing or commercial space, including mobile home parks. No extra charge can be levied because of the dog's presence. A landlord, however, is not responsible to modify the premises or maintain a higher standard of care than provided other tenants, and the dog guide user is responsible for any damage to property that the dog may cause.

No fee can be charged for licensing a dog guide, but the first time a dog guide is registered, the town clerk should be shown written evidence, such as an identification card, that the dog has been specially trained. (Section 22-345)

Public accommodations include hotels, inns, restaurants, stores, places of amusement, public buildings, and any other facility offered to the public. (Section 22-346a)

Public transportation includes trains, buses, and all other modes of transit offered for public use, (Section 22-346a)

Commercial housing or property includes publicly assisted housing and commercial property, except two family houses in which the owner or his family reside or a private dwelling in which the owner lives but also rents rooms. The statute covers mobile home parks, and deals with both sales and rentals. (Section 22-346b, Section 46a-64)

Violation: Violation of the above rights is punishable as a Class C misdemeanor. (Section 22-346c)

DELAWARE

The state of Delaware has no legal provisions for a hearing impaired person to be accompanied by a dog guide.

DISTRICT OF COLUMBIA

District of Columbia, Section 6-1702 through 6-1707

District of Columbia law guarantees a deaf person the legal right to be accompanied by a specially trained dog guide in its public buildings and its public facilities, and in all public accommodations and on all public conveyances. The right to equal accommodation in all public and commercial housing is also guaranteed to a dog guide user. No additional charge can be levied because of the dog guide's presence, but the dog guide user is liable for any damage the dog may cause to the premises. Landlords are not required to modify the premises nor are they responsible for maintaining a higher degree of care than that provided other tenants. (Section 6-1702-B)

Public accommodations include hotels, restaurants, stores, places of resort and amusement, and all other places to which the general public is invited . (Section 1702A) Equal access for people with dog guides to public buildings and housing shall not be denied. (Section 6-1706B)

Public conveyances include boats, trains, buses, streetcars, taxis, airplanes, and all other modes of transportation offered for public use. (Section 6-1702A)

Housing includes all accommodations offered for rent, lease or compensation within the jurisdiction of the district. (Section 6-1706)

Violation: Any person or agent thereof who denies or interferes with the above legally established rights is punishable with imprisonment up to 90 days, or a fine not to exceed $300 or both. (Section 6-1707)

FLORIDA

Florida Statutes 1982 Supplement, Section 413. 08, Subsections 1, 2, and 4.

Florida statutory law guarantees a deaf person the legal right to be accompanied by a specially trained dog guide in all public accommodations and on all public conveyances. Florida statutory law also guarantees a dog guide user the legal right to equal accommodation in all commercial housing. No extra charge can be levied because of the dog's presence, but the dog guide user is liable for any property damage the dog might cause. Landlords are not required to modify the premises nor are they responsible for maintaining a higher standard of care than that provided to other tenants.

Public accommodations include hotels, lodging places restaurants, stores, places of resort and amusement, and any other place to which the general public is invited. (Section 413.08, Subsection 1a)

Public conveyances include all common carriers, airplanes, boats, trains, buses, taxis, and any other mode of transportation offered for public use. (Section 413.08. Subsection 1a)

Commercial housing covers any real property or portion thereof that is offered for rent, lease, or compensation as a residence or sleeping place, but does not include private single family dwellings in which the occupants have offered no more than one room for rent. (Section 413.08. Subsection 4a, b,c)

Violation: Any person, firm, corporation or agent thereof who denies or interferes with the above enumerated rights is guilty under Florida law of a second class misdemeanor and punishable in accordance therewith. (Section 413.08, Subsection 2)

GEORGIA

Official Code of Georgia Annotated. Title 30, Chapter 4, Code Sections 30-4-1 through 30-4-3

Georgia statutory law guarantees a deaf person the legal right to be accompanied by a specially trained dog guide in all public accommodations and on all common carriers. Also guaranteed by Georgia law is the legal right of a dog guide user to equal accommodation in all commercial housing. No extra charge can be levied because of the dog guide's presence, but the dog guide user is liable for any damage to the premises that the dog might cause. Landlords are not required to modify the premises, nor are they responsible to maintain a higher degree of care than that provided for other tenants.

Dog guide users employed in vending stands have a legal right to have their dog with them, with the limitation that the dog cannot be within twenty-five feet of the food being vended. (30-4-1 [c])

Public accommodations include hotels, restaurants, stores, places of resort or amusement and any other place to which the general public is invited. (30-4-1 [a])

Commercial housing includes all real property or a portion thereof offered for rent, lease or compensation as a residence or a sleeping place, but does not include a private single family dwelling in which no more than one room is offered for rent. (30-4-2 [a])

Violation: Any person, firm, corporation or agent thereof who denies or interferes with the above enumerated rights is guilty of a misdemeanor and punishable by a fine not to exceed $100 or by imprisonment for no more than ten days, or both. (30-4-3)

HAWAII

The state of Hawaii has no legal provisions for a hearing impaired person to be accompanied by a dog guide.

IDAHO

The state of Idaho has no legal provisions for a hearing impaired person to be accompanied by a dog guide.

ILLINOIS

Illinois Revised Statutes, Chapter 23 Paragraphs 3361 through 3366; Illinois Revised Statutes, Chapter 38, Paragraph 65-1 and 65-26

Illinois statutes guarantee a deaf person the legal right to be accompanied by a specially trained dog guide in harness in all public accommodations and on all common carriers. A dog guide user also has the legal right to equal housing accommodations in regard to both rentals and sales. No extra charge can be levied because of the dog's presence, but the dog guide user is liable for any damages the dog might cause to the premises. A deaf person may be asked to present credentials for inspection issued by a school for training dog guides approved by the U.S. Veterans Administration. (Chapter 38, Paragraph 65-1)

Public accommodations include public facilities, hotels, restaurants, stores, places of amusement and resort and all other places to which the public is invited. (Paragraph 3363)

Common carriers include trains, airplanes, boats, buses, taxis, and all other modes of transportation offered for public use.(Paragraph 3363)

Housing includes all rental property and other real property offered for sale, but there is no requirement that property be modified nor is the owner responsible to provide a higher degree of care than that furnished other persons. (Chapter 38,

Paragraph 65-26)

Violation: Any person, firm, corporation or agent thereof who interferes with the above legal rights is guilty of a Class A misdemeanor and is punishable under the appropriate civil or criminal statute. (Paragraph 3364)

INDIANA

Indiana Code: 16-7-5-1 through 16-7-5-3

Indiana law guarantees a deaf person the legal right to be accompanied by a specially trained dog guide in all public accommodations and on all public conveyances. No extra charge can be levied because of the dog's presence, but the dog guide user is liable for any damage the dog may do to the premises.

Public accommodations include hotels, restaurants, stores, places of amusement and resort and all other places to which the general public is invited. (16-7-5-2)

Public conveyances include airplanes, buses, trains, boats, taxis, and all other modes of transportation offered for public use. (16-7-5-2)

Violation: Any person, firm, corporation or agent thereof who denies or interferes with the above enumerated rights can be fined up to $100, or imprisonment up to three months or both. (16-7-5-3)

IOWA

1983 Iowa Acts, Chapter 46, Sections 1 and 2; Iowa Code Supplement 1983, Sections 6011.7 and 6011.8; also Iowa Code 1983, Sections 601D.3 through 601D.5

Iowa statutory law guarantees a deaf person the legal right to be accompanied by a dog, under control and specially trained at a recognized training facility, in all public accommodations and on all public conveyances. No extra charge can be levied because of the dog's presence, but the dog guide user is liable for any damage caused to the premises by the dog.

Public accommodations include public facilities, hotels, restaurants, stores, places of amusement and resort, and all other places to which the public is invited. (601D.3 and 601D.4)

Public conveyances include airplanes, trains, boats, taxis, elevators, and all other modes of transportation offered for public use. (601D.3 and 601D.4)

Violation: Any person, firm, corporation or agent thereof who interferes with the above enumerated rights is guilty of a simple misdemeanor. (6011.8)

KANSAS

Kansas Statutes Annotated, 39-1101 through 39-1107

Kansas statutory law guarantees a deaf person the legal right to be accompanied by a specially trained dog guide in all public accommodations and on all common carriers. No extra charge can be levied because of the dog guide's presence, but the dog guide user is liable for any damage to the premises that the dog might cause.

Public accommodations include public buildings, hotels, lodging places, restaurants, stores, places of resort and amusement and all other places to which the general public is invited. (39-1101)

Common carriers include boats, airplanes, buses, trains, taxis and all other modes of transportation offered for public use. (39-1101)

Violation: Any person, firm, or corporation or agent thereof who interferes with the above enumerated rights is guilty of a misdemeanor and punishable accordingly under Kansas law. (39-1103)

KENTUCKY

Kentucky Revised Statutes, Chapter 258, Section 500, Subsections 1 through 9, Penalty 258.991

Kentucky statutory law guarantees a deaf person the legal right to be accompanied by a dog guide, trained by a recognized dog guide school, in all public accommodations and on all public transportation. The dog must be in harness and in the custody of the dog guide user. The dog guide user also must have verification of the dog's training such as an identification card issued by the training school. The dog may not occupy a seat on a public conveyance, and the common carrier cannot levy an additional charge because of the dog guide's presence.

Public accommodations include public buildings, restaurants, theaters, places of amusement, stores, hotels, and all places to which the public is invited. (Subsection 1)

Public transportation includes trains, buses, airplanes, taxis, public elevators, and all other common carriers. (Subsection 2)

Violation: Any person who violates the above enumerated rights is punishable by a fine of not less than $25, nor more than $100, or by imprisonment for not less than 10 days, nor more than 30 days, or both. (258.991)

LOUISIANA

Louisiana Revised Statutes, Title 46, Chapter 23, Section 1951 through 1954

Louisiana statutes guarantee a deaf person the legal right to be accompanied by a specially trained dog guide in all places of public accommodation and on all public conveyances.

No extra charge can be levied because of the presence of the dog guide, but the dog guide user is liable for any damages the dog might cause to the premises.

Public accommodations include hotels, lodging places, restaurants, stores, places of resort and amusement and all other places to which the public is invited. (Section 1952-B)

Public conveyances include trains, buses, airplanes, taxis, street cars, boats and all other common carriers. (Section 1952-B)

Commercial housing includes any real property or portion thereof which has been offered for rent, lease or compensation as a home, residence or sleeping place, but shall not include single family residences which offer not more than one room for rent, lease or furnish for compensation. (Section 1953-A through D)

Violation: Any person, firm or corporation who interferes with the above rights is guilty of a misdemeanor and punishable by a fine of not less than $100 or more than $500. In addition, the deaf individual who has been discriminated against may sue for $500 damages for each offense in any court of competent jurisdiction. (Section 1952-D)

MAINE

Maine Revised Statutes Annotated, Title 22, Section 3611 through 3614

Maine statutory law guarantees a deaf person the legal right to be accompanied by a specially trained dog identified by a bright orange collar and leash in all public accommodations and on all modes of public transportation. The dog guide user shall also carry an identification card issued by the Bureau of Rehabilitation. No extra charge can be levied because of the presence of the dog guide, but the dog guide user is liable for any damage the dog might cause to the premises.

Public accommodations include hotels, lodging places, restaurants, stores, places of resort and amusement, and all other places to which the public is invited. (Section 3612)

Public conveyances include airplanes, trains, buses, street cars, boats, taxis, and all other modes of transportation offered for public use. (Section 3612)

Violation: Any person or his agent who interferes with the above enumerated rights is guilty of a Class E crime. (Section 3614)

Any person who fits a dog with a bright orange collar and leash in order to represent that the dog is a hearing ear dog is guilty of a civil violation and punishable by a fine not to exceed $100. (Section 3614)

MARYLAND

Maryland Statutes, 1982 Cumulative Supplement, Article 30, Section 33; Article 56, Section 192

Maryland statutory law guarantees a deaf person the legal right to be accompanied by a specially trained dog guide in all public accommodations and on all forms of public transportation. The dog guide is identified by an orange license tag or an orange collar and leash. Maryland law also guarantees equal housing accommodations to a dog guide user in commercial housing. No extra charge can be levied because of the dog's presence, but the dog guide user is liable for any damage the dog might cause to the premises. A landlord is not required to modify property or to maintain a higher degree of care than that provided to other persons.

Maryland exempts dog guides from a licensing fee. (Article 56, Section 192)

Public accommodations include hotels, restaurants, public buildings, stores, places of resort and amusement, and all other places to which the general public is invited. (Article 30, Section 33)

Commercial housing includes all property offered for rent, lease or compensation which is designed to be a home or sleeping place, but does not include a single family dwelling whose occupants offer no more than one room for rent. (Article 30, Section 33)

Violation: Any person, firm, corporation or agent thereof who interferes with the above enumerated rights is guilty of a misdemeanor and punishable by a fine not to exceed $500. (Article 30, Section 33)

MASSACHUSETTS

Massachusetts General Law, Chapter 272-98A

Massachusetts law guarantees a deaf person the legal right to be accompanied by a dog guide in all public accommodations and on all public conveyances. No extra charge can be levied because of the dog's presence. Muzzling can be required. Also, the dog guide user can be required to produce identification such as the identification card furnished by the dog guide school from which the dog was obtained.

Public accommodations include hotels, restaurants, stores, places of amusement, and all places to which the public is invited. (Chapter 272-98A)

Public conveyances include trains, airplanes, buses, taxis, and all common carriers. (Chapter 272-98A)

Violation: A person who interferes with the above enumerated rights is punishable by a fine not to exceed $300. (Chapter 272-98A)

MICHIGAN

Michigan Compiled Laws of 1970, Section 287.291 and 750.502c

Michigan statutory law guarantees a deaf person the legal right to be accompanied by a dog guide wearing a blaze orange collar and leash in all public accommodations and educational institutions and on all public conveyances.

Michigan law exempts dog guides from a licensing fee. (287.291)

Public accommodations include stores, theaters, movies, hotels, restaurants, barber shops, places of recreation, and other places to which the public is invited. (750.502c)

Public conveyances include trains, buses, taxis, elevators, boats and other common carriers. (750.502c)

Violation: Any person who interferes with above enumerated rights is guilty of a misdemeanor. (750.502c)

MINNESOTA

Minnesota Statutes, Chapter 256C, 1971, Sections 01 through 06

Minnesota statutes guarantee a deaf person the legal right to be accompanied by a dog guide in all public accommodations and on all public conveyances. A dog guide user is also guaranteed the right to equal accommodations in commercial housing. No extra charge can be levied because of the dog guide's presence, but the dog guide user is liable for any damage the dog guide causes to the premises. A landlord is not required to modify the property nor to maintain a higher standard of care than that provided other persons.

Public accommodations include hotels, public buildings, restaurants, places of resort and amusement, stores, and all other places to which the public is invited. (256C.02)

Commercial housing includes any real property offered for rent, lease or compensation. (256C.025)

Violation: Any person or agent thereof who interferes with the above enumerated rights is guilty of a misdemeanor. (256C.05)

MISSISSIPPI

Mississippi Code Annotated (1972) Sections 43-6-1 through 43-6-13

Mississippi statutory law guarantees a deaf person the legal right to be accompanied by a specially trained dog guide on a blaze orange leash in all public accommodations and on all public transportation. No extra charge can be levied because of the dog guide's presence, but the dog guide user is liable for any damage the dog might cause to the premises.

Public accommodations include hotels, inns, restaurants, stores, places of resort and amusement, and all places to which the general public is invited. (Section 43-6-5)

Public transportation includes boats, airplanes, taxis, trains, buses, and all other common carriers. (Section 43-6-5)

Violation: Any person, firm, or corporation or agent thereof who interferes with the above enumerated rights is guilty of a misdemeanor and punishable by a fine not to exceed $100, or imprisonment for not more than sixty days, or both. (Section 43-6-11)

MISSOURI

Missouri Statutes, Sections 209.150 and 209.190

Missouri statutory law guarantees a deaf person the legal right to be accompanied by a specially trained dog guide in all public accommodations and on all public transportation. A dog guide user also has a legal right to equal accommodation in all commercial housing. No extra charge can be levied because of the dog's presence, but the dog guide user is liable for any damage the dog might cause to the premises. A landlord is not required to modify the property nor to provide a higher degree of care than that provided other tenants.

Public accommodations include hotels, stores, restaurants, places of resort and amusement and all other places to which the general public is invited. (209.150. Subsections 1 and 2)

Public transportation includes airplanes, buses, boats, trains, taxis, and all other modes of conveyance offered for public use. (209.150. Subsection 2)

Commercial housing includes real property or a portion thereof offered for rent, lease or compensation as a home, residence or sleeping place, but does not include a single family dwelling whose occupants offer not more than one room for rent. (209.190, Subsections 1-4)

MONTANA

Montana Code Annotated, Sections 49-4-202 through 49-4-217

Montana statutes guarantee a deaf person the legal right to be accompanied by a specially trained dog guide in all public accommodations and on all public transportation. A dog guide user also has a legal right to equal housing accommodation in all commercial housing. No extra charge can be levied because of the dog's presence, but the dog guide user is liable for any damage a dog might cause to the premises. A landlord is not required to modify the property nor to provide a higher degree of care than that provided other persons.

Public accommodations include hotels, public buildings, stores, restaurants, places of resort and amusement, and all other places to which the general public is invited. (49-4-211, 49-4-214)

Public transportation includes trains, airplanes, buses, boats, taxis, and all modes of transportation offered for public use. (49-4-211, 49-4-214)

Commercial housing includes any real property or portion thereof which has been offered for rent, lease or compensation as a home, residence or sleeping place, but does not include single family dwellings, the occupants of which have offered not more than one room for rent. (49-4-212, 49-4-214)

Violation: Any person, firm, or corporation or agent thereof who interferes with the above enumerated rights is guilty of a misdemeanor. (49-4-215)

NEBRASKA

Nebraska Revised Statutes (1981 Cumulative Supplement), Chapter 29, Sections 20-126 through 20-129, and 20.131.01 and 20.131.04

Nebraska law guarantees a deaf person the legal right to be accompanied by a specially trained dog guide in all public accommodations and on all public transportation. A dog guide user also has a legal right to equal housing accommodation in all commercial housing. No extra fee can be charged because of the dog's presence, but the dog guide user is liable for any damage the dog might cause to the premises. A landlord can require a security deposit against damage, but the deposit cannot exceed one-fourth of one month's rent.

Public accommodations include hotels, public buildings, stores, restaurants, places of resort and amusement, and all places to which the public is invited. (20-127)

Public transportation includes trains, airplanes, boats, buses, taxis, and all other modes of conveyance offered for the public use. (20-127)

Commercial housing includes all property designed as a home or sleeping place, and offered for rent, lease or compensation, but does not include single family dwellings. (20.131.01-and 20.131.04)

Violation: Any person, firm, or corporation or agent thereof who interferes with the above enumerated rights is guilty of a Class III misdemeanor, punishable by a maximum of three months imprisonment or a fine of five hundred dollars or both.

NEVADA

Nevada Revised Statutes, 118.105; 426.081; 426.091; 426.510; 426.515; 426.790; 651.070; 651.075; 651.080; 704.143; 704.145; 706.361; 706.366

Nevada statutes guarantee a deaf person the legal right to be accompanied by a specially trained dog guide from a training school that has been approved by the Division of Rehabilitation in all public accommodations and on all public transportation. A hearing dog will be identified by a blaze orange leash. No extra charge can be levied because of the dog's presence, but the dog guide user is liable for any damage the dog might cause to the premises. A dog guide user has a legal right to equal housing accommodation and can enforce this right through injunctive relief with damages.

Public accommodations include hotels, restaurants, stores, places of resort and amusement, and all places to which the general public is invited. (651.070; 651.075)

Public transportation includes trains, buses, airplanes, taxis, and all other forms of public conveyance offered for public use. (651.070; 704.143; 704.145; 706.361; 706.366)

Commercial housing covers rental properties. The statute contains a provision that the law is to be interpreted liberally. (118.105)

Violation: Any person who interferes with the legal rights of a deaf person as outlined under Nevada law is guilty of a misdemeanor.(651.080)

NEW HAMPSHIRE

New Hampshire Revised Statutes Annotated, Chapter 167-D, Sections 1 through 9

New Hampshire statutes guarantee a deaf person the legal right to be accompanied by a specially trained dog guide from a generally recognized agency involved in the rehabilitation of the deaf in all public accommodations and on all public transportation. A hearing dog will be identified by a bright yellow leash and harness. No extra charge can be levied because of the dog's presence, but the dog guide user is liable for any damage a dog might cause to the premises.

Public accommodations include hotels, public buildings, trailer camps, stores, restaurants, places of resort and amusement, and all other places to which the public is invited. (167D:1)

Public transportation includes trains, airplanes, buses, taxis, and other modes of conveyance offered for public use. (167D:1)

Violation: Any person who interferes with the above enumerated rights is guilty of a misdemeanor. (167D:9)

NEW JERSEY

New Jersey Statutes, 4:19-15.3 and 10:5-29 through 10:5-29.6

New Jersey anti-discrimination laws guarantee a deaf person the right to be accompanied by a dog guide in all public facilities, in employment, and on all public conveyances. No extra charge can be levied because of the dog's presence, but the dog guide user is liable for any damage the dog might cause to the premises. A deaf person with a dog guide has a legal right to equal housing opportunity in the rental or leasing of housing and cannot be charged extra because of the dog guide's presence. A landlord is not required to modify the premises, nor to provide a higher standard of care than that offered other tenants.

Public facilities include stores, boardwalks, places of recreation, education institutions, camps, restaurants, hotels and all other places of public accommodation where the public is invited. (10:5-29)

Public conveyances include airplanes, trains, buses, boats, taxis, and all modes of transportation offered for public use. (10:5-29)

Housing accommodations include any property designed for residential use, whether for rent, lease or sale, except for single family private dwellings, whose occupants offer no more than one room for rent. (10:5-29.2)

Violation: Any person who violates the above enumerated rights is subject to a fine no less than $100, and no more than $500 for each offense.

NEW MEXICO

New Mexico Statutes, Article 11, Section 28-11-1

New Mexico statutory law guarantees a deaf person the legal right to be accompanied by a specially trained dog guide in all public accommodations and on all public transportation. No extra charge can be levied because of the dog guide's presence, but the dog guide user is liable for any damage the dog might cause to the premises.

Public accommodations include hotels, restaurants, stores, public buildings, places of resort and amusement, and all places to which the general public is invited. (Section 28-11-1)

Public transportation includes trains, airplanes, buses, boats, taxis, and all forms of conveyance offered for public use. (Section 28-11-1)

Violation: Any person, firm, or corporation or agent thereof who interferes with the above enumerated rights is guilty of a misdemeanor and subject to a fine of not more than $25. (Section 28-11-1)

NEW YORK

New York Statutes: Civil Rights Law, Article 4-B, Section 47a through c, 1979. Human Rights Law, Article 15, Section 290-296

New York law guarantees a deaf person the legal right to be accompanied by a dog guide in all public accommodations and on all public transportation. No extra charge can be levied because of the dog guide's presence, but the dog must be properly harnessed. Muzzling can be requested by a common carrier. A deaf person who possesses a dog guide is entitled to equal housing accommodations and cannot be charged a fee because of the dog guide.

Public accommodations include resorts, theaters, restaurants, stores, hotels, places of recreation and all other places to which the public is invited. (Section 47)

Public transportation includes taxis, subways, trains, buses, boats, airplanes, and all other modes of conveyance offered for public use. (Section 47)

Violation: Any owner, manager or employee who interferes with the above enumerated rights is subject to prosecution under several New York State statutes. (Section 47-c)

NORTH CAROLINA

North Carolina General Statutes, Chapter 168, Sections 168-1 through 168-9

North Carolina statutes guarantee a deaf person the right to be accompanied by a specially trained dog guide in all public accommodations and on all public transportation. No extra charge can be levied because of the dog's presence, but the dog guide user is liable for any damage the dog might cause to the premises. A dog guide user has the legal right to equal housing accommodation. The dog guide owner must have an identification card issued by the North Carolina Council for the Hearing Impaired.

Public accommodations include hotels, restaurants, stores, places of resort and amusement and all other places to which the public is invited. (Sections 168-3, 168-4.1)

Public transportation includes airplanes, trains, buses, taxis and all other forms of conveyance offered for public use. (Sections 168-3, 168-4.1)

Housing includes leased or rented properties and specifically covers residential communities, homes and group homes. (Section 168-9)

NORTH DAKOTA

North Dakota Century Code, Sections 25-13-01 through 25-13-05, North Dakota Administrative Code, 69-03-04-05

North Dakota statutes guarantee a deaf person the legal right to be accompanied by a specially trained dog guide in all public accommodations and on all public conveyances. No extra charge can be levied because of the dog's presence, but the dog guide user is liable for any damage the dog might cause to the premises. Muzzling can be requested by a common carrier. (69-03-04-05)

Public accommodations include hotels, lodging places, places of resort and amusement, stores, restaurants and other facilities to which the public is invited. (Section 25-13-02)

Public conveyances include trains, airplanes, taxis, buses, boats, and other modes of transportation offered for public use. (Section 25-13-02)

Violation: Any person, firm or corporation or agent thereof who interferes with the above enumerated rights is guilty of a Class A misdemeanor. (Section 25-13-04)

OHIO

Ohio Revised Code, Section 955.011, 955.43, 955.99

Ohio statutory law guarantees a deaf person the legal right to be accompanied by a specially trained dog guide in all public accommodations and on all public conveyances. No extra fee can be levied because of the dog guide's presence. A dog may not occupy a seat on a common carrier, and dog guides are exempt from licensing fees.

Public accommodations include hotels, restaurants, stores, places of resort and amusement and all other places to which the general public is invited. (Section 955.43)

Public conveyances include taxis, trains, airplanes, buses, boats, and all other modes of transportation offered for public use. (Section 955.43)

Violation: Any person who interferes with the above enumerated rights is guilty of a misdemeanor. (Section 955.99)

OKLAHOMA

Oklahoma Statutes 1981, Title 7, Section 19.1 and 19.2

Oklahoma statutory law guarantees a deaf person the legal right to be accompanied by a specially trained dog guide in all public accommodations and on all public transportation. No extra charge can be levied because of the presence of a dog guide, but the dog guide user is liable for any damage the dog might cause to the premises. A dog guide shall be required to wear a yellow identifying collar.

Public accommodations include stores, restaurants, hotels, cafes and all other places to which the public is invited. (Section 19.1)

Public transportation includes public elevators, trains, airplanes, boats, buses, taxis and all other modes of public conveyance. (Section 19.1)

Violation: Any person who interferes with the above enumerated rights is guilty of a misdemeanor. (Section 19-2)

OREGON

Oregon Revised Statutes 346.640, 346.650, 346.660 and 346.991, 609.105

Oregon statutory law guarantees a deaf person the legal right to be accompanied by a specially trained dog guide on an orange leash in all public accommodations and in all public transportation. No extra charge can be levied because of a dog guide's presence, but the dog guide user is liable for any damage the dog might cause to the premises. Dog guides are exempt from licensing fees.

Public accommodations include restaurants, stores, hotels, and all facilities to which the public is invited. (Section 346.640)

Public transportation includes buses, trains, taxis, airplanes and all other conveyances offered for public use. Exempt is a parlor, lounge, or club car on a railroad. (346.640)

Violation: A person who interferes with the above enumerated rights is guilty of a Class C misdemeanor. (346.991)

PENNSYLVANIA

Pennsylvania Statutes Annotated, Title 18, Section 7325

Pennsylvania statutes guarantee a deaf person the legal right to be accompanied by a dog guide in all accommodations which are made available for public use. The statute further guarantees equal housing accommodations to dog guide users in both the rental and purchase of commercial housing.

Public accommodations under Pennsylvania law and regulations include restaurants, hotels, places of resort and amusement and public transportation.

Commercial housing includes rentals and leased residential property, as well as negotiations covering the purchase of property.

Violation: Any person who practices unlawful discrimination is guilty of a misdemeanor.

RHODE ISLAND

General Laws of Rhode Island, Section 31-18-14, 39-2-13, and 39-2-14

Rhode Island statutes guarantee a deaf person the legal right to be accompanied by a specially trained dog guide wearing a yellow harness in all public facilities and on all public transportation.No extra charge can be levied because of the dog's presence, but the dog guide user is liable for any damage the dog might cause to the premises.

Public facilities are any buildings open to the public. (Section 39-2-13)

Public transportation includes buses, trains, airplanes, taxis, elevators and all other modes of conveyance offered for public use. (Section 39-2-13)

Violation: Anyone who interferes with the above enumerated rights is guilty of a misdemeanor and punishable by a fine of $500. (Section 39-2-14)

SOUTH CAROLINA

Code of Laws of South Carolina, 1976, 43-33-10 through 43-33-70; Cumulative Supplement to Code of Laws of South Carolina, 1982, 43-33-10 through 43-33-70

South Carolina statutes guarantee a deaf person the legal right to be accompanied by a dog guide in all public accommodations and on all public transportation. Dog guide users are also guaranteed equal housing accommodation. No extra charge can be levied because of the dog guide's presence, but the dog guide user is liable for any damage the dog might cause to the premises. Landlords are not required to modify their property, nor to provide a higher degree of care than that provided other tenants.

Public accommodations include stores, hotels, restaurants, places of resort and amusement and all other places to which the public is invited. (Section 43-33-20)

Public transportation includes taxis, trains, airplanes, buses, and all other forms of transportation offered for public use. (Section 43-33-20)

Housing accommodations include all property offered for rent or lease as a residence or sleeping place, except for a single family dwelling, whose occupants offer no more than one room for rent. (Section 43-33-70)

Violation: Any person who interferes with the legal rights enumerated above is guilty of a misdemeanor. (Section 43-33-40)

SOUTH DAKOTA

South Dakota Annotated Laws, Volume 7, Section 20-13-23.1, 20-13-23.5 and 20-13-23.6

South Dakota law guarantees a deaf person the legal right to be accompanied by a specially trained dog guide in all public accommodations. A dog guide user also has a legal right to rent or lease an apartment or other residential housing without discrimination. No extra charge can be levied because of the dog guide's presence, but the dog guide user is liable for any damage the dog might cause to the premises.

Public accommodations include hotels, restaurants, stores, and all other places to which the general public is invited. (Section 20-13-23.1)

All modes of transportation are generally included with the definition of public accommodations. (Section 20-13-23.1)

TENNESSEE

Tennessee Code Annotated, Section 62-7-112

Tennessee statutory law guarantees a deaf person the legal right to be accompanied by a specially trained dog guide in harness in all public accommodations and on all public conveyances. The dog guide user may be requested to present for inspection the identification card furnished by the dog training institution.

Public accommodations include such facilities as stores, theaters, motion picture houses, elevators, public transportation, restaurants, hotels, public educational institutions and other places to which the general public is invited. (Section 62-7-112)

Violation: Anyone who interferes with the above enumerated legal rights is guilty of a misdemeanor and punishable by a $50 fine. (Section 62-7-112)

TEXAS

Texas Human Resources Code, Title 8, Chapter 121, Section 121.001 through 121.006

The Texas anti-discrimination statutes guarantee a deaf person the legal right to be accompanied by a specially trained dog guide in harness in all public facilities. The owner of the dog must also have completed a specific training course in the use of the dog as a communication aid. A dog guide user has a legal right to equal housing accommodation in all housing offered for rent, lease or compensation. The landlord need not modify the premises, nor is a higher standard of care required than that provided other tenants. No extra fee can be levied because of the dog guide's presence, but the dog guide user is liable for any damage the dog might do to the premises.

Public facilities include hotels, stores, restaurants, college dormitories, places of resort, recreation and amusement, public buildings, railroads, buses, boats, airplanes, taxis and all other common carriers or places to which the public is invited. (Sections 121.002 and 121.003)

Housing accommodations include any real property, in whole or in part, which is designed or used as a home, residence, or sleeping place, except for a single family dwelling, the occupants of which offer for rent no more than one room. (Section 121.003)

Violation: Any person,firm, association or agent thereof who interferes with the above enumerated rights is guilty of a misdemeanor and is punishable by a fine of not less that $100 or more than $300.

In addition, the dog guide user whose civil rights have been violated may proceed in any court of competent jurisdiction to recover personal damages with the presumption that at least $100 worth of damage has been sustained. (Section 121.044)

Any person who unlawfully represents his dog as a specially trained dog guide is guilty of a misdemeanor and punishable by a fine of not more than $200. (Section 121.006)

UTAH

Utah Code Annotated 1983, Section 26-30-1 through 26-30-4

Utah statutory law guarantees a deaf person the legal right to be accompanied by a specially trained dog guide in all public accommodations and on all public transportation. No additional charge can be levied because of the dog guide's presence, but the dog guide user is liable for any damage the dog might cause to the premises. The dog guide user may be asked to present for inspection the laminated identification card provided by the dog guide school from which the dog was obtained.

Public accommodations include stores, restaurants, hotels, lodges, public buildings, places of resort and amusement and all other places to which the public is invited. (Section 26-30-1)

Public transportation includes airplanes, buses, boats, taxis and all other modes of transportation offered for public use. (Sections 26-30-1, 26-30-2)

Violation: Any person or agent of any person who interferes with the above enumerated legal rights is guilty of a Class C misdemeanor and punishable accordingly. (Section 26-30-4)

VERMONT

Vermont Statutes, Chapter 31, Section 1451

Vermont law guarantees a deaf person the legal right to be accompanied by a dog guide in all places of public accommodation. The dog must be in harness and proper identification of the dog may be required from the dog guide owner. No extra charge can be levied because of the dog's presence.

Public accommodations include any establishment which offers services, goods, or facilities to the public. The term public accommodation covers stores, restaurants, hotels and common carriers. (Section 1451)

Violation: Vermont law prohibits interference in the exercise of the above enumerated rights by any owner, operator, employee or agent of a public accommodation. (Section 1451)

VIRGINIA

Virginia Statutes, Article 3, Sections 63.1-171-1 through 63.1-171.8

Virginia statutory law guarantees a deaf person the legal right to be accompanied by a specially trained dog guide on a blaze orange leash in all public accommodations and on all public transportation. The dog guide user shall obtain an identification card from the Virginia Council for the Deaf upon presentation of identification of the dog from a recognized training center. A dog guide user is also guaranteed equal housing accommodation, but the landlord is not required to modify the property or provide a higher standard of care than that provided other tenants. No extra charge can be levied because of a dog guide's presence, but the dog guide user is liable for any damage the dog might cause to the premises.

Public accommodations include hotels, stores, restaurants, places of resort and amusement and any other place to which the general public is invited. (Section 63.1-171.2)

Public transportation includes airplanes, boats, trains, buses, taxis, common carriers and all other modes of conveyance offered for public use. (Section 63.1-171.2)

Housing accommodations include any real property or portion thereof designed or used as a home residence, or sleeping place offered for rent, lease or compensation, except for a single family dwelling, the occupants of which offer not more than one room for rent. (Section 63.1-171.7)

Violation: Any person, firm, corporation or agent thereof who interferes with the above enumerated rights is guilty of a Class 1 misdemeanor. The above rights are also enforceable through injunctive relief. (Section 63.1-171.4)

WASHINGTON

1981 Revised Code of Washington, Chapter 70.84, Section 010 through 900

Washington statutory law guarantees a deaf person the legal right to be accompanied by a specially trained dog guide in harness in all places of public accommodation and on all public transportation. No extra charge can be levied because of the dog's presence.

Public accommodations include hotels, restaurants, stores, public buildings, places of resort, amusement, and assemblage and any other place to which the general public is invited. (Section 010 and 030)

Public transportation includes trains, buses, airplanes, boats, taxis and any other common carriers or modes of conveyance offered for public use. (Section 010)

Violation: Any person, firm, corporation or any agent thereof who interferes with the above enumerated rights is guilty of a misdemeanor and punishable under Washington law accordingly. (Section 070)

WEST VIRGINIA

West Virginia Annotated Code (1983 Cumulative Supplement), Article 15, Section 5-15-1 through 5-15-8

West Virginia law guarantees a deaf person the legal right to be accompanied by a specially trained dog guide in harness in any public accommodation and on all public transportation. No extra charge can be levied because of the dog guide's presence, but the dog guide user is liable for any damage caused by the dog. The dog guide user may be asked to present for inspection the identification card provided by the dog guide school from which the dog was obtained.

Public accommodations include hotels, restaurants, stores, places of resort and amusement and all other places to which the public is invited. (Section 5-15-4)

Public transportation includes trains, boats, buses, taxis, airplanes and all other common carriers and modes of conveyance offered for public use. (Section 5-15-4)

Violation: Any person, firm, corporation or agent thereof who interferes with the above enumerated rights is guilty of a misdemeanor and subject to fine. (Section 5-15-8)

WISCONSIN

1981-82 Wisconsin Statutes, Sections 174.055 And 174.056

Wisconsin law guarantees a deaf person the legal right to be accompanied by a specially trained dog guide in harness in all public accommodations. The dog guide user can be requested to submit for inspection the identification card that is provided by the accredited training school to the dog guide owner. Dog guides are exempt from a licensing fee.

Public accommodations under Wisconsin law include hotels, inns, stores, restaurants, public conveyances on land and water, places of resort and recreation and all other facilities and places to which the general public is invited. (Section 174.056)

Violation: Any person or owner, lessee, employee or agent of a public accommodation who interferes with the above enumerated rights may be fined up to $100, or imprisoned for 30 days, or both. (Section 174.056)

WYOMING

1983 Session Laws of Wyoming, Chapter 88, Sections 42-1-26 through 42-1-129

Wyoming statutes guarantee a deaf person the legal right to be accompanied by a specially trained dog guide in all public accommodations and on all public transportation. No extra charge can be levied because of the dog guide's presence, but the dog guide user is liable for any damages the dog guide causes to the premises.

Public accommodations include hotels, restaurants, stores, public buildings, places of resort and amusement and any other place to which the public is invited. (Sections 42-1-126, 42-1-129)

Public transportation includes buses, trains, taxis, airplanes, boats and any other mode of public conveyance offered for public use. (Sections 42-1-126, 42-1-129)

Violation: Any person, firm or corporation or agent thereof who interferes with the above enumerated rights is guilty of a misdemeanor and punishable by a fine for each offense. (Sections 42-1-128, 42-1-129)

Suggested reading:

Brickel, Clark The therapeutic roles of cat mascots with a hospital based geriatric population: A staff survey. *The Gerontologist,* 1979, 19, 368-372.

Lee, Ronnal, et al. Guidelines: Animals in nursing homes. *California Veterinarian,* 1983, 3, Supplement.

Olsen, Geary, et al. Pet-facilitated therapy: A study of the use of animals in health care facilities in Minnesota. In Katcher, Aaron and Beck, Alan (eds.), *New perspectives on our lives with animal companions.* Philadelphia: University of Pennsylvania Press, 1983.

Quigley, Joseph, et al. A study of perspectives and attitudes towards pet ownership. In Katcher, Aaron and Beck, Alan (eds.), *New perspectives on our lives with animal companions.* Philadelphia: University of Pennsylvania Press, 1983.

Robb, Susanne, et al. A wine bottle, plant and puppy: Catalysts for social behavior. *Journal of Gerontological Nursing,* 1980, 6, 721-728.

Tolliver, L.M.P. Perspectives on aging and the role of companion animals: An overview and future needs. In Anderson, Robert, et al. (eds.), *The pet connection: Its influence on our health and quality of life.* South St. Paul, Minn.: Globe Publishing Co., 1984.

Section III
Programs in Action

8

Companion Animals for the Blind

Jennifer Bassing

"...effective and proven mobility..."

The relationship between dogs and men is not one with roots entirely based in affection. Early dog, a wild and different-looking creature from what we recognize as today's dog, was viewed first as a pest—an animal that stole food from man's campsite. But that introduction, almost certainly initiated by dog, gave our human ancestors something to think about.

The dog's scenting and tracking abilities made it difficult to hide stores of food from it. Its pack connections gave it a unified strength that easily made up for the loss of a single animal. And the dog's persistence in following man from cave to hut to house showed a loyalty that could not be defeated by man's threats or rejection.

It is, perhaps, this lack of defeatist attitude on the part of both dog and man that finally caused the two to form an early truce in their common struggle for survival. At some point it must have seemed simply easier to join forces.

And, so, the dog became a hunting partner and a camp guardian. Its life was not an easy one. It bred, lived and died without benefit of special care or comforts. It was a tool. Without even realizing it, man was fashioning that tool into the elements that would eventually earmark the dog as an animal that would achieve a unique status—the service dog.

Other animals of higher intelligence than the dog were, possibly, too smart for man. The apes that did not descend from the trees kept their

Jennifer Bassing is a writer specializing in animal-related topics. She is the development officer for Guide Dogs for the Blind, Inc., in San Rafael, Calif., where her constant companion is a Black Labrador Retriever named "Puka." She is a member of many animal and writing groups, including the Dog Writers' Association of America, the Marin Dog Training Club and the Public Relations Society of America.

distance. They may have thought their ground-bound cousins foolish for making fire and cooking food when fruit and roots and nuts were plentiful. The felines, suspicious of even their own kind, had little interest in an alliance with man.

From hunters to herders, it was man and dog who discovered each other's strengths and weaknesses and played on those to get what each wanted. Without prejudice the dog quickly accepted man as leader. It is, in fact, dog's greatest modern tragedy that there are humans who do not recognize the dog's need and desire to be led. Modern "problem" dogs are mainly those who have not had the benefit of a kind but strong leader.

Left to its own devices in these times, the dog is confused. By its nature, the dog wants to belong. It cannot tolerate isolation or lack of direction. Tied to a post all day, it will howl or bark. Locked alone behind a fence, it will jump out in search of companionship. Given an inkling that it is the master, the dog will become a dictator, biting, snarling, defecating and digging at will. In short, the dog wants to be incorporated into its human family pack, no matter whether it be one dog and one person or a family filled with children, adults and other animals.

It is this eagerness on the part of the dog to participate, to belong, that has enabled human-service programs to train the dog to be of specialized assistance to people. In this chapter, devoted to dog guides for the blind, the evolution of this specialty will be described and current programs discussed.

It is important to point out that the term "dog guide" is the generic expression used to describe all dogs that are trained in this particular field. Terms such as "Guide Dog" or "Seeing Eye Dog" reflect the names of the various schools specializing in this training.

Early literature on the subject is scant. Nelson Coon in *A Brief History of Dog Guides for the Blind* traces dog guides largely through works of art. A fresco dating from 79 A.D., uncovered among the ruins of Pompeii, depicts a marketplace at which a blind man with a staff is being led by a small dog. A 13th century Chinese scroll painting, "Spring on the Yellow River," which is housed in the Metropolitan Museum of Art, offers a similar scene. In it a blind man carrying a staff in his right hand is being led by a dog with his left hand.

Other paintings from the 14th through the 19th centuries give evidence of the dog in the role of a guide to the blind. In many cases, notably the painting of a "Beggar" by Rembrandt, the dog was employed less as guide than as a beggar's assistant.

The 19th century engraving by Dibart of "Le Chien de L'Aveugle" clearly shows the dog in the act of soliciting alms. In that engraving the dog holds a dish in its mouth while dancing to the tune its blind master plays on an oboe-like instrument. A George Willie engraving done in Paris in 1801 shows blind beggars, each with a staff and a dog, approaching one another with cups held forth.

It was Rembrandt who demonstrated in his painting, "Tobias," that the dog was suited for more than begging. In that painting a small dog tries to direct its blind master toward a door opening by tugging at the master's robe.

Personal attempts at training dogs to act as guides were probably numerous. One such account comes from Joseph Reisinger, born in Vienna around 1775. Reisinger, who lost his sight at age 17 due to an infection, trained his Spitz to stop at doorways and to avoid obstacles. This dog served Reisinger for 16 years until its death. Reisinger trained two other dogs who gave him a combined 27 years of guide service until Reisinger was physically unable to train another animal.

The formalized training of dogs as guides was recorded by Father Johann Wilhelm Klein of Vienna in his *Textbook for Teaching the Blind,* published in 1819. In his book, Klein describes the training of dogs by

Different breeds of dogs may serve as guide dogs for the blind. From left, a German shepherd, yellow Labrador retriever, black Labrador retriever and golden retriever all demonstrate their attentiveness. *(Photo by Thom Ainsworth)*

sighted people for the specific purpose of guide work. A preference for poodles and German shepherd dogs is stated and the training method outlined is strikingly similar to that used by many schools today:

"One leads him [the dog], many times, on the same road and drills him, particular attention being paid to places where through turning, through slow pace, through standing still, or through other movements which might be useful to the blind in situations such as the turning of a street and in the avoidance of obstacles that lie ahead—through all this the dog will be made alert to various kinds of danger situations."

In 1845 the blind Jacob Birrer of Germany introduced the training he gave his dog guides by writing:

"I feel it a duty therefore to my blind colleagues who want to be guided by dogs, to give instructions based largely on my own practical experiences for training the dogs."

Using the poodle and Spitz breeds, Birrer described a method involving repetitive travel over the same area using consistent commands to get the desired performance from the dog. Birrer closed his diary-style account with:

"However no one should think, regardless of what species the dog is, that it can be trained only by being beaten; on the contrary, every trainer should make it his duty, when his animal has done well in his exercises to pet him and make him a faithful friend, now and then giving him some delicacy to eat."

It took World War I to hasten the further development of training service dogs not only for use as guides for the blind but as messengers, for sentry duty, in rescue work and for other tasks. The Germans were particularly successful in this type of training and in 1916 a program was started at Oldenburg to train German shepherd dogs as guides for the blind. The dogs learned to avoid traffic and obstructions, to stop at curbs and stairs, to move out rapidly and to alert pedestrians by barking.

A second training center opened at Wurttemberg and at the close of the war there were two more centers added at Potsdam and Munich. Following the war, training was expanded to include civilian blind as well as blinded war veterans.

An American, Dorothy Harrison Eustis, who had been breeding and training German shepherd dogs at her Fortunate Fields Research Center on Mount Pelerin above Vevey, Switzerland, learned of the German successes in training dog guides for the blind. Mrs. Eustis described the program in 1927 in an article published by the *Saturday Evening Post* entitled "The Seeing Eye."

Word of the program reached Morris Frank of Nashville, Tenn., a blind

19-year old, who wrote to Mrs. Eustis asking if dog guide training was available for blind people in America. As a result of his inquiry Mrs. Eustis decided to attempt the training of a dog guide and blind person team at her research facility in Switzerland.

Frank arrived in Vevey in April of 1928 where he trained with a female German shepherd dog named Buddy I. After five weeks of successful training, Frank and Buddy sailed back to the United States as the first American-trained person-dog guide unit.

The success of Morris Frank and Buddy encouraged Mrs. Eustis to follow through with her plan to establish a dog guide center in the United States. In 1929, The Seeing Eye, America's first dog guide program, was incorporated in Tennessee, where it stayed until 1931 when the program moved to its present location in Morristown, N.J.

There are currently about 10 dog guide programs or schools in this country. Training facilities flourish in England, Australia, South Africa, Sweden, Holland, Italy, Norway and Denmark, among other countries. While a common thread runs among all of these schools in that they train dogs in the task of guiding blind people, there are distinguishing differences among breeding programs, testing and training techniques, application procedures and follow-up programs.

For example, most schools, such as Guide Dogs for the Blind, Inc., in San Rafael, Calif., operate an in-residence program for the blind person in training. However, some schools, such as Fidelco Guide Dogs in Bloomfield, Conn., provide home-based training. Certain schools use only purebred American Kennel Club (AKC) registered animals while others accept mixed breeds. In fact, there are schools which use only dogs produced by their own select breeding stock and other programs which will use adult pet dog rejects.

Funding is another area where differences exist. There are schools that depend exclusively on private donations and charge no fees for their services. Other schools may charge the blind person a nominal amount. Standards for the trainers of both dogs and people vary from school to school. California is currently the only state requiring that dog guide instructors be licensed. The instructor must complete a three-year apprenticeship at a dog guide school and then pass a rigorous California state board examination which includes working a dog guide over an unpracticed area while under blindfold.

But the most essential part of the program—the decision to employ the dog as a mobility tool—is one upon which all dog guide programs agree. The dog is an effective and proven mobility tool—more complex to use than the long cane, but, certainly, more companionable.

As a staff member of Guide Dogs for the Blind, Inc., in California's Marin County, it is only logical for me to allow that particular program to serve as the descriptive basis for much of the following discussion of dog guides. And while the staff experience of Guide Dogs for the Blind, Inc., has instilled me with a point of view, it has not caused me to lose my journalist objectivity. With that in mind, close your eyes and imagine.

Imagine what it is like to have never seen anything. Not your parents. Not your teachers. Not your playmates. Not dogs, cats, birds, or flowers. It is difficult to imagine. It is something I cannot do.

Imagine, instead, having seen, what it would be like to lose your sight—suddenly, perhaps as the result of a traumatic injury, or slowly, due to the progression of a disease like diabetes. In the case of trauma, there is no getting used to the idea of blindness. One day you can see and the next you cannot. It may have been a car accident or an industrial injury that destroyed your sight. About 40,000 Americans experience impaired vision as the result of injuries each year.

Surgery can repair the skin but there is no vision-giving replacement for the eyes. Prosthetic eyes can make a difference in how the sighted world views a blind person. Modern artificial eyes are made of plastic and are so highly crafted that it is difficult to distinguish between the real and the substitute.

This is a good time to point out that not all blind people are without sight. To be legally blind means that the individual has a maximum degree of corrected vision of 20/200 in the better eye or has a visual acuity better than 20/200 but with a field of vision no greater than 20 degrees at its widest point.

Dog guide schools, in general, will not accept a candidate for training unless the applicant is legally blind. Aside from the obvious need of the institution to establish admission criteria by accepting only legally blind individuals, the students at the dog guide schools can be very critical of one another. Blindness almost becomes a badge of honor and those seemingly "less blind" are viewed as not quite legitimate.

Returning for a moment to the loss of sight, consider what it would be like to know that one day you will no longer be able to see your family, your friends, your home, your clothes, the food you eat. One day I complimented a diabetic blind young man on the shirt he was wearing. He was pleased with the compliment and replied, "This was the last shirt I bought for myself before I went blind."

It isn't merely the glorious sunsets that blind people remember. It is the day-to-day humble sights, such as clothes on a rack, that they recall. And it is exactly the daily chores of shopping, walking, and working that can be opened up to them through the use of a dog guide.

At Guide Dogs for the Blind a general information sheet is kept on each applicant. It is a way to keep track of each step in the application process. On it is listed the reason why the applicant wants a Guide Dog. On every sheet I have seen the answer is always the same: For Increased Mobility.

Now this is not to say that the blind person is somehow a prisoner without a dog guide. A dog guide represents a *choice* among mobility tools. In fact, less than one percent of the U.S. blind population of 500,000 have elected to use a dog guide as a means of mobility.

The decision to use the particular mobility tool of a dog is not one that can be reached through pressure from family or friends. The individual must not only want a dog guide but must also be physically strong enough to handle one. As blindness is often a secondary problem resulting from the primary disease, or is combined with other syndromes, the

Dog guides afford the blind considerable mobility and the opportunity to pursue normal lives. "Ranger" helps guide Carol Rainbolt to a student dormitory on campus where she is a student.
(Photo by Thom Ainsworth)

prospective dog guide user's physical condition must be taken into account. The typical pace the dog guide user will travel at is between two and five miles per hour.

Another consideration for the person thinking of obtaining a dog guide is the responsibility he or she must accept for the animal as a living mobility tool. If the blind person cannot invest the time or energy in caring for the animal's physical and emotional needs, then, certainly, a dog guide is the wrong tool to choose.

At Guide Dogs for the Blind the dogs are given no rewards during training other than physical and verbal stroking. This reward system, while seemingly simple, does imply a degree of sophistication in understanding the nature of dogs. To the person who has never had a dog before and may have never actually *seen* a dog, the physical display of praising the dog may be a difficult requirement to follow. It is common to hear the instructors saying to the blind person in training, "Praise your dog."

And, so, before describing the creation of a person-dog unit, it must be stressed that a dog guide from Guide Dogs for the Blind or from any other similar program may not be the appropriate mobility tool for every blind person. But if that is the tool a blind person truly wants and is physically and emotionally able to handle, then getting a Guide Dog is not as difficult as some may think. The dog, the training, plus years of follow-up service, are completely free at Guide Dogs for the Blind. All that a qualified, legally blind person must do is to ask.

The Guide Dogs for the Blind school has an active social services department that processes all inquiries and applications. Each applicant is interviewed at his or her home. The waiting time from point of inquiry to actual class placement is about six months. Every effort is made to accommodate special schedules. For example, classes during the summer months are often filled with college-age people who want to train during the summer break. Guide Dogs for the Blind also offers special "replacement classes" for individuals whose Guide Dogs have died or have been retired due to illness or age.

The first-time Guide Dog user must participate in a 28-day in-residence program at the school's campus in San Rafael, Calif. The replacement class is a two-week resident course. But before the blind person sets foot on the Guide Dog campus the groundwork for developing a solid person-dog team has already been laid, starting with the whelping of Guide Dog puppies in the school's maternity kennels.

Guide Dogs for the Blind maintains its breeding stock in private homes within a 50-mile radius of the school's 11-acre campus. Only three breeds are used: golden retrievers, Labrador retrievers and German shepherds.

These breeds were selected for their willingness to work, ease of grooming because of their short to medium coats, even temperaments, and medium size. Other programs have used and still use various other breeds, including boxers, Doberman pinschers and poodles.

The litters of Guide Dog puppies are registered with the AKC and detailed breeding records are maintained. The pups remain in the Guide Dog kennels for three months. During that time the pups undergo weekly testing by a crew of volunteer puppy testers, some of whom have been with the puppy testing program for 30 years!

The puppy testing techniques and criteria at Guide Dogs were developed by Clarence Pfaffenberger who served as regional director at the Dog Training and Reception Center for Dogs for Defense and the Army in San Carlos, Calif., during World War II. Pfaffenberger observed that among the thousands of dogs donated to the military, the ones best suited for service work were those that had been raised in a socializing environment.

After the war, Pfaffenberger joined the board of Guide Dogs for the Blind and later became a staff member. He decided to pursue information on breeding and raising dogs with an eye toward puppy selection for guide work. Working with scientists at the Roscoe B. Jackson Memorial Laboratory in Bar Harbor, Maine, Pfaffenberger learned that not only do genetic behavioral differences exist in dogs but that those differences are developed and influenced by environmental factors.

Over the course of a 13-year research project, scientists, notably Dr. John Paul Scott and Dr. John L. Fuller, determined that puppies passed through critical developmental stages. Experiences that took place during those critical periods affected the animal's later behavior in accordance with its genetic disposition. This information was applied to the breeding, testing and rearing program at Guide Dogs for the Blind and has served as a model for puppy testing in other service dog organizations, such as the California Rescue Dog Association.

Today's Guide Dog puppy represents the best product of breed and environment. After the testing period, during which time the pup is checked for distraction level, come and fetch instincts, reactions to noise and other stimuli, the young animal is placed in the home of a volunteer puppy raiser. The pup is generally three months old when this occurs and the foster homes are primarily those of 4-H members located in the far Western states.

The responsibility of the puppy raiser is to housetrain the pup and to introduce it to as many socializing influences as possible—public transportation, shopping centers, other animals, other people, etc. These activities permit the dog to experience many of the real-life stresses and situations that it will encounter when working as a guide.

It is also during this early period that the dog makes its first solid human-animal bond. The puppy raiser plays a significant role in shaping the personality of the Guide Dog.

When the dog is about 18 months old it must be returned to the school to begin formal training in guide work. This is a difficult time for the puppy raiser, the dog and the Guide Dog instructor, for it is a time of transition of loyalties. The youthful puppy raiser must give up an animal that has been part of the family for more than a year. The dog leaves the family setting and returns to the Guide Dog kennels where it will be incorporated into a training string of about 28 to 30 dogs. The instructor must get to know the new dog's personality in order to understand how best to develop its potential as a Guide Dog. The instructor must give the dog balanced support that will enhance its chances to succeed at the training while avoiding creating over-dependence on the trainer.

The dog entering formal training is first placed in an orientation kennel where it stays for a short period while it adjusts to its new surroundings. Hip x-rays are taken and a dog may be dropped from the program because its hips fall below the standards acceptable for guide work. Any dog rejected from the program is offered back to the person or family who raised it. In the rare instance that the family cannot take the dog back, the dog will become part of the Guide Dog pet stock. Few dogs ever remain pet stock, as the list of potential adoptors is hundreds and hundreds of names long.

The next step is several months of intense individual training of the dog by the Guide Dog instructor. This is when the second bond—that of instructor and dog—is formed. If the first bond, that of raiser and pup, was meant to supply the dog with input on family life, then the second bond, of teacher and dog, is meant to give the dog excellent working skills. Ideally, the total experiences the dog gains from both of these bonds will be integrated by the dog to form the basis for its third, and most important, bond—that of Guide Dog and blind person.

The period of development of the second bond of Guide Dog-in-training and instructor is a time of rapidly accelerating education for the dog. It moves quickly from obedience to harness work to actual guide work. After 15 individual workouts with the instructor, the dog is given its first real test as a guide. The instructor dons a blindfold and works the dog in downtown San Rafael, a suburban town outside of San Francisco with a bustling business section.

It will take at least 40 more full workouts before the dog can be considered ready to enter class with a blind person. By then the Guide Dog will have led its instructor safely through the streets of San Francisco. It will be comfortable working in stores and office buildings, on elevators and stairways, and on public transportation. The Guide Dog will have learned to avoid obstacles, including overhead ones that it could easily pass under. It will be able to determine when it is safe to cross a street and will disobey any command to cross an intersection when it is not safe to do so.

The Guide Dog will become a "thinking dog" and only 50 percent of all the dogs who enter formal training will ever achieve the status of Guide Dog. Again, those dogs that fail the rigorous Guide Dog training are offered back to the puppy raisers as pets or become part of the school's pet stock.

To be rejected as a Guide Dog is no shame. The reasons for rejection may include excessive shyness or overaggressiveness. Even size or cosmetic reasons can be causes for rejection. For example, if the ears on a German shepherd fail to stand erect, the dog will not become a guide even though it is adequate in every other way.

Lay people may be surprised by the stringent requirements that apply even to a dog's ears; however, most blind people are extremely sensitive to physical appearances. If a dog is not fully representative of its breed the blind person may be subjected to ridicule at worst or to innocent queries as to why the dog looks the way it does. Rather than leave any question open in the mind of a blind person as to how good a dog looks, the Guide Dog school has decided to add the requirement that a Guide Dog be truly characteristic-looking of its breed.

Finally, after five to six months of specialized training, the successful Guide Dog candidate is ready to progress to the third major bond it will share. The Guide Dog is ready to meet its blind partner.

At Guide Dogs for the Blind the issuing of the dog to a blind person is a rite of passage that carries with it all the subtleties that mark any major change in a life. In this case, several lives are affected by what takes place on dog-issuing day. The puppy raiser has been advised by the school that his or her dog has entered class and, certainly, there must be intense curiosity as to what type of person will receive the precious gift.

The instructor who has fed, watered, nursed, trained and loved the dog for many months must now hand over the lead to a relative stranger. The Guide Dog instructors are philosophical about the nature of their work. Most of them come to it with an intense love of animals but as they grow in their jobs, their knowledge and feeling extends wholeheartedly to the blind people they must teach to use the dogs they have trained. Yet, it would be unnatural to expect that as the leash passes from one hand to another that it goes without all the worries and hopes any dog lover feels in turning over the trust of an animal to someone unskilled in its full use.

The blind person enters into the new bond with, perhaps, the greatest fears of all. Their questions are of a common strain: Will the dog like me? Will I be able to learn to handle it? Can I take care of all of its needs? Will it really give me the extra mobility I seek?

And, finally, there is the dog. So many changes . . . so many things to have learned . . . so many people to have loved and to have been loved by. Is this too much to ask of any animal, even our dearest friend, the dog?

The blind students arrive at the Guide Dog school on a Sunday. On Monday and Tuesday of their first week at the school they go through a form of training called "Juno" work. Juno is a unique "dog". He looks human, for it is the instructors who assume the role of dog these first two days, but Juno acts and reacts just like a regular four-footed canine. Juno's job is to give the students a preview of what it will be like to work with a real Guide Dog. The instructors lead the students at the end of a harness, going gently at first, but then increasing in the demands that they make on the students. Juno requires direction and correction. Juno needs praise and support. Juno is, in every sense, the true spirit of the dog he represents.

Wednesday of that first week is known as "dog day" on the Guide Dog campus. It is an exciting day for everyone at school. A meeting takes place that morning in the office of Benny Larsen, the school's executive director. And in that meeting the determination is made as to which Guide Dog will be matched with which blind person enrolled in the class.

A young student who travels on buses or subways will need a dog that excels at work on public transportation. An elderly person who wishes to shop and stroll may need a more sedate animal. A mother will want a dog who is excellent around children. An office worker will need a dog whose nature is compatible with long periods spent in a down-stay.

The students are interviewed by the instructors prior to dog-issuing day and their individual needs are discussed openly at this most important dog-pairing meeting. No detail is ignored. Does the blind person have other pets? Has he or she ever used a dog guide before? What is the climate like in the blind person's environment? These and many other questions are considered.

Recommendations are made by the instructors as to which student will get which dog. The most difficult match to make is that of pairing the right dog with the weakest student in class—not necessarily a person who is physically weak, but one who may be the most insecure. Although all the Guide Dogs about to be matched with a student are considered top quality, obviously one dog will always stand out as the best. That dog always goes to the weakest student. This one simple policy of the Guide Dog school may best express the dedication of its training staff, for among lay people the wish is that the best goes to the best. But at Guide Dogs it is known and accepted that the person who needs the most help must get the animal that will be the most helpful.

Lunchtime on dog day is filled with excited chatter. The students always leave the dormitory dining room earlier than usual to head back to their rooms where they will await word of their new Guide Dogs. After lunch the instructors gather the students and tell the group the name, breed and sex of each student's Guide Dog.

The students return to their rooms and wait once again to be escorted to the instructor's quarters where they will meet their new guides. One by one the students enter the instructor's room. When the student hears the pat-pat-pat sound of the dog's feet in the hallway, all the preparation for this moment of introduction suddenly seems to move in the direction of 50 to 80 pounds of dog. Into the room comes the dog, nose working full force, head bobbing back and forth, as it recognizes the instructor and wonders who the tense stranger is sitting in a chair. Most of the dogs will first approach the instructor, nudging the instructor's knee or hand in greeting.

Guide dogs are not only working pets but also friendly companions. Frank Hodges relaxes with "Dale" on campus. *(Photo by Thom Ainsworth)*

The instructor gently encourages the student to call the dog's name and the dog, being dog, rarely refuses this invitation of friendship.

After the initial hands-on contact between the student and dog, the instructor tells the student to hook the leash to the dog's collar. In ritual, it is similar to placing a golden band on the finger of a loved one.

The final phase of the introduction is a full physical description of the dog given by the instructor to the student. The details of the dog from the color of nose leather clear down to tip-of-the-tail markings are described thoroughly. The instructor may take the student's hands and place them over the dog's ears saying, "Feel how soft they are."

The rest of the afternoon of dog day is spent by the students and their dogs back in their dorm rooms where the two are given time to get acquainted. Playing, grooming, touching, hugging and licking, are the agenda items for dog day afternoon. Walking down the hallway of the dormitory, one can hear the words, "Good dog. What a good dog," coming from behind closed doors. It is the most highly personal time the student and dog will ever have in their lives together. It is their time to make whatever private pledges people and animals make that speak of respect and care, hopes and love. The Guide Dog, in a compliant way, must let its new partner know that it is safe to trust its instincts and skills. The blind person must reassure the dog that though trust may come slowly, there is, at least, the promise to try.

And the trying begins the very next morning when, bright and early, the duo is up and ready to start the work of becoming a true person-dog unit. For the remainder of the 28-day resident course at Guide Dogs for the Blind there is no separation of person and dog. They sleep in the same room; they attend evening lectures together; they participate in rigorous workouts six days out of every seven. Every part of the training of the unit is geared toward duplicating the real-life situations the blind person and Guide Dog will encounter on their home territory.

Practice sessions take place in office buildings where students and dogs use revolving doors, elevators, and stairs. Visits to shopping malls and shopping districts of towns and cities are part of the schedule. A real test of the unit's abilities takes place in San Francisco's winding Chinatown district abounding with pedestrians, automobiles, fresh fish, meats and produce. The smells and sights alone would be enough to distract the most aloof dog.

One of the more difficult things the student must learn is to give the dog a correction. The corrections are performed by a sharp jerk on the leash which is connected to a specially designed safety choke collar. The links of the collar are made in a way that allows the handler to give a firm but humane correction.

There is a natural hesitancy on the part of some students when it is necessary to make a correction. The physical correction must be coordinated with a firm "No," and succeeded by the proper command. Praise must always follow a properly executed command.

Other students are reticent in giving praise to the dog. For some blind people the Guide Dog is their first canine contact and they must learn a whole new relationship system in addition to learning all that is specific to using a dog guide.

The "how to's" of relationship-building are clearly outlined to the students throughout the month-long course at the Guide Dog school. Lectures on grooming, dog care, and features of the Guide Dog program are part of the regimen. But the fine-tuning of the person-dog unit is a progressive endeavor that will continue for the working life of the dog.

The dog, as a guide, has a clearly defined role to perform. That part of the program can be planned and studied and adjusted. The dog *guide* part of the human-animal bond can, to a large degree, be controlled by the programs that provide this service. But the part of the blind person-Guide Dog relationship that is limited only by individual enthusiasm and concern, is the part that is simply person and dog. It is here that the two can remain a highly-effective, safe-traveling unit, or they can go beyond that and become the best of friends.

With so much to learn in the month-long course at the Guide Dog school it is not possible for the person-dog unit to reach its full potential during that time. The school staff advises students that it generally takes six months for both sides of the unit to fully adjust as a team.

At the end of the course Guide Dogs for the Blind has an informal graduation ceremony. Not all dog guide schools do this but at Guide Dogs for the Blind the feeling is that the graduation gives all those involved in the creation of the person-dog unit a sense of completeness and readiness. The graduation is not so much a way of saying goodbye as it is a way of acknowledging a beginning.

The person who raised the student's dog as a puppy is invited to attend the ceremony to make the official presentation of the dog to the graduate. Does the dog remember its raiser? Of course it does. There is great jubilation when the two meet. But despite the deluge of dog kisses and the beat of a wagging tail when it is reunited with the person who raised it, the dog moves back and forth between old friend and new partner as if to say, "I'm so glad to see my old friend but I know I've got an important job to do." This meeting helps the blind person to understand a little more of his or her dog's background. It shows the blind person the history of love that has gone in to making his or her Guide Dog.

Families of the raiser and the student are welcome at this event as are members of the public. Alumni of the school often return to attend the graduation. And, of course, the instructors and other staff members are present and though they may have been through it many times before, there is always a bittersweet pang as the ceremony closes.

The day after a graduation the cycle begins all over again when new students arrive at the Guide Dog campus to receive and train with Guide Dogs. But those students who have graduated and gone back to homes and jobs and schools are not forgotten or ignored. The Guide Dog school is one of the few that has an extensive follow-up program that includes a visit to each of its graduates at least once a year. If the graduate needs special help, such as learning new routes after moving, the school will send a member of its training staff to assist the graduate. In a one-year period alone, Guide Dog staffers logged over 400,000 miles in travel to visit graduates across the U.S. and Canada.

Many graduates keep the school informed of their activities through letters, Christmas cards, newspaper clippings and photographs. The vast majority of the news is good. The Guide Dogs are leading their blind partners to offices, laboratories, restaurants, libraries, department stores, supermarkets, parks and beaches all across North America. Guide Dogs can be found at newspaper copy desks, in law firms, at counseling centers, beside computer terminals, by teachers' desks and at a variety of other business locations.

The dog, by itself, does not change a blind person's life. It is the blind person who decides to make the changes that include the use of a dog guide. There are many blind people who lead full, useful and happy lives without a dog guide. The dog guide is not the only answer for an individual seeking a mobility tool. And for a few people who obtain dog guides, the dog can create problems that did not surface earlier.

There are cases of married people who trained with a dog guide and returned home to discover that the spouse could not accept the partner's new increased mobility. One sighted partner of a guide user complained, "She's always out. I never get to see her any more."

For other people the dog guide becomes the object of jealousy. The praising, grooming and attention that the guide user must shower on the animal gets misinterpreted. It is seen not as a necessary part of the dog's support system but as an emotional overindulgence that detracts from relationships with human friends and family members.

The dog guide that was meant to *add* to the blind person's life can end up in the position of *taking* from that life by forcing the user to choose between friend, husband, wife or dog. It has happened. And the choices have gone both ways.

The majority of the dog guide users, however, are committed to life with their new mobility tool. So committed, in fact, that many of them return to the school several times to train with replacement dogs as their old guides die or retire. The working life of a dog guide is about eight to 10 years. The retired dog may live as a pet dog with its blind master or mistress, or it may go back to live with the family that raised it. The decision to retire a dog and train with a new one is almost more difficult for a blind person to make than was the original decision to become a dog guide user. It is impossible not to make comparisons, not to feel sad about working a new dog while the old one stays at home. But having experienced life with a guide, it is a rare individual who opts for life without one.

The dog guide is a special "breed," indeed. More than a pet, it falls into that area that was once the territory of early dog. It reminds one of the dog that came to man's campfire and refused to leave—the dog that showed man they could think, act, work and live better together than they could apart. The dog guide with all of its marvelous senses and patient dignity seems to say, "Use what I am to make your life a little better." It may not be the perfect solution but ask any dog guide user just how wonderful imperfection can be.

Dog Guide Programs In The United States

GUIDE DOGS FOR THE BLIND, INC.
P.O. Box 1200
San Rafael, CA 94915 — 415-479-4000

GUIDE DOGS OF THE DESERT
P.O. Box 1692
Palm Springs, CA 92262 — 714-329-8998

INTERNATIONAL GUIDING EYES, INC.
13445 Glenoaks Blvd.
Sylmar, CA 91342 — 213-362-5834

FIDELCO GUIDE DOGS
P.O. Box 142
Bloomfield, CT 06002 — 302-243-5200

EYE OF THE PACIFIC AND MOBILITY SERVICES, INC.
2723 Woodlawn Drive
Honolulu, HI 96822 — 808-988-6681

LEADER DOGS FOR THE BLIND
1039 Rochester Road
Rochester, MI 48063 — 313-651-9011

THE SEEING EYE, INC.
P.O. Box 375
Morristown, NJ 07960 — 201-539-4425

GUIDE DOG FOUNDATION FOR THE BLIND, INC.
371 E. Jericho Turnpike
Smithtown, NY 11787 — 516-265-2121

GUIDING EYES FOR THE BLIND, INC.
Yorktown Heights, NY 11375 — 914-245-4024

PILOT DOGS, INC.
625 West Town Street
Columbus, OH 43215 — 614-221-6367

Suggested reading:

Coon, Nelson *A Brief History of Dog Guides for the Blind.* Morristown, N.J.: The Seeing Eye, Inc., 1959.

Hartwell, Dickson *Dogs Against Darkness.* New York: Dodd Mead & Company, 1942.

Gibbs, Margaret *Leader Dogs for the Blind.* Fairfax, Va.: Denlinger's Publishers, Ltd., 1982.

Curtis, Patricia *Greff: The Story of a Guide Dog.* New York: Lodestar Books, E.P. Dutton, 1982.

Rappaport, Eva *"Banner, Forward!"* New York, E.P. Dutton, 1969.

9

Companion Animals for the Handicapped

Bonita M. Bergin

"Life can still be positive despite limitation..."

Did you know there are over 21.9 million people in the United States with a disabling condition? Of those:

... over 1.6 million people have a disability involving deafness or serious hearing impairment.

... over 3.5 million people have a disability involving loss or lack of physical mobility.

... over 5.5 million people have a disability involving blindness or serious visual impairment.

Did you know dogs have been working for and with man in varying capacities for 15,000 years, and they derive personal pleasure and satisfaction from that working relationship? These roles have included:

... hunting with man by tracking prey, pointing out and retrieving game, and herding livestock.

... guarding hearth and home, working with police and local law enforcement agencies, sniffing out narcotics, participating in search and rescue operations, and leading the blind.

Did you know the canine's role has now been expanded to embrace the needs of a still larger segment of the disabled population? This includes:

... the physically disabled in wheelchairs who are now being pulled long distances and up inclines and ramps formerly too difficult for them to traverse, having items they dropped and cannot reach picked up and given to them, having lights they are unable to reach turned on and off for them,

Bonita Bergin, founder and executive Director of Canine Companions for Independence, conceived and pioneered the Service Dog concept to train special dogs to assist people with disabilities to live independent lives. She holds an M.A. in early childhood and special education from Sonoma State University and is a doctoral candidate in education at Nova University. Based in Santa Rosa, Calif,. CCI has placed hundreds of dogs in the U.S. and several foreign countries.

and having "new doors" literally and figuratively opened for them by this unique and dedicated servant, the dog.

...the deaf and hearing-impaired who are being alerted to sounds in their environment such as the doorbell, the smoke or fire alarm, a baby's cry, and other daily-living or lifesaving sounds they are unable to hear.

...the elderly and convalescing, the retarded and autistic, the mentally and emotionally disadvantaged, whose recovery is hastened through an interaction known as "pet-facilitated therapy"

...the elderly and convalescing who are being given new reason to live; the retarded and autistic who are improving IQ levels and reaching out to connect with a world they left behind; the mentally and emotionally disadvantaged who are finding barriers lifted and new social interactions available with the dog working as a classroom or nurse's aide, co-therapist, or friend.

For thousands of years dogs have had a serious working role in hunter-gatherer and agrarian societies. Gradually, after World War I, their role was reduced to family and house pet. "Elevated" to a family and house pet, some would say, and many would agree with this perspective. However, those intimately involved with the canine's physical and psychological makeup may tend to support the contention that dogs lost a portion of the respect and appreciation formally held by them in a society whose need for their services placed them prominently in the forefront of the community of animal workers.

While the former traditional role and need for the dog began its decline, another concept began to grow. In the late 1920's in Germany, a program evolved that began to train German shepherd dogs to work as guides for the blinded veterans of World War I. An American living in Europe at that time, Dorothy Eustis, brought that concept to this country, and with the valuable assistance of Morris Frank and Jack Humphries, developed Morristown, New Jersey's Seeing Eye program, the first formalized dog guide program of its type in the United States. Other programs followed, and the dog became recognized for its versatility and usefulness to the visually impaired population of this country. *(See Chapter 8)*

For several years the canine's adaptability to serve the disabled population in capacities other than dog guides for the blind was limited to the creative use by individuals in their own home setting. But in 1975, the Minnesota Society for the Prevention of Cruelty began an involvement which created a new working role for the canine, by training dogs to act as the ears of deaf persons. The specific origins of the hearing dog concept can be traced to a call from a deaf woman in Minnesota to a local radio station. True to its nature her dog had adapted itself to accommodate her disability by letting her know when sounds in the household were occurring. When her dog was killed, she asked the radio station over the air for knowledge of any formal schools that trained dogs for the deaf and hearing-impaired. The director of the Minnesota Humane Society was made aware of this need and took up the challenge by assigning a staff person, Agnes McGrath, to develop a feasibility study on the implementation of such a program.

The year 1975 was spent developing the concept of the hearing dog, at which time it became evident that real success could be achieved. As demand for trained dogs increased, the Minnesota organization questioned its own ability to continue a high level involvement, and in 1976 the American Humane Association (AHA) adopted the program and moved it out to Colorado. Prominent implementations followed with the AHA devising ways to meet the needs of the deaf community while also finding homes for abandoned and abused animals.

From 1976 to early 1983, the AHA continued its valuable contribution to the development of a program to train rescued dogs to alert the deaf to critical sounds. As the AHA worked to develop these concepts, it collaborated closely with SPCAs and other humane programs around the country to coordinate efforts and foster the work throughout the United States. Of late, this organization, which had spent several years developing and promoting the concept of the training of rescued, shellter animals for this exciting and useful role, has backed out of the formal training process to act as a clearinghouse and an information and retrieval center for the many programs in effect all across the United States. AHA has recently published a summary of legal rights of dog guides for the deaf. *(See Chapter 7)*

As the Minnesota program struggled to develop the concept of using rescued dogs to work with deaf and hearing-impaired individuals, a different program in California was also being born. This program took the fledgling concept of dogs working for the deaf and began to expand it by exploring all breeds from around the world to find an animal that had the natural abilities for the type of work involved, thus making use of the dog's instinctive behaviors to work toward a higher rate of success and lessen the need for follow-ups and heavy retraining.

This program, Canine Companions for Independence (CCI), had as its birthplace a lecture hall in a master's program in early childhoood special education. As founder and executive director of Canine Companions for Independence, I conceived the idea of training dogs to help the physically disabled become more independent while participating in discussions concerning the plight of the disabled population during master's degree coursework at Sonoma State University. The obvious needs and less obvious abilities of this special population became an issue in these class discussions, which so often centered around concepts of what housing facilities and meal planning services could best help improve the quality of life for these individuals. Having witnessed numerous incidents in Asia of individuals with these same disabilities forced through the economic and social fabric of the country into finding a means to "do for themselves," I found myself mentally searching for ways to facilitate this group's ability to further its own independence and achieve an economic role in our society.

The memory that kept coming to mind was of viewing, from a rooftop restaurant in Ankara, Turkey, a man dressed in a business suit, dragging his entire body down a sidewalk in the modern business center of the city,

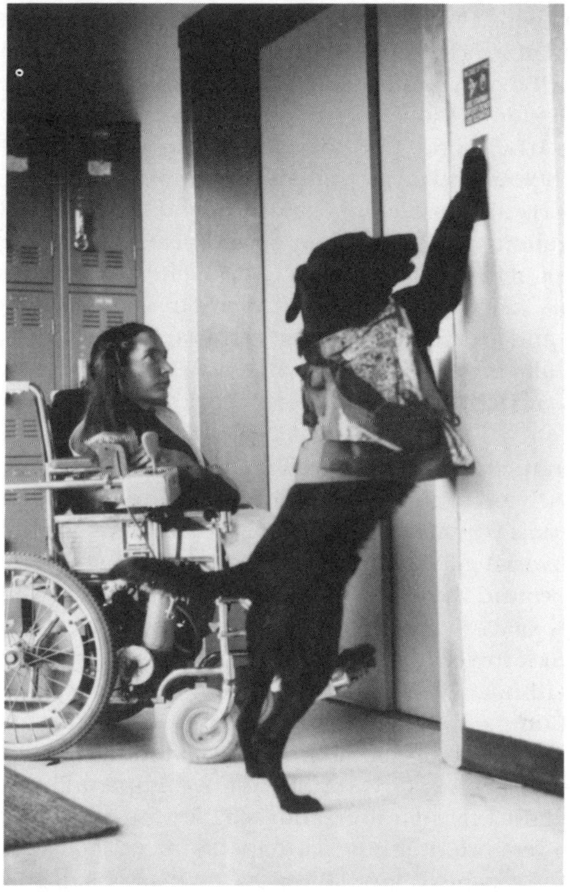

Abdul, first service dog for Canine Companions for Independence, provides many unique services and opportunities for Kerry Knaus. In addition to tasks, Abdul brought her companionship and self-confidence.

across a six-lane freeway, propelling himself with his elbows and hips, making every part of his usable body function to get to where he was going. That memory, coupled with numerous experiences of donkeys and burros carrying wares to be sold on street corners, supporting the weight of disabled individuals while progressing slowly down the dirt roads to their assigned spots, solidified the germination of the idea to develop a way to help the disabled population to do for themselves and to make use of their own capabilities with other people simply providing them the means to do it, not doing it for them. Obviously donkeys and burros would not meet our country's health standards, but a dog could. Thus was born the concept of CCI and the Service dog.

The initial months of 1975 were spent studying and researching the feasibility of a program of this type and searching for suitable breeding stock with desirable temperaments, tractability, and the necessary physical qualifications for the work involved. Much time was also put into the need for a prescribed program of puppy rearing so that the "optimum" Canine Companion would result. Simultaneously, an intensive study of dog training under several renowned trainers was begun until enough knowledge had been gained to teach a dog to serve as a Canine Companion to a disabled individual.

Working with the knowledge of the completed master's course work and the dog training experience, the next step was to develop a program that would meet these goals and objectives. It was decided that the disabled participant should take part in the training of the dog for two reasons: first, there was no facility in which to raise and train such a dog, and second, by participating, the disabled individual would benefit from the experience and knowledge gained so that at a future time, more training could be put on the dog by the participant as the need arose. This plan turned out to be successful in many ways, both anticipated and not; however, certain drawbacks were encountered. At this time the program trains dogs on the present facility site, then places them with the disabled participants.

Over a period of two years' training time with sessions at regular intervals, Kerry Knaus, the first participant, whose disability is so severe that she has only minimal hand movement, learned to be in complete control of her dog, Abdul. Abdul, in turn, has been trained to open the doors of a variety of elevators Kerry is physically unable to reach herself. He turns lights on and off for her, carries a pack which allows her to reach her materials without the aid of an attendant, and picks up things she drops or needs and brings them to her on command. He turns on the heater in a van she acquired. Abdul also attended college classes with her, carrying her supplies, and at one point, made it possible for her to go to work in a building that was not accessible by learning to operate the touch sensor elevator button. Her confidence and self-esteem having grown with the success of his training, it became apparent just how useful Abdul would be to her.

In addition to the tasks that Abdul did for Kerry, he brought her a companionship and confidence to be home alone and to go places by herself. Her life opened up to one of assertive interaction rather than passive acceptance of a disability that need not limit the scope of her involvement in activities. This unanticipated value is best expressed by the many changes in Kerry herself, who says, "I used to look at things and tell myself that I couldn't do them. Now I look at those same things and ask myself how I am going to do them."

As the success with Kerry and Abdul became known, applications for dogs appeared and interest grew, statewide, then nationwide. The Social (pet therapy) dog and Signal (hearing) dog were added to the program. Many individuals throughout the state volunteered to help train. With the limited resources available to CCI at that time, it was impossible to institute a full-fledged volunteer training program; thus, only individuals with extensive dog training experience were utilized. These AKC obedience judges and licensed trainers found their lack of experience with disabilities to be a severe deficiency and their volunteer status did not allow for the heavy demands that were made upon them by participants during the initial stages of the training. CCI responded to these problems by drawing back to a small physical area with a core group of volunteer and paid trainers in order to be more easily managed. At that time a plan was implemented to train the Canine Companion Service, Signal, and Social dogs at the newly established training center before placing them with their disabled partner.

Since its birth in 1975, CCI has virtually outgrown its 4,000 square-foot facility in Santa Rosa, Calif. which houses 50 adult dogs preparing for the intensive two-week "boot camp" prior to each quarterly graduation ceremony. The willingness and excitement these dogs feel as they couple up with their new partners is equalled only by the staff's and the participant's excitement at stepping into the relatively new and thrilling experience of pioneering an independence provided through the dynamic relationships of dog and man.

Service Dogs: Arms and legs for the disabled

This newly created concept of a dog working to increase the physical mobility of someone in a wheelchair or on crutches, to increase the independent living skills of paraplegics and quadraplegics, has caused the need for a whole new set of tasks and commands to be put together to produce the quality performance the canine is capable of achieving. The Service dogs are trained to fetch and return dropped or needed items, and to pull wheelchairs distances the disabled participant is incapable of attaining in a timely manner, as well as up ramps, inclines, curb cuts and, for the more adventurous, curbs themselves. These amazing dogs also turn lights on and off, open elevator doors, hand paperwork to tellers and receptionists, carry materials and supplies in a reachable position in a specially designed backpack, pick grocery items off the shelves, and act as an extension of limb for those individuals with little or no arm movement.

As if that were not enough, these dogs also protect the physically immobile person when needed. They supply the warmth and friendship so lacking from a society when one's body structure is not of the norm, and give the average man on the street a reason or an excuse to make contact with the disabled minority via the dog, a contact that is educational and beneficial to both the disabled individual and the society of able-bodied people. For disabled persons to be casually included in a street-corner conversation puts them in touch with and makes them recognized as bona fide members of this culture. For the able-bodied community, an awareness is developed that life can still be a positive and fruitful experience despite limitations put upon one's physical body, a condition that so frequently mars the aging process as paralysis suddenly requires the care and manipulation of others—independence of choice and activity having literally flown out the window. The Service dog provides what the weakened limbs cannot: a way to go out, to do things that would normally require the presence of another person to accomplish, the ability to continue to do things and go places, and to be an equal in a society which demands movement for survival and acceptance.

Canine Companions for Independence, in researching and experimenting with this concept, has settled on five basic breeds for the Service dog, though we continue to try new breeds at the rate of two a year with the intent of locating other capable breed types with the necessary qualities. Presently the core breeds used in the program are: German shepherds, golden retrievers. Labrador retrievers, smooth-coated collies, and Dobermans. Evaluative criteria for breed selection include: size, temperament, tractability, enthusiasm, willingness, freedom from common faults such as hip and elbow dysplasia (common in most large dogs), wet mouths, back problems, proneness to bloat, hereditary visual impairments, skin allergies, and other genetic problems. The animals cannot require excessive grooming or other care which would be difficult for the disabled participant to do or would become burdensome to have done. However, in single instances, standard poodles have been used with disabled participants who need the hyperallergenic coat and the unique workmanship they have to offer.

Since their inception in 1975, Service dogs have received the same rights as guide dogs in California, North Dakota, Arizona, Alaska, New Jersey and Nevada. Other states are making rapid advances in updating their legislation to meet the growing demand for legal rights assigned to these valuable workers, as more and more individuals across the nation acquire a Service dog. In 1979, a young American exchange student's Service dog gained admittance to Sweden as a "handicapped dog" and was able to avoid the long quarantine required upon entrance to the country.

Signal Dogs: Ears for the deaf

Signal hearing dogs have gained more acceptance across the United States in direct proportion to the number of programs producing these dogs for hearing-impaired and profoundly deaf individuals. The worth of this dog cannot be over-rated in terms of the valued changes it makes in the lives of individuals with this disablity. Deafness is sometimes thought of as

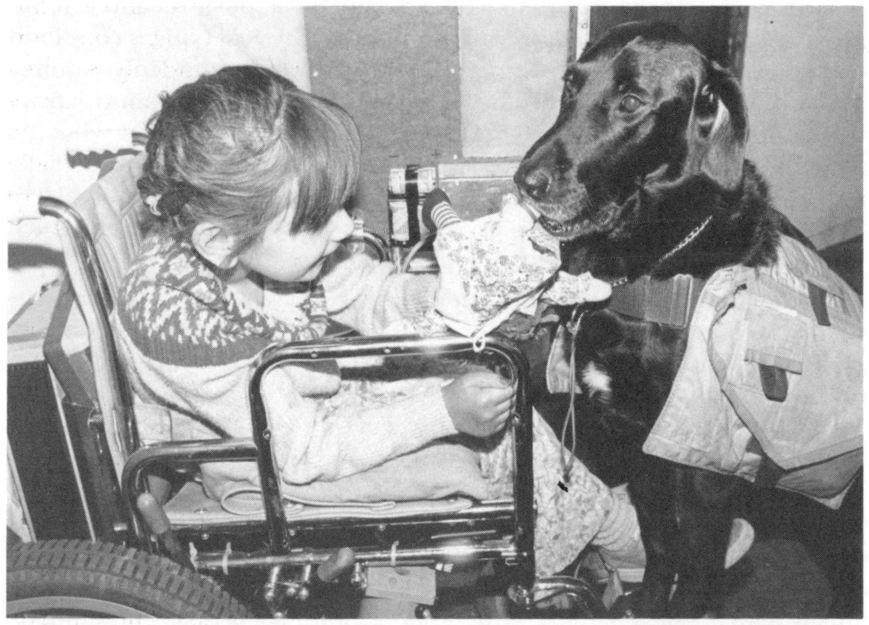

Service dogs provide many unique services to their masters—including picking up a doll for a disabled child. *(Photo by Ron Dickey)*

the most critical of all disabilites because those involved are not immediately recognizable. Thus, in many instances these individuals lack a following of knowledgeable people who empathize with their plight. At the same time, these people are often cut off from main sources of cultural interaction, social contact, sharing, and love. Divorced from this most important communicational mode, essentially set apart from people and society, the kinship and intimacy that is shared with a dog reduces the isolation, helping erase the alienation, paranoia, and resulting social indifference.

Living in a world devoid of sound, experiencing reduced social contacts, and facing the notable psychological problems of hearing impairment, places individuals with this disability in a direct line for the "pet therapeutic" function imbedded within the terms Signal/Hearing dog. These animals add a completeness to the lives of the aurally impaired by giving and receiving the love and companionship that help to establish and maintain a perspective for human interaction, in addition to alerting them to necessary sounds in the environment. Not only are deaf and hearing-impaired individuals now able to experience and respond to these everyday sounds, such as the doorbell, the crying baby, or the smoke alarm, but they can sleep soundly knowing that their Signal/Hearing dog will bounce them out of bed in the morning with a cheerful lick and a tail wag. For those with partial hearing loss, sounds such as the telephone are of a pitch not easily discerned. Their Signal/Hearing dog enables them to maintain the normalcy of everyday existence in both the work and home environments.

Some of the Signal/Hearing dog programs across the country require that the dogs pick up anything that is dropped by deaf participants (such as a set of keys) since they are unable to hear the item drop and the loss might pass unnoticed otherwise. Many of the programs training hearing dogs have added their own special flavor to the concept. For example, some programs are training dogs belonging to the deaf individual, while others, following the AHA's lead, are rescuing dogs from shelters, training them, and placing them with hearing-impaired persons. Canine Companions for Independence to date is the only program breeding carefully selected stock for the role, though other programs are considering this as a possiblity.

Probably the most significant characteristics thought to make a good Signal/Hearing dog are its eagerness and enthusiasm, high-level response to food, and qualities of endurance. Food, playing, and love are the most common reward systems used to reinforce the work role, but each program has its own specialized techniques and methods. The American

Humane Association is planning to put together a pamphlet of training methods for individuals and programs wishing to prepare Signal/Hearing dogs for the deaf community. A common denominator felt by most programs are the needs for the deaf and hearing-impaired participant to do follow-ups and continued training of the dog to insure that the animal's response to the sound is ongoing and consistent in nature.

Canine Companions for Independence has, at present, identified three breeds for Signal work, though the program continues to explore other breeds for traits and abilities which will help to decrease the need for follow-ups and continual training. The schipperke, Pembroke Welsh corgi, and the border collie have shown themselves to have the talent to respond consistently and eagerly to sounds in the environment and the desire to share that information with the home inhabitants. Unfortunately, as with all work of this type, it is necessary to take into consideration not just the breed but the lines within the breed and individual temperaments. Other breeds suitable for this work will be considered at such time as the difficulties involved in coat care or health problems within the breed are resolved. A most exciting aspect of breeding for this work is the ability to continually improve the stock in training. However, much can and has been said about the immense value of using rescued dogs from shelters. Statistics have shown that a full quarter of all puppies adopted as pets by the American public get returned to shelters or abandoned on country roads because they have become a problem in the home as they become "teen-agers." The need for programs to train and place these newly "mature and responsible" dogs with a public thirsting for well-behaved dogs is critical, and programs such as the AHA's Hearing Dog program do just that.

Social Dogs: Companions for the lonely

Social dogs, well-known for their roles in the human/companion animal bond concept of "pet-facilitated therapy," bridge the gap between a limited mind or limited body and the external world. Through their loving, non-judgmental interaction, these dogs share the joy of life and love with individuals who have rejected the world or feel that the world has rejected them. These specialized animals work with the retarded and autistic, the elderly and convalescing, the mentally and emotionally impaired, and the institutionalized. They provide general socialization, stimulating conversation or physical activity for those involved. Acting as a valuable link in the lives of lonely people, the Social dog shares those minutes, hours, and days in a complete and sincerely companionable way. By interacting and providing a loving warmth and trusting devotion, these dogs help give a reason for living to those who have lost the will to live, while extending purpose and direction to those who have begun to feel useless in their declining years.

The training of these wonder-furry additions to the lives of many who are seeking a fulfillment not easily derived from the social life of an institution or convalescent hospital is very specialized and differs from program to program. Canine Companions for Independence breeds and trains these dogs on the facility grounds and places them in schools, institutions, convalescent hospitals, and group homes. The particular breed in use differs with the setting; generally, a standard poodle is used in

Service dogs protect the physically immobile person and supply the warmth and friendship often lacking in society. They also give the average person on the street an excuse to make contact with the disabled minority.

nursing homes and convalescent hospitals since there are no problems with shedding and coat allergies. Gregarious, physically tough Labradors are used most frequently in the schools and group homes whose population makeup is predominantly aggressive in nature. Golden retrievers are more frequently used in quieter social settings where their sensitive nature responds to the needs so successfully.

The Canine Companion Social dog goes through as intensive a training program as Signal and Service dogs, responding to a minimum of 75 single or combined commands. When told to "say hello," the Social dog rests its head directly on the lap of the appointed individual to be fondled or just gazed upon. The interaction must be intimate but appropriate to each person's need within a group setting; a variety of commands are employed to assure that these specialized requirements are met. A teacher in a class of developmentally disabled children may ask the Social dog to take a toy over to one youngster or go lie down beside an autistic child whose need for tactile, visual, emotional, or physical stimulation may awaken a long-forgotten experience with human contact or instill a trust and desire for such. The "visit" command in a convalescent hospital sends the dog in to put its front paws on the bed and visit with a bed-ridden patient. The visit and antics of the resident Social dog become the basis of conversation between the patient and a visitor that help "break the ice" and allow conversation to flow smoothly and enthusiastically between grandparent and grandchild, parent and children.

Speech and physical therapy sessions at convalescent hospitals housing a Social dog have chosen to incorporate the dog into these programs. The activity directors and physical therapists have found that much of the difficulties they have had to overcome in involving patients in group sessions is dispelled when the dog is utilized. Speech therapy frequently encourages patients who have simply quit speaking to give commands to the dog and results in a significant rate of response. Physical therapy sessions, both formalized classroom and informal individual activities, involve the patients and dog in throwing, catching and retrieving a ball, pulling with the wheelchair, tug-of-war, walks or simply using the dog as the reward for a specified activity. These dogs also begin to take some responsibility for the patients by acting as caretakers. For example, in one convalescent hospital's physical therapy class, the CCI Social dog began to bark inappropriately. After repeated attempts to quiet the dog, the instructor gave up and went to put the dog outside. However, when she opened the door, she found that a patient had fallen on the other side of the door and was helpless to right herself. The Social dog had only been trying to alert the instructor to the occurrence. All the training in the world could not have guaranteed this animal would have taken the responsibility to make this situation known to that instructor; therefore, it must be noted that the selection of dogs who can make decisions and take responsibility is as much a criterion for developing a successful program as is the training program itself, though a proper course of training can increase the occurrence of incidents such as this.

Dog training is an art as well as a science and not an easy subject to address; however, there are certain commonalities to be found through all programs in the area of dogs working with disabilities. First, it is acknowledged that the dog has to have matured enough to face the responsibilities of its job expectations before being trusted at any significant level to carry out an intensive role. Most dogs mature between the ages of one and three years, with smaller dogs thought of as maturing sooner. Second, four to six months of intensive advanced training seems to be the norm for all programs that have a specific set of commands

Signal dogs are the ears of the deaf, alerting the hearing-impaired to hazards, obstacles, or someone at the door.

requiring mastery. Of course, the number and complexity of the skills involved contribute to that determination. Third, the disabled individual or group care person absolutely must take responsiblity for the animal and its care and feeding, and make certain that it maintains a standard of excellence in the task performance. Fourth, the average working life of the canine trained for these roles seems to be between eight and ten years depending on the breed, age of placement and the activity involved. Thus, a Social dog experiencing aging may be capable of working longer in that setting than a Service dog whose need to pull wheelchairs may be impaired by an increasing arthritic condition.

Specific methods to train these dogs vary from group to group and individual to individual. For example, in training Signal/Hearing dogs, some use a pulley set-up to teach the dog a pattern of response, others have made food treats available with each intersecting pattern, while still others use corrections solely to guide the incorrect responses. Most probably it would be safe to say that a combination approach works best if it is made adaptable to each individual dog in training and geared to that dog's prime motivations. Obviously, each trainer can only truly be successful with a method that he or she believes will work, so leeway must also be available to allow for a trainer's personality as a factor in program success.

The basic training cycle for CCI Social, Service and Signal dogs takes one and one-half to two years, including the first 12 to 15 months the puppies spend in foster homes. Much attention is paid to those early puppy developmental stages from six to 16 weeks of age and a serious monitoring program of puppy classes and carefully designed puppy experiences is an integral part of the program as well. Once returned to the facility for their advanced training, dogs are cared for by volunteer puppy walkers who take over the intense and vital job of exposing these pups to any outside elements that could be misconstrued by the young dogs as a distraction. The dogs then move fluidly into the five-day-a-week intensive training program in preparation for placement as a Service, Signal or Social dog.

As graduation draws near, carefully screened and interviewed applicants arrive for their two-week-long intensive work session held at the facility. At that time, a determination is made suitably matching participants and Canine Companions, with personalities, working capabilities, needs and life styles taken into account. At the completion of the two-week core program, each pair is ready to start a life together which CCI monitors at regular intervals with evaluation forms and visits. When necessary, a training team is sent in to assess and revamp problem areas, though the intent is to prepare the participants to trouble shoot and be capable of reinforcing or retraining whenever necessary. The majority of participants experience a growth in self-confidence and self-worth as they assimilate the necessary skills required to successfully work with their dogs.

Over the years since the role of the canine in aiding the disabled has expanded, many programs have been developing certain specialized approaches to fulfilling the needs of the disabled community, as more and more people become aware of the endless possiblities available through a partnership with the canine. In New Jersey, for example, Therapy Dogs International has developed a program which certifies dogs to work in a pet-therapeutic role. Chapter affiliations are available with memberships nationwide. This program allows motivated individuals with well-trained pets to gain certification attesting to their team workmanship as qualified to make visits with their pets to convalescent hospitals and other social settings. These dogs work primarily in a "social" role in the numerous institutions and nursing homes that they voluntarily visit. Programs of this type give a formal structure and encourage the lay person with a good heart and a desire to make a difference to make these visits which mean so much to the confined.

Handi-dogs of Tucson, Ariz., represents a totally different approach. It specializes in teaching the disabled to train their own dogs rather than having a third party do the training. The goals of the program include providing dog obedience classes for the deaf, disabled, and senior citizens who may have some difficulty in dog club obedience classes. Handi-dogs teaches special exercises that will make the dogs more useful to their owners, such as picking up dropped objects, and it works to make the sporting aspect of dog obedience available to the disabled.

All this wonderful work is not limited to the dog, however. For example, Canine Companions is experimenting with cats in convalescent hospitals and nursing homes to reach the needs of "cat" people who have spent a lifetime receiving enjoyment and stimulation from the feline species. The visual stimulation from such a placement should provide a touch of home welcomed by that segment of the convalescing society, while providing a form of pet therapy to those places with neither the means nor ability to sanction a canine.

Programs that continue to grow in success and value include horseback riding for the physically disabled, putting individuals with limited mobility on a horse who happily moves for them. These programs are now gaining such acceptance that rescued horses are being donated to continue this marvelous work, as well as tried and true top-notch working or show quality horses whose age and body can no longer handle the intensity of trail or competitive forms of exercise. The thrill of being on the back of the strong, willing animal that conquered the West leaves a sense of well-being that flows through the veins for days on end. *(See Chapter 12)*

It is impossible to note all the worthwhile and exciting programs making significant contributions to human society. Excellent ones have undoubtedly been overlooked. Many come and go while trying to meet the needs of their target population financially and physically. Funding difficulties abound with major income sources being individual donations, group and service club contributions, memberships, foundation and corporation grants, and fund-raising activities. At present there are no national or local evaluative measures which rate quality or accredit these programs (except for equestrian therapy activities). Potential information sources regarding programs include disabled groups and independent living centers, dog clubs, and local human services agencies and humane societies.

Along with the physical assistance these specially trained animals provide disabled individuals comes an added confidence which encourages them to move into new areas. This confidence helps these

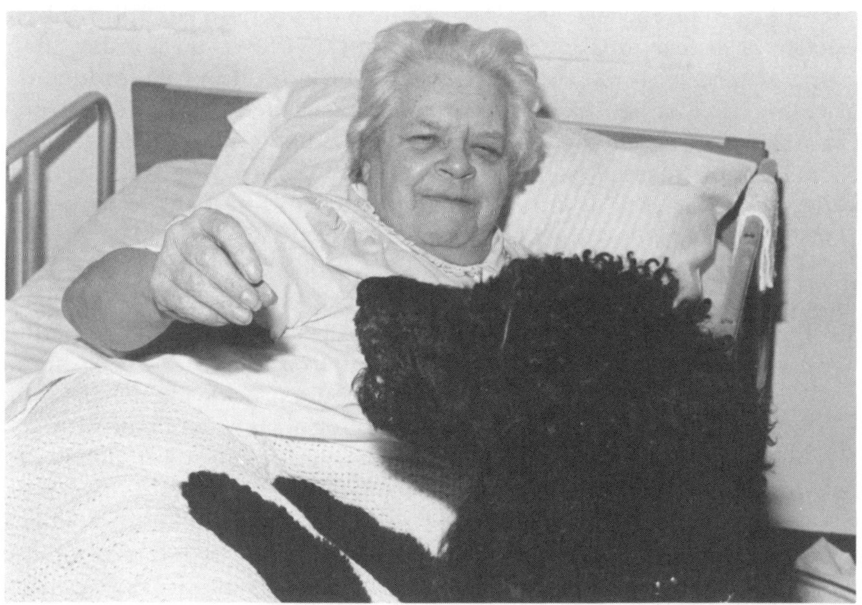

Social dogs, like "Lora," visit the bed-ridden elderly. They share the joys of life and love with persons who have rejected the world or who feel the world has rejected them. *(Photo by Ron Dickey)*

people take part in vocational training and jobs, reducing the cost of financial support from government sources.

There is little that awakens one's appreciation of life more than seeing someone who would otherwise have little or no hope of making a significant contribution to life able to go to work, to live alone, to interact on a peer level with able-bodied individuals and to truly feel and be a part of life. Having a specially trained dog allows the disabled population to depend more completely on themselves for those critical life needs and enables them to be in a position to share with and care for others.

Directory of Training Centers For Dogs Helping the Hearing-Impaired and Physically-Limited

American Humane Association Hearing Dog Program — (303) 695-0811
9725 E. Hampden Ave.
Denver, Colo. 80231

Applegate Behavior Station — (503) 899-7177
13260 Highway 238
Jacksonville, Ore. 97530

Assistance Dogs International
527 Madison Ave.
New York, N.Y. 10022

Audio Canes, Inc., Training School — (313) 352-0997
Box 1185
Berkley, Mich. 48072

Canine Companions for Independence — (707) 528-0830
P.O. Box 446
Santa Rosa, Calif. 95401

E.A.R. Foundation — (615) 327-4870
Baptist Hospital - West Building
2000 Church St.
Nashville, Tenn. 37236

Ears for the Deaf — (616) 455-2537
P.O. Box 8482
Kentwood, Mich. 49508

Feeling Heart Foundation — (301) 228-3689
RFD 2, Box 354
Cambridge, Md. 21613

Great Lakes Hearing Dog Program — (414) 463-8300 VOICE
5800 North Lovers Land Rd. — (414) 463-1990 TTY
Milwaukee, Wis. 53225

Handi-Dogs — (602) 326-3412
P.O. Box 12563
Tucson, Ariz. 85732

Hearing Dog, Inc. — (303) 287-3277
5901 East 89th Ave.
Henderson, Colo. 80640

Hearing Dog of Columbus, Inc. (614) 471-7397
c/o Mrs. Mary Jane Stickdale
290 North Hamilton
Gahanna, Ohio 43230

Hearing Dog for the Deaf (616) 468-6154
6940 48th St.
Coloma, Mich. 49038

Hearing Ear Dog Program (617) 829-9745
c/o Bryant Hill Farm
76 Bryant Rd.
Jefferson, Mass. 01522

Red Acre Farm Hearing Dog Center (617) 897-5370 VOICE
Box 278 (617) 897-8343 VOICE/TTY
109 Red Acre Rd.
Stow, Mass. 01775

Residential Dogs
2716 Community Park Drive
Matthews, N.C. 28105

San Francisco SPCA Hearing Dog Program (415) 621-1700 VOICE
2500 Sixteenth St. (415) 621-2174 VOICE/TTY
San Francisco, Calif. 94103

Support Dogs for the Handicapped (614) 878 2127
6901 Harrisburg Pike
Orient, OH 43146 - 9409

Therapy Dogs International (201) 968-0086
1536 Morris Place
Hillside, N.J. 07205

Other Training Programs

Helping Hands: Simian Aides for the Disabled (212) 430-9230
(Capuchin monkeys trained to help quadriplegics)
2425 Kingsland Ave.
New York, N.Y. 10469

10

Companion Animals for the Elderly

Dan Lago and Barbara Knight

"...part of a comprehensive service system..."

Introduction

Her face was buried in the ruff of Jody's neck. She looked up at me, her face beaming and said, "This idea of giving pets to old people is wonderful. I don't know what I would have done without Jody." I snapped her picture then with Jody in her lap, the sun in her smiling face, her fingers wrapped in the dog's fur. It's a warm and compelling image and one that most of us share when we think of pets and the elderly. This image works at an emotional level, rather than a rational one; and we tend to see what we want when we see an older person with a pet, rather than accurately judge from the person and animal's actual behavior just how satisfactory the relationship is.

Much of the power of this image comes from the symbolic pairing of two major sources of personal ambivalence and fear in this culture. Both the elderly and pets are overwhelming us with sheer numbers. Both the elderly and pet animals are loved and honored in the abstract, but are often poorly treated by the hard priorities of scarce resources. We are often

Dan Lago, Ph.D., is assistant professor of human development and assistant director of the Gerontology Center at the Pennsylvania State University. Barbara Knight, MPSS, is on the staff of the Gerontology Center at West Virginia University. Since 1980 they have directed a demonstration research project to place pets with the elderly and to document the effects of pets on the elderly's health and well-being. As part of that program they established PACT (People and Animals Coming Together), a non-profit organization devoted to supporting responsible pet ownership among the elderly, which won a national Model Program Award.

forced by both pets and the elderly to accept that we are powerless to significantly change the basic conditions we encounter. Our fear of death, often preceded by extensive pain and suffering, is the cultural bedrock that connects pets and the elderly. We seek a moment of happiness and pleasure in viewing the relatively grim future most of us see for the elderly (including ourselves) and for homeless pets. In a sense, we cling to the image of a happy elder and happy pet to reassure ourselves more than we rationally consider helping an older individual or specific pet.

To be sure, there is growing evidence and practical experience to demonstrate that pets can have an extremely beneficial impact on the lives of certain older persons. However, a rational approach consistent with professional human services models will, in the long run, be more effective in integrating pets into the health and social care systems for older persons. Until the benefits that pets can provide and the means by which those goals are to be achieved in a reliable fashion can be documented, the interest in pets will remain a volunteer adjunct rather than an integral part of comprehensive services for the elderly. It is the purpose of this chapter to outline briefly the demographic changes associated with our aging population and their implications for animal programming and to describe some of the common needs of the elderly and the extent to which those needs can potentially be met by animal companionship programs. Finally, we suggest the variability of the roles that pets may play in the lives of older persons and how those differences and changes ought to be considered in developing programs using pets with older persons. This chapter, while providing some generalizations about the elderly and the relationships of pets with the elderly, urges an individualized functional assessment approach in considering pet interventions with a given older person.

Demographic changes

The United States and most Western cultures are categorized by the United Nations as "aged societies," since greater than 7% of our populations are over age 65. In 1900, people over 65 accounted for only 4% of the United States' population, whereas in 1980 the elderly accounted for over 11% of the total population. With over 24 years of average life expectancy being added for all persons at birth, this century has seen greater increases in average expected lifespan than in the previous 19 centuries combined. An increased standard of living and reduction in infant mortality are usually cited as the primary reasons for our increased probability of living to a ripe old age.

This increase in the aging population has been accompanied by two other demographic trends of interest. First, urbanization, the growing centralization of people in cities and suburbs rather than on farms where the majority of the population traditionally lived, has occurred. Along with the departure from the farms and frequent working contacts with animals, there has been an explosion in pet keeping. While urban and suburban living arrangements clearly discourage certain kinds of animal husbandry, pet keeping has grown to be a basic aspect of American family culture. This trend, coupled with casual ownership practices, has resulted in huge populations of dogs, cats, and other animals throughout America, and in the public health and safety problems arising out of pet ownership. Thus, in the last 80 years we have seen explosions in the elderly population and in the animal population, increasingly within an urbanized setting.

Pet ownership and interest in pets varies greatly with geographic

The vast majority of the elderly live in their own homes. While concerns over pets in health care facilities are valid, the largest group of pet owners reside in the community. *(Photo by Dave Rains)*

regions. Several studies have documented pet ownership rates among the elderly between approximately 10% in urban settings and approximately 30% in rural areas. Several local surveys of public housing residents have indicated that approximately 15% of residents of a given public housing project would want to own pets if they were permittted.

Sex differences are also important when estimating the effects of these demographic changes, with women living an average of approximately eight years longer than men. More and more we are dealing with larger and larger groups of very aged women. (The average age of widowhood in the USA is age 56. By age 75 over three-quarters of older women are widowed.) For people who have traditionally lived alone, and for widowed persons, the preferred living arrangement is to keep their own home, to live independently as long as possible. At the present time over 42% of elderly women live alone. This trend has been increasing for the last 15 years and is expected to continue.

Approximately 5% of the elderly are institutionalized in nursing homes or long-stay hospitals. An additional 4% of the elderly live in special public group housing for the elderly or handicapped. The vast majority of elderly live in their own homes or apartments within the community. Therefore, while concerns over pets in institutionalized settings and public housing are valid, it is obvious that the largest group of current and potential owners of pets reside independently in the community.

The expected, explosive growth in the elderly population will continue until after the World War II "baby boom" generation has completed its lifespan, approximately the year 2040. Given the smaller numbers of births in the years following the "baby boom" generation, it is clear that there will be an increased social burden in caring for an aging population that is large relative to the younger generations. Recognition of uncontrolled costs of the health and medical care systems have caused extensive examination of alternatives to institutionalized long-term care of aging persons. In the future, a great many more older people will remain at home for as long as possible, having services delivered to them in their own homes through a combination of the efforts of family, informal and formal service programs.

This means, of course, that older pet owners, and older pets, will be spending more time together under conditions of increasing impairment and variable supervision or assistance in their own household. Increasing numbers of these older persons will be women (who are more likely to be pet owners), will live alone, and will have to rely to a greater extent on their own resources in coping with the predictable social, biological and functional crises that inevitably occur with advanced age. Clearly, problems in owning and responsibly caring for a pet can be expected to occur in this context, though they have not been systematically recognized to date in the vast majority of aging services or humane society programs.

The picture is not all grim. Older individuals will have increasing periods of time that they can allocate personally as they wish. This leisure time offers great potential for recreation, for productive effort, and is in many quarters considered one of our largest underutilized social resources. The coming cohort of elderly people represents the best-prepared cohort in history. These people are a tremendous resource for program development with their peers. While emphasizing the resources and capabilities of the large majority of elderly persons we also must recognize that there are predictable problems consistently experienced by large numbers of elderly persons.

Needs of the elderly

While there are common problems associated with aging, it is extremely important to recognize that individual older persons will vary tremendously in the problems they experience. Some people in their late 50s are at greater risk and more impaired than people in their 80s and 90s, some of whom act much as we would expect people in their 50s to act. A judgment in working with older persons should be based on actual abilities of the person rather than on some presumed age category. This means that very detailed, very skillful *behavioral and functional assessment* is important in identifying what needs an older person actually has that can be met by services. Further, when most older individuals have problems, they have multi-problems. It is rare to find an older person with just one thing wrong, and it is not likely to expect that any one thing is going to solve all the problems. Interventions, including pets, must be coordinated and seen as part of the teamwork approach in helping an elderly person maintain her or his abilities.

Even more basic than the specific needs which an older person might experience is the manner in which help is provided. Any person has a right to receive any services in a way that helps her or him to retain a sense of self-respect and personal control in coping with problems. The circumstances of elderly people, and the good intentions and powerful status of prospective helpers, often combine to deny older people their rights in making decisions and to place them in a dependent condition. A great many older people resist help and resist services because they inherently recognize that accepting help carries with it, in many cases, the assumption of a second-class status.

The needs of older people can be described in categories of physical, biological, psychological, social and economic needs. Physical health problems are extremely common among the elderly with over 85% of the elderly reporting at least one physical impairment and over 60% with multiple impairments. Decline in physical health and increases in the prevalence of chronic disease occur steadily with advancing age. Approximately 40% of those in their late 60s and early 70s experience some limitation in their ability to carry out activities of daily living. Nonetheless, almost 40% of those over 80 years of age indicate that they are not restricted in their daily activities. Maintained physical activity and exercise are shown to be valuable in coping with chronic illness and prolonging the ability to live independently. The beneficial role of pets in encouraging, even requiring, additional physical exercise is one of the most salient aspects of pet-owning among the elderly.

Nutrition and appropriate medication, when required, are aspects of biological functioning that are strongly influenced by social and environmental situations. Pets also appear to be useful in a home as a stimulus for food intake for the older person and more generally for environmental caring behaviors by the older person. Several studies have also shown that pets can be a powerful force in rehabilitative medicine and care planning. Pets' abilities to not only assist with the maintenance of a healthy life style, but also to be associated with speeded healing or more complete recovery, are significant aspects of the importance of pets in responding to the physical needs of the elderly. Of course the widely cited reports of the ability of pets to produce reduction in blood pressure and heart rate and conditions of deep relaxation and pleasure for humans, represent important means by which pets might assist in meeting the health needs of elderly persons.

The psychological needs of the older person are diverse, yet three basic aspects can be pointed out. First, psychological functioning usually is defined as including personality in the sense of one's self-esteem and personal satisfaction that one is a complete, competent human being. For many older persons there appears to be a need to review one's life, to accept one's current status and accomplishments in the context of a whole life, and to evaluate one's current ability and situation against one's expectations. Pets can play an immediate and important role in these executive processes of life, helping to give a sense of value and meaning to life's last stages.

Psychological needs also usually concern cognition, the ability of a person to think and to perform intellectual processes necessary to carry out activities in environments. Pets can provide sensory stimulation and a subject for thought that might help keep particularly isolated or more regressed older persons in touch with reality.

The fun and interest of watching pets as they explore their environment or play represents an important aspect of the beneficial effects of having animals present. Pets serve as distracters from our own concerns. They help an individual by reducing the person's preoccupation with her or his own problems. Pets are very good as distracters; they break into a situation and in many cases demand attention. Their occasional high activity levels and riveting appeals for care aid older persons in turning their attention from other concerns to carry out reassuring activities.

This help with avoiding "a preoccupation with self" is also useful in maintaining mental health. One of the most serious problems encountered among the elderly is the increasing prevalence of mental illness. Depression, constant worries and anxieties and paranoid reactions are common affective mental problems in old age. Among community-dwelling elderly, depression has been diagnosed in approximately 10% of the population and it is estimated that significant symptoms of mental illness are experienced by between 15 and 25% of the population. The incidence of senile dementia and other causes of chronic mental confusion vary from approximately 5 or 6% in the community, to estimates as high as 50 to 70% in nursing home facilities. It is in these affective disorders that pets can play an especially important role in helping conquer that sense of hopelessness that so often accompanies multi-problem situations.

The social needs of older persons are increasingly being recognized. However, this is an area where there is little consensus on what is actually best for older persons; there is tremendous variability in the social relationship needs of older persons. Certainly some elderly people enjoy solitude and prefer little social contact. Nonetheless, most people appear to benefit from participating in both intimate, close social relationships and a larger, more casual network of social acquaintances, as well as a series of structured social roles with expectations from other members of a social group. Especially for those elderly living alone, pets appear to substitute for lacking social contacts. The most important of the social needs, especially for elderly women, appears to be the need to feel valued for providing care to others. Pets are less demanding in their care needs, are easier to manage and are accessible. Caring for children is much more demanding and the children are usually under somebody else's ultimate authority. Owning and caring for pets provides elderly people of even very limited social roles with a clearly dominant social position in at least one relationship.

It would not be appropriate to paint a picture of a vast group of isolated elderly persons. Most estimates of the seriously lonely are 10% of the elderly population although the figure may rise in certain rural isolated areas. Appropriately 80% of the elderly have a younger family member living nearby who visits on a weekly basis. The efforts of families are progressively being recognized and integrated into formal systems of caring for elderly persons with serious needs; however, it should be pointed out that not all older persons have families and that increasing family mobility and changing work career patterns serve to weaken the ability of the family's social support system to provide certain kinds of social support. Increases in women working particularly jeopardize traditional informal support arrangements. In some families contact seems to become much more ritualized and much more routinized in terms of providing only certain relationship functions or services, or in visiting only at certain holidays, etc. Tensions are often evident in these family relationships, though it is very clear that in the vast majority of cases, both adult children and parents attempt to meet high personal

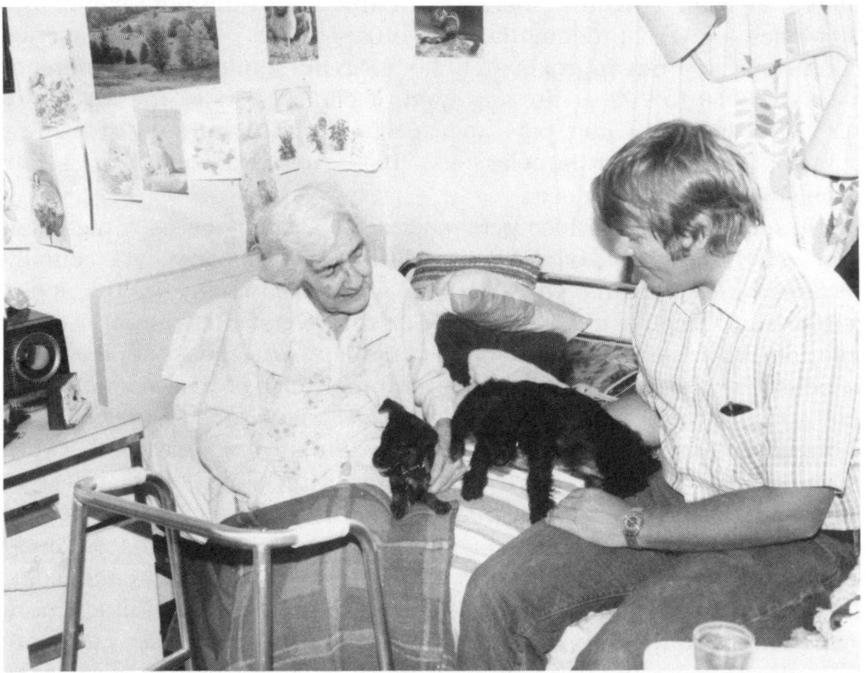

Many humane societies have popularized bringing pets to visit the elderly, an image symbolically pairing two major sources of fear and ambivalence in our culture. Both the elderly and pets are revered in the abstract, but often treated harshly in reality. *(Photo by Phil Arkow)*

codes of conduct.

Nonetheless, it becomes clear that social relationships with non-family members, with friends and with some other group are also very important in the sense of social well-being of an older person. Pets can serve as this external individual and help to provide a buffer for the elderly person living with relatives. Additionally, simply by being in a home so that a person can recognize that she or he is not alone, pets provide a sense of emotional security. Pets not only help keep a house from feeling empty, they also serve to structure the daily rituals and routines that drive a house and provide a rhythm for the day. Among centenarians, such a personally defined daily predictable routine is, along with not smoking, one of few behavioral correlates of reaching advanced age.

Pets also serve as a means of facilitating pleasant social interactions. It has been demonstrated that people like to talk with individuals walking pets, and that conversations about pets are an easy way to start a relationship. Possession of an especially good-looking or well-trained animal serves to increase the status of its owner and provides some social rewards for an elderly person. Consider for example the 90-year-old man who is routinely the center of attention in his neighborhood bar because of the unique abilities and language of his 90-year-old Amazon parrot.

Economic needs

Approximately 13% of the elderly are classified as below the poverty level; however, a significantly larger group struggles along with marginal incomes that are not adequate to meet their needs. Certainly, many elderly are financially well off, as the increases in retirement travel and elderly consumerism demonstrate. However, these general patterns must be interpreted on a personal level, comparing available resources with required expenditures. Some individuals, counting their homes, appear to have adequate resources until it is recognized that their resources are not easily translated into cash, and that they may have unbelievably high expenses, due largely to chronic health care costs.

With increasing economic burdens, some people surrender their pets. Most, however, maintain their pets as cost-effectively as possible. While most of the stories appear apocryphal, there can be little doubt that some elderly owners provide for their pets by neglecting some of their personal needs. In our research only three people have actually requested assistance with routine pet food cost, but yearly costs of keeping a pet average only approximately $250. This low cost reflects the fact that almost 75% of elderly owners do not incur any yearly veterinarian fees; they tend to avoid that expense. On the other extreme, one owner reported expenditures in excess of $1,000.

For some elderly people, especially in rural areas, animals represent a source of economic return. Raising chickens for eggs and butchering other small animals is the kind of husbandry that provides both traditional, meaningful activity and economic return. Similarly, pet-sitting and other services can supplement the income of older animal lovers.

The roles of pets in the lives of older persons

It is clear that pets mean different things to different owners. It is also clear, although not well documented, that pets mean different things to the same person at different points in her or his lifespan. Consider the potential differences of the role of a pet in the home of the "young old" person in their early 60s, compared with the same pet in the household of a terminally ill 90-year-old. While basic attitudes towards animals are probably quite stable and formed early in life, the meaning of pets does change over time for some older persons. There are certain life events that are often associated with changes in pet ownership: having children, the children leaving home, retirement, acute health crises, widowhood, divorce and dying are clear examples.

The timing and impact of these changes on animal ownership is not at all clear or predictable. Some otherwise happy pet owners stop keeping pets as an aspect of "launching" their grown children. Some of these people return to owning pets after a period of active retirement and travel. Others never again own pets, but put pet ownership behind them, like the Little League. Similarly the pet ownership response to acute health crises is not predictable. A relatively small group of non-owners acquire pets as a means of coping with this crisis. More commonly, other family members or the older person decide the pet adds an unnecessary burden, and it is sold, given away, or euthanized. Some older persons refuse to give up owning pets until they die, while others surrender pets early in a health crisis. One older woman of our acquaintance who lived alone with many pets correctly predicted her pets would have to eat her body for food if nobody found her soon after she died.

A developmental perspective is essential for understanding the role of a given pet in the social world of a particular older person and why individual relationships turn out so differently. This change-oriented view is also essential in considering appropriate kinds of pet interventions with the elderly at different points in the aging process.

Within a shorter time perspective, the process of developing a relationship with a pet is also a critical, but poorly understood process, for the elderly as well as other age groups. The issues of sharing experiences, negotiating expectations and behavior and developing emotional bonds are just as likely to characterize getting attached to a pet as they are to a spouse. It is in these initial interactions that the course of the relationship is largely defined and whether a bonded relationship forms or fails to form. Certainly, the accumulating evidence of significant numbers of dissatisfied or worried pet owners and the large number of pets which are surrendered to shelters, indicate that relationship development is a complex process with frequent characteristic problems.

While there is inadequate evidence to say decisively, it appears that older persons who own pets tend to have fewer problems than many younger owners in actually controlling or relating to the pet. Experience and self selection have combined to produce older pet owners who are, for the most part, more skilled and knowledgeable pet owners, within their own perspective.

It is this perspective, the attitudes and expectations of the elderly owner and those of significant others, that exerts the most influence over the future of the relationships. Pets are acquired for various reasons, with the potential owner selecting quite specifically what she or he wants, modifying the environment and exercising authority over the pet in particular situations, consistent with her or his expectations of the animal's role.

Thus, a big German shepherd tied outside a building for an older man concerned with security is treated roughly and becomes a "watch dog", a fluffy Pekingese, combed with bows in her hair and with her own special bed and eating spaces, becomes a "companion and family member" for an older single woman.

However impressive the influence the owner exerts, the control is certainly not complete. The animal itself exerts a significant influence on how its role will be defined. Even within breeds of animals there are major differences that are not apparent at the time a commitment to ownership is made. Some watch dogs beguile their owners and are elevated to housepets, while many housepets fail or refuse to live within the owner's expectations and are consigned to a kennel or worse. Certain pets gain status and receive more attention with advancing age. Experiencing concern over the geriatric pet's care needs deepens the owner's commitment, both emotionally and financially and causes the older pet to be regarded as special and worthy of more favor, because it has survived a rough early life.

Much has been said of the ability of puppies and kittens to solicit care and affection, but the elderly often seek and acquire mature animals and appear to be more sensitive to the metaphor describing their own circumstances in the care and eventual death of their old pet. Numerous owners have said they haven't got time for a puppy, worrying that "all that training and I might not be around to enjoy the results." Approximately 20% of the new owners avidly seek puppies and kittens. They don't want "other people's mistakes and cast-offs"; they want a "fresh young life" to keep them "active and thinking younger." Most older pet owners reflect back over the lifespans of six to 10 well-known pets. Mature animals, closer to the person's own stage of life, are preferred by the majority. For approximately 5% of elderly owners, the death of a close pet hurts so much that they refuse to ever own pets again. That decision ages them and helps define a preparation for late life, or for their own death. As a depressed widower said in refusing his son's suggestion of getting a puppy, "NO! no way. One wife, one dog; it's all over for me." Repeatedly, others have said, "No, my pet-owning days are over."

Older persons in our research have reported acquiring pets for a variety of reasons:

Pets can provide sensory stimulation and a subject for thought for the elderly—They serve as distracters from our own concerns.
(Photo by Phil Arkow)

- As companions, to have something else alive in the house
- As an aid in physical rehabilitation
- As an aid in improving mental health
- For personal security
- As utilitarian workers, catching rodents or aiding with poor vision or poor hearing
- As a charitable obligation
- As a valuable possession and status symbol
- As a hobby or an interesting project
- As an economic venture or husbandry
- Habit, tradition or part of the definition of a home
- To admire the beauty of the animal

Certainly, other motivations could be identified. Nor should it be assumed that pets are always acquired with a rational, internally consistent set of reasons in mind. The set of other major determinants of the relationship between older owners and animals are generally described as the physical and social environment.

The importance of living arrangements has already been discussed in terms of the increased companionship role of the pet with an elderly person who lives alone, particularly when the individual is under stress. Within larger social groups however, the animal's role can become very complex. Most older married couples enjoy the company of mutually owned pets with little discord, though in some cases disagreements over a pet's status and proper care occur frequently. In our research approximately 9% of pet owners report conflict with their spouse over the pet and 10% report conflict with adult children over pets. It is very clear that it is much harder to successfully introduce pets into married households than to those who live alone. This might be because the married have more social options and less need for company; their schedules appear busier and they report less time to care for pets. Or it might be simply that it is easier for an animal to learn to please one owner than two or more. Whatever the reasons, the character of family attitudes and behavior toward pets will have a major impact on the role the pet plays.

Conflict with neighbors over pets was reported by only 2% of owners in our research. Far more common were reports of neighbors assisting with each other's pets, including transportation to medical care, pet sitting, feeding treats, etc. The extent to which an older person is embedded in a supportive social network that is geographically accessible becomes more important as the older person's functional ability declines. The relationship that the pet, as well as the older owner, maintains with these supporting friends is critical. If the person or pet are not rewarding, it is probable that the support will deteriorate as the need for it increases.

The presence and characteristics of other animals in the household influence both the time available for relating to an individual pet, the degree of control the animals will exert over each other and their orientation toward the owner. The relatively few situations when older owners fail to control the size of their pet population, or when dog packs attack humans, represent the damaging impact of animal social structure on our lives.

The physical environment of the older person affects overall patterns of ownership and the kind of relationship that develops between a person and a given animal. Rural settings are sufficiently sparse that very casual animal ownership is possible; urban ownership, especially in apartment or congregate housing, increasingly requires an owner committed to active care and control of the pet at all times. The local environment directly constrains the choice of many species and suggests criteria for selecting pets.

The local physical environment, at the neighborhood level and in the design and layout of the property, home or apartment, can be

Older persons acquire animals for a variety of reasons. For some, a mature pet is preferred; others seek puppies and kittens.

(Photo by Phil Arkow)

characterized as facilitating or impeding animal ownership. For example, well-designed, sanitary indoor areas for animal elimination requirements would greatly reduce the burden of ownership on infirm older owners. Resourceful older and handicapped individuals have devised all sorts of tools and systems to ease their pet chores. Use of fences, exercise lines, double-door systems, indoor kennels, self-feeders, grooming stands, high beds and feeding tables, retracting leads, transmitters, etc., can make ownership feasible and help to compensate for the person's reduced ability level.

With advancing age and disablity, large numbers of older people have to relocate to more supportive living environments, such as apartments in town, public housing, personal care homes, nursing homes, etc. Often, regulations in these facilities prohibit or discourage pets and cause crises for elderly pet owners. While other chapters in this book document striking progress on some of these fronts, it is not clear that animal companionship programs are being integrated into the main elements of the community-based aging services programs. *(See Chapter 7)*

Issues in programmatic use of pets and aging services for community-dwelling elderly

The primary issue is translating recognition of the roles of animals in the lives of a significant minority of elderly people into a series of service policies and programs that support both responsible ownership and bonded relationships with pets, but at the same time protect the interests of the animal and other community members. At the present time the major elements in the community aging services system (the Area Agencies on Aging, their subcontractors, home health agencies, and hospitals) have not integrated animal concerns into their casework intake and assessment interviews or developed animal-related referrals or programmatic resources. As Leo Bustad pointed out in his book, *Animals, Aging and the Aged,* a few simple questions would assist greatly in identifying problem situations before they cause serious hardships:

- Do you have pets or animals at home?
- Is someone taking care of them now? (for hospital admission)
- Are you having any problems with your animals?

When problems are discovered, aging services caseworkers should be knowledgeable about animal care resources in the area and work to integrate that help into the older person's comprehensive care plan. Indentifying local animal care resources and linking them into a service plan for a particular individual might be relatively easy in some situations, especially where special purpose groups like PACT (People and Animals Coming Together) or a local humane society are well organized, and where the size of the community provides more extensive resources. In some communities however, resources will be very few and the programmatic ability to meet older owners' problems will be small. However, any response is better than simply ignoring the fact that a large number of older people live with animals.

As resources permit and information grows about priority local needs, more precisely focused programs can be developed and a more responsive and appropriate referral network can be established. This local process of bridging aging services with animal care resources involves choosing from a growing array of program options including working animal programs (seeing eye/hearing dogs), animal-facilitated therapy, bonded ownership training, responsible ownership training, home and institutional visitation, senior animal hobby clubs, cruelty prevention and control programs, Extension Service and 4-H programs, etc. It is clear that while companion animal owners represent a growing segment of the elderly owners, particularly with advancing age, the community's response capacity should be broader than just that group. Certainly, elderly citizens are just as offended by violation of animal control and cruelty laws as other community groups. The primary issue remains that in the past it is the "companion group" of elderly owners who have been harmed and ignored by aging services' policies, while the relatively few irresponsible owners have been taken as a stereotype of the elderly pet owner.

In the operation of a community-based program, the most common serious issues revolve around deterioration of an older person's ability to care for a pet, with value judgments required of appropriate risk levels, rights of owner, rights of animals, and of the neighboring community. Some third party judgment, and eventually active support and animal care, must be provided, but in most communities there is no response until the owner's problems are out of control. Then in a "raid" fashion all animals are forcibly removed. Early insertion of concerned "sponsors" could avert many of the most serious excesses in overpopulation and aid the owner through a transition to a more responsible sustainable style of ownership. Such out-of-control pet owners are usually vulnerable, multi-problem people and their obvious affection for animals can become a key to enter a needed service planning process.

At much-reduced levels of ability, particularly mental disability, pet ownership becomes impossible unless daily care is the total responsiblity of a third party. Visitation programs and institutional residential programs become appropriate, as well as an attempt to shift attention to animals that require only observation for enjoyment—fish, birds, caged mammals, etc.

Most of the time, animal programming appears to provide simply a stimulating and diverting activities program. In many cases particular therapeutic goals, such as psychological or physical recovery or speech therapy, can be effectively approached through using pets with older persons who have strong feelings about animals.

When individuals reach their levels, pets can be integrated into hospices and the dying process at home, as a means to relax, comfort and palliate the older person's last weeks.

The references in this book will direct interested people to a growing set of specific program models and resource organizations to aid in developing animal-related service, education and control programs. It is well beyond the scope of this chapter to document the available resources. Instead, the focus has been placed on considering more rationally the range of factors affecting the diversity of the relationships among elderly people and their pets and their diverse impact on the well-being of older persons; life-saving in some situations, life-threatening or fatal, in others. An objective assessment of the older person's desires and needs is therefore necessary prior to intervening. Indeed, more than we initially imagined, sometimes the correct thing to do is to remove, not place a particular pet.

Finally, this chapter has stressed the need to view animal-related programs as part of a comprehensive service system meeting the needs of older pet owners, rather than as a monolithic belief that somehow owning a pet is supposed to help every older person. Through cooperation with local aging services, providers and public health officials, interested community members and animal care groups can establish a strong network of referrals and shared understanding that will provide a foundation for maintaining and supporting animal relationships for those elderly who value them.

Suggested reading:

Aging Magazine (September-October, 1982) Washington, D.C.: Administration on Aging.

Bustad, Leo K. *Animals, Aging and the Aged.* Minneapolis: University of Minnesota Press, 1980.

Hines, Linda M. *The People-Pet Partnership Program.* Alameda, Calif.: The Latham Foundation, 1980.

Katcher, Aaron and Beck, Alan *New Perspectives on Our Lives with Companion Animals.* Philadelphia: University of Pennsylvania Press, 1983.

Knight, Barbara, Lago, Dan, and Rohrer-Dann, M. *PACT: Promoting bonded relationships between pets and the elderly.* University Park, Pa.; Pennslyvania State University, 1984. Available from: PACT, 101-B Myra Dockhouse, University Park, PA 16802.

11

Companion Animals in Institutions

Dave Lee

"... feasible in any institution..."

The use of pet animals as companion therapists to inmates and patients can be one of the most effective programs within an institution.

The clearest success is with chronic depressed and suicidal cases. Patients believed to be unreachable through such means as chemotherapy, ECT and a variety of "talk" therapies have literally been turned around simply by properly introducing a pet into their lives.

Overall goals set when introducing a pet with a patient include:

1. Improving the patient's self-esteem
2. Providing the resident with non-threatening, non-judgmental affection
3. Stimulating a responsible attitude with the pet caretaker
4. Providing the patient with a necessary diversion from normal hospital routine
5. Providing the patient with needed companionship

The reference I must use for this writing is the pet program at the Lima State Hospital for the Criminally Insane in Lima, Ohio. The use of pets at the hospital began in January, 1975, as a 90-day experiment. The program started on one ward using three parakeets and an aquarium. But its immediate popularity caused a snowball effect on other wards who requested similar programs, partially because of patient pressure but mostly because it was considered a "hassle-free" program that blended well with already existing activities.

David Lee is a psychiatric social program specialist at the Oakwood Forensic Center (formerly the Lima State Hospital for the Criminally Insane) in Lima, Ohio, where he pioneered the nation's first PFT program in a state mental hospital. A graduate of Defiance College, he has been featured in numerous magazines and TV reports in connection with the Lima PFT program.

Within a year there were visible changes in many of the depressed, non-communicative patients. Instead of endlessly pacing up and down the

Smaller animals, such as birds, can be quite valuable as therapeutic aids in an institution. Although a cell is unthinkable for a dog, it can be a paradise for a cockatiel or a parakeet. *(Photo by Allan Kain)*

ward hallways, many had found an interest object (the pet) who had no demands or interest in the patient's past activities. Most importantly, the pets broke the daily routine which all institutions guarantee.

Without doubt, a pet therapy program is feasible in any institution that is interested in helping its clients.

The types of pets which may be introduced to such a program depend on the size of the institution, the age range of inmates served and the interest of the staff. A wide variety is possible.

Almost all institutions of our type are divided into wards housing a set number of clients. Each client has his or her own area, either a cubicle or a cell, perhaps six feet by 12 feet. Although a six-by-twelve cell is unthinkable for a pet dog, it is a virtual paradise for a parakeet, cockatiel, or hamster.

When institutions first consider the feasiblity of having pets, they usually think of dogs and cats and the potential problems these animals may bring. But smaller animals can be quite valuable. One of the most important aspects of using companion animals as therapy is the close physical proximity between client and pet. Within the institution where space is limited the smaller pets appear to have the best results, as they can stay with the client especially when he or she is troubled. Almost instinctively, a troubled client will retreat to his or her area and the importance of having a valued companion at that time can be significant.

At Lima State Hospital, chronic (long-term) patients keep their personal pets with them, living in the actual cells. More acute cases, who are staying for short terms before being returned to Corrections (prison), get to visit and work with other animals such as deer, goats, ducks, geese and rabbits. A smoother transition is achieved by using farm-type animals during the short-term clients' recovery process: the patients reach their described goals without a high attachment level.

Even though the pet program at Lima began somewhat by accident, it developed under a very structured set of guidelines. In late 1974, a group of depressed and suicidal patients on one ward jointly risked punishment by hiding an injured wild bird in a mop room and feeding it scraps from the dining hall. It was clearly unusual for the residents of this ward to be concerned about *anything* except their own problems.

Although that bird died of its injuries, the cohesion it created during its short stay was not forgotten and a formal 90-day trial proposal for the introduction of pets was made. This eventually developed in a formal program now over eight years old and using more than 170 pets.

However, the use of pets within an institution is not without opposition. As a rule, state institutions are opposed to many changes as the staff invariably find that most changes involve one sure thing—more work.

Those in opposition to the use of pets as therapy also usually argue the hygiene problems outweigh the benefits. This is why any program using pets needs consistent monitoring systems and set clean-up schedules.

Like similar programs using pets, Lima State Hospital had its share of opposition and failures. For example, the attempt in 1981 to use chimpanzees on one of the wards was a complete disaster. The eight-year-old female chimp was subject to violent temper tantrums which, on several occasions, "cleared the dayhall." The use of wild turkeys as courtyard pets in 1982 led to attacks on patients attemping to feed them. Eventually, the turkeys were returned to freedom in the wild.

Fortunately, the successes far outweigh the failures. Patients who were totally uncommunicative due to depression have been successfully treated using pets as catalysts. Often, patient letters can be a good indication of success.

One 63-year-old, serving time on four counts of first-degree murder, wrote to a friend, "I wouldn't have nothin' to do without pets. It's the last of my family."

A 20-year-old man, imprisoned for armed robbery but having been in institutions since the age of eight, wrote to the director of the zoo in Columbus, Ohio, about his parrot, Missy, which had been donated by that zoo. "I guess I can say that Missy has helped me more than any doctor has ever done, for one reason: she cares. I know she can't help me with my problems that I've had since childhood, but in something I lack she's there and she helps."

Individual patient successes are too numerous to mention. Patients you just don't think will ever respond seem to react to that something special a pet can provide.

Studies and research often have a tough time measuring the success of pet therapy because there are so many variables within the institution. One study conducted at Lima in 1981 compared patients on one of the six "pet" wards with one of the six without animals. Both wards had equal status and population. The patients with pets needed half as much medication, had drastically reduced incidents of violence and had *no* suicide attempts during the year-long comparison.

The ward without pets had eight documented suicide attempts during the same year.

There appears to be something about inmates of state facilities which makes them an appropriate target audience for a program using pets. There is so much loneliness and rejection in an institution that pets can have a real impact, for when a patient becomes very depressed there is something non-threatening for them to turn to.

Much of this loneliness occurs when treatment staff are not present, such as over weekends or late at night. It is at these times that the pet truly

Wild animals can be included in a therapeutic program. Deer kept in an outside area can be a successful adjunct to other treatments. *(Photo by Allan Kain)*

earns its keep.

The actual starting of a pet therapy program is not as easy as one would think, especially in an institution. Using the Lima State Hospital pet program as a guide, the beginning steps for another facility could be:

1. Write up a beginning proposal for the introduction of pets, in detail.

2. Together with representatives from the humane society, a veterinarian and interested others, formally present the ideas to the administration and seek a commitment from them for a certain time period for trying pets.

3. Start small on one receptive ward or area. One successful approach is to introduce a small pet in an office where escorted patients can go at first to visit. Then, work up to a structured program where the patients can help share responsibility for the pet. The patients must demonstrate responsibility first, like helping daily with the farm-type pets or helping care for ward pets and aquariums. Only then should arrangements be made for a personal pet.

4. Constant documentation on progress (or lack of progress) for both the patient and the pet must be conducted.

5. Establish a firm policy of taking *no* risks with the pets. The animal's safety and humane care precedes any therapeutic goals.

6. Incorporate close monitoring and structure into the program.

Structurally, a pet program needs to provide a consistent, well-integrated service delivery system. This begins with a uniform referral system, for use on all wards, which includes questions as to pet preference and past pets and psychological testing to reflect what goals are to be sought. At Lima, for instance, each patient receives as a part of his admissions psychological testing a depression inventory to gauge his depression. This same test is administered when starting the patient in pet therapy, again at every six-month interval, and at the point of discharge.

When a patient is referred to the program or requests to be involved, a complete write-up, including a sketch of his history, his problems and anticipated goals, is completed and filed. Every month the goals are reviewed and a note showing progress or lack of progress is made. Upon discharge or removal from the program a full discontinuation note is done.

Monitoring at the state institution is extremely important. Lima State Hospital's monitoring includes:

1. Daily rounds by the pet therapy coordinator.
2. Daily rounds by attendant and nursing staff.
3. Weekly documentation by the pet therapy coordinator in each participant's nursing notes.
4. Monthly meetings between ward staff and each client.

5. Monthly updates to administration staff.
6. Monthly updates to a variety of local and national humane societies.
7. Monitoring through weekly club meetings with participating residents.

This weekly club grouping of pet caretakers is conducted primarily to discuss pet-related problems, as well as to set new policies and to determine whether existing hygiene policy is being followed.

The actual selection of pets can be the key to success. Because institutional overcrowding is commonplace, the smaller pets seem to work better without having to restrict the animals' mobility. Although a cockatiel or parrot provides less contact comfort than a dog, it can be a very loving pet which responds well to kind treatment. Most importantly, it can do this in a limited space.

At Lima, the selection of pets includes a wide variety of small animals which have been both donated and purchased. Three years after the program started, *disadvantaged* pets were also introduced, including a one-footed finch, a one-eyed parrot and a self-abusing cockatoo. These animals had surprisingly good results.

The patients felt empathy for the disadvantaged pet and had a greater feeling of accomplishment in *saving* the animal. This led to obtaining parakeets from breeders, but instead of purchasing the young, patients adopted the old breeder parakeets who were unproductive and were about to be destroyed. Although not as long-lived as a conventional parakeet, these older birds helped the patients feel better about keeping animals, due to their disadvantaged conditions.

The benefits which an institution can receive by implementing a pet therapy program include:

1. A comfortable atmosphere.
2. An improved sense of patient self-worth.
3. A necessary diversion.
4. Providing companionship.

These benefits far outweigh the problems such as monitoring pet hygiene. In fact, documentation at Lima concluded that, in many cases, personal hygiene *improved* following the insistence that pet hygiene standards be maintained.

Even if the suicide attempts were decreased by one, a pet program would be well-founded.

It is genuinely felt that the use of pets within the institution is a therapeutic technique that helps decrease suicidal depression in many cases and at worst does no harm to any particular case, providing that the program is properly structured and monitored.

Suggested reading:

"Hi Ya, Beautiful," and *"Five Years After"* (documentary films) Alameda, Calif.: The Latham Foundation.

Curtis, Patricia Animals are good for the handicapped, perhaps all of us. *Smithsonian,* July 1981, 48-57.

Rosenblatt, Rae Marie Pets Are Therapists at Lima State Hospital. *National Humane Review,* August 1976, 19-20.

Hines, Linda "Pets in Prison: A New Partnership." *California Veterinarian,* 5/1983, 6-17.

12

Equestrian Therapy

Lida L. McCowan

" 'I can ride a horse!' "

Beginnings

Through the ages, man has attributed therapeutic benefits to horseback riding. Medical writers of centuries past, Orebasius and Galen, have alluded to riding therapy. In 1670, Lord Thomas Sydenham, an early English physician wrote, "There is no better treatment for the body and soul than many hours each week in the saddle, riding the horse."

Equestrian therapy, as we know it in this century, had a more formal introduction when Mme Liz Hartel of Denmark rehabilitated herself from wheelchair to horseback and then, in 1952, entered the Olympic Games in Helsinki. Riding her horse, Jubilee, Mme Hartel won the silver medal in dressage, the most difficult of all riding forms. Since that day, riding as therapy is practiced worldwide with many countries, including the United States, having their own national riding-for-the-handicapped associations. Most of these organizations were established as governing bodies to assist in organizing programs, provide guidelines for operations, accredit existing programs, provide insurance and offer instructor examinations. All of this is done to assure the handicapped they will receive the best instructions available under the safest possible conditions. In the United States, the national organization is known as NARHA, the North American Riding for the Handicapped Association. At the present time, over two hundred programs are registered as members.

When a new group joins NARHA, it is given a six-month "grace period" before it has to apply for accreditation. NARHA realizes that it takes at least six months to get a program started and in operation. After the six months,

Lida L. McCowan is director of the Cheff Center for the Handicapped in Augusta, Mich., one of the most noted equestrian therapy programs. She is co-founder and former president of the North American Riding for the Handicapped Association, serves as an accreditor for NARHA, and has written several equestrian therapy training manuals.

the program is visited by a NARHA'approved accreditor who will see if the program is being conducted in a safe and structured manner. Only the programs that are accredited can continue to have NARHA insurance, advertise in their literature that they are an approved center, or remain a NARHA member. This is done solely to protect the handicapped and to further assure them of receiving quality instruction.

Pros and cons

Though comparatively new in the United States (starting on a formal basis in the early 1960s), riding therapy has already become a controversial subject among some physicians who have been asked to refer a patient for riding lessons. Having no research to honestly back the claim "that riding is beneficial," many physicians are afraid to refer their patients for fear that the patient would suffer further injury. This has not been the case, however, in NARHA-approved centers and most of the doubting physicians have changed their opinion that riding is too much of a risk and have sent patients.

For those physicians still not sure, the situation may change in the near future, as in April, 1983, the American College of Orthopedic and Pediatric Surgeons hosted an invitational seminar for the disciplines involved in recreation and competitions for physically handicapped children and young adults. Horseback riding was included as one of these disciplines. This is the first time that I know of that a seminar of this type has ever been held in the United States. Out of that seminar came recommendations as to what types of handicaps could be accepted in a horseback riding program

A class is mounted and ready to ride at the Cheff Center. For centuries, man has known of the therapeutic value of horseback riding to the body and soul.
(Photo by JMT Studio)

and what handicaps would not be recommended for riding. Individualized programs could be developed for special cases that were not totally contraindicated as non-riders. Chart I shows the list of acceptable handicaps, the ones requiring individualized programs and the contraindications for others.

Chart II, though not discussed at the invitational meeting, was compiled from physical and occupational therapists' records from the programs of horseback riding in which they are involved.

The accident rate of riders in NARHA-approved programs is minute compared to accidents through bicycle riding, playgrounds, falling out of wheelchairs, off crutches, or others involving the handicapped. The benefits in Chart II far outweigh any small risk that could be involved.

CHART I
Handicaps and Horseback Riding Programs

RECOMMENDED	INDIVIDUALIZED	NOT RECOMMENDED
A. Neuromuscular System		
1. Cerebral Palsy		
2. CVA and Brain Injured		
3. Spinal Cord* and Spina Bifida	X	*Quadraplegics above T-5 or T-7
4. Multiple Sclerosis		
5. Muscular Dystrophy	X	
B. Skeletal System		
1. Arthritis*		*Contraindicated during acute exacerbation (flare-up)
2. Amputations	X	
3. Congenital Dislocations	X	
4. Osteogenesis Imperfecta**	X	**At young age because of maximum multiple fractures
5 Arthrogryposis	X	
C. Emotionally Impaired		
D. Mentally Impaired*		*Profoundly not recommended
E. Autism	X	
F. Deaf and Blind	X	
G. Learning Disabled		

CHART II
Benefits of Equestrian Therapy in Selected Handicaps

TYPE OF HANDICAPPED	BENEFIT FROM EQUESTRIAN THERAPY
A. Cerebral Palsy	Relaxation and stretching of spastic and rigid

	muscles. Reinforcement of normal movement patterns. Increased coordination. Good balance - Good posture. Independence - Stimulation of hypotonic and flaccid muscle groups. Spatial awareness.
B. CVA - Brain Injured	Relaxation and stretching of spastic muscle groups. Prevention and correction of contractures. Muscle strengthening. Improved balance and coordination. Independence - Stimulation of flaccid muscles.
C. Spinal Cord and Spina Bifida	Maintain mobility - trunk control with correct alignment. Balance - maintain good posture. Physical independence. Spatial awareness. Increased cardiopulmonary output. Proprioceptive stimulation.
D. Multiple Sclerosis	Prevent abnormal movement patterns. Maintain muscle strength and control. Maintain normal movement patterns. Increase endurance and improve balance. Physical independence prolonged.
E. Muscular Dystrophy	Minimize muscular deterioration. Minimize loss of balance and prevent contractures. Maintain muscle strength. Stimulate cardiopulmonary output. Maximize motor functions. Strengthen trunk and pelvic muscle groups.
F. Arthritis	Joint mobility - muscle strength and endurance. Return of coordination. Maximize physical independence. Exercise with frequent rest periods.
G. Amputations	Increase muscle strength. Good balance. Good stump function. Physical independence.

	Good coordination. Use of prosthesis.
H. Congenital Dislocations (Hips)	Maximize abduction. Muscle strengthening. Good posture and balance. Normal movement patterns. Normal functions and independence.
I. Osteogenesis Imperfecta* *Contraindicated at an early age because of multiple fractures	Strengthen muscles Gain mobility of extremeties after multiple fractures. Prevent contractures. Develop normal movement patterns. Improve cardiopulmonary output. Good posture and balance. Good function. Independence without fractures.
J. Arthrogryposis	Gain joint mobility. Develop muscle strength. Maximize function in extremities. Develop good posture within range of mobility. Maximize independence.
K. Mentally Impaired	Balance, flexibility, spatial awareness, receptive and expressive skills. Improved attention span. Sensory awareness.
L. Emotionally Impaired	Spatial awareness. Control of fears. Positive self-esteem. Memory, visual, learning, improved attention span, self-control, thoughtfulness.
M. Autism	Thoughtfulness, verbalization. Visual and auditory learning. Self-control. Spatial relations. Cooperation. Getting and keeping attention for longer periods of time. Positive self-esteem.

N. Deaf and Blind	Balance, posture, relaxation, coordination. Improved self-image.
O. Learning Disabled	Relaxation. All learning problems. Self-control. Visual and auditory perceptions. Attention span. Coordination, balance, posture, motor development (both fine and gross).

Precautions

Unfortunately, there can be complications in an equestrain therapy program, but most complications can be avoided by being extremely selective of the program itself.

Like any other non-regulated sport activity, riding programs for the handicapped are cropping up everywhere. Many of these programs have not sought out the information available on a well-run program, and more or less, just open their doors. Every week or so a publication from somewhere will arrive on my desk showing a riding program. Some of these articles are about excellent programs; others are about programs that should not be in operation at all.

Just recently, I was shown a full-page spread on a riding program that truly appalled me. No student (there were eight in the class) wore helmets. One leader was leading her horse in her bare feet and another child (obviously a very severe spastic cerebral palsy) was being mounted on a very large and wide horse in a similarly large western saddle. With those circumstances, complications could easily develop, not the least being just what physicians are fearful of: further damage to the cerebral palsy child through excessive stretching of the adductor muscles and possible hip dislocation. This program is not a NARHA member, but, unfortunately, persons looking for a handicapped riding program most of the time don't even ask if a program is approved. Until the public is made aware of the dangers in this type of program, these programs will continue to operate.

One of the first things a well-run program insists on is a physician or appropriate medical referral. If the student is physically handicapped, he or she is evaluated by a physical therapist. The therapist then discusses the disability with the riding instructor. They decide on the mounting procedure, type of horse or pony, exercises that will be used, and what special equipment will be needed, such as Devonshire boots, fleece pad on saddle, saddle or bareback pad, a waist safety harness, handhold and of course, always a helmet. Every aspect is thoroughly discussed before the student is ever mounted. He or she may have one or two sidewalkers but always a leader in the beginning stages. Progress reports will be done regularly. At any time the child undergoes surgery, a new referral form will be required. Many children are on prescribed drugs and it is important to know what drugs they are on. Some do produce side-effects and if not taken as prescribed, some seizure control drugs will allow the child to have a seizure on the horse. If the instructor is not trained to handle these situations, an injury could definitely occur.

Other complications can be caused by placing handicapped riders in a precarious position because of a lack of horse knowledge by the instructor. No one should ever be strapped to a horse or a saddle that is already strapped to a horse.

The disability will be the deciding factor in choosing the proper horse. If a student has extremely tight adductors, then a fairly narrow horse or pony should be chosen. If the child has muscular dystrophy, a very wide horse or pony is needed. The instructor must have a knowledge of horses and handicaps to be able to choose the right animal for the rider.

If you are looking for a program for yourself, or you are a parent of a handicapped child who wants to take riding lessons, be sure you ask questions before starting your child or yourself. Is the program a member of a national organization? Are the horses specially trained for this work? What are the instructor's qualifications? Do they have a physical therapist on staff? Do they require medical forms? Do they require each student to wear protective headgear with properly fitted chin strap? Is the facility clean? Do they have a mounting ramp?

If the answers are evasive or administrators avoid answering at all, please look elsewhere for a program. Why accept anything but the best for your riding instruction?

Exciting happenings

If you asked any instructor of a riding program if they have had a real success, I don't think anyone would answer no. So-called "miracles" do happen. I will tell you a story in which I was involved personally and have never forgotten.

When Cheff Center first started back in 1970, we had an eight-year-old autistic girl named Rose. Rose did not verbalize, had the characteristic rocking motion, was totally withdrawn but not uncontrollable or abusive; instead, Rose stayed to herself and didn't like to be touched or handled. At orientation, I noticed Rose did look at the ponies and horses as they were led from their stalls. She seemed interested to the point her eyes followed their head movements. The following week, we had little difficulty in getting Rose to mount, but once on, the rocking motion continued; reins were frequently thrown down or placed in her mouth and her helmet was frequently unfastened and thrown on the ground. Patience in working with Rose became the key. Discipline was also administered when she would not keep her helmet on.

Soon, Rose began to react to certain directions from the instructor that were reinforced by her volunteer. She would actually scoot in her seat when told to do so.

In almost every lesson, she would try at least once to turn her pony and stand up over the poles on the ground. Her teachers were beginning to see more attentiveness in her and also less withdrawal from the school group. A new student instructor even laid her arm across Rose's shoulder and Rose did not pull away.

One day, some six months after Rose started the program, she did not return to the lounge area after her lesson. No one missed her until the loading of the school bus, then we knew she was gone. To say we were frantic is a gross understatement. Horses in the pasture, a nearby lake, dogs running loose—anything could have happened. I started down the aisles of the barn, first on one side, then the other. Others were outside

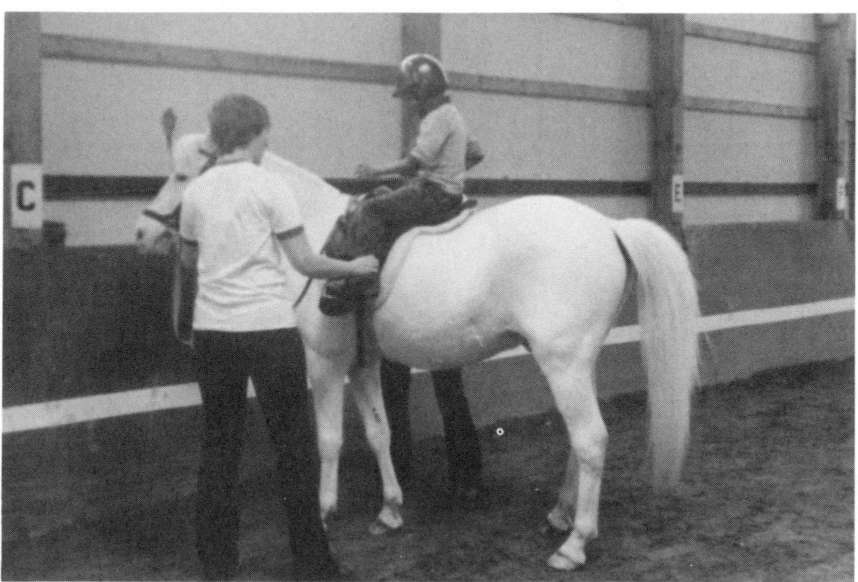

A young rider is shown the correct position during an "Around the World" exercise during which he turns completely around on horseback.

searching around the building. On my second trip through the stall area, I thought I heard a child's voice. It can't be Rose, I thought to myself, she doesn't talk, but I kept going in the direction of the voice until I came to Billy's stall. Sitting between Billy's front legs was Rose. With both hands rubbing up and down his legs, she kept saying, "Nice pony, Billy," over and over again. I couldn't believe what I was seeing and hearing so I backed quietly away, then ran and got the school teacher. Still standing in the same spot was Billy, still sitting was Rose. The teacher started to yell but I stopped her, as that could have frightened Billy. I called out Billy's name as I slowly opened the door to his stall. He never moved until the teacher lifted Rose to her feet.

Rose continued in the program for another three months, making steady improvement. She would try to say "Walk on," and "thank you," but always would say "Nice pony, Billy," no matter which horse she rode. At school she began speech therapy and was moved to a different group. The next year she did not return to Cheff and I was told she had been moved to a regular school and a resource room.

Six years later, I was announcing our program for the Open House demonstrations, when a girl of about thirteen or fourteen asked, "Mrs. McCowan, how can I get to ride again?" I looked for a minute, not recognizing the girl and she knew it. She turned and said, "Mrs. McCowan, I'm Rose W----, my sister is out riding in the class now." I couldn't believe it; here was a girl who had been truly autistic and was now a normal fourteen-year-old in junior high school. After that time, I never saw Rose again, but somehow I think Billy and the other ponies at Cheff Center had a lot to do with her becoming a pretty normal young adult. That is only one of many stories that can be told, but it shows a very positive benefit of equestrian therapy.

Research

Research is being started by some members of NARHA and by NARHA itself. Probably the most sophisticated research project has been started in Colorado by Marvin Lutlges, Ph. D. This research is designed to measure objectively the therapeutic values of horseback riding for disabled persons. The testing will be done at the Colorado Therapeutic Riding Center, Inc., a fully accredited NARHA center.

The organization of an equestrian therapy program

Too often, persons wanting to start a riding program put "the cart before the horse" and consequently, what could have been an excellent program fails before it gets started. The dictionary gives the following definition of "organize": "To unite separate elements into a smoothly working unit."

There are many excellent programs in operation throughout the United States. Above all else, avail yourself of the information that these programs can provide to you. The complete list of NARHA programs can be obtained by writing to Leonard Warner, Executive Director, NARHA, Box 100, Ashburn, VA 22011. NARHA also holds workshops in various areas of the United States and Canada and Warner can give you the information on these workshops and their locations.

Step one - establishing need

Determining the need for such a program in your area can be done very simply by contacting your local chapters of United Cerebral Palsy, March of Dimes, Easter Seals, Crippled Children and Adults Association and Association of Retarded Citizens. You may also contact the local medical society and your schools. They will be able to give you an idea of the numbers of handicapped that could be served by a program. You can decide by these numbers approximately the size of program that would best serve the needs of your community. However, in any case, starting small is the best policy.

Do not consider just the numbers of handicapped who can be served, but also the number of volunteers needed for a program. Is the community, as a whole, civic-minded? Do people support already existing programs by volunteering in them, or do those programs have some difficulty getting support? Talk to persons involved in other programs for the handicapped, such as bowling and swimming and ask them if they receive community support. Remember, deciding to operate a program is not the total answer; you have to look ahead and be able to count heavily on volunteers. Not one program in this country could operate without the total support of volunteers.

Step two - locating a facility

Absolutely nothing could be accomplished, even if you have everyone excited about a therapeutic riding program, without having a facility in which to operate. If you own such a facility, that is great—you can skip this step. But if you have to locate one that will be suitable, not to buy but to lease, then you definitely have to think of accessibility for your students. Is it near your targeted group? An hour's ride in a car can be very tiring for the handicapped. Does it have bathrooms that are accessible to wheelchairs? Will they lease you horses, saddles and bridles? Will they allow your instructor to work with the horses so they may be specially trained for this work? Can you have a stall or other area that can be locked, so the special equipment needed will be readily available for classes? Will you be able to use the ring with no others expecting to use it at the same time? Can you build, and have available, a mounting ramp?

Make sure that, before you lease any facility, everything is written down and all parties understand exactly what is expected of them and agree on the price. Charges will vary greatly from one section of the country to another. I won't get into discussing what I personally feel is a fair price, but I do know that some programs have signed leases that I feel are entirely out of line. One such lease costs a program $2,000 a month for a two-day-a-week program, serving 24 students and this does not cover helmets, ramp, special equipment, or any salary for an instructor. To me, that is exorbitant.

You can do without some luxury as long as the area of teaching is safe. You can buy a portable handicapped toilet that is very workable and accessible for wheelchairs. You don't need an indoor arena if you are in the South. There are ways to cut expenses. Don't sign a long-term lease unless you feel there is no other way of finding another suitable facility at a later date. Once locked into that type of lease, you may have some difficulty getting out of it if you want to. Make sure you have an attorney study the lease before the final signing.

Step three - incorporation

Now that you have decided there is a need for a therapeutic program in

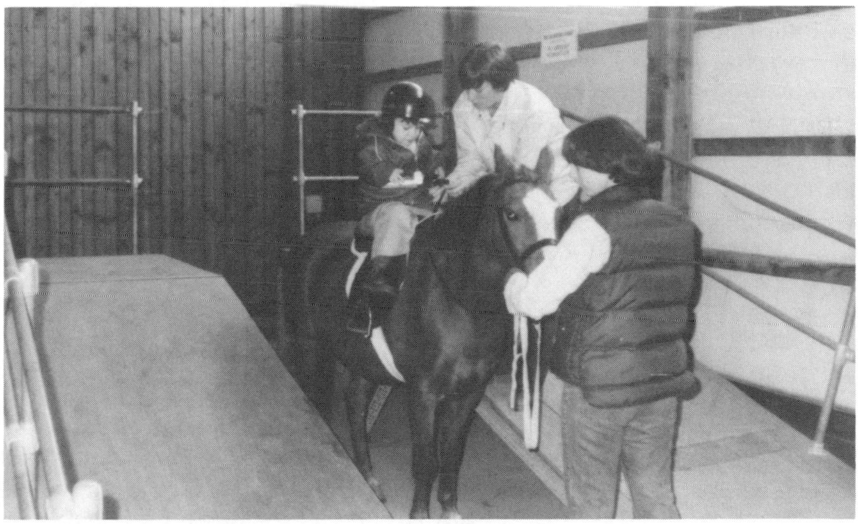

Each rider's equipment must be individually adjusted. In the case of an amputee, fixing the reins takes special care.

your area, that you will be able to recruit volunteers and that you have a facility, it is time to attack the legal matters. Most programs in this country operate as non-profit, tax-exempt foundations or agencies. To do this, your first step must be to contact the Secretary of State in your state capitol to see what is required for incorporation in your state as a non-profit corporation.

After receiving this information, if you know an attorney personally, solicit his or her expertise to help you on the Articles of Incorporation. You will also need at least three people as the incorporators. These may be people who will later serve as part of your Board of Directors. At the same time, your attorney can also apply to the state and federal governments to become a tax-exempt corporation. Each state requires its own form. The U.S. Internal Revenue Service requires that you prove to them you are a non-proft corporation registered in your state and an approved charity under the IRS Code. They will recognize you as a Private Foundation or 501 (c) (3) organization, allowing you to give receipts for tax purposes for gifts you receive.

To go one step further, you can apply to become a Public Foundation or 509 (a) (2) organization under the 501 (c) (3) statute. To do this (besides proving you are a worthwhile charity), you must prove that one-third of your support comes from the public. For new charities, the IRS will give you 90 days to operate as a Public Foundation, but it will be quickly taken away from you unless, within the 90 days, you can meet the support test and have filed necessary papers to show them that you have done so. The donor is the one who will profit by your being a Public rather than Private Foundation. I won't go into the explanation here of why that is so, but your attorney can explain it to you.

Once you have taken care of the state and federal requirements, it is time to move on. Being a non-profit, tax-exempt organization does not mean you cannot charge a fee for your services. It does mean, however, that you cannot make a profit on your operations. Many programs do charge a small fee for those who can afford to pay and charge nothing to those who cannot afford to pay.

Step four - board of directors

Probably the most difficult step in the organization of a therapeutic riding program is putting together a working board of directors. May I suggest, before you even begin, to read "The Board Member", available from Han-Mar Publications, P.O. Box 60143, Sacramento, CA 95860. It is an excellent little book and will give you good ideas of what a board member is expected to do. At a later date, after you have acquired your board, you might have it available for each board member to read.

Just being interested in helping you may not be what you need in a person to serve on your board. Two very important things to consider are a person's community involvement and occupation. An attorney may not be able to attend every board meeting, but his or her serving the organization with legal expertise and volunteered services would certainly qualify for board membership. Diversity of occupations and the acceptance of serving the community in other capacities would also weigh your decision. You need doers on a board, you need decision makers, you need leaders and you need hard workers. Interest, of course, should be considered. Certainly, if someone doesn't like horses and has never been involved in working for the betterment of the handicapped, it might be best not to consider that person for your board.

Remember, your board is the governing body of your organization. It will make, and see to it that all major decisions are carried out the way it has directed them to be done. It will make the budget for the program and handle the financial affairs of the group. I cannot tell you too many times how carefully you should select your board. Don't start with too many people. The three chosen incorporators can be a beginning, then add slowly. My favorite saying is, "God so loved the world He didn't send a committee." A good decision-making board can be six or eight people. It gets to be unruly when it reaches 20 or 30. Your board will also draft the by-laws of your organization and determine their terms of service as board members. Make sure you will be able, at a later date, to get rid of members if they are not good. Missing so many meetings without a valid excuse is one way of being able to dismiss a board member. Just make sure you are not locked into one board year after year, when possibly its usefulness to the organization is past history.

Step five - the instructor

Now, you'll have to make the all-important decision of who will be your instructor. Are you, personally, an excellent rider, know stable management and experienced in teaching regular riders? Possibly, you have been a pony club instructor or a 4-H horse leader. Maybe you have already taken a course for instructors of therapeutic riding, or have passed the NARHA certification examination. If you haven't maybe you should consider getting the training, or sending the person who is to be your instructor to get the training. Be honest with yourself: unless you are a physical therapist or occupational therapist and an excellent rider, a course is the way to learn the complexities of the different handicaps and how you evaluate them for riding. You are doing the handicapped an injustice if you try to learn about them through trial and error. Don't short-change them. They are deserving of the best.

Now, if you don't intend to be the instructor, how should you go about getting one? First, write out a job description thoroughly. Then look at all candidates' knowledge very carefully. Check their credentials. Give them screening tests to determine if they are the excellent riders they say they are. Do they show ability to relate to people? Remember, they will not only work with your board and take directives from it, but they also will be working with parents, educators, students and volunteers. Do they have the ability to handle criticism? Can they accept orders and follow through on those orders? Your instructor is the single most important person in the program. On his or her shoulders is success or failure. Make absolutely sure the person chosen can do the whole job, not just parts of it.

In the job description, you not only outline the instructor's duties, but what you will do in return. Be sure it is all written out and don't expect someone to work until 10:00 p.m. when the job description says the day ends at 5:00 p.m. unless you have stated that extra hours may be required. If attendance is required at all functions your group plans to have, make sure that is written into the job description. Make it simple, but effective. Remember, the instructor will be the most important member of your

Soloing is frightening for anyone. Riding alone for the first time is exhilarating and a tremendous boost of self-confidence.

group. Don't employ one unless that person is fully qualified to do the job you intend to do.

Step six - recruiting students

There are many organizations that you can contact to help you recruit students. Among the better known are: United Cerebral Palsy Association, Easter Seals, Association for Retarded Citizens, Exceptional Children, and Crippled Children and Adults Association. There are also many singular organizations, such as Muscular Dystrophy Association, that you can call upon for assistance in locating students. Other groups are social services agencies, schools and physicians.

When starting Cheff Center, we found that placing an article in the local newspaper brought us no end of requests from parents to enroll their children in the program. But, because it was so new, long explanations had to be given to the physicians before they would sign the referrals. Many of those doctors came to the Center to see the students we did have from the schools before they would give their permission for their patients to ride. Fortunately, the schools had their own physicians, so they agreed to participate with those students on a trial basis. They never were taken out of the program; in fact, that same school still participates weekly at the Center. Student recruitment is probably the easiest part of the organization steps. It is only difficult in getting physicians to do proper referrals.

Step seven - selecting horses

The selection of the horse or pony to be used in a riding program for the handicapped is second in importance only to the selection of the instructor. Together they make a working team. There are definite requirements in selecting a horse, the most important being the temperament. A horse that bites, kicks, or rears has no place in a therapeutic riding program. It could cause serious injury to your students, volunteers, or to the people who will be caring for the horses. Don't accept this type of horse no matter what the previous owner or stable manager tells you. There is no excuse for bad behavior in this type of program.

Also, the "spirit" or energy level of the horse should be considered. If a horse or pony is too "hot blooded," the term given to thoroughbreds, it may be too spirited for your program. You certainly don't want a horse or pony that won't move at all, for it will be useless; but neither do you want one that may run off every time a brace or heel touches his sides.

Make sure the instructor rides the horse before you buy it or lease it for your program. A donated horse should never be accepted without a two- to four-week trial period. This gives you the needed time to see if it will adjust to all the new happenings that will occur in a riding program for the handicapped.

Next to be considered is the size of your mounts. A good range will be 12 to 15 hands. You should also try to find narrow- to wide-shouldered horses and ponies so that a wide range of disabilities can be handled. Size is important also for volunteer sidewalkers. If a very tall rider is placed on a 16-hands horse and needs sidewalkers, it will be very difficult for them to protect him or her from a fall: if their straightened arms come even with the rider's back, it will be no problem to hold on. I have always believed in ponies for children and this program is certainly no different; a small cerebral palsied child should be mounted on a suitable small, narrow pony. The fear is lessened, the child can learn control easier and it is much safer, with no excessive stretching of already tight muscles.

Most riding instructors feel every horse and pony should have three distinct gaits: the walk, trot and canter. However, for paraplegic riders or those with spina bifida or even some polios, possibly the walking horse types would be more comfortable to ride. Those disabilities are not going to be concerned about posting the trot, so those types of horses should not be excluded. Be very careful, however, that you select the horse that will be most frequently used, not just standing in the stall. Unless you are limiting your program to disabilities that won't be trotting, it would be quite expensive to keep walking horses. Three distinct gaits are desirable for most riders to afford them the maximum opportunity for exercise and therapy.

What ages should your mounts be for this type of program? Most programs have horses with a range of ages between five and 20. For acceptance as a donated horse or one you will lease or buy, I would look for it to be between seven and 14. At seven, they are settled, their youth of bucking and playing around is usually behind them and if they have been well trained prior to your acquiring them, they should be good mounts. The upper age of 14 is looking to the future and how many more years you will have without constant veterinary care. Many programs have excellent older horses in their programs that require no more care than the younger ones, but as they get older you have to realize you will be having problems. Soundness of limbs is usually one of those problems. Be very careful in selecting your horses no matter what age.

Soundness is a subject many persons don't seem to know what to do about. First, a horse that cannot pass a veterinary check for soundness does not belong in your program. Enough problems will develop after they are in the program without starting out with a horse that is not sound. Any number of persons who want to give you a horse will say, "He is fine at a walk, he is only lame at a trot or canter." Even navicular horses cannot pass a veterinary check, so just don't take them. Be sure you see a complete health record on any horse for your program. Has it been wormed on a regular basis and are all the protective immunizations up to date? What past illnesses has the horse had? It is important that you know all of the details. Veterinarians are expensive. Don't buy, lease, or accept a donated horse that is not perfectly sound: the bills will come sooner than you expect if you do.

Last but not least is sex. It goes without saying a stallion should never be used in a therapeutic riding program. Most breed associations never allow a stallion to be shown by anyone under 18. That gives you a valid reason in itself to say no to a stallion. They are often very unpredictable. Geldings are probably the most desirable, but don't overlook mares. They may have to be turned out for a few days each month while they are "in season," but they are very dependable all other times. A mare or gelding needs to be turned down only if it doesn't meet the other qualifications.

No matter how many horses or ponies you plan to have, please remember selection is the key. Ride and try them in all situations they may encounter.

Step eight - recruiting volunteers

Recruiting volunteers depends a lot on where you live, whether rural or city. In a city, you may have a Voluntary Action Agency which will be glad to assist you in getting volunteers. Of course, publicity in daily or weekly newspapers and TV and radio announcements will also be a great help. Don't discount any service organization or church group. Also, ask other programs how they recruited their volunteers.

It may be more difficult in a rural area. You may have to put announcements in your local grocery stores, drug stores or any place which allows posters announcing your needs.

Be specific as to what you require of volunteers and don't just limit it to sidewalkers and leaders. Maybe you will need a part-time secretary, a baby-sitter (for those volunteers with younger children), a good person to work with the stable management program and grooms. People who don't mind getting their hands dirty can clean tack and be in charge of keeping the equipment in order. Make a list of all the people you might be able to use as volunteers. Give them a telephone number where they can call and set up a specific time for a training session. Once started, we have found word-of-mouth is a good way of getting others. Good volunteers can recruit others for you, but dissatisfied volunteers will usually leave. Once recruited, training is important.

Step nine - fundraising

Most small programs, operated mostly by volunteers, with possibly one paid instructor, don't need a great deal of money, just enough for care of their mounts, needed equipment, insurance and extras for telephone, paper, etc. A lot of the above can be acquired through donations if you are good at asking for help. Horse clubs in a local area are usually more than willing to help organize a horse show or ride-a-thon. Service clubs will often be willing to sponsor a student for so many lessons or to help purchase equipment. Charity fairs are great because you can involve eveyone: parents, students and volunteers. It is work, but $10,000 can be realized from just one fair, if handled properly. Raffles are always a good way, but make sure you have a tax number or else you can't run a raffle. In some states (Michigan is one), you have to have a Charity Solicitation License before asking for donations or having any activity to raise funds.

Large sums can be raised from a garage sale or an auction of services, such as, painting a fence, baby-sitting, washing windows, fixing an entire meal for eight (they supply the food), cleaning up after a big party, cutting grass, cleaning out a swimming pool, or acting as a groom at a horse show. You can hold bake sales or an antique valuation day with a local antique dealer volunteering to place values on antiques brought to a certain place. You can charge so much a piece and limit the number of pieces people can bring and what type of antique, furniture, glass, etc. Another idea is a progressive dinner where eight or nine people each do a course and you sell tickets for the entire meal. One person has cocktails (limit one) and hors d'oeuvres, one has soup, one salad, one entree, one vegetable and one dessert. There are books you can purchase to assist you and a good one is *The Art of Fundraising*, by Irving Warner, published by Harper and Row, New York.

Fundraising can be difficult or easy, frustrating or rewarding, depending on the person or persons involved in doing it. A "think" session with your board, volunteers, parents and staff will come up with unique ideas. Schools in Michigan have raised as much as $15,000 by taking orders for submarine sandwiches. I wouldn't suggest this, unless you have many, many workers to take and fill the orders. I've only skimmed the surface on this type of fundraising. I'm sure there are many more ideas, but remember one very important thing: you must make a budget even for fundraising activities, as well as why you want the money. Always have a specific project in mind before starting to raise the money.

NARHA accreditation procedures

Equestrian therapy is one of the fastest growing recreations and therapies for the handicapped today. The accreditation procedure that NARHA has initiated for member programs is done to assure the handicapped that their instruction, the horse or pony they ride and the facility are of the highest quality. The accreditation procedure is also a tool that can be used to improve the program. The accreditor has a list of things to be checked, such as volunteer training, equipment, first aid procedures, horses and ponies, the facility, the lesson quality and overall safety. Weaknesses and strengths are discussed with the coordinator and instructor after the testing and before the accreditor leaves. If the program passes with an overall score above 85, it becomes a full-accredited NARHA program. Unless the instructor changes, it may not be seen again for two years. If the instructor changes, the program must reapply to NARHA immediately. If the score is below 85, but higher than 70, the program receives provisional status which allows it to keep insurance. Within three months, it must reapply and if it does not receive full accreditation on the second visit, it is dropped as a NARHA member.

Safety is, of course, the main concern, with the instructor's ability to teach to the ability of the student as second most important. NARHA expects its member programs to meet certain standards of excellence, to assure physicians, parents, students, educators and others that a NARHA program will provide the handicapped, no matter what their disability, with a well-thought-out and well-designed program to fit the students' needs.

Conclusion

A bond develops between horse and rider. The horse is totally dependent on others for the care it receives and the student, by assisting in that care, realizes he or she is needed. They develop a friendship. A horse or pony doesn't talk back nor can it give thought-out negative responses. A heel is touched to its side, it moves forward; a rein is pulled towards the right, the horse turns right. Given the right commands, it obeys. It is a positive experience; even mounting a horse for the first time creates a success. Too many times, the handicapped are programmed to failure. To even make a horse move, the student has to do it, so the experience becomes an instant success. Games, exercises and just learning the rudiments of riding can all create a wholesome attitude. Add that to helping care for the horse itself and you have an unbeatable combination.

Yes, a bond between the horse and its rider exists; they are a team. The horse provides the rider a way of improving, not only physically in balance, posture and coordination, but even more by giving the rider a sense of worth, of belonging, of being someone. "I can ride a horse" is a positive statement and they find that if they can ride a horse, they can accomplish even more feats that seemed unattainable. A bond develops and matures, hopefully under the best possible circumstances, in a well operated, approved program.

Suggested reading:

McCowan Lida *It Is Ability That Counts.* Olivet, Mich.: Olivet College Press, 1972. $9.00.

Davies, John A *Reins of Life.* London: J.A. Allen &. Co., 1967.

Haipertz, Wolfgang *Therapeutic Riding: Medicine, Education, Sports.* Ottawa: Canadian Equestrian Federation, 333 River Road, 1982. $10.00

Hulsey, Robin *Horseback Riding for the Hearing Impaired.* Chesterfield, Mo.: Riding High, 609 Thunderbird Ct., 1979. $5.00.

Small, Mary *And Alice Did the Walking.* London: Oxford University Press, 1978.

"Ability, Not Disability" (documentary film) Alameda, Calif.: The Latham Foundation.

McCowan, Lida, et al.: *Aspects and Answers: A Training Manual on Therapeutic Riding.* $16.50. Cheff Center, Box 171, Augusta, MI 49012.

13

Companion Animals on the Farm

Stanley L. Diesch

"Farm animals for therapy... appears to be of great value."

A bond exists between people and farm animals, such as cattle, sheep, goats and swine. However, a more definitive bond has been identified between people and their companion animals, such as dogs, cats and horses. In the literature there is evidence of man's companionship with livestock since the beginning of domestication.

During my youth I had the opportunity to live on a southern Minnesota livestock farm. Here the "pet" farm animal was never home-slaughtered for meat. The milk cows were given names such as "Peaches and Cream" and "Popeye." It is still common practice for farm people to give names to their livestock from dairy goats to purebred boars. A definitive bonding occurs between young people and their 4-H club and Future Farmers of America livestock. Many owners exhibit and express a feeling of loss when selling or parting with their animals.

The relationship between the farmer and livestock exists in management, production, husbandry, and the prevention, diagnosis and treatment of animals for diseases. For several years I practiced large animal medicine and surgery in Iowa and Illinois. In veterinary medical practice the family farm owner and employee related health and disease problems to me, not only from an economic approach, but with expressed concern for the well-being of their animals. To date, information is primarily anecdotal. This whole spectrum is inadequately defined and needs

Stanley L. Diesch, D.V.M., M.P.H., is former director of CEN/SHARE, the Center to Study Human-Animal Relationships and Environments, at the University of Minnesota, where he is also a professor in the Department of Large Animal Clinical Sciences in the College of Veterinary Medicine. He has served on the Board of Directors of the Delta Society and is a member of numerous national veterinary councils.

additional scientific research and evaluation.

For most farmers, economics is of major importance. Farmers strive for efficient production and satisfactory economic return for the livelihood of their families. In the U.S. these factors have resulted in intensive livestock production. However, varying degrees of relationship beyond economics exist between people and farm animals.

Review of the literature

In a literature review *"Human-Animal Bond: Historical Perspectives."* Dr. Leo Bustad and Linda Hines indicate that throughout history there is evidence that the purpose of domestication of farm animals has been more than economic exploitation; a utilitarian explanation alone is not sufficient. Some of the examples they present include: the Chinese kept cattle for hundreds of years but never milked cows or other livestock; people bred sheep but some never produced wool nor were consumed for food; in Burma and Africa, poultry were kept but rarely consumed. Pigs were kept by many cultures including prehistoric Egypt, but there is little evidence that they were eaten or worked in any way. The time when pigs were utilized as beasts of burden or to plant seed appears to have been short-lived. Historically, there is extensive evidence that people have lavished much affection and care on animals, especially those regarded as pets and which were not utilized as food.

In pastoral societies people extensively depended on animals in life and death. Animals had great cultural and economic value. People spent much time with their animals, working with, grooming and talking to them. Conversation of animal owners often would be about their animals. In some cultures animals were buried with their owners. Many of these behaviors are common today.

Bustad and Hines report that in 1867, Bethel, in Bielefeld, Germany, was founded and that animals were an integral part of the enterprise. It began as a home for epileptics but now is a center of healing for disadvantaged people, with over 5,000 patients and more than 5,000 staff. Farm animals, cats, dogs and horses are evident in many residences and other sites in the "institution without walls." A wild game park on the facility attests to the human-animal relationship and the environment.

Dr. Calvin Schwabe, describing what he calls "the most intense man-animal bond," writes that scholars argue on the origins of cattle-culture pastoralism but many agree that domestication of cattle in Asia Minor, adjacent Europe and perhaps elsewhere developed by at least 6000 B.C. for religious reasons relating to man's admiration for strength, speed, bravery and libido of the largest and most powerful animal of the region. Cattle culture religions emerged from Egypt, Greece and the Mediterranean islands in the West through Iran and India in the East. He further indicates that sheep cultures were probably the first to possess behavioral qualities considered humane as distinguished from bestial.

Recent information exists on how farm people relate to animals. Dr. Marvin Samuelson, a veterinarian, indicates that people in a community have varying ideas, notions and feelings toward animals. He feels that there are two major groups. The first group tends to think of animals as living creatures with feelings and certain ethical rights; this group could be called humanistic or moralistic. The second group thinks of animals as owned, personal property with some practical value or usefulness; this group is often called utilitarian or dominionistic. His experience is that veterinarians' attitudes towards animals vary widely. Veterinarians with a wider "more professional view" are apt to see animals as contributors to life quality for humans. Whether their role is for companionship, food, or service makes little difference. It is Samuelson's opinion that humane care of non-human animals comes naturally.

Temple Grandin, a knowledgeable animal scientist in livestock handling, recommends well-designed and maintained equipment for the reduction of stress and injuries to livestock during movement through stockyards, veterinary facilities, slaughter plants and loading on trucks. She reported on the human/livestock interaction in handling at the 1983 Conference on the Human-Animal Bond at the University of Minnesota.

In an earlier report, Grandin found that observing cattle behavior could lead to design of handling facilities in commercial operations which result in facilities which can handle larger numbers of cattle with fewer people. Facility design based on sound ethological principles reduced the incidence of alarmed, excited cattle and employee accidents.

An example of behavioral production research is that of Dr. Bill Hall, a veterinarian at the University of Minnesota. His research attempts to answer questions concerning the well-being of animals. Hall has researched three different types of farrowing housing for pregnant sows prior to farrowing and for the period of lactation. This was evaluated using behavioral, physiological and production measures. The three housing types were: a large pen with straw bedding; a standard farrowing crate which allowed the sow a limited degree of movement; and a modified farrowing crate which allowed the sow a limited degree of movement. Preliminary measurements indicated little difference in the measurements between the three types of farrowing.

Dr. Jack Albright, Professor of Animal Sciences, published on the behavior and management of high-yielding dairy cows. He states that behavioral characteristics of the high yielding cow (more than 40,000 pounds of milk) include: aggressive eating habits, consuming large amounts of high quality alfalfa hay; excellent temperaments, personalities and responses to close relationship with their caretaker(s); they all have names and nicknames; they all are broke to lead and respond to the halter for purposes of handling; and they have strong pedigrees. He further states that the high-yielding dairy cow is a composite of unique behavioral characteristics. She must fit well with her herd mates as well as handlers. Proper mental attitude of her caretakers must blend in with skillful management and humane care in today's highly competitive technological society.

At the 1983 Minnesota Conference on the Human-Animal Bond, Albright reported that calves raised individually formed a closer bond with people, that cows liked comfort and that reactions of cows depend on the mood of people.

Dr. Ingvar Ekesbo, a veterinarian and professor at the Swedish University of Agricultural Sciences, has conducted research on preventive medicine and studied the relationship between environment and health. He defines health in animals as physical and psychological well-being and not as "production." Ekesbo believes that to achieve this definition of health, animal behavior must be given serious consideration.

New Zealander, Ron Kilgour indicated five foci for the welfare of farm animals: use behavior and stress to identify areas of concern; pre-condition stock to housing and husbandry; design housing and feeding to fit the animal; select strains to breed and match the farm conditions; and prevent disease and accidents. These should also serve as areas for farm animal welfare in therapeutic settings.

Use of livestock and farm animals for therapeutic purposes

In the 1940s the first recorded use of farm animals in therapy in the United States occurred at Pawling, N.Y., at an Army Air Corps Convalescent Hospital. During World War II the Pawling Center received Air Corps personnel from throughout the world. The patients were recovering from effects of operational fatigue or convalescing from injuries. They needed restful activity rather than continued intense medical care. An academic program was designed to keep their minds active and also to give them release from war and its activities. The patients were encouraged to work at the Center's farm with cattle, hogs, horses and poultry. They also benefited from snakes, frogs, turtles and other creatures of the nearby fields and forests. The experiment was successful, but the Center was later closed as an economic measure.

In recent years there has been an increasing use of pets and farm animals in therapy for the mentally retarded, emotionally ill, those maladjusted to society and the lonely and isolated. The impact of pets and farm animals on the "normal" individual or families is generally accepted, but poorly documented from a scientific approach.

In Minnesota, the majority of state institutions developed from 1890 to the early 1900s had facilities and acreage to implement an agricultural program. Many state institutions in Minnesota had farm and horticulture programs for a large portion of their existence. The farm and horticultural programs were diversified so the institution could be as self-sufficient as possible.

At one state mental hospital in Minnesota there was no exception to farming at a self-sufficient level. For years there were a variety of livestock, crops and vegetables produced. The longest running enterprises were the dairy and swine programs. The dairy program had approximately 60 milking cows and 20 to 30 young stock. The swine operation had 200 to 300 head. Both of these programs had purebred stock and exchanged breeding stock with other state institutions. Other livestock included flocks of turkeys, chickens and geese. At the peak of the horsepower era the farm had 12 teams of draft horses. The horticulture program worked hand in hand with the livestock portion of the farm. Large gardens, fields, a greenhouse and an apple orchard were all considered part of the farm.

The farm and its activities were an integral part of many patients' lives. Those patients who were allowed to work on the farm participated in all areas of the production, care and maintenance of the animals and maintenance of the buildings and machinery, with the exception of running large machinery. Several examples of patient/animal interaction were described by five individuals, four of whom were employees of the state hospital, to Debra Pangerl. These five were a registered nurse, a business manager, two medical assistants and a local farmer who had had business dealings with the state hospital farm. Although Pangerl's interviews were not a scientific study, the retrospective information suggests that the farm of the state hospital played an important part in the lives of patients for many years. According to some people it had positive therapeutic value.

Pangerl's interviews related the following interactions:

1. One patient slept in the turkey barn at night to monitor the barn's temperature.
2. Patients would run their fingers through the chicken feed to break up clods of feed, thereby encouraging the chickens to eat more.
3. Patients would gather the eggs.

4. Each team of horses had assigned patients who were responsible for their care and grooming.
5. Farrowing time often had two patients assisting one sow.
6. Herding the geese was one of the farm jobs.
7. Feeding the livestock was an important job of the patients.
8. Members of the milking crews had specific jobs and worked together as a team to get the milking done.
9. Plowing, planting, hoeing and harvesting were all tasks on which the patients worked.

When asked about the therapeutic aspect of the farm, all five of the persons interviewed thought the farm held such a value for the majority of the patients, though they recognized that it could have been non-therapeutic if handled improperly. The benefits mentioned included improved communications, even among patients who were most often uncommunicative. Some patients working on the farm became easier to work with in other areas. Work on the farm and with the animals allowed the patients a feeling of worth and of being needed.

The farm changed with time as did the herdsmen in charge. In the 1940s the large dairy barn burned and was not rebuilt. The dairy operation continued but at a lower production level. Gradually over the years individual programs were discontinued. By 1963 the dairy and swine enterprises were the only remaining aspects of the farm. In the fall of 1963 an auction was held at the State Hospital and all the livestock and machinery from that and other state institutions were sold. In response to the question of why the farm was closed, the former business manager cited two possible reasons: one being economics, the other being the negative opinion that the staff psychiatrist had concerning patients working on the farm.

The close of the farm affected many patients. Most did adjust to the change; however, to some, the farm had become more than a daily activity and their adjustment was much slower. Some of those interviewed recalled patients being "lost" without their work on the farm.

Although economics played a role in the closing of farms associated with many state institutions, the time also coincided with the pharmaceutical development of tranquilizers and other medications coupled with overall changes in treatment methods of the mentally ill. There is evidence that work and responsibility have curative aspects and are needs of most people. Removal of animals from the previously mentioned farm most likely was of extensive importance to a number of people associated with that institution.

The importance of farm animal therapy is again emerging. In 1979, the

Minnesota state legislature recognized that there is interdependence between the elderly and their animals and passed a law allowing animals to be on the premises of nursing homes and boarding care homes. This law was signed by Governor Albert Quie, a person with a farm animal background and an equine enthusiast. Minnesota became the first state in the United States to recognize, through legal means, the existence of a human-animal bond. *(See Chapter 7).*

In 1981, Geary Olsen surveyed 744 administrators of health care facilities in Minnesota. These facilities were categorized as nursing homes, supervised living facilities, boarding care homes, nursing and boarding care homes and convalescent and nursing care units. Of the health care facilities, 47.9% were utilizing animals. Of those utilizing farm animals,

A wide variety of animals have been used successfully in institutional visits. For elderly residents, raised in a rural environment, the presence of farm animals can bring back fond memories and reminiscences. *(Photo by Susan Reardon)*

21.03% were using baby farm animals and 14.75% adult farm animals.

The advantages perceived in utilizing pets (including farm animals) in health care facilities were: entertainment and enjoyment, outlets for expression of human feelings, rekindling pleasant memories and providing a more home-like atmosphere. Major disadvantages included: sanitation and hygiene, extra work required by the staff, fear or non-acceptance of the animal by the residents or staff and the potential for injuries to residents. At present, no further definitive information is available on the utilizations of farm animals in Minnesota health care facilities.

Throughout the United States a number of farms, ranches and camps have been established which give people an opportunity to associate with farm animals. At Camp Courage, in Golden Valley, Minn., each year more than 1,000 children and adults with physical and communication disabilities are given a chance to make new friends, learn about nature and participate in a variety of activities at the camp, including becoming acquainted with domestic farm animals and wild animals in a zoo. Horseback riding ranks as second most popular activity at the camp. Eleanore Thompson, the Pony Express coordinator for the Courage Center, says that the camp farm has horses, sheep, goats, pigs and calves. These animals are of real importance to the senior citizen campers as well as to the young people. Many of the seniors were former farm folk and enjoy being a part of the atmosphere of "farm life."

"The Ranch," founded in 1964, is located at Menomonee Falls, Wis. It is an urban/rural day services rehabilitation center on 58 acres of farm land. Facilities include a farm, stable and a production shop worksite for the handicapped and developmentally disabled of Wisconsin who may not benefit from traditional work programs that emphasize benchwork activities. The Ranch is a provider of supportive services to help the handicapped achieve personal and vocational independence. According to Dr. Paquette, clinical psychologist and director of services, the farm environment allows the staff a unique opportunity to utilize farm animals as "support staff' in education, training, and therapy.

An active farm making therapeutic use of animals with children is the Green Chimneys Children's Services of Brewster, N.Y. This is a non-profit, multi-service voluntary child care agency providing year-round education and mental health services to youth and their families in the New York metropolitan area. The program was founded in 1947 by members of the Ross family. Pioneering work has been done in helping people develop emotionally through therapeutic activities that include caring for animals and participating in the running of the farm. Dr. Samuel B. Ross, Jr. is the Executive Director.

Green Chimneys uses farm animals and horticulture as an integral part of its therapeutic program. All resident children are exposed to the farm program through animal husbandry, horseback riding, farming and gardening. The program serves 88 boys and girls between the ages of six and 16. Staff work with youngsters with emotional problems often combined with learning disabilities.

In 1978 a program called Using Talent with Animals and Plants was successfully launched with the help of the Western Connecticut Association for the Handicapped and Retarded. The goals and objectives were to allow Green Chimneys' students the opportunity to share and be of service to others. In 1981 and 1982 Green Chimneys implemented a program aimed at training older youths in Putnam County who were on probation as aides for the handicapped. This introduced them to career opportunities with plants and animals and provided them with first-hand experiences with therapeutic riding and farm chores.

In discussing the roles of animals, Ross notes that ownership and care of a pet may aid in the development of sound personality traits and that nurturance and companionship heighten the capacity to be loved and to give love. He further states that in many cases, animals have helped a child work through feelings of rivalry, possessiveness and jealously and in turn this helps provide the basis for wholesome feelings toward siblings and adults. Ross concludes that pets and animals serve a variety of needs of children and their families; various inter-relationships can occur as a result of the human/pet bond.

In 1978 the Syosset School District of Nassau County, N.Y., obtained a 20-acre parcel of land to develop a farm program to educate disabled children. Animals included were sheep, cattle, ducks, chickens, ponies, goats, rabbits and also a cat, donkey, piglet and dog. Children are involved in the farm operation. Delores English, describing the Developmental Learning Farm, reports beneficial experiences and concludes that the sure-fire ingredient is the animal.

Safety considerations

In utilizing farm animals in therapy, potential injuries and safety of the people must be assessed. This information has not been adequately documented. However, some information exists concerning injuries to farmers by their animals. In 1979 an American study revealed that in one out of every eight farm injuries reported, animals were a factor: however, machinery ranked first.

Kilgour of New Zealand reports the causes of 432 farmers in hospitals with injuries from stock: horses 82%; cattle 12%; sheep 3%; dogs 2%; and pigs 5%. During a three-year period, body injuries from stock were reported from farmers, veterinarians and others: hands and fingers 46%; legs and feet 33%; body 5%; face and head 6%; eye 4%; and infectious diseases 6%.

In developing guidelines and selection of farm animals for therapeutic uses in institutions, camps and other facilities, veterinarians, animal husbandrymen and others must be actively involved in evaluating the animal's behavior in addition to nutrition, housing, breeding and physical health. Sometimes what is termed a behavioral problem may be normal for the animal, but it may be inconsistent with the owner's expectations. Consideration must be given to the safety of both people and animals.

The facility must have assurance that the animals are free of, or protected from zoonotic diseases (those diseases that are naturally transmitted between vertebrate animals and man). Approximately 40 diseases of this nature are potential in the United States. Diseases such as brucellosis, leptospirosis, toxoplasmosis, salmonellosis, rabies and ringworm are reported. At present there is lack of adequate assurance that the farm animals selected for visits to institutions are free of zoonotic disease. Allergies resulting from contact with animals must also be considered.

Institutionalized people who previously lived in an environment with farm animals may prefer companionship with farm animals rather than dogs, cats, or other species. On a visit, young farm animals would be the most satisfactory and safest to use in order to prevent injury, as they are easier to manage. Partly because of size and management, it appears that baby pigs and lambs are better suited to visits than calves or colts. However, a new environment, handling and transportation can cause stress and unusual behavior in animals. People with mobility can make external visits to a farm. Unless these facilities are in a rural setting or people have access to farms, it is unlikely that large metropolitan areas will be able to develop successful programs with farm animals. People are traveling for a day or longer to rural farm environments, such as has occured at Camp Courage, The Ranch and Green Chimneys. There is an increase in numbers of petting zoos in shopping centers, using grown and baby farm animals for people—contact. This trend is likely associated with the statistic that only 5% of the U.S. population are now farming. For longer term association, whether therapeutic or casual, continued development of farms for visits appears likely.

With increasing research and documentation of the value of small companion animals (dog, cat, goldfish, etc.) to people, the need for therapeutic use of large farm animals will be questioned and must also be evaluated. Individual people have definite animal species preferences. People with a rural background have a varying degree of attachment to farm animals. Other non-farm people, through media or intermittent contact, have acquired an attachment. The human/animal bond began with domestication and has evolved since that time. Increasing use of farm animals for therapy is emerging and appears to be of great value to many. However, well-designed epidemiologic research and quantitative documentation need to be addressed. This type of research will support continued development and growth of the companionship of people and farm animals.

Suggested reading:

Diesch, S.L., Johnson, D.W., Martin F.B., Christensen, L.T., Revsbech, R., and Therrien, T.M.: *Project Report, Validation of the Minnesota Food Animal Disease Reporting System*, October, 1981.

Diesch, S.L. and Ellinghausen, H.C., Jr.: *Leptospirosis in Diseases Transmitted from Animals to Man*, 6th Edition, Eds.: Hubbert, McCulloch and Schnurrenberger. Springfield, Ill., Charles C. Thomas, 1975.

Diesch, S.L., Pomeroy, B.S., and Allred, E.R.: *Survival of Pathogens in Animal Manure Disposal* (three-year project report), Environmental Protection Agency, June, 1975.

Diesch, S.L.: Should Wild-Exotic Animals be Banned as Pets? *California Veterinarian*, December, 1981, 13-18.

Diesch, S.L., Hendricks, S.L. and Currier, R.W.: The Role of Cats in Human Rabies Exposures, *J.A.V.M.A.*, Vol. 181, No. 12, 1510-1512.

Houpt, K.A. and Wolski, T.R.: *Domestic Animal Behavior for Veterinarians and Animal Scientists.* (Ames: Iowa State University Press, 1982.)

Section IV - Perspectives

14

The Veterinarian's Role in the Human/Animal Bond

James M. Harris

"We are healing arts professionals..."

The role of pets in our lives and its effect on veterinarians

Evidence suggests that in prehistory man first sought the companionship of animals. As time passed and cultures developed, man "used" animals. Advanced technological society has had a marked depersonalizing effect. There has been a breakdown of the nuclear family unit and discomfort with and isolation of the aged, injured, deformed and handicapped. In this contemporary setting man has an increasing need for emotional support from and physical contact with other living things. It is no wonder then, that having come full circle, man again looks to other animals for companionship, affection, diversion, entertainment and at times as substitutes for a variety of human relationships.

Given the importance of these relationships and the emotional value placed on these companion animals, a high level of expectation often exists on the part of clients when seeking professional medical and/or counseling service for his or her companion animals. Contemporary times have also seen a trend towards the ethics and practice of humane stewardship which, when carried to an extreme, becomes "animal rights" rather than the traditional "human rights" approach of dominionistic ownership. Neither, in the extreme, is acceptable, practical, nor realistic. But both are presented, day in and day out, to this nation's veterinarians,

James M. Harris, D.V.M., is a practicing veterinarian in Oakland, Calif. A graduate of Michigan State University, he chairs the Human/Animal Bond Committee for the California Veterinary Medical Association, and is on the AVMA Human/Animal Bond Committee. He is a certified grief and bereavement counselor.

who are caught at the forefront of a changing spectrum of societal values. Every day we face clients who feel they have an inalienable right to do whatever they want with their property; alternately, we face others who argue that their pets are "free spirits," who ask how can one living thing own another? Do not all species have a right to habitat and continued existence?

Man, as well as all the other life forms present on this planet, have equal importance. Man must remind himself that he is not the most successful life form existing today, but is surely the most destructive. Our existence is dependent on all other life forms, both plant and animal. Without them we would perish. We are not more important; we are perhaps as important as other life. In learning to respect, care for and help other life survive, man may develop the skills needed for his own survival.

Veterinarians, in their role as licensed animal health practitioners, have great demands placed upon them by their clients. Often these demands are excessive, unreasonable and impossible to comply with, let alone satisfy. Instant diagnosis, prognosis, cure, low- or no-cost treatment and correcting existing conditions that are incompatible with life are not often possible to accomplish. Anxiety levels run high, as is the case with most medical contacts in our society and this, combined with the level of attachment often associated with the human-animal bond, puts further pressure on the veterinarian who is expected to be available 24 hours a day wihout a wait, 365 days a year, always correct in his or her clinical judgments and be able to cure everything. In reality only patients cure themselves and practitioners observe, notate and occasionally influence the process.

The success of the client-practitioner relationship is dependent upon trust, skill, good communication and demeanor, i.e., "bedside manner." Under the most ideal conditions it is at best difficult to maintain ongoing success. Considering the adversities and pressure under which practitioners are often placed, it is a wonder that success occurs at all. It is not surprising, therefore, to see the results of the stress to which the veterinarian is exposed. "Burn out" is common. Depression, suicide, divorce, alcoholism and drug abuse are well-documented occurrences. In California, a state with approximately 4,400 veterinarians, the state veterinary association's Committee on Alcohol and Drug Abuse receives between 80 and 100 referral calls per year. One wonders how many others should call for help. International Doctors in Alcoholics Anonymous has estimated that 12-15% of all medical practitioners have some alcohol/drug-related impairment and 10-11% are frank abusers of alcohol and/or drugs. These figures are considered to be conservative. In the county in which I practice we have about 100 veterinarians. In the past two years we have had one successful suicide and one attempted suicide. The demands of clients and those self-imposed add fuel to the fire. In an effort to be successful and popular we actually try to comply with the unreasonable requests and expectations of clients.

We have only recently come to study the human/animal bond and the practitioner/client/animal bond. We also need to direct efforts and time to studying the veterinary practitioner.

The psychological, emotional and physiological aspects of a client

Psychiatrist Michael McCulloch has estimated that veterinarians in companion animal practice have 100,000,000 human contacts yearly. Clients who have placed high priority on their companion animals will call their veterinarian when they perceive that their animals have medical needs long before they will consider "disturbing" their pediatrician, dentist, or physician. Many people use their animals as a "ticket of admission," a means by which they gain access to a nonthreatening professional authority with a sympathetic ear. The veterinary practitioner becomes a gatekeeper of mental health observing varying degrees of human psychopathology. Often, the veterinarian is the only person privy to these phenomena and all too often is unprepared or unable to deal with them.

The presenting client is often anxiety-laden and apprehensive with any medical visits. The pet, an extension of the owner/client, when taken to the veterinarian, sets off the client's own fears of medical and dental service. In turn, the companion animal, especially when encouraged or trained to protest, senses the level of apprehension, is on guard and can be a source of potential physical danger to the practitioner. Clients often respond to their animals' protective and/or aggressive actions by reassuring them. "It's O.K.," an often-heard comment from clients who are really trying to reassure their pet and themselves that the medical visit is pleasant and the doctor is a good person, is in fact a verbal approval of the animal's behavior which further encourages the animal's undesirable examination room protectiveness and/or aggression.

Many clients present animals which, for some reason of the owner's psychological or emotional needs, are overly and often deliberately, aggressive. In many sub-cultures, large and vicious dogs, not to mention rare and exotic animals, are signs of "macho" status and are believed to enhance the owner's self-esteem. Consequently, veterinarians and their support staff are often bitten and/or scratched by patients. One could avoid this by never having physical contact with animal patients or by always using safety muzzles, but for most patients this is unnecessary and it is certainly not a technique readily accepted or appreciated by clients. I personally know one veterinarian who started an exclusively feline practice as the result of receiving numerous bites from large aggressive "watch dogs" kept by his clients in the suburban area where he practiced.

In any case, a thorough, competent physical examination requires a hands-on approach. Injuries can be minimized by a knowledge of animal behavior and principles of dominance and aggression. Prolonged eye contact with dominant dogs may result in a dog at one's throat. Assuming

In many sub-cultures, rare and exotic animals are signs of "macho" status and are believed to enhance the owner's self-esteem. Despite warnings by veterinarians and animal shelters, lions and other dangerous animals find their way into American cities.

(Photo by Phil Arkow)

a dominant position with a similar dog may likewise set off an untoward response. Sudden movements around felines can trigger fight-or-flight reactions, especially with subjects that have well-developed predatory instincts. The animal-wise practitioner can minimize personal injuries, but never totally eliminate them. Studying the incidence of animal-related trauma to veterinarians and their staff is appropriate, as would be the development of strategies to prevent these incidents.

Clients need continued reassurance and often place unreasonable demands on their veterinarians. As I alluded to previously, diagnostic, therapeutic and prognostic information is expected instantly. The concepts of "I don't know" and "I am unable to predict" do not sit well and are rarely accepted by clients. Although this is no different than with human health care, the veterinary client seems to assume that we should know and predict. Perhaps this is an irrational compensation to make up for the fact that their companion animals cannot verbalize their discomfort, pain, or problems to them. Actually this does occur, but in a non-verbal way. Because we deal with "dumb" animals, veterinarians are apparently supposed to be god-like, having some special undefined ability to communicate with "all creatures great and small." James Herriot's books have not helped this situation either. These lovely descriptions and reminiscences of rural Yorkshire of the 1930's have also encouraged an increased romanticization of veterinary medicine. This image on the part of the clients adds further stress and handicaps to an already difficult job.

Clients' psychological and emotional needs for love, recognition, success and power are often so strong that they totally out-weigh and overshadow potential and real dangers to their physical well-being and health. Clients with aggressive pets will often hold on to the relationship in spite of repeated physical attacks and trauma to themselves and/or their children inflicted by their animals. An individual with severe allergies may be most willing to give up strawberries or feather pillows, but will hide a pet's existence from his or her physician during history-taking when animal allergies may produce unacceptable advice from the doctor. Unfortunately, doctors often exclude animal data in histories. Zoonoses, often life-threatening, are not uncommonly ignored by clients. It is not uncommon to find an owner who finds it inconceivable that his bird could be carrying psittacosis or his pet skunk rabies.

I am not suggesting that all animals harbor zoonotic problems, but that the potential does exist and needs to be dealt with in a rational, reasonable manner. Neither am I suggesting that all clients have an irrational or neurotic approach to their pet ownership, but rather that unusual situations do occur frequently and that the psycho-social dimension of pethood in American society is greater than we previously thought. Without being overly judgmental, how can the veterinary profession better come to terms with these phenomena?

What veterinarians are and are not taught in school

The veterinarian is a healing arts professional providing service. The privilege of practice is licensed and regulated by government. To meet the requirements for licensing and to become proficient in the medical care of their patients, students enroll in formal training programs. For some four years they study and learn traditional technical medicine. They study anatomy, physiology, pathology, parasitology, bacteriology, surgery and medicine. They are helped and prodded to reach the current level of the medical field as it exists at that moment in time. I would hope that the realization of the need for constant study, change and growth is also ingrained so that the matriculated student can indeed keep up with the field in a self-motivated, disciplined way. The profession, aware of this need, provides continuing education programs. These also generally cover traditional topics and disciplines and at this time are still by and large elective and voluntary. Practitioners are not required to have a minimum number of continuing education hours for relicensure at this time.

The reality of the veterinarian's world, though, is more than technical medicine. People are all highly complex social creatures with great social, psychological and emotional needs. People interact with great intensity on many levels. When veterinarians provide service to clients, to other people, they are in the people business. In fact the people business (i.e. social service) consumes most of our time. It would therefore seem logical to prepare the veterinary student for social service, rather than concentrating solely on anatomy, physiology, pharmacology and the like. The inexperienced practitioner should not be cast unprepared upon the uncertain currents of human emotion and frailties. Veterinarians need all the help we can get if we plan to have a long and productive career in practice. To this end the social service aspects of practice need to be presented to students in detail and students need adequate time to absorb, assimilate and incorporate the material. In short, the students need more time and faculty members must support these activities. At this time this is not the case. Sociology, psychology, psychopathology, psychotherapy, philosophy, anthropology, all need to be incorporated into our training programs and continuing education presentations.

Unfortunately, at this time veterinary training institutions by and large still do not see the value of this material and their faculties are generally disinterested in these subjects. Although some veterinary colleges are making efforts towards this end, the efforts seem to be just lip service rather than dedicated commitments. The University of California School of Veterinary Medicine, with encouragement from the state veterinary association, did offer such a course to students. This non-credit course, offered at night, was organized by two faculty members. In spite of long days of classes and clinics some 80-90 students did attend. Most lectures and presentations were provided by guest speakers. Attendance by faculty, other than the organizers of the course, was non-existent. Recently the course was dropped, then offered again as an elective. Plans were made to include it, starting in the fall of 1984, as a required course in the veterinary college curriculum during the students' freshman year.

Human health care training programs may not do much better, but at least there is a strong humanistic tradition and role modeling in human medicine. This is sorely lacking in veterinary medicine with its origins in agriculture. Institutions of formal training must accept the responsibility of providing the material and keeping students for the additional time that is needed. Society will have to accept the burden of educational cost necessary to train professionals who will be capable of fulfilling that society's needs. Veterinarians need to study, learn, change and therefore grow as individuals and as an organized profession.

This process needs to begin early in the training program if not in the pre-professional training of students. Students represent a captive audience. We need to take advantage of this and blend the traditional coursework with the social sciences and related humanities. Students need strong humanistic models to role-model after. The graduate is a different matter; as he or she is harder to round up, material can be presented only at infrequent intervals in continuing education programs and many organizers of these programs seem reluctant to include these topics out of fear of poor attendance. Surprisingly, the California veterinary association conference in 1983 started its program with a half-day presentation on the human-animal bond, an overview of the topic and a presentation on grief and bereavement. Much to the surprise of the organizing committee this session was very well attended and a dramatic change from previous efforts. I would hope that this signals a change and that more veterinarians will become acquainted with the psychological and emotional aspects of the human/animal bond and the human health implications of veterinary medical practice. *(See Chapter 19)*

The effects of euthanasia on clients and practitioners

Legal killing is an awesome responsiblity. Death does not sit well with any of us, whether client or practitioner and is accompanied by grief with its feelings of guilt and anger and reminds us of our own frail temporary existence. In our culture losing a family member to "natural causes," accident, or sudden illness does not have the impact of a death that is planned, prepared for and instituted by human choice. Humans do take their own lives, but our Judeo-Christian ethic places a stigma on this practice. So strongly ingrained is this in our culture that the mercy killing of a human causes court actions of great magnitude and the practice of executing criminals in recent times has triggered numerous court cases, political action and a society divided into opposing camps. It is no accident that the recent "animal rights" movement should follow so closely behind several decades of social awareness in which open discussions and protests on such issues as capital punishment, human euthanasia and abortion are seen frequently in the mass media.

Because we live in a very homocentrically controlled world we are often faced with the task of killing or participating in the process of killing other species under our care. Our society says that, under certain conditions, killing of other animals is acceptable whereas killing human animals for the same reasons is not. Western man talks about a reverence for life, but by and large really means a reverence for human life.

There is still, subliminally within our culture, a deep discomfort with animal killing. To overcome this, society creates approved executioners. Slaughterhouse workers kill animals for human consumption. Hunters kill animals to thin herds. Animal shelter personnel kill surplus companion animals. And veterinarians kill pets. When a companion animal is terminally ill or in intractable pain, when there is no longer a reasonable quality of life, or when a veterinarian making the rounds in an animal shelter must select today's list of those doomed to die because the facility is overcrowded, man as the controlling agent may elect euthanasia. For veterinarians making this decision it can be tremendously stressful.

Sometimes, however, euthanasia can be an easy way out and in our throw-away society this is not an uncommon occurrence. Clients tiring of a companion animal request euthanasia. Families at a time of break-up, crisis, or moving euthanize pets. People faced with costly medical care of an animal often request euthanasia. Some veterinarians faced with a difficult medical case may encourage a euthanasia decision from their client as an easy way to cover up their lack of skill or their unwillingness to be inconvenienced by a difficult or unpleasent case. Improved medical capabilities, cooperative emergency facilities operating during off-hours and health insurance for animals may help to change this.

Lacking a reverence for life, a client may be desensitized and dehumanized enough not to feel grief or have a natural period of bereavement. This may be further exacerbated in our culture where public mourning over the loss of an animal is considered strange and abnormal. This may also apply to some veterinarians. Practitioners working in food inspection, research animal control and even private practice may be so overwhelmed by the frequency of death or so burned out that they become desensitized to it. By and large veterinarians do have and maintain the reverence for life and do not take death lightly. For them the burden is heavy, the responsiblity great. They are aware of the moral and ethical aspects of their acts. They are aware that they are one of only a few professions legally sanctioned to slaughter animals.

In addition to resolving their own feelings of loss, practitioners must also reach out, support and facilitate resolution of their clients' grief. Unfortunately, very few veterinarians are trained to do this. To provide this support is truly social service.

We ask our fellow man to be stewards of other creatures rather than have dominion over them. In doing so, we increase sensitivity in us all. To the person sensitized to this humane stewardship, there is even greater need for receiving social service from veterinarians. Extreme animal rightists and irresponsible people who treat animals as throwaways, two extremes in clients, are, depending on the veterinarian's viewpoint, often handled differently. Approval of or rejection of requests from clients for euthanasia service does occur. I will not perform convenience euthanasias, but on the other hand I have with great patience spent considerable time convincing a client that a totally non-functional companion animal in great distress would be best euthanized.

As more institutions and individuals become aware of the human health and social service implications of veterinary medicine, there may be a greater trend towards including veterinarians in these interdisciplinary fields. The Arthur D. Little report, prepared for the American Veterinary Medical Association, stated that by 1985 there will be a surplus of 3,900 veterinarians in the U.S., a figure which will increase to 8,300 by 1990. Animal-related social service activities may be one way of providing gainful employment for these new graduates.

Prescribing pets

We are groping in a time of great stress and rapid change. The trend today in veterinary practice is towards medical specializations similar to those in human medicine and group practice. The high cost of construction, equipment and setting up is prohibitive to starting a solo practice. Group practice as we know it today comprises a number of generalist and Board-certified veterinary practitioners working in the same facility. Unfortunately, "groups" are still generally composed of healing practitioners who are all in the same discipline with similar educational training, predisposed to prescribing drugs and medicines. They often practice in a vacuum, removed from other disciplines, soloing in their considerable skills.

We are now beginning to appreciate the benefits of the companion animal to many patient populations. One natural direction therefore is to start "prescribing" pets. I would suggest that pet prescription is far more complex than any drug or medicine and requires an interdisciplinary group practice approach for success. Physicians, veterinarians, mental health personnel and social workers all need to practice together. Perhaps in the future the "prescription pet" will be one of the major factors in bringing all the healing arts together. My personal opinion is that this would be a step forward, but man's provincial and conservative nature will probably resist this innovative idea for "group" practice.

Veterinarians, with the aid of the above-mentioned professionals, would be most suited to facilitate prescription pet selection, care, counseling and placement. From the aspect of professional challenge this area may well be

Veterinary medicine is more than technical medicine. The practitioner must interact with clients on social, psychological and emotional levels. Veterinarians are in the people business of social service, and community outreach programs such as this educational display are one way of reaching current and potential pet owners. *(Photo by Phil Arkow)*

one of the most complex, sophisticated and rewarding experiences. Training and skill in husbandry, ethology, behavior and medicine (to name only a few of the areas) of the varied species suitable as prescription pets give the veterinarian the unique opportunity and responsibility to lead the team. Many of the aspects to be considered by veterinarians in this task are discussed in other chapters of this book as well as in other current publications. It is sufficient to say that consideration of all aspects of placement, including chances of success, availability of back-up supports and community support systems, needs to be made.

Pets as alter egos

Non-conventional bonds between humans and animals are frequently encountered in veterinary medical practice. Animals may be considered as child substitutes, spouse substitutues, parent substitutes, lovers and some people comprise pets as alter egos. Although this can at times be humorous as, for example, the suppressed client who teaches his parrot to swear and say things that the client himself would never be heard uttering in public, many of these relationships have no humor and are of great potential danger to animals, clients, veterinarians and society. Meek clients acquire animals with aggressive propensities and then encourage this trait in the animal. Needless to say, the physical risk of working with these animals is high. During my practicing years I have been bitten more than once by pit bull terriers, German shepherds and other aggressive dogs as well as by a cayman, raccoon, wolf and numbers of exotic wild *felidae.*

These animals often create great problems if, for any number of reasons, there is a transfer of stewardship. On the humorous side is the client presenting the Panama green parrot of great age, handed down from his great-grandfather, who, much to the client's consternation, swore from dawn to dusk in some six languages. I was not able to convince the bird to "clean up its act." Another example is the dog encouraged to exhibit overt sexual behavior by one caretaker: this was not appreciated by other relatives when they acquired the animal. On a more serious note, the attack-trained dog, a lethal weapon at best in unknowing, untrained, or irresponsible hands, is a great liablility and danger to all. Exotic animals are often kept as alter egos. Poisonous reptiles, wolves, raccoons, African lions, pumas, ocelots and other wild cats, to name a few, have all been presented to me by clients for medical care. This practice, the keeping of non-domestic animals as pets, needs to be discouraged. There is a moral question regarding the attempted domestication and pethood of wild animals. It is also an extremely high-risk practice and for the protection of both the animal and the human steward it needs to be stopped. Ideally this would best be accomplished by education, but from the practical point of view cessation could occur through governmental regulation and control by law and statute.

The veterinarian's responsibility in human health

The veterinarian is deeply involved in human health. Four areas are involved: zoonoses, physical trauma, hypersensitization and emotional disturbance.

In traditional veterinary medical training the student learns some three hundred infectious diseases of which approximately ninety are transmissable to humans. The veterinary practitioner's duty is to be constantly diligent and observant for signs of the presence of these zoonotic diseases. Although some of these diseases are of rare occurence, many are frequently encountered. Parasitic infestations such as visceral larval migrans, echinococcosis, giardiasis, strongyloidiasis, scabies and toxoplasmosis, to name a few, need to be screened for and controlled. Rabies is a constant potential in all susceptible species and can be effectively prevented. Psittacosis can be detected; latent carriers as well as active cases can be treated prior to exposure to humans. This is particularly important in older and debilitated patient populations who are at a higher risk if infected. Dermatomycosis spread from kitten to client is well represented in practice experience as is salmonella infection from reptiles. Not only does the veterinarian need to monitor and screen for these potential problems, but when they are suspected he is obliged ethically and legally to discuss his suspicions with the client and with public health officials when appropriate.

When there is physical risk to a client or others from a companion animal, the veterinarian is obliged to notify the client of this fact. It is important that this information be noted on medical records for the veterinarian's own protection in case of legal actions. This is especially true in behavioral work with aggressive animals. One can never guarantee that an animal which has bitten or inflicted physical damage will be totally safe in the future. The reality is that the great majority of these animals are destroyed in spite of any efforts at retraining.

Hypersensitization of clients to animals is common. Some physicians are eager to blame animals for allergies without conclusive tests, although often tests do show animals to be a problem. The veterinarian is in a position to help counsel clients on alternate companion animals and to outline husbandry and housing strategies resulting in less antigenic exposure. Veterinarians need to receive this training in school.

Finally we are healing arts professionals. Our goal is to do no harm, relieve suffering and pain, provide succor for both patient and client and to do some good. A bleeding patient gets a bandage. The psychologically bleeding client should at least receive an emotional band-aid and ideally, as much help as we can comfortably and competently give within the limits of our own abilities. Emotional distress and grief are recognizable conditions in clients. Sadness, crying and anger, to name a few, are easily recognized signs that signal problems.

We sell our time. Why not sell time to help facilitate resolution of these conditions? If unable to do so we should at least have resources available and be able to refer clients to help and assistance when it is needed. The development and utilization of this sort of network would be an interdisciplinary approach to health care. The severly emotionally disturbed client certainly would benefit from this resource. Those unwilling to be helped might still be helped through discreet inquiries. The average client with a basic bond can certainly be helped in times of psychological distress by veterinarians providing "curbside service." This occurs daily in companion animal practice. The most useful tool in this activity is bedside manner. Listening, really concentrating and hearing, watching and being concerned and truly sympathetic to clients, their feelings, emotions and needs are skills that can and should be taught. In human medicine, physicians learn this skill by role-modeling. During medical school, internship and residency, ample opportunity exists for this to happen; this is not so in veterinary medicine, where a student might get a glimpse of this art only if he or she is lucky. As new practitioners there might be some opportunity to learn from a senior practitioner or employer. By and large, bedside manner is self-taught. This is a great educational failure and needs to be rectified for veterinary students choosing practice careers. This would truly be responsible to human health requisites.

Suggested reading:

Neiburg, Herbert A. and Fischer, Arlene *Pet Loss.* N. Y.: Harper and Row, 1982.

Fogle, Bruce (ed). *Interrelations Between People and Pets.* Springfield, Ill.: Charles C. Thomas, 1981.

Anderson, R.S. (ed). *Pet Animals and Society.* London: Balliere Tindall, 1975.

Harris, James M. "A Study of Client Grief Responses to Death or Loss in a Companion Animal Veterinary Practice."

Katcher, Aaron and Beck, Alan, (eds.) *New Perspectives on Our Lives with Companion Animals.* Philadelphia: University of Pennsylvania Press, 1983.

Harris, James M. "The Nonconventional Human Companion Animal Bond, Death and the Veterinary Practitioner-Client Relationship."

Kay, William, et al., (eds.) *Pet Loss and Human Bereavement.* Ames: Iowa State University Press, 1984.

AVMA guidelines for veterinarians: Animal-facilitated therapy programs

Statement of position

When the AVMA officially recognized the importance of the human/animal bond to client and community health in 1982, it really acknowledged that the human/animal bond has existed for thousands of years and that this relationship has major significance for veterinary medicine. As veterinary medicine serves society, it fulfills both human and animal needs. The veterinarian, as an individual and a professional, is in a position to provide community service and to aid in the scientific evaluation and documentation of the health benefits of the human/animal bond.

Animal-facilitated therapy

Today, animals provide many positive human health benefits: companionship, a friend to care for and to keep one occupied, something alive and warm to touch, a focus of attention, a reason for exercise and to provide protection. Therapy programs using animals have evolved worldwide in many forms and with many names whenever a need or an opportunity has arisen. Usually these programs are directed toward people with health problems requiring rehabilitation, such as the elderly, physically handicapped, deaf, blind, emotionally or physically ill, or persons in correctional institutions. However, most individuals and families can and do benefit from human/animal relationships.

Locations

Programs may take place at home on a one-to-one basis with a hearing-ear dog, at a nursing home with an animal-visitation program, at a correctional institution with a resident mascot, or at a horseback riding center for the mentally or physically impaired.

Veterinary involvement

Veterinarians may be asked to participate in programs in a variety of ways:

1) Approached by a client that has read about animal-facilitated therapy, wishes to start a program for a parent in a nurjsing home and asks a practitioner for advice.

2) Approached by the director of a nursing home or day care center, who wishes to develop a program and seeks guidance from a local veterinary medical association.

3) Approached by the director of a humane society or animal shelter, who wishes to use adoptable random-source animals in a program and would like the veterinarian to aid in animal selection and provide health care for the animals.

4) As part of a community service project, a veterinarian may initiate a visiting pet

*Reprinted from the *Journal of the American Veterinary Medical Association,* Vol. 184, No. 2, January 15, 1984.

program by encouraging the cooperation of the local veterinary association, a humane society, a scout troop and a health-care facility.

The field of animal-facilitated therapy is open to innovative and creative thinking. Many situations exist in which animal-facilitated therapy has yet to be tried.

How to get started

An animal-facilitated therapy program should be started only after there has been adequate advanced preparation and discussion by everyone that will be involved. Simply bringing animals in contact with the target population is not sufficient. On the other hand, programs can become so structured with regulations that they never get off the ground or subsequently flounder. Each program has its own potential benefits and problems.

Animal selection

Animals should be selected on the basis of type, breed, size, age, sex and especially behavior appropriate for the intended use. The animal should be chosen with the target population in mind. Experience shows a boisterous, overactive dog may be friendly but inappropriate for a nursing home in which most patients are using walkers. A visiting calf or lamb may be more effective with patients who have rural background than would a caged rodent.

Health care

1) Animals that are healthy, well trained, temperamentally suitable and appropriately immunized should be selected.

2) A health-care plan is needed to prevent and/or to minimize the risk from common zoonotic diseases such as rabies, psittacosis and salmonellosis, as well as internal and external parasites.

3) The current *Compendium of Animal Rabies Vaccines* (prepared by the National Association of State Public Health Veterinarians Inc, PO Box 13528, Baltimore, MD 21203 and published yearly in the *Journal of the AVMA*, and/or state guidelines should be followed.

4) Humane animal care should include appropriate grooming, feeding, watering and exercise schedules. Animals should be monitored for clinical signs of stress and their well-being should be ensured.

Client education

No one is in a better position than the veterinarian to monitor the health and welfare of the animal used in an animal-facilitated therapy program. Fundamental animal handling, behavior, housing and husbandry may have to be explained. Feeding, watering and exercise schedules should be established. A specific individual, such as a staff member, should be responsible for the animal and its well-being. Animals should be monitored for clinical signs of stress and their humane treatment should be ensured. Potential health hazards of common zoonoses should be discussed and evaluated with the facility staff.

Fundamental steps

1) Become informed about animal-facilitated therapy concepts and current programs.

2) Be knowledgeable about local and state laws concerning use of animals in the designated facility. Federal regulations do not prohibit use of animals in federally funded health-care facilities.

3) Contact and encourage cooperation and participation of facility directors, activities directors, and facility staff. This is vital to a successful animal-facilitated program.

4) Establish realistic program goals. An unstructured rush of enthusiasm can lead to early people burnout and abandonment of the program.

5) Employ a team approach. Recruit help from community resources, such as psychiatrists, psychologists, social workers, occupational therapists, humane groups, 4-H clubs, riding clubs, civic and church groups, foundations, nurses and *your clients.*

6) Talk about it.

Suggested reading:

1. Arkow P: *"Pet Therapy": A Study of the Use of Companion Animals in Selected Therapies.* The Humane Society of the Pike's Peak Region, PO Box 187, Colorado Springs, CO 80901—price $10.00
2. Bustad LK: *Animals, Aging and the Aged.* Minneapolis, University of Minnesota Press, 1980, vol 5.
3. Bustad LK: The Veterinarian and Animal-Facilitated Therapy. *J Am Anim Hosp Assoc* 16:477—483, 1980.
4. Fogle B: *Interrelations Between People and Pets,* Springfield, Ill, Charles C. Thomas, Publisher, 1981.
5. *Guidelines: Animals in Nursing Homes.* California Veterinary Medical Association, File No. 3758. PO Box 6000, San Francisco, CA 94160—price $3.00.
6. McCulloch M: Animal Facilitated Therapy: Overview and Future Direction. *Calif Vet* 8:13—24, 1982

15

The Shelter's Role in the Bond

Phil Arkow

"In too many cases the bond is broken."

In California, a couple undergoing divorce proceedings engage in a year-long custody battle over their cockapoo, "Runaway." The husband flies in his sister from Paris to testify about his character and offers his wife $20,000 to buy out her "share" in the dog, before the judge, obeying state child custody laws, awards joint custody to the feuding couple.

In New York, a veterinarian with a nationally-syndicated pet care column describes his experiences at an animal shelter where people brought in their cats and placed them up for adoption because they had recently redecorated and the cats no longer matched the furniture.

These two extremes—utter, eccentric devotion and unfeeling disposability—represent the dilemmas with which the humane community is confronted in its approach to the Human/Companion Animal Bond (H/CAB). For while humane societies and SPCAs are traditionally perceived as fostering good, quality homes for orphaned and unwanted animals in their communities and as standing up for the rights of animals in general, the reality of American life in the latter part of the twentieth century is that many factors combine to create a modular, throwaway pet, the last priority in a culture of disposables. The no-deposit/no-return puppy is an unfortunate victim of American life today and in too many cases the unique "bond" between people and animals either never has a chance to develop and mature, or is broken. We "trash" millions of animals each year, animals who kept their part of the bond and

Phil Arkow is director of education and publicity at the Humane Society of the Pikes Peak Region in Colorado Springs, Colo., where he pioneered human-companion animal bond programs with the successful "Pet-Mobile" nursing home visitation program. A graduate of the University of Pennsylvania and former newspaper reporter, his "Pet Therapy": A study of the use of companion animals in selected therapies *is an on-going, frequently-updated chronicle of developments in the H/CAB field. He is active in numerous state and national animal care and control organizations, and served as editor of this book for the Latham Foundation.*

expected us to keep ours.

Historically, humane societies and SPCAs have been at the leading edge of awakening public conscience and consciousness and of spearheading some of the morality-based issues of the day. Though a relatively recent phenomenon in Western culture, humane groups have played important parts in the legal, legislative, communications and activism spheres to make the public aware of conditions which touch a raw nerve in the community's conscience. Without knowing it, the pioneers and earliest leaders of the humane movement were extolling the virtues of the human/animal bond, a term which has become popular and generic only in recent years. It is no small surprise, therefore, that many humane groups have perceived the H/CAB and its related issues and activities as the new wave of "humaneness" as we enter the twenty-first century. Likewise, humane groups are continuing their traditional roles in serving to catalyze other groups into action and to create new spin-off groups to deal with the new specializations of an emerging field of widespread concern.

Humane history: early bond programs

The first humane societies in this country were as concerned with child abuse as they were with animal protection. Modeled to some degree after the Royal Society for the Prevention of Cruelty to Animals, chartered in England in the 1830s, animal protection societies emerged in the years immediately after the Civil War "to promote kindness toward all living things" or "to provide protection to less fortunate creatures, especially animals and children." Working under a Victorian-era concept that someone who was kind to animals and children would eventually translate that kindness into compassion for his fellow man, humane societies tried to build a "humane" society—one in which everyone exercised respect for everyone else.

The charters and statements of purpose of some of these groups are quite revealing. The oldest American humane society, New York City's American Society for the Prevention of Cruelty to Animals was founded in 1866. Even today, the ASPCA professes:

> By encouraging the humane treatment of animals, the Society promotes the noblest instincts of mankind and seeks to enhance the quality of life.

The concern for animal welfare spread rapidly. Within a decade of the ASPCA's founding, 27 local humane organizations were in operation from New Hampshire to California, prompting the formation of a group in 1877 which came to be the American Humane Association. AHA President

William O. Stillman reflected in 1913 on the Association's origins:

> For ages humanity, as an active social force, was only a dream of idealistic philosophy. The Nineteenth Century made it a reality. The Eighteenth Century presented the recognition of the "Rights of Man" as its greatest contribution to human progress. The Nineteenth adopted the doctrine of the right of the weak and oppressed to protection as its noblest conception of human duty.

As time passed, the humane movement grew. By the turn of the century, 161 local humane organizations were in operation and education came to be seen as the keystone of human and humane progress. One pioneer group, the Latham Foundation for the Promotion of Humane Education, was formed in 1918 and even today:

> The Latham Foundation unequivocally believes that mankind is best served by a clear understanding of the vital importance of universal kinship and respect for all life. Latham believes that a child taught to respect animals and all living things will grow to respect his fellow man as well.

The "no-deposit/no-return" pet is an unfortunate victim of American throw-away society. Millions of pets are "trashed" in our shelters each year, animals who kept their part of the human/animal bond and who expected us to do the same.
(Photo by Phil Arkow)

New technology brought terms such as "ecosystem" and "Spaceship Earth" and the humane movement continued to grow and promote the unique kinship, or bond, between people and animals within new cultural frameworks. The Humane Society of the United States, organized in 1954, expresses its concept of the "bond" in terms of moral responsibilities:

> Man has been uniquely endowed with a sense of moral values. For this reason we believe he is responsible for the welfare of those animals that he has domesticated and those upon whose natural environment he encroaches. As the dominant intelligent life form on earth, we are accountable as a species. All life possesses an inherent value and is thus deserving of this consideration.

Though different ages have presented different needs, the humane movement continues to grow and enter new fields of involvement—most notably, the human/companion animal bond. Though the original humane motivation may seem to some today to be somewhat idealistic or simplistic and to others it may be the reverse of W.C. Fields' famous comment ("Anyone who hates children and dogs can't be all bad"), several thousand local and national animal protection programs are in place today to protect less fortunate creatures. Though only a half-dozen humane societies still conduct child-abuse work (the rest of the task having been taken over by government agencies), many groups see the potential of the H/CAB as the next logical step in carrying forth their original purposes of promoting "kindness toward all living things" into the twenty-first century.

In the early 1970s, a small but influential number of humane societies inadvertently stumbled into programs which came later to be grouped under such terms as "Human/Companion Animal Bond," "Pet Therapy," "Pet-Facilitated Therapy," or "Animal-Assisted Therapy." Working independently at first and financially deprived of the resources which could lead to full-scale, clinical research into exactly what was going on, humane societies began bringing animal visitors to nursing homes and convalescent centers. These visits, it was argued, were beneficial to the animals under the humane societies' care and thus part of the humane purpose: visits gave animals human love and kindness and improved behavior during the puppies' and kittens' socialization periods. They diversified the societies above and beyond their traditional programs of sheltering, adoption, rescue and cruelty prevention. And they raised the public's level of awareness of the humane societies' role in the community.

But these programs also indirectly expanded the definition of a "humane" society and extended the original charters of these groups.

Handicapped, elderly and other institutionalized people with special needs—long the targets of other caring professions—were now included within the traditional definition of kindness "to all living things" and "less fortunate creatures." Volunteers, both children and adults, recruited into the institution visit programs observed the ravages of aging and the realities of Down's Syndrome and Alzheimer's disease and could not help but feel compassion for their fellow man.

As the field proliferated, specializations, by necessity, began to emerge. One group, the Minnesota Society for the Prevention of Cruelty, concentrated on training and placing "hearing dogs" to help the hearing-impaired, similar to guide dogs which had helped the blind for half a century. Later, when the demand for these dogs outstripped the capabilities of the St. Paul shelter to conduct the program, it was turned over in 1976 to the American Humane Association for national coordination. Later, regional chapters and local splinter groups were formed. *(See Chapter 9)*

Many humane groups see the potential of the human/animal bond and pet-facilitated therapy as the next step in carrying out their charters to promote kindness toward all living things—particularly those less fortunate than the majority. *(Photo by Phil Arkow)*

Other programs were created to deal with different aspects of the "bond." The San Francisco SPCA initiated a "Pets & Older People" program, coordinating several animal-related services for senior citizens. Low-cost adoptions, medical care, housing, free pet food, free transportation, hearing dogs, education, membership services and volunteering opportunities were all arranged "to encourage the mutually rewarding bonds that can develop between older people and animals." The Humane Society of the Pikes Peak Region in Colorado Springs, Colo., began chronicling the development of the field and networking information to assist others in "pet therapy," and pioneered nursing home visits with its highly successful "Pet-Mobile" program. Numerous societies turned to the legislative arena and promoted bills in Arizona, California, New York, Connecticut and elsewhere to allow senior citizens in low-cost housing projects, under controlled conditions, to keep their pets which, in many cases, had been their only friends or "family." Others worked on legislation to allow or encourage nursing homes and other health care facilities to keep residential mascots or visiting animals. Still others worked with the scientific and research communities to document the therapeutic benefits and define the human and animal behavior patterns within the "bond." Others initiated equestrian therapy programs. In some communities, government-run animal control agencies (the animal counterparts to the earlier child abuse programs) followed suit and began conducting their own pet-facilitated therapy programs. And the field is still growing....

The humane catalyst

Humane societies have always had a unique perception of the needs of society, starting from their baseline of recognizing animals as a touchstone of human existence. Within the declared goal of trying to achieve a more "humane" society by caring for animals lies a tacit assumption that animal behavior somehow mirrors our own; within the cry for moral responsibility lies a recognition that there is a unique bonding process between man and beast. Humane groups have always been working toward the advancement of the H/CAB, although that specific term has been used only in recent years. The scientific community is now quantifying and qualifying the issues which the humane movement has brought to public attention; this pattern has persisted throughout the relatively brief existence of humane societies and SPCAs. Whether calling for reforms in interstate animal transportation or decrying the definition of children as property, whether lobbying for humane slaughter or organizing animal relief efforts during wars and natural disasters, whether attacking the new issues which arise with each new generation, such as the sealing and whaling industries, rodeo, dog fighting and dozens of other issues, the humane movement has launched many new offshoots which, it is hoped, will eventually lead to that "humane" society. The scientific recognition, demonstration and ensuing public awareness of the therapeutic value of animals is one of the newest such offshoots, a direction which will lead to a greater compassion for and kindness toward our animal friends and better understanding of our fellow man.

The paradox of humane work

But humane societies and animal protection agencies are caught in a cruel double bind. As their reputation and numbers spread as caretakers of society's unwanted animals, they became overwhelmed with the jetsam of a highly mobile society with disposable animals. The organizations chartered to save animals' lives now find themselves inundated with more animals than they can possibly care for and are forced to defend mass euthanasia as a necessary evil. The Hawaiian Humane Society in Honolulu has theorized that the rate of pet disposability is linked to disposable money and the Consumer Price Index. Others have speculated that surges in unwanted pets are tied in with baby booms, the shift from an industrial to post-industrial economy, movements to the suburbs, movements to the Sun Belt, higher family mobility, divorce rates, marketing techniques in the pet and pet food industries and dozens of other factors.

Whatever its cause, the humane community must cope with the issue of animal "overpopulation"—a surplus of dogs and cats for which there are and probably will never be enough suitable homes. Accurate national figures are hard to come by, but estimates range as high as 25 per cent of all the dogs and cats in America will pass through a shelter each year and as many as 90 percent of them will be put to death there because no one wants them. Officials at private humane shelters and public governmental animal control agencies have become urban game wardens, allowing for the culling of a percentage of the pet population each year so the rest can survive on limited resources.

This double bind has been troubling to the humane community and some see the Human/Companion Animal Bond as a way out. Humane societies, chartered to prevent cruelty, today are forced to kill millions of animals and justify it by saying "euthanasia is better than suffering." Even within the humane community, this argument is disturbing: as noted pet columnist and humane spokesman Roger Caras has said, "The movement that was born to save horses now kills cats and dogs. Something is out of alignment." The argument is even more disturbing to the general public, particularly in an age when issues such as abortion, human euthanasia and capital punishment have heightened the levels of awareness and concern.

Many humane societies have turned to H/CAB studies as a means of alleviating pain and suffering among animals and less fortunate humans—and also to realign themselves in a changing era. Changing times dictate changing programs if any organization is to adapt and survive: this was foreseen by Bill Barrow, then director of the Kentucky Humane Society, who wrote in 1979:

> When the public thinks about shelters it is faced with an inherent paradox: animals are sheltered from harm, yet most of them end up being killed. People pay lip service to the "good work" the shelter does but feel that the whole thing is somehow inhumane in principle. One is reminded of the statement mady by an army commander during the Vietnam war: "We had to destroy the village in order to save it." The challenge is not just that animal control will assume a function traditionally performed by humane societies, but rather that the local societies will lose their reason for being. They will not only lose their highly visible base of operations—which is at best a mixed blessing—but they will lose their symbol of individual animal rescue. What else can they do? Rescue cattle from the slaughterhouse? Barge into the local laboratory research facility? Legislation and education are fine, but will they be enough to satisfy the need to touch and see the animal whose suffering is being alleviated?

Whether the directors of humane societies pursuing H/CAB programs are aware of it or not, the fact remains that pet-facilitated therapy programs are slowly helping to turn around the image of shelters from "humane slaughterhouses" to new positive, natural outgrowths of the original purpose for which SPCAs were chartered.

Shelters also see the negative side of the "bond," the human/companion animal connections which fail to take hold or mature. A few shelters have publicly declared they will no longer kill any "healthy" animals or will place every animal they receive. (What they fail to tell the public is that they do not accept every animal they are offered and while their adoption rate may be 100 per cent their unaccepted pets become the problem of some other shelter.)

But the majority of the nation's shelters accept every animal given up and mass euthanasia becomes a way of life—and death. Why should this be? Again, figures are difficult to obtain, but one study found some unusual indications of the extent to which many Americans see their animals as readily disposable when family conditions change, or when the "bond" fails because the animal failed to perform to what had been the owner's levels of expectation.

This study, conducted by the National Animal Control Association in 1981, surveyed 918 people surrendering their dogs for adoption at 13 shelters in eight states. The study generated a situational stereotype of the conditions under which a dog is perceived to be readily disposable: the dog was obtained free of charge, usually from a friend or neighbor, as a puppy and kept about 17 months before being surrendered due to changes in the family's lifestyle, real or perceived behavioral problems, or requiring too much time and responsibility. The more the dog had cost, the longer the family kept it before disposal; more than two-thirds of the dogs received had been obtained free of charge. For many people, then, the degree of attachment and the depth of the "bond" is directly related to financial investment.

Thus, animal shelter personnel daily deal with both sides of the "bond"—the successful adoptions and the unsuccessful rejects dumped on their doorsteps in alarming numbers. But there are other links between these employees and volunteers and the H/CAB, links which desperately need review and study by the scientific community. For example, what "bond" links humane personnel with their own and their shelter's animals? How do shelter clerks, kennel attendants, cruelty investigators and animal control officers go home to their own pets each night after facing dozens or hundreds of abandoned animals and people who "didn't have time" for their responsibilities each day?

And what of the toll taken by euthanasia? At present, animal shelter and slaughterhouse workers and veterinarians are the only professions permitted to euthanize animal life in routine, daily massive scale. Court battles, insurance claims, public debate and intra-professional censure all confront the doctor, minister, or medical technician who chooses to "pull the plug" on a human being condemned to artificial life-support systems or who arranges an abortion. Hangmen and executioners are almost extinct in the wake of recent court and legislative decisions. Prison execution procedures often ensure that no one individual is responsible for snuffing out another living being's life. But daily, tens of thousands of puppies, kittens, dogs and cats are routinely euthanized by humane society, animal control and veterinary personnel. The field has, by necessity, developed its own "gallows humor" and jargon, as these workers avoid the awesome reality of their responsibilities by speaking in such euphemistic terms as "put to sleep," "XT," "dispatch" or "destroy."

Shelter workers invariably receive a minimum of technical training—if they receive any at all—on the methods of euthanasia. For some, a class or two with a veterinarian or at a training school is all they get; others rely strictly on on-the-job experience. But neither shelter personnel nor veterinarians have, until recently, received any schooling in the emotional aspects of their work: the effects on their own minds of euthanasia and the management of grief in the animals' owners. As veterinarian Marc Rosenberg, a leader in the movement to provide grief counseling instruction to veterinarians and veterinary students has written, euthanasia is "the one time when the veterinarian must treat the human patient rather than the pet."

The Hard Part of the Job

Come here, boy,
And please don't lick my hand.
Don't look at me that way
It's almost more than I can stand.

I'm sorry this has to happen
And that this was your last home.
I wish you'd had owners that loved you
And hadn't let you roam.

You'll never fetch another stick
Or make a little boy smile.
I hope your life was a happy one—
The life you had for such a short while.

I wish that people would realize
That your life is as important as theirs.
At times like this I wonder
If anyone really cares.

He opens the door slowly
And sets the dog inside.
He notices that the dog shivers
And his eyes are open wide.

He flips the switch, and the gas rushes in
As he watches another life die.
He then turns around, and leaves the room quickly
So that no one will see him cry.

Chris Trujillo
Animal Control Officer
Sandy City, Utah

Shelter workers labor under the additional handicap that, in too many case, the owners are not grief-stricken: they neither know nor care about the death of their pets. In addition, public revulsion over the reality of mass euthanasia is such that humane workers are frequently victims of mass media campaigns against the relative "humaneness" of the particular method employed. All of these conditions cannot help but affect the performance of the worker; accelerate the burn-out process that accompanies any profession with high levels of stress, care and frustration; and distract from the true goal of affirming, initiating and developing successful human/companion animal bonds.

How to start a H/CAB program

For the humane group or animal control agency wishing to become involved in the growing field of H/CAB studies, there are a number of possible approaches. Do you want to be active on the *institutional program* level, bringing animals to hospitals, nursing homes, prisons and institutions to let the residents benefit from the presence of pets? Perhaps a *community-based program* is more appropriate, given the needs of your locale and the resources of your agency; for example, providing foster pet care and pets' "meals on wheels" for house-bound or hospitalized senior citizens. Perhaps you want to enter the *legislative* arena and work for the encactment of local and/or state laws to facilitate the controlled keeping of pets in institutions, public housing or households where special conditions apply. Or perhaps you want to use your unique position within the community as a *resource* to bring together the veterinarians, health care professionals, social workers and other interested individuals who can create a comprehensive community-wide program.

Whatever your direction(s), it is imperative that the group take a needs assessment study first, chart its goals and objectives and determine its capabilities. "Just doing good isn't good enough any more," says Larry Brown, director of child protection services for the American Humane Association. "Accountability is the byword of modern management. Don't think that because you do good you can afford to do it badly."

A pet-facilitated therapy (PFT) or H/CAB program, regardless of its name, should be started *only* after considerable advance preparation. The following premises are generally regarded as prerequisites:

1. PFT is not a panacea for medical or social problems. At best, animals in therapeutic programs are an adjunct to other professional treatments.
2. The welfare of all animals, patients and others affected by the presence of animals must be considered and common sense can

avoid abuse and disappointment.

3. Planning and evaluation are essential.

Here is an outline the animal care and control agency can follow in setting up a H/CAB program:

I. Needs Assessment

Does a need exist for H/CAB programs in your community? What is it?

Does a need exist for H/CAB programs in your organization? Why?

There are a number of ways to obtain this information. Your agency may have received some inquiries or requests for service which are currently not being provided. You may schedule a council meeting of leaders from a variety of institutions and community programs to see if animal-related activities and needs are currently being included. You may take a survey and send a questionnaire to nursing homes, hospitals, doctors, psychologists, orphanages, mental health facilities, senior citizen referral services and others actively involved in social care to determine whether they could or would use H/CAB programs.

You should also gain input from your staff, administration, board of directors and membership. Does your group need and want to enter H/CAB programs? If so, why? How does your group perceive the H/CAB and its role within it? What types of programs, if any, are you best equipped to provide? How much of a commitment, in terms of time, personnel, man-

Animal shelters struggle to cope with pet overpopulation—the jetsam of a highly mobile society with disposable animals. It is estimated that as many as 25% of the dogs and cats in America will pass through shelters each year.

(Photo by Phil Arkow)

hours, resources, money and in-kind services, are you prepared to expend?

An animal protection agency need not have a full-scale, fully-staffed, daily program in order to be successful. In most cases, it is actually better to start small and "test the waters" first. Also, many agencies, particularly those based largely on volunteer help, may not be equipped to conduct regular H/CAB programs. Suffice it to say that whatever your level of commitment, your programs will be another step forward in carrying out the traditional definition of humaneness to new audiences and animals in need of humane activities.

II. Goals and Objectives

> *What do you hope to attain by implementing PFT or H/CAB programs? Why?*

An animal protection agency need not sit down and write a formal Management By Objectives plan detailing its proposed activities (although this is certainly a help, especially if you intend to write grants and seek outside funding for your activities). But the agency should be able to define its purpose in conducting these programs for a number of reasons: to explain the purposes to the public and the organizations served; to avoid criticism; and to keep on track when personnel and programs change with time. Needless to say, a certain amount of flexibility must be allowed for, as conditions will change. But the group should have some idea of where it and the H/CAB programs are going and what it hopes to achieve. *(See Chapter 20)*

An important part of Goals and Objectives is the development of measurement indicators. How do you plan to assess the successes and failures of your program?

III. System Analysis

> *What laws affect your proposed program?*
> *What animals, personnel, vehicles, finances, housing facilities, trainers, and other considerations are available to maintain a program?*
> *What characteristics of the institutions and populations to be served will positively or negatively affect the program?*

An agency planning H/CAB programs needs to be aware of the in-place systems which can facilitate the "bond" and the procedures for creating new systems as needed. Local and state laws and institutional policies may affect the program. *(See Chapter 7).* Available resources need to be determined and solidified. An organizational infrastructure may need to be created to organize, maintain and accept the reponsibility of the program; such a management chain may need to be created within either the humane society, the institutions to be served, or both.

The society should carefully review its own structure and that of the institutions to be served, all involved parties' capabilities and attitudes towards the program and the specific problems to be addressed. Input from all parties involved is essential to become familiar with differing perspectives and to avoid overlooking potential mistakes. Everyone must consider possible risks involved: danger to the animals, to the residents or inmates, to the care-givers and to innocent by-standers. Possible dangers include, but are not limited to:

- allergies
- bites, scratches and other injuries inflicted by animals
- zoonotic diseases transmitted from animals to humans
- inappropriate animal or human behavior
- tripping, falling and other accidental injuries caused by animals present
- concerns over sanitation and sterility, particularly in an institution
- noise, odor waste and other pollutants
- pet reproduction
- grooming
- death of the animal (or of the human recipient)
- psychological rejection
- adverse impact on others in the facility
- insurance liabilities
- financial constraints

Virtually all of the considerations can be eliminated or minimized with adequate planning, realistic expectations and a proper degree of flexibility designed into the program.

The first major consideration once all systems appear to be "go," is *proper selection of animals* for type, age, temperament and training. At this point in the development of H/CAB studies, common sense is as good a guideline as any, although some researchers are attempting to design computer-generated models of ideal animals for model situations. Animals chosen for any program must be appropriate and specially-trained if necessary, for the individual or institution to be served and for the animal's particular needs and capabilities. Such selection must include criteria such as: species; breed; age; housebreaking capabilities; potential for allergenic reaction; size and durability; temperament; danger of inflicting injury on the program recipients; and likelihood of being abused by program recipients.

There are no set rules. Numerous workable models suggest a variety of animals may be used depending on circumstances. Horses work quite well in equestrian therapy programs. Livestock and farm animals are suitable for juvenile delinquents doing alternative service work or for petting zoos. Puppies and fully-grown dogs are suitable for visit programs, though older dogs—already housebroken—work better as in-residence mascots. Kittens are better than older cats for both visiting and residential programs, although they are more likely to inflict scratching injuries than are dogs. (One humane society in New York minimizes this danger by trimming the cats' claws before starting the visit; others use declawed cats). Small rodents, rabbits and reptiles may not provide as much tactile stimulation and may not be as universally popular among recipients, but may have a place in certain programs. Farm animals may be meaningless to urban residents, but can be highly stimulating to people from rural backgrounds. Fish and birds require less care and cost but do not provide much tactile stimulation; however, they can provide a calming effect and an aesthetically pleasing visual and auditory atmosphere.

Proper pet selection and training are also important if animals are to be successfully integrated with other, existing, treatment modalites. Humane groups considering these programs must be aware of two medical oppositions to their efforts:

1. PFT is, at best, an adjunct to existing therapies (physical, occupational, recreational, group, individual, pharmacology, medical, etc.) It is not a panacea and will not correct defects in other areas, such as poor institutional organization or communications, low staff-to-patient ratio, poor program design and bad attitude.
2. The scientific and medical communities take great exception to anyone, especially untrained, unschooled and overly enthusiastic volunteers, arbitrarily labelling an untested regimen a "therapy."

Consequently, humane societies starting programs should be aware that not everyone will view their efforts with the same degree of enthusiasm. This is not to quash your hopes, but instead to encourage you to work with other groups in a cooperative way whereby each side understands the other's view. A second key to successful programs is *realistic expectations.* For all the charm, allure, and kindness exhibited by successful PFT programs, there is still little documentation as to actual psychological or physiological benefit. Several studies indicate that pets rarely create permanent personality changes among patients; at best the animals are seen as at least not causing any harm. Some studies emphasize that animals, at best, "enhance the treatment milieu" or make a nursing home what it is—a "home." Pets can stimulate recipients' capabilities for warmth and empathy and can be catalysts for social interaction. By establishing realistic goals and objectives and by understanding what PFT programs can and cannot do, the humane society can implement a more successful program.

A third key, and the element common to all successful programs, is *supervision.* One person must be assigned overall responsibility for the animals in a facility and other personnel in the institution must be aware that the animals are to be treated as regular parts of the facility's activities. Provisions must be made for weekend and holiday care. The animals must be under adequate supervision at all times and must also have a secure, somewhat isolated, area to which they can retreat for rest and avoid the stress of so many people present.

What bond links shelter personnel with animals? How does a humane officer go home each night to his own pets after facing hundreds of abandoned animals all day?
(Photo by Phil Arkow)

Supervision can also help minimize the most common objection to animals in an institution—that coming from housekeeping staffs who maintain the pets will create more work. To date, there has been little evidence to document this allegation and in fact some studies have shown that residential pets create less demands on housekeeping staffs. By helping to take care of the patients' affectational needs, the animals free the housekeeping staffs to attend to their traditional responsibilities.

Two important responsibilities of the supervisor and two additional key elements to a successful program are *orientation* and *training*. People are naturally fearful of the unknown. To medical personnel keyed towards sterility, to institutionalized residents (and their families) unsure of their own capabilities and to humane workers thinking solely in terms of animals, the concept of PFT may be too new to be immediately grasped. Successful programs must have at least the tolerance, if not the enthusiastic approval, of all concerned and the endorsement of administrative personnel. The perspectives of those actively and justifiably opposed to animals in an institution must be considered. An orientation session conducted prior to the introduction of animals and repeated as needed can do wonders to explain the purposes, expectations and goals of a seemingly radical idea.

Similarly, on-going training may be necessary to acquaint volunteers, staff and the animals involved with the rigors and goals of the program. Animal training may take several forms and presupposes a proper selection and subsequent conditioning to deal with the specific conditions of the institutions involved. *(See Chapter 5).*

To date, *costs* have not appeared to be significant stumbling blocks for humane groups or health care delivery systems operating PFT programs. Donations of money and in-kind services appear to be available from memberships, support groups, service clubs, community agencies, veterinarians, private individuals and others to help offset any costs incurred. (One SPCA charges the nursing homes $50 per visit, since the visits occur at night and the animal ambulance drivers are union personnel who must be paid overtime; this, however, appears to be an exception rather than the norm.)

However, groups should be aware that costs may arise, including: vehicles and gasoline; uniforms; training; animal food; veterinary care; pet procurement; licensing and registration; temporary or permanent housing facilities; pet accessories; and personnel costs (overtime, etc.) In some cases, such as Lima, Ohio's famed State Hospital program, some costs can be offset by selling pet offspring or by-products.

Special insurance coverage, for the shelter or the institutions served, does not appear to be necessary, as these programs should be covered underexisting policies. However, concerned administrators may wish to check with their insurance carriers to be certain.

Another important element of a successful program is adequate *documentation.* In addition to the Needs Assessment surveys and Goals and Objectives statements mentioned earlier, several written documents may be required to define, clarify, and continue a program. The institution should have a written policy regarding the animals in residence. *(See Chapter 16).* Likewise, the humane group should have a policy statement about its role in H/CAB programs. Job descriptions for both volunteers and employees in both the humane society and the institution served should be written to define areas of responsibility. A budget for the program may be necessary. Particularly in a health care facility, residential animals may need a chart detailing their veterinary care and daily nutritional, medical and exercise regimens. Other records collected by the humane group and the institution should include staff and administration anecdotes, reports and insights to assist programmers in evaluating the operation.

Finally, conditions must be established to assure the *welfare of the animals* in any program. Residential pets must have suitable quarters and appropriate opportunity for exercise. They also need access to areas for solitude and sleep. Adequate nutrition and a constant supply of water must be maintained. (Actually, a problem reported consistently to be more common than the lack of food is the overabundance of it and care must be taken to prevent obesity. Many patients cannot resist the temptation of feeding scraps to a residential pet and some animals, especially dogs, cannot resist the treat either. Over-feeding should be monitored by staff members and the residents made aware of the health dangers of overfeeding.) And, of course, no abuse, trauma, stress, or mistreatment of the animal will be tolerated.

Here are some common-sense suggestions for a successful visiting animal program at a long-term health care facility:

1. Keep the animals out of food preparation and serving areas and other places where sanitation and sterility is a greater factor (medication and laundry rooms, etc.) This ban may also be mandated by law. *(See Chapter 7)*

2. Select animals which are clean, healthy, appropriately vaccinated and which have suitable and predictable temperaments. Animals should be friendly, calm, controllable and react well to strangers. *(See Chapter 5)*

3. Expect urination, defecation and vomiting and take appropriate precautions. Carry clean-up materials with you, exercise the animals before arriving, avoid feeding the animals prior to transporting them and

avoid carpeted areas in the institution where clean-up is difficult.

4. Keep larger dogs under control, preferably on a leash, and carry smaller animals in portable cages if appropriate.

5. Know which people in the institution are allergic or antipathetic towards animals and avoid them.

6. Minor injuries (bites, scratches) may occur and should be reported to nursing or administrative staffs immediately. Any animal observed to have greater potential for inflicting injury should be returned to the transport vehicle as soon as possible.

7. Be punctual and regular in your appointments so as to not disappoint waiting residents and staff members who may be coordinating your visit with other activities.

8. Schedule visits so as to not conflict with other activities, particularly meals and naps.

9. Familiarize volunteers with what they can expect at the facilities to be visited (types of residents, common physical conditions of the residents and coping with people with limited sight, hearing and mobility). Be certain the volunteers know what their responsibilities are.

10. Introduce yourselves to the residents and get to know them. Likewise, let them get to know you.

IV. Evaluation

One of the most challenging aspects of PFT is attempting to document its effectiveness. Though most humane society workers conducting programs have an intuitive sense that something positive is happening and though the smiles on the faces of residents visited in nursing homes and other institutions are warm and readily photographable, there is, at this point in the development of the field, little conclusive, scientific data to define what is specifically occuring between pets and people. Most of what data exists is anecdotal in nature, though some attempts have succeeded in measuring changes in human and animal blood pressure, survival rates after heart attacks, responses to questions and degree of social interaction when animals are present. Some researchers have postulated that the presence of animals may decrease patient dependency on drugs or make the patient more self-reliant and less dependent on the institution.

Persons conducting PFT programs should attempt to evaluate their successes and their failures. Such instruments as patient charting, questionnaires, videotaping, surveys and formal research may be appropriate. Likewise, the behavior, selection and performance of the animals used should also be under on-going evaluation.

A number of intriguing possibilities for scientific research into H/CAB programs have been suggested, in addition to the increasing number of research programs already under way. Humane groups wishing to start or expand PFT activities are encouraged to seek out the assistance of the scientific community for the unique contributions to the field which this sector can provide.

Evaluation, like the PFT program itself, is an on-going process. As with any new discipline, H/CAB studies are currently undergoing rapid change and development of specializations. Both the humane groups and institutions conducting PFT activities should analyze the outcomes of PFT and refine the programs as necessary. Trial-and-error is a necessary part of the program at this stage and groups should be prepared to learn from their mistakes. Failures should be documented to form an important record for the group's own needs and to assist others across the country. Documented failures can demonstrate areas in which PFT is not useful or appropriate and situations where a systems breakdown occured which is correctable. All too often, groups and institutions suffering an early failure tend to overgeneralize from the mistake and condemn an entire program, rather than see where the mistake occurred and attempt to correct it in future activities.

It should further be noted that there is a strong, genuine and enthusiastic bias within the humane community that PFT "works," although the community is not quite sure what it means by "works." The humane movement, as it enters its second century of caring for less fortunate creatures and preventing their suffering, will not be able to prove its intuitive assumptions to the scientific and health care professions until documentation and evaluation confirm the informal observations and years of anecdotal information. This, too, is a challenge facing the humane movement and a challenge, which like so many other areas of the "bond," will be successfully overcome.

Suggested reading:

Anderson, R.K., et al. (eds.) *The Pet Connection: Its Influence on our Health and Quality of Life.* South St. Paul, Minn.: Globe Publishing Co., 1984.

Arkow, Phil *"Pet Therapy": A Study of the Use of Companion Animals in Selected Therapies.* Colorado Springs, Colo.: Humane Society of the Pikes Peak Region, 1983. $12.00.

Dow, Shelby and Arkow, Phil *Turn-Over Study.* Colorado Springs, Colo.: National Animal Control Association, 1982.

Levinson, Boris Nursing Home Pets: A psychological adventure for the patient. *National Humane Review,* July-August and September-October, 1970.

Lynch, James *The Broken Heart: The Medical Consequences of Loneliness.* New York: Basic Books, 1977.

Wolff, Ethel *A Survey of the Use of Animals in Psychotherapy in the United States.* Denver: American Humane Association, 1970.

Pets in Society: The Social Importance of Pets in an Aging Society. *Proceedings.* Toronto: Pet Food Manufacturers Association, 1982.

Arkow, Phil: "The Humane Society and the Human-Companion Animal Bond: Reflections on the Broken Bond. "*Veterinary Clinics of North America: Small Animal Practice* — Vol. 15, No. 2, March, 1985.

16

The Nursing Home and the Bond

Cappy McLeod

"Continuing life's experiences..."

It's not uncommon today to visit a nursing home and discover a dog chasing a ball in the backyard, birds singing in the aviary, or a cat curled up on the lap of one of the residents.

These animals are part of the increasing pet therapy programs practiced in skilled and intermediate nursing homes. In most facilities, the pet program comes under the direction of the activity coordinator. It is a structured program, closely working with the medical and administrative staffs.

Today's definition of activities is "continuing life's experiences." The activity director writes up a history on each resident, noting work experience, family relationships, community involvement, types of vacations and leisure time hobbies and special interests. It's the responsibility of the nursing home to provide an atmosphere that meets each resident's personal needs and interests.

Allowing animals in the nursing home is one way the facility can meet the needs of many residents. Most individuals grew up with pets, owned them as adults, or worked with animals on ranches and farms. As people grow older, many losses are experienced: loss of home, work, family and health. An animal can't replace those losses, but it can help provide a normal, everyday way of life. There's companionship, concern, motivation, attention and enjoyment for many when a pet is part of the program.

Adopting an animal into a nursing home requires complete dedication

Cappy McLeod's background includes extensive work with animals and people at the San Diego Zoo, media relations and promotions of various sorts. She was director of activities at the Garden of the Gods Care Center in Colorado Springs, Colo., which formed the basis of this chapter and her book, Animals in the Nursing Home: Guide for Activity Directors.

and a structured program. *(See Chapter 20)* The following guidelines and regulations are recommended.

Guidelines for adoption

1. The administrator and owner of the facility must be in total agreement.

2. Communication is essential. The residents, staff and residents' families should be informed of the adoption before the pet arrives.

3. Assign a responsible staff member for the pet's care.

4. Select a local veterinarian.

5. Plan for housing. If it's a dog, a fenced yard must be provided, with a well-sheltered doghouse. A cat must have a sleeping area away from residents' private rooms. All other animals must have proper cages.

6. All animals must be currently licensed if required by the city or county. Necessary vaccinations should be under the supervision of the veterinarian. Certain species of birds are restricted by state health laws due to psittacosis and other diseases. Most cage birds such as parakeets, canaries, budgies, etc. may be considered safe.

7. A file must be kept on the animal's health records.

8. State, county and city health requirements must be met.

9. No animals are allowed in the kitchen and food areas, tub rooms, nursing stations, or isolation areas. Animals are allowed in the activity room and in residents' rooms (providing permission from the resident and family is granted.).

10. A budget for food and health care must be provided.

11. Selection of individual animal must be discussed: If a dog is desired, my personal suggestion is a homeless dog from the local humane society. Females seem to be more gentle and less likely to roam. Mixed and "working" breeds seem to work out best. Plan to spay or neuter the pet. A grown dog, already housebroken, is easier to accept than a puppy requiring several months of training.

12. Plan the activity program involving the new animal (grooming sessions, walking, making a photo album, etc.) The pet will take on individual interaction on its own. The animal will also be able to recognize who does and who does not wish its company.

Welcoming the new addition

Once the animal is selected and adopted by the facility, it's best to schedule an "open house" for residents, families, staff and friends. An informal talk by the pet's veterinarian, or better yet, someone involved in existing pet therapy programs, is a good "ice breaker." The goal of the gathering is to inform everyone of the role the pet will be taking—the vital interacting between residents and the animal. It's also a good opportunity to answer questions and take suggestions. Adopting a pet into the facility will undoubtedly bring some negative response from some of the staff, some residents and families. Their concern is important and each individual should be able to voice any doubts. Good communication will help and time will be the best way to make the new adjustments. Regular staff in-services are suggested, utilizing animal experts from the community: veterinarians, humane society personnel, physicians, physical therapists and other professionals. Many are "prescribing" pets in daily living. The in-services will help the staff recognize the vital role the animal is playing.

Providing a homelike atmosphere will certainly be fostered with the addition of a pet. Needless to say, there will be some pros, some cons. But, just like a family of four with a new puppy, a nursing home with over 50 residents can adjust together and enjoy the love of a pet.

There might be little "accidents" on the floor, "first night" howling and other new-pet problems. The activity director or other staff responsible for the pet's discipline can begin to schedule regular dog training sessions, allowing interested residents the opportunity to help or observe the lessons.

Young animals may have the tendency to jump up on people, or get underfoot. Proper scolding and a firm "no" will soon teach a pup manners. Some nursing homes have attached a bell to the collar of their dog, so residents can hear clearly where the dog is. In each case, the dog soon learns to steer clear of walking individuals and oncoming wheelchairs. Most dogs seem to learn their role in the nursing home and sense that good manners are essential.

If a dog doesn't work out, try to find it another home with the family of a resident; perhaps the large family in the nursing home doesn't work out. Locate another dog and try again.

One of the most satisfying moments I had while activities director at Garden of the Gods Nursing Center in Colorado Springs, Colo., was when a doctor approached me at the nursing station one day. He told me that from the beginning he had been opposed to having Lucky, the resident dog at the nursing home. "It just isn't the place for pets," he had thought. He then told me he had been wrong in judging so quickly. One of his patients, a woman in her eighties, had been very passive, withdrawn, a picky eater and not interested in anything. But her attitude and behavior had changed. For the last three months she had been ambulating, dressing herself, eating well, putting on needed weight and feeling better. He discovered the positive changes in her were due to the dog. Slowly, a friendship began between Lucky and the woman, with Lucky visiting her room daily. The nurses and aides saw the improvement and were delighted when she decided to take her meals in the dining room. The doctor told me had taken her off most of her medications. He attributed it to the rapport she had with Lucky—her feeling of being needed and the exercise she received daily from walking Lucky. I felt as if another rung in the ladder of awareness of pet therapy had been reached that day. I thanked the doctor and asked him to chart his discovery in her records.

It's important to note all activities, both positive and negative, with the pet and individual residents. One question about animals which is asked frequently is, what if the pet dies? The emotions of an animal's death can be devastating to anyone who has loved a cherished pet. Children experience this sadness, as do adults. The elderly have had to deal with this probably many times in their lives. It is part of life. It is an emotion, with

Activities programs continue life's experiences for nursing home residents. Allowing pets to visit or stay in the home can continue experiences with which many residents are familiar.
(Photo by Phil Arkow)

tears and a feeling of loss. I believe the elderly can handle the situation better than most young people will give them credit. Why cheat them out of not having a pet, only because of thinking about its death? After all, isn't that "continuing life's experiences?" In due time, like times in the past, another pet will win their hearts.

Animals in the nursing home can be possible, with a good activity program, a structured schedule, communication and the good sense that animals can fit into the daily lives of nursing home residents.

Animal activities for nursing homes

Care, feeding and grooming of resident pet

Build, paint and insulate a doghouse

Schedule pet training sessions with a local dog trainer, coordinating daily practice sessions between lessons.

Exercise the pet daily... walking with leash, throwing frisbee or ball.

Rent or borrow films on wildlife, pet care and individual animals.

Build book shelves and stock a section with animal-related stories.

Photograph residents with the pet, keeping a scrapbook.

Schedule animal experts to speak on various subjects.

"Adopt" a zoo animal if the local zoo has such a program.

Field trips: zoo, humane society, pet stores, animal parks

Hold a pet show and invite local scouts to participate. Entry fees can cover costs of ribbons, refreshments and possible donation to local humane society.

Pet-Mobile visits regularly from Humane Society.

Create, stitch, embroider, knit, etc. animal pillows, catnip bags, or stuffed toys for gifts, resale in nursing home gift shop, or donations to local hospitals.

Volunteer time and manpower (from the residents) to help local animal organizations with special projects, i.e., stuffing envelopes for humane society's annual reports. Materials can be delivered to facility, residents can stuff envelopes, put on labels, etc. A worthwhile community involvement project.

Make scrapbooks for local pediatric wards in hospitals. Each one can be filled with clippings of animals from magazines, pet care notes, etc. Books can be presented with a dedication page from the residents participating.

Involve children whenever possible with these activities. Local scouts can hold regular meetings at nursing home, working on a project together. Activity coordinator should send press releases out on all community-involved projects and on the progress of the pet at the facility.

Why have animals in a nursing home?

The conditions in a long-term health care facility would appear to be ripe for the introduction of residential and visiting animals. Despite the best efforts of nursing home administrators and staff to provide for the physical and emotional needs of their residents, the populations served by these programs could easily be seen to need desperately the companionship which animals can provide.

Early pioneers in human/companion animal bond work, Dr. Samuel A. Corson and his wife, Elizabeth and associates at Ohio State University, have written extensively on the success and potential of animals in nursing homes. In several writings they have described "the psychosocial milieu of a nursing home" as follows:

> Loneliness, depression, hopelessness, helplessness, boredom and low self-esteem are characteristics shared by many residents in all custodial institutions, particularly in those catering to the aged. The social structure of a custodial institution tends to perpetuate and exacerbate the very deficiencies which brought the residents to such an institution in the first place. Thus, a vicious cycle of debilitation and social degradation and dehumanization is established.
>
> The social structure of a typical nursing home (in an industrial society such as the U.S.) generally has the following characteristics:
>
> 1. It is essentially a closed social group.
> 2. It has a low staff/resident ratio, thus making it difficult to individualize treatment.
> 3. It is a highly regimented social organization, leaving very little room for the retention of a sense of individual responsibility and a feeling of dignity.
> 4. It is a mass-oriented social organization, leaving very little room for privacy and initiative.
> 5. The residents tend to lose an important life-sustaining and life-enriching driving force: the sense of purpose and the engagement in satisfying goal-directed activities.
> 6. It fails to furnish an environment conducive to the maintenance and development of positive affective states, a feeling of being needed and respected and a feeling of being loved and an opportunity to reciprocate such feelings.

7. The residents lack socially sustaining tactile contacts.
8. Many of the residents may suffer from varying degrees of sensory deficits particularly in the visual and auditory modalities. These losses contribute to further tactile and social isolation, thus leading to a vicious cycle of social deprivation and psychological-emotional disintegration and disorientation.

Given these characteristics, it is easy to see how the introduction of a new, living element, which can provide individual affectational support, touch and other sensory stimulation, responsibilities, ego strength and a sense of purpose, can be a vital link to break through barriers, a catalyst to social interaction and an important adjunct to traditional modalities.

"Lucky," resident mascot at a nursing home, needs a break from her duties, too. When a senior transportation service van comes to take the ambulatory residents shopping, "Lucky" often goes along for the ride. *(Photo by Phil Arkow)*

Pet Policy in the nursing home

Any institution considering the addition of in-house, residential animals for therapeutic or recreational purposes should have a policy, in writing, to aid in establishing and maintaining the program and to protect the people and animals involved.

The following Pet Policy was written by Cappy McLeod and staff members while she was activities director at the Garden of the Gods Nursing Center in Colorado Springs, Colo. The policy was written after the center adopted Lucky from the humane society as a residential mascot. The center also has other animals in residence: Mittens, a calico cat also from the humane society; and several birds, both individually-owned and institutional.

PET POLICY IN THE NURSING HOME

PURPOSE

An animal can reach an individual in many ways and does not expect anything in return except love. It can fill a void of loneliness and can give a sense of belonging to someone else. Not all residents can or desire an attachment to the dog, but as with all activities, they are based on individual needs.

PHILOSOPHY

Companionship - friendships can be formed between resident and pet

Concern and motivation - caring for the pet, i.e., grooming, feeding etc., gives the residents a feeling of usefulness. It provides for something else to think about besides themselves.

Touch - petting and stroking the animal provides good sensory stimulation and physical exercise

Attention - watching the activities of the animal gives the resident something to observe, something to do and is a soothing pasttime

Exercise - the animal can provide healthy movement when going on a walk with residents

Social influence - staff, administration, resident and visitors can become involved with something in common

Homelike atmosphere - having an animal within the facility can bring back memories of pet ownership in the past

LEGAL AND PUBLIC REQUIREMENTS

The dog must be currently licensed in Colorado Springs, be spayed, have all necessary vaccinations and be under the supervision of a veterinarian.

The cat must also meet all health vaccination requirements and be spayed. Because cat litter can be a potential health hazard the cat has been trained to eliminate outdoors.

Certain species of birds are restricted by state health law due to psittacosis and other disease problems. Most small cage birds such as parakeets, canaries, budgies, etc., may be considered safe. Birds must remain caged and cage waste must be cleaned regularly.

HOUSING

The fenced-in yard between the dining room and the north wing has been designated for the dog's living quarters. The gate is locked at all times to prevent the dog from wandering away from the property and from coming inside the facility at the improper time. There is a dog house for sleeping, providing warmth and shelter during all types of inclement weather. The yard is large enough for exercise.

FEEDING

All food and water for the dog is provided within the fenced yard. Under no circumstances is she to be fed elsewhere. She is now considered an adult dog and needs to be fed once a day. She receives dry kibble. She is also given chew sticks and dog biscuits and her water is changed daily.

The cat is fed and watered daily and her food provided for her in the housekeeper's utility room. The birds are fed and watered daily within their cage.

DAILY TIME SCHEDULE

The dog is to remain in the yard during the night, sleeping in her house. She may come into the facility between mealtimes for the residents (9:00 a.m. to 10:45 a.m., 1:30 p.m. to 3:45 p.m, and at 6:30 p.m. until bedtime, usually 7:30 p.m. to 8:00 p.m.) Under no circumstances is she allowed to come in at mealtime. She is to be put in the yard by the responsible staff member, not just let out the door. No animal is allowed in the kitchen at any time.

WALKING THE DOG

If the residents wish to walk the dog, they may request the leash which is kept in the office. The staff member will unlock the gate (two keys are provided, one at the nurses' station and the other in the office). After the walk, the staff member is responsible for returning the dog to her yard.

VISITING AREA

Acceptable visiting areas for the dog are the hallways, residents' rooms (except those not wishing her in their rooms), the office and activity area. This applies to the cat as well. When the dog is outdoors outside of her yard she is to be on a leash and attended by a resident under the supervision of a staff member.

No animal is allowed in the kitchen area, nurses' station, utility room or tub rooms. Animals are not allowed up on chairs or on other pieces of furniture.

RESPONSIBLE PERSON

The staff member responsible for the overall care and supervision of the pets and pet therapy is the Activities Director. She is to delegate responsibility to another employee on her days off from the facility.

Nursing home animal visitation regulations and program guidelines

Many nursing homes, long-term health care facilities and other institutions receive animal visitors on either regular or occasional bases, from local animal shelters, veterinary groups, or others interested in the human/companion animal bond. The following Regulations and Program Guidelines, to assist both those bringing the animals and those working and living in the facilities, were prepared by PACT (People and Animals Coming Together), in State College, Pa. *(See Chapter 10).* The Regulations and Program Guidelines were developed in conjunction with activities directors Audry Woodle, at State College Manor, State College, Pa., and Karen Soebel, at Centre Crest, Bellefonte, Pa.

ANIMAL VISITATION REGULATIONS AND PROGRAM GUIDELINES

I. *GOALS OF THE PROGRAM*

Goals can be identified for all parties in the visitation program:

A. *Residents*

1. Should attend and enjoy visitation programs.
2. Develop pleasant social relationships with particular pets and volunteers.
3. Develop improved social relationships with fellow residents.
4. Residents should experience a sense of affection, good conversation and good humor during the program.
5. Increase residents' sense of personal ability, control and self-esteem.
6. Individual goals may be developed with particular residents and staff.

B. *Staff*

1. Orient and inform staff on program operations, goals, benefits and limitations.
2. Provide staff with reliable, well-trained help in using community animal resources in nursing home activities and therapy programs.
3. Staff should enjoy the program, attending when they are able, and observing how residents under their care interact with visitors and pets in a relaxed setting.
4. Identify residents who appear to have either a noticeable benefit or disturbance from participating in the visitation programs and for whom specialized goals seem appropriate. Work in cooperation with Activities Director to develop animal treatment plans.
5. Staff bring in their animals for use in programs; a team approach.

C. *Volunteers* (children and adults)

1. Develop an improved social competence, through talking with both residents, staff and other volunteers during visits.
2. Develop positive attitudes and behavioral habits toward aging and death, and nursing homes as a care setting, through getting to know elderly residents personally.
3. Gain skill in controlling and training an animal for proper behavior in a social situation.

D. *Animals*

1. Animals should become confident and skilled in initiating social contacts; making friends with strangers and accepting affection from impaired older persons.
2. Should not display any disruptive behavior toward people or other animals in attendance in a social situation.
3. Animals should develop improved obedience to owner commands and voice signals.

II. *VISITING PETS: PROCEDURE GUIDELINES*

A. All "Visiting" pet owners shall sign in at the facility's "Pet Registration Roster" at the beginning of each visit.

B. Visiting Animals shall:

1. Have up-to-date vaccinations for all diseases of the species that are of local concern. Animals should be healthy and be under the care of a veterinarian; (See Section IV. Requirements)
2. Shall be free of serious internal and external parasites;
3. Be licensed and wear an identification tag on the collar, choker chain, or harness, stating the dog's name, the owner's name, address and phone number;
4. Be immediately removed from the premises and taken to a cooperating licensed veterinarian for examination if infested with internal or external parasites, vomit or have diarrhea, or show signs of a behavioral change or an infectious disease.

C. Volunteers and animals should wear name tags.

D. Residents' name tags should be more visible.

E. Both volunteers and visiting animals should be introduced at the beginning of each session, with some information about them shared with residents.

F. Conduct a brief formal program and group discussion at the start of the program (approximately 10-15 minutes.) Topics may vary widely, but should show an interesting aspect of animal behavior and care and be related to the background and interests of the group members. Encourage volunteers not to continue private conversations and visiting, but to direct residents' attention toward the program.

G. Animals holders then begin to rotate pets around the room, letting each animal greet and visit with each resident, if they wish.

1. When volunteers are visiting, they should strive to make conversation and develop relations with residents, not simply to present and supervise

the visiting animals. The pet aids you in starting a conversation, but from there you can develop a variety of topics with the person. (See Volunteer Training)

2. Depending on the goals identified for each resident who regularly attends the program, the animals should be moved around frequently from resident to resident and shared among residents in subgroups. In a few cases, an exclusive concern with a given pet might be a desirable goal for a resident; in most cases, however the goals will also include increasing social interactions with fellow residents and volunteers.
3. Strive to increase the resident's sense of personal control and responsibility for the visiting pets. Encourage them to handle, hold and talk to the pet. Very well trained, voice controlled pets could be let off leash, so that residents could have a greater sense of freely choosing to interact with certain pets of their choice, calling and coaxing them to come, etc.

H. Provide caregiving equipment (brushes,combs) and snack foods, that residents may use in their interactions with the pets.

I. Make certain all pets have eliminated recently before the program begins to the extent possible. Be alert for signs of need to go; take outside.

J. The rights of residents who do not wish to participate in the pet program must be respected. Patients not wishing to be exposed to animals must have available a pet free area within the participating facility. A patient's desire not to have a pet in their room must be respected by all participants, including roommates. Do Not Force Participants.

III. *ROLE SUMMARY OF VISITING ANIMAL HANDLERS*

A. Participate in an orientation/training program to learn how to responsibly use pets in a nursing home.

B. Be certain your visiting pet meets the criteria outlined above in order to retain your privilege of bringing the animal into the health care facility.

C. Adhere to scheduled times for visits. Arrive early to aid in reducing confusion at the start of each visit. When you interact with residents, tell them of your next planned visit so they have something to look forward to and can predict your visits. Following up on these promises is the most direct path to building a satisfying relationship with the residents and gaining their trust.

D. Document your visit. If you are part of a larger group program, *be certain to sign the registration form so there is a permanent record of what animals and people were in the health care facility on a given day.* If you are visiting alone, with a single resident, be certain to announce your arrival in the facility with the Activities Director or designated staff member and enter the visit in a log book that they keep.

E. Maintain a regular communication with the Activities Director and PACT's coordinator of visitation. Keep people informed of your plans and experiences. Remember you are part of a team.

F. Use the pet as a point of conversation—an icebreaker to help you talk more comfortably with the resident. Don't let the pet do all the work. If you are there and do not speak, it alienates and disappoints the resident.

G. Several skills will aid you in speaking with residents who have speech/hearing impairments:
   1. Do not yell to make yourself heard. Contrary to belief, loud volume often makes hearing even harder.
   2. Speak slowly and clearly while looking directly at the person.
   3. Slow your pace of conversation to accommodate to the resident's needs and do not be anxious or interrupt if they speak slowly.
   4. Nonverbal communication, touching, smiling, good eye contact and a relaxed posture help greatly in sending a message of acceptance and interest to the resident.
   5. Avoid the temptation to ask questions, since they are hard to respond to. Share a story or incident from your experience.
   6. Careful listening is an essential skill in understanding the speech (or attempts at speech) of seriously impaired persons. If you stay relaxed, communication will become established. (TRAINING RESOURCE MATERIALS ARE AVAILABLE.)

H. Do not treat residents like children; it is demeaning. Remember, they are simply older adults with health problems.

I. Respect the preferences of individual residents; some may only like cats, or some dogs. Some will not want any animals near them. This is their right and pets should not be forced upon them. If a roommate does not want a pet to enter their room, even if the other resident has requested it, they are within their rights. Take the interested resident to a neutral location where they may interact with the pet without disturbing the roommate

J. Avoid providing personal care for residents. You are not properly trained for that task and incur a personal liablity, plus increasing the nursing home's liability. If you see something that needs to be done, contact a staff member and request they help the person.

K. Remember, the staff of the nursing home is extremely busy and burdened with the care of a difficult population. Strive to obey their requests and do not argue with them. If a problem does need to be resolved, speak with the visitation coordinator of PACT and the issue will be addressed with staff supervisors. We must remember we are there as guests to aid the residents (and the staff) in feeling better about where they live and work.

L. If you find you do *not* enjoy the visitation experience, please withdraw. Residents pick up your dissatisfaction and it defeats the purpose of our visits.

IV. *GENERAL REQUIREMENTS - ALL PETS*

A. All state and local ordinances on animal control, licensing and care apply.

B. Companion pets must not pose a threat or nuisance to the patients, staff, or visitors because of size, odor, sound, disposition, or behavioral characteris tics. Aggressive or unprovoked threatening behavior will mandate the pet's immediate removal.

"Pet-Mobile" visits from the local humane society can bring an enjoyable afternoon activity to residents. Some prefer puppies, while others await the return of an older, fully-grown friend, "Falstaff," who makes regular rounds to visit.

(Photos by Phil Arkow)

C. Animals which may be approved include: dogs, cats, birds, fish, hamsters, gerbils, guinea pigs and rabbits. Other pets may be appropriate if proper guidelines are followed. Wild animals such as turtles, reptiles and carnivorous birds are not permitted.

D. All dogs and cats are preferred to be neutered. In fact, animals are prohibited from the facility while in estrus (heat).

E. Without exception, pets must be effectively controlled by leash, command, or cage.

F. Sanitary constraints:

   1. All animals shall be clean and groomed.
   2. Pets are prohibited from the following areas:
      a. food preparation, storage and serving areas with the exception of the participant resident's bedroom;
      b. areas used for the cleaning and storage of human food utensils and dishes;
      c. vehicles used for the transportation of prepared food;
      d. employee's toilet, shower and dressing rooms;
      e. nursing stations, drug preparation areas, sterile and clean supply rooms and areas where open wound precautions are in effect;
      f. areas where soiled or contaminated materials are stored.

If the puppies can't come to visit the residents, why not bring the residents to visit the animals? A field trip to the local animal shelter can give both pets and people a break from the routines of their lives.
(Photo by Phil Arkow)

3. All pet utensils, food and equipment used for maintenance of pets are prohibited from patient food preparation and serving areas. The exception shall be the participating resident's bedroom.
4. Food handlers shall not be involved in animal care, feeding, or clean-up of animal food or waste.
5. Spilling or scattering of food and water shall not lessen the standard of housekeeping or contribute to an increase in vermin, or objectionable odor.
6. Dogs and cats must be effectively housebroken and provisions shall be made for suitably disposing of their body wastes. Cats must have 24 hour access to an appropriate litter box area.
7. Proper and frequent hand-washing shall be a consideration of all persons handling animals or animal products.

G. Any animal bites of humans shall be promptly reported by telephone to the local county health officer. Bite wounds shall be promptly and thoroughly washed with soap and running water. Mild disinfectants may be applied to the wound. Residents who are bite victims must be seen within 24 hours by a physician. Non-residents shall be advised to be seen by a physician.

H. The person or persons in charge of pets who are unable to demonstrate adequate control of a pet may, at the discretion of the facility Administrator, or his designee or a health official, have their privilege for participation in this program suspended or revoked.

V. *ADMINISTRATION, DOCUMENTATION*

The Activities Director, or other delegated staff member, is primarily responsible for the conduct of the program within their particular facility. PACT will appoint a Coordinator for each nursing home who will be responsible for ongoing programming, scheduling of volunteers and assurance of animal/program standards.

A. Copies of the health records of each visiting animal should be on file not only in PACT's records, but also in the Nursing Home Activities Director's files. File information should include volunteers' name, address, phone, and animal's name and description, vaccination record (updated annually).
B. Chronological person and animal visitation records should be maintained on file documenting the volunteers who were at each visit.
C. Logbooks should be kept by the PACT coordinator for each facility, documenting the program and any notable incidents.
D. The Activities Director and other appropriate staff as they become identified, will keep additional case files on individuals attending, developing a background of animal-related programming attitudes, preferences, participation record and any desirable or undesirable outcomes.
E. Individual volunteers are also urged to keep logs and document their view of the program and its effects on each participant.
F. Use of cameras, movies and videotape are encouraged in evaluating programs.

Suggested reading

McLeod, Cappy *Animals in the Nursing Home: Guide for Activity Directors.* Colorado Springs, Colo.: By the Author P.O. Box 9334, 1982, $8.50.

Lee, Ronnal, et al. *Guidelines: Animals in Nursing Homes.* Moraga, Calif.: California Veterinary Medical Association, 1983.

Yates, Elizabeth *Skeezer: Dog With A Mission.* New York: Harvey House, 1973.

Corson, Samuel Pets as Mediators of Therapy. *Current Psychiatric Therapies,* 1978, Vol. 18, 195-205.

PACT (People and Animals Coming Together) *PACT: Promoting Bonded Relationships Between People and Animals.* University Park, Pa.: PACT and Pennsylvania State University, 1983. Available from: PACT, 101-B Myra Dock House, University Park, Pa. 16802.

17

What the State Needs

Clarice Seufert

"... delicate balance between protection and freedom."

It may be helpful if I identify my role in the Minnesota Department of Health to explain my involvement relating to pets in health care facilities. My responsibility as a Health Program Manager is the area of licensing and certification of health care facilities, i.e., hospitals, nursing homes, boarding care homes and supervised living facilities. Included in my functions is the task of rule development and ensuring the enforcement of these rules.

Although our 1972 rules permitted pets to visit nursing homes, the rule did ban the long-term care facility as being a permanent home for pets. At the time of the public hearing relating to these rules in 1972 there was some objection to the ban, but the Department felt the ban was appropriate since there was a risk to residents from germ transmission, fleas, hygiene, etc.

In 1975, the Department undertook revision of the existing nursing home rules with our early drafts containing a provision which would allow a nursing home to have pets. The proposed draft contained rules governing the care of pets and the types of pets that could be allowed since some restriction seemed necessary to assure for the well-being of the residents.

In 1979, the Minnesota State Legislature passed a bill which would permit health care facilities to keep pets on the premises, as follows:

HOSPITALS, NURSING HOMES, ETC.—PETS
CHAPTER 33
S.F.No. 307
[Coded]

Clarice Seufert is chief of the Survey and Compliance Section of the Health Resources Division of the Minnesota Department of Health in Minneapolis. She has been active in working with the Veterans Administration and other groups in designing programs incorporating animal-facilitated therapy in health care facilities.

An Act relating to health: permitting placement of pets in certain institutions: amending Minnesota Statutes 1978, Chapters 144, by adding a section; and 144A, by adding a section.

Be in enacted by the Legislature of the State of Minnesota:

Section 1. Minnesota Statutes 1978, Chapter 144A, is amended by adding a section to read:

144A.30 Pets in nursing homes

Nursing homes may keep pet animals on the premises subject to reasonable rules as to care, type and maintenance of the pet.

Sec. 2. Minnesota Statutes 1978, Chapter 144, is amended by adding a section to read:

144.573 Pets in certain institutions

Facilities for the institutional care of human beings licensed under Minnesota Statutes 1978, Section 144.50, may keep pet animals on the premises subject to reasonable rules as to the care, type and maintenance of the pet.

Approved April 23, 1979.

This law was subject to the development of reasonable rules as to the care, type and maintenance of the pet, to be developed and enforced by the Minnesota Department of Health. As a result, we have been evaluating the effects of pets on residents with a consideration for the safeguards felt neccessary to protect the residents, staff and visitors. These rules were finally adopted in June, 1983 and will be presented later in this chapter.

It is not that the concept of pets in a nursing home has a negative connotation, but in the process of rule-making it is necessary to put aside any biases we have and approach this process in terms of the welfare of those living or working in the nursing home.

First, consider the reasons a person enters a nursing home. The primary reason relates to problems of health; that is, the person requires medical, nursing or supportive health care for prolonged periods of time. As a result of the health problem the person experiences inability for continued independent living and self-sufficiency; a determination made either by the resident or someone else.

Second, consider the characteristics of physiological changes which have occured in these persons: decreased capacity to re-adjust to change such as temperature change; increased susceptibility to diseases; and notable changes in the nervous system with the result that their reaction time and speed movement slow down.

These physiological manifestations of the elderly will not disappear by the addition of a pet. Conversely, these characteristics may well become the deciding factors in a facility's denial of pets in the home.

In addition to the physiological needs, the resident's psycho-social needs require consideration. Again, what is the impact of this admission upon the resident? The nursing home becomes an intervention in the person's life. It becomes a person's home and community as long as he or she is there. What specific attitudes might the adult resident experience? It's probably the first major loss of autonomy and self-direction. He or she experiences a changed and lessened status in life, a loss of touch with developments in family, neighborhood and community. Limitations are placed upon the person's movements and actions with accompanying confinement and restriction. There is a loss of self-esteem with a feeling of helplessness and uselessness. Two very basic psychological needs are threatened: the feeling of importance and independence. It has been the Department's experience relating to the admission of residents to a nursing home that many of them often exhibit social withdrawal.

A pet in a nursing home may well ease the transition from community life to institutional setting. The essence of this therapeutic argument is summarized in two quotations:

> "Pets have kept a lot of us out of mental institutions. The family pet—dog, cat bird, hamster, even a snake—is a cure for worry that's worth a fortune. Pets relieve anxiety. They act as emotional stabilizers because of the way they unconditionally accept you."
>
> Dr. Wesley Young
> Los Angeles Zoo

> "Pets upgrade the quality of life, bring us closer to nature, provide companionship and emphasize the fact that animals must be accepted as desirable participants in society."
>
> Dr. Boris Levinson
> Child Psychologist

Both state and federal regulations for nursing homes require the provision of resources which will assure that the residents have adequate recreational and physical therapies. A frequent complaint, however, is that there often is a lack of responsiveness to their psycho-social needs. The introduction of pets into the nursing home environment may have a therapeutic benefit by providing companionship, warmth and a feeling of contributing since caring for a pet provides the resident with some self-direction and thus, some control over a part of his or her life.

The Department, in its awareness of the apprehension and resultant depression often experienced by the elderly, has long recognized the potentially positive aspect of pets in easing the transition from community life into an institutional setting. This was evidenced in the 1972 nursing home licensure rules in which the Department, in an effort to be responsive to this concern, permitted the visiting of pets in a nursing home, although the rule did not permit the pets to permanently reside there.

The 1979 statute was the result of successful lobbying by individuals and a widespread belief that pets can be a source of therapeutic recreation and stimulation for people who have either had animals throughout their lives or for whom animals may be the only source of affection left to them. The statute also reflects an attempt on the part of consumer groups and the Health Department to afford nursing homes with a flexibility which allows them to provide the resident with as home-like a setting as possible. With five per cent of the U.S. population aged 65 and over now living in nursing homes, the new law means that approximately 40,000 senior citizens in Minnesota will now have the opportunity to enjoy the warmth and friendship which a pet can provide.

Concerns of the department

In drafting regulations of any kind, the Department is concerned with appropriateness and reasonableness. Because we are charged with protecting the interest of Minnesota's citizens residing in health care facilities we must, of course, be primarily concerned with the impact pets may have on the health and safety of the nursing home residents. This is

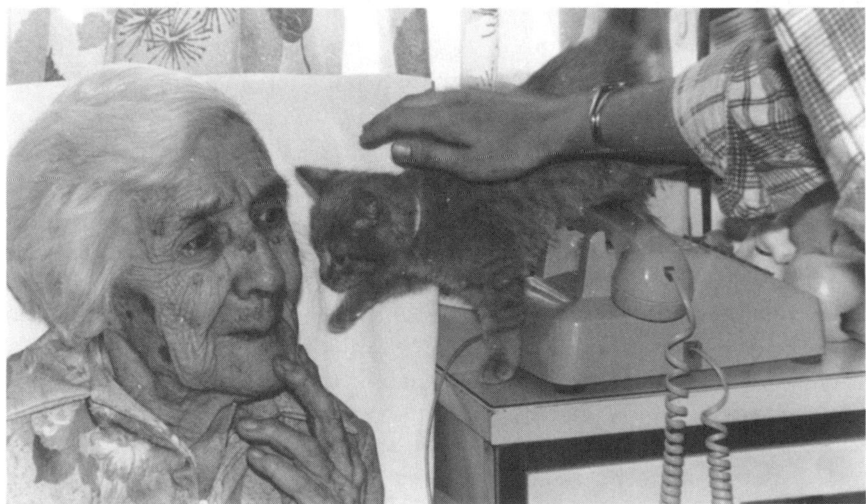

Elderly persons admitted to a nursing home experience a loss of autonomy and self-direction, a changed and lessened status in life, and limitations. Animals in the nursing home may ease the transition from community life to institutional setting. *(Photo by Phil Arkow)*

not to minimize the need to address the animal's welfare as well. Certainly factors such as abuse must be assured. However, in view of the Department's responsibility my emphasis is upon safeguarding the resident.

In considering pets in nursing homes it is necessary to evaluate the public health risks to what is, in the main, an at-risk population. Veterinary science has minimized the risks with proper immunizations but how can we be sure that animals receive proper care and treatment? Animals must be free of communicable or infectious diseases. Cooperation and support from staff will be necessary to assure visits to veterinary clinics for routine immunizations as well as for care when ill. We must assure that pets in the facility will not pose a health hazard. To that end, there must also be restrictions on the areas where pets can be allowed, e.g., in food service or preparation areas, or in the nursing station or areas where clean linen and sterile supplies are stored.

If pets are permitted the Department has the responsibility of assuring that written policies and procedures for the housekeeping and maintenance of nursing homes includes care of the animal(s). Provisions must be made for maintaining sanitary conditions in areas where the pets are located. This would include cleaning of cages, fish tanks, yard, combating odors and vacuuming up shed hair, controlling noise, etc. These things impact adversely upon the health (physical and emotional) of residents and must be under control at all times.

Another issue is that of nuisance. Ideally, we need to require that the nursing home be accountable to its residents and staff in some manner which includes them in the decision of whether or not to maintain a pet. In reality, the Department of Health can not prescribe management of such a decision; however, since supervision and management of a pet must be a coordinated effort it would seem that this should be a joint decision.

In drafting rules of any kind the Department must be concerned with the appropriateness and reasonableness of the rule. We thus must find that delicate balance between protection and freedom. The issues we've identified relate to health and safety and specifically, to the controls necessary for enforceable regulations.

The rule that has been developed starts with the basic premise that the decision to have or not have pets is up to the facility. The administrator of the facility has the responsibility to operate and govern the affairs of the facility on a day-to-day basis and it will ultimately be up to the administrator to weigh the pros and cons of having pets. We encourage that the final decision on this issue be based on input from the staff and residents of the nursing home and advice from a veterinarian. However, the over-riding consideration must acknowledge the resident's right to as *safe* as well as home-like an environment as possible.

To this end, the Department will need to safeguard the residents and assure that we can justify these regulations and controls on the basis of being reasonable mimimum standards. Our surveyors must evaluate the nursing home's compliance with regulations through licensing visits and unless the rules can be enforced through our survey techniques they become meaningless. We are constantly striving to reduce ambiguity in the regulations both to help the nursing homes and the surveyors, so it's necessary to consider the ability of the surveyors to enforce controls. This will, of course, depend upon clarity of rules and documentation of animal records plus the implementation of the home's policies concerning animals. Some judgment concerning cleanliness and odors is likely to be required on the part of surveyors. Subjectivity enters in and will certainly cause some problems with uniformity in the survey process.

The most appropriate resource for information on pets would be the veterinarian; we see the role of the veterinarian in helping the nursing home as absolutely essential. The nursing home choosing to house pets will be encouraged to develop and maintain a working relationship with a veterinarian, who can assist the home in complying with regulations through education in proper care and handling of pets. If a nursing home decides to permit pets, my own opinion is that they should have a written agreement with a nearby veterinarian to provide in-service programs for staff and residents and pet emergency services when needed.

It would seem also appropriate that the veterinarian have a role in providing advice and recommendations to a facility concerning whether or not to allow pets; and if the decision is to permit one, advising what types of pets should be restricted, helping to select a pet that will fit into the environment of the home and helping the facility assure that the pet is healthy.

To properly provide this assistance, the Department would consider it essential that the veterinarian be knowledgeable regarding any special considerations which impact upon animals dwelling in a nursing home setting. To this end, we would encourage veterinarians to visit long-term care facilities, particularly nursing homes, to assure their own awareness of the environmental considerations and potential complications at issue in the implementation of a pet therapy program.

The adopted rules

The first draft of the proposed rules relating to the keeping of pets in health care facilities was accompanied by a Cost Analysis and a Statement of Need and Reasonableness. Following the presentation of these documents, there was a public hearing and report from the hearing examiner. The rules were amended somewhat and finally adopted on June 8, 1983, and later re-codified.

Adopted Rules Relating to the Keeping of Pet Animals in Health Care Facilities

CHAPTER 4638 DEPARTMENT OF HEALTH
HEALTH CARE FACILITIES GENERALLY

NOTE: Under Minnesota Statutes, section 144.011, the State Board of Health was abolished and all of its duties transferred to the commissioner of health.

4638.0200 PET ANIMALS IN HEALTH CARE FACILITIES.

Subpart 1. Definition. As used in this part, "health care facility" means a hospital, nursing home, boarding care home, or supervised living facility licensed by the Minnesota Department of Health under Minnesota Statutes, sections 144.50 to 144.56 or 144A.01 to 144A.17.

Subp. 2. Written policy. Every health care facility shall establish a written policy specifying whether or not pet animals will be allowed on the facility's premises. If pet animals are allowed on the premises, the policy must specify whether or not individual patients or residents will be permitted to keep pets. This policy must be developed only after consultation with facility staff and with patients or residents, as appropriate.

Subp. 3. Conditions. If pet animals other than fish are allowed on the premises, the following requirements must be met:

A. Written policies and procedures must be developed and implemented which specify the conditions for allowing pet animals on the premises.

B. The policies and procedures must:

(1) Describe the types of pet animals allowed on the facility's premises. This policy must be developed in consultation with a veterinarian and a physician.

(2) Describe the procedures for maintaining and monitoring the health and behavior of animals kept on the facility's premises. These procedures must be in accordance with a veterinarian's recommendations. A copy of these recommendations must be maintained in the facility.

(3) Identify those areas in the facility, in addition to those areas described in item F, where pet animals shall not be permitted.

C. Regardless of the ownership of any pet, the health care facility shall assume overall responsibility for any pets within or on the premises of the facility.

D. The health care facility shall ensure that no pet jeopardizes the health, safety, comfort, treatment, or well-being of the patients, residents, or staff.

E. A facility employee shall be designated, in writing, as being responsible for monitoring or providing the care to all pet animals and for ensuring the cleanliness and maintenance facilities used to house pets. This rule does not preclude residents, patients, or other individuals from providing care to pet animals.

F. Except for guide dogs accompanying a blind or deaf individual and except in supervised living facilities with a licensed bed capacity of 15 beds or less, pet animals shall not be permitted in kitchen areas, in medication storage and administration areas, or in clean or sterile supply storage areas.

Cost analysis

A major concern, of course, was the fiscal impact of pets in health care facilities, both upon the facility itself and upon the Department. A cost analysis statement was presented by the Department and is reprinted here:

It must be emphasized that this rule does not compel a health care facility to keep pets on its premises. The statute and the rule expressly indicate that the decision to keep pets must be made at the facility level. The only mandatory obligation is contained in the provision requiring a facility to develop a policy specifying whether or not pets will be permitted. The development of such a policy would not increase a facility's cost of operation. The licensee of a facility is already charged with the responsibility to develop policies and procedures relating to the facility's operation. Thus, a mechanism is already in place in each facility for policy development and compliance with the rule will not require additional expenditures.

However, if a facility does decide to allow pets to be kept on the premises, costs relating to the care of the pet may be incurred. However, the multitude of variables relating to these costs makes it impossible to develop a prospective fiscal analysis. A pet could be donated to the facility or could belong to a specific resident. In these instances, there would be no initial acquisition cost. Since the facility has almost unlimited discretion in selecting a pet animal, the costs for obtaining a pet will vary based upon the selection made by the facility.

Since the keeping of pets is optional, any costs incurred will be the result of the facility's decision and not directly related to mandatory compliance with the rule. Again depending on the type of pet selected, the costs for the care of the pet, e.g., veterinarian fees, grooming fees, food, shelter, etc. will vary. Since these costs are so variable, the Department is unable to definitively provide any cost estimates which would be more than pure conjecture.

The rules require that any pet kept in the facility be in good health and properly cared for. The rules also require that the facility initiate any necessary steps to assure that a pet does not become a nuisance or otherwise jeopardize the well-being of residents in the facility. However, the costs associated with meeting these outcomes will only be known after the facility has decided to allow pets and has selected the type of pet(s) that will be appropriate. Since the care and feeding of a pet would not be reimbursable under the provisions of the Medicaid program, the state's or a county's contribution to the program will not be affected. The keeping of pets will have to be financed solely by the facility. Thus, it is reasonable to expect that a facility would carefully evaluate the fiscal impact that a pet will have on its operation. This decision must be left to the facility since only the facility will be in the position to obtain the necessary facts to accurately assess those costs. Since the rule does not impose a mandatory requirement on the facility, the Department does not believe that a cost analysis is required. It is also the Department's position that the conditions contained in the rule could be implemented by the facility through the appropriate utilization of existing staff resources. Therefore, even if a facility allows pets to be kept on the premises, additional staffing would not be required.

While the rule will necessitate additional monitoring activities by the Department, this review would be included in the ongoing survey activities of the Department and handled by present staff. Thus, no increases in the Department's budget will be required.

Statement of need and reasonableness

Accompanying the proposed rule was a Statement of Need and

Conditions for animals in health care facilities—both resident pets and visiting ones—must be sanitary to avoid adverse impact on the physical and emotional health of residents, staff, and visitors. *(Photo by Phil Arkow)*

Reasonableness which commented on the specific provisions of the rule. Excerpts from this Statement are reprinted here:

> Section B.1 requires that each health care facility establish a written policy specifying whether or not pet animals can be kept on the premises. The establishment of the written policy will provide an assurance that this issue has been carefully considered by the licensee of the health care facility.
>
> Section B.3. requires that the development of the policy be based on consultation with the facility staff and with the facility's residents and patients, as appropriate. The Department believes that the need for obtaining input from staff and residents is important. Numerous articles have promoted the benefits to be gained by allowing pets to be kept on the premises of a health care facility. However, despite these benefits, it must also be kept in mind that the keeping of pets on the premises will involve work and will require that staff supervise the care of the pets. In addition, the health and sanitary aspects of having pets housed in a health care facility must also be carefully evaluated. Residents may be allergic to certain types of animals and since the primary goal of a health care facility is to promote and protect the health of its residents, these concerns cannot be ignored. In addition, staff members and residents may have adverse feelings about allowing pets on the premises on a permanent basis. Residents may not like pets and these concerns must be weighed in reaching a decision in this matter. Staff may not wish to be involved in the care of the animals or may feel that animals will not be appropriate or beneficial in the facility. Since the policy finally adopted by the facility will be a standard of conduct to be followed by facility staff and residents, the Department believes that this rule requiring staff and resident input is appropriate and necessary to assure that the feelings and concerns of staff and residents are considered.
>
> If the health care facility allows pets to be kept on the premises, Section B.2. will require the policy to specify whether or not individual residents will be allowed to keep pets. Residents and prospective residents have the right to be informed if the facility will prohibit or permit them from keeping indivi dual pets in the facility. This position should be known to avoid any misunderstanding as to the nature of the facility's policy and this issue should also be carefully considered by any facility that will allow pets to be kept on the premises. The Department has approved a number of specific waiver requests which, with the approval of the facility, allowed individual residents to retain pets in the facility. These requests were primarily based on the therapeutic benefit that the retention of the pet would provide to the individual resident.
>
> Section C. of the rule establishes the conditions that must be followed by any facility electing to maintain pet animals on its premises. This section contains subsections relating to the types of pet animals, the health of the pet animals and the facility's responsibility for the care of the pets.

While the Department does not dispute the beneficial and therapeutic effects that pet animals could provide in a health care facility, the Department must also assure that the health, safety and well-being of the residents is not threatened by allowing pets to be kept on the premises. The conditions contained in this section establish reasonable controls to be followed and at the same time, do not create barriers which would unreasonably preclude the keeping of pets in the facility.

The types of animals that could be retained in a health care facility are virtually unlimited. For that reason, it will be necessary for the facility to carefully consider this issue and then, once a decision is made, to inform the residents. In determining the types of pets which will be allowed to be kept in the facility a number of factors must be considered: the types and needs of the residents, the physical surroundings, the costs of caring for the pets, the willingness and ability of staff to care for or to monitor the care of the pets; and the risks associated with keeping pets on the premises. Any pet selected must also be compatible with the residents and must not pose a health or safety factor. The animal must be emotionally stable and adaptable to the purpose that it will serve in the facility, e.g., will the animal come into close contact with residents, will the animal be handled by many individuals, etc.

Since the types of animals available for pets are numerous and since the Department cannot predict the purpose that an animal will serve in a particular facility, it would not be feasible for the Department to develop a specific listing of "approved" pets. In fact, while a dog or cat may be appropriate in a particular facility, differences in the size of another facility or the characteristics of the resident population could make the dog or cat completely unsuitable as a pet in another facility. For these reasons, the rule will require that this policy be developed in consultation with a veterinarian and with a physician. The veterinarian has the expertise to advise the facility as to the appropriateness of different types of animals to be considered as well as possibly suggesting various breeds of animals that would be suitable to a specific facility. The physician, along with the veterinarian, would also be able to inform the facility of those pets that pose a higher risk of transmitting diseases to human beings. Veterinary medicine has greatly reduced the risks of disease transmission to a human being by developing various immunizations and providing proper treatment of the animals. However, these risks should not be minimized and expert advice will be important in properly selecting the type of pet to consider. The physician would also identify problems that the keeping of pets on the premises might create. Facility residents, especially those in nursing homes are a greater risk of disease than the average population. Residents could have allergies or other respiratory diseases that would be compounded if certain pets were retained For that reason, the impact that particular types of pets might have on the resident population must be considered. The physician and the veterinarian will be able to provide the necessary advice in these important areas and this will help to assure that an appropriate type of pet animal is selected.

Since the residents may have less than optimum physical health, the Department is concerned with the resident's susceptibility to animal transmitted diseases and infections. It is for this reason that any pet animal brought into the facility must be healthy in order to reduce the possibility of any disease transmission to the residents. The rules also require that the health care facility assume the responsibility for assuring that the pet is examined and receives any necessary immunizations in accordance with the veterinarian's recommendation. The veterinarian has the training and expertise to assure that pets are in good health and to establish a schedule of regular examinations and treatments to maintain a pet in a healthy condition. It would only be through these regular examinations that a determination as to the pet's health status could be ascertained. These examinations and treatments will protect residents from the possibility of receiving an infection or disease from the pet animal.

The facility has a responsibility for the care and maintenance of the pet. The Department believes that it is necessary to require the facility to assume this responsibility in order to assure that the interests of the residents are protected as well as to assure that the pet is properly cared for. The facility is responsible for the care of the residents and this responsibility also includes assurances that the rights and interests of all facility residents are protected. Thus, even if residents are permitted to keep their individual pets on the premises, the facility must assume the responsibility for any pets kept on the premises. Even if the resident cares for the pet, the facility must monitor the provision of the care and assure that the resident's pet does not interfere with the rights of other residents or disrupt the activities of the facility. If the facility did not assume this control, it would not be possible to properly monitor the pets in the facility and if other residents also kept pets, problems in controlling the pets would occur.

It will also be important to assure that the welfare of any pet animal is also taken into consideration. Since the facility will be required to assume the responsibilitty for the pet animal, facility staff will be in a position to monitor the care and feeding of the pet. This would include the furnishing of suitable living quarters, adequate nutrition and the avoidance of abuse. Since the facility will have the option to allow pets to be kept on the premises, the Department does not believe that this rule is unreasonable. The facility is responsible for the well-being of all residents and since the retention of pets on the premises could jeopardize that well-being, the facility must be in the position of overall responsibility to curtail any problems that might develop. Even in situations when a pet is owned by a specific resident, the Department does not consider this rule to be a violation of that resident's right. The facility will be required to develop policies relating to the keeping of pet animals and the responsibility of the facility should be clearly stated within that policy. This policy will be available for the resident's review and if a resident wishes to bring a pet into the facility (assuming this would be permissible under the facility's policy), the resident would be notified of this restriction. As previously mentioned, the rule is not intended to exclude or limit a resident's involvment with the pet. In fact, the interaction between the resident and a pet is one of the benefits to be gained by allowing pets in the facility. Since the facility staff has responsibility for the residents, this responsibility extends to all aspects of the facility's programs.

Another factor that is of critical importance is any impact that the keeping of pets would have on the health and safety of the facility's residents. Residents could be allergic to certain pets or may have respiratory problems that could be complicated if pets are kept on the premises. While restricting pets to specific areas may solve this problem, the health of the residents must be carefully considered. Pets that have freedom to roam around the facility also become an obstacle for residents, especially those residents with visual handicaps or whose ability to walk is limited. Staff reaction must also be considered since pets could create similar problems for staff members. The facility will have to assure that appropriate measures are taken to prevent pets from becoming a nuisance and to assure that the interest of staff and residents are protected

In order to assure that the facility's responsibility is effectively carried out, it will be necessary to require that a facility carefully plan its program and provide an organized mechanism to implement the program. For that reason, the Department believes that is necessary for a specific facility employee to be designated to care for the pet animals. The designation of a specific individual will assure that appropriate accountability is maintained and will also provide a uniform approach for caring for the pets and monitoring the pets in the facility. In no circumstance should pets be permitted in a facility unless provisions for adequate supervision and management are in place. The individual designatd by the facility will be assigned the responsibility for the day-to-day care of the pets. While specific chores for caring for the pet can be delegated, the staff member will be responsible for assuring that these chores are completed. In the event that these chores are not completed, it will be the responsibility of the staff member to take the necessary steps.

It is obvious that the keeping of a pet on the premises could lead to problems with sanitation, particularly with hair, food and body wastes. The rule requires that the facility be maintained in a clean and sanitary condition and since pets could create problems, the designated individual will be required to assure that these problems do not occur. The welfare of the pet animal must also be considered and the selection of one individual to monitor the care of the animal will help to assure that the animal is fed, groomed and appropriately cared for. This individual will also be responsible for following the facility's policy and procedures concerning the keeping of pets and for assuring that the provisions of the policy and procedures are implemented.

Hearing examiner's report

The report of the Hearing Examiner on the rule, the submitted Statement of Need and Reasonableness and Cost Analysis, and public comment made some intriguing comments. The report noted the lack of clear definitions of such words as "care," "maintenance," and "pet," and conflicting opinions as to whether fish were to be considered as pets in the context of the rule. It affirmed the authority of the Department to adopt and enforce the rule.

It also raised the question as to whether visiting pets should be treated differently than residential ones. Referring to B.1., and following the testimony of Ruth Stryker-Gordon and Dr. R.K. Anderson of the University of Minnesota School of Public Health, the proposed rule wording about whether pets could be "kept" was amended to read whether pets would be "allowed." The Hearing Examiner noted:

> Pets may create a health or safety risk to a facility's patients or residents. They may carry a disease or be of such a size or temperament that they pose a threat to patients, especially the elderly, who can, for example, be more easily knocked down by a rambunctious dog and who because of their age are particularly susceptible to, or more seriously threatened by; common heatlh hazards. In fact, it would appear that strange dogs, for example, who visit a facility may be a greater threat to the residents' health and safety than dogs who live on the the premises because the temperament and habits of visiting animals are not known and their health may not be monitored, as would be the case with resident pets under the proposed rules. Consequently it is concluded that an amendment recognizing the hazards posed by visiting animals is necessary and reasonable and consistent with the Department's authority to protect the health of residents or patients and to regulate the maintenance of pets. Although the word "maintenance" suggests some kind of permanency, the repeated or even occasional visiting by pets is as much keeping of pets as is having them and it would be wholly inconsistent with the purposes of the law to ignore the risks posed by visiting animals.

The Hearing Examiner also raised the question about the removal of animals from a health care facility, if this became necessary. The report stated:

> The Legal Advocacy for Older Americans Project noted that human beings can form strong attachments to their pets and that in order to protect their rights, facilities should be required to provide a procedure for the removal of pets in the written policy developed. The Department did not specifically

> respond to this comment and it is urged to do so. The Department's failure to include a provision requiring the adoption of procedures for the removal of pet animals is not arbitrary or unreasonable and it can leave such decisions to the facilities. However, a strong argument can be made that a formal procedure for pet removal be adopted in order to protect the patients and the residents. If such a procedure is required by the Department, it would be a necessary and reasonable exercise of its discretion and within the scope of its delegated authority to regulate the maintenance of pets.

Finally, the Hearing Examiner raised some interesting points about the prohibition of pets in certain areas:

> Except for guide dogs, pet animals are not permitted in kitchen areas, medication storage and administration areas or in clean or sterile supply storage areas. This requirement was questioned by several commentators, especially as it would apply to the kitchens of supervised living facilities, or group homes for mentally retarded individuals, which house less than 15 residents and frequently less than six. These group homes are often single-family dwellings and are structured to provide a home-like atmosphere. In such homes, it is difficult to close off kitchen areas from the rest of the home. It is clear that the presence of pets in kitchen areas may be a health hazard, especially where the pets have access to counter tops and could contaminate foods or food preparation surfaces. However, kitchen areas are commonly used to isolate pet dogs during toilet training and other periods to prevent the soiling of carpeting. In a typical home, pets normally have access to the kitchen. For this reason and since the residents do not suffer from the same health hazards as the elderly, the Department is urged to consider excepting group homes from the prohibition of pets in kitchen areas or consider excepting such homes for particular pets such as dogs which would not have access to counter tops or direct access to food storage areas or food preparation surfaces. The rule ultimately adopted whether it allows such an exception or not is necessary and reasonable, however, and within the scope of the Department's expertise and reasonable discretion.

Section V - Carrying It On

18

Publicizing the Bond

Hugh Tebault

"... tremendous potential for helping an agency ..."

A sound, workable public relations program is as important a need for a progressive organization as is a competent staff. If the public is not made privy to the purposes and functions of an operation the unknown often becomes the mysterious and upon contemplation, mysterious things frequently tend to stimulate images of nefarious activity. Just as a dark alley or house is forbidding and when well-lit unthreatening, a well-conceived and implemented public relations program will provide the necessary enlightenment to engender a favorable public image.

In the absence of an effective public relations program, far too many human and animal service agencies find themselves engaged in otherwise unecessarily enervating efforts in defense of their policies, programs and in some cases their very existence. The public record is replete with evidence of encounters which are costly in both time and money. In this regard, nursing homes are frequently spoken of as impersonal domiciles into which worthy elderly citizens are placed to vegetate and die. Veterinarians are seen as business entrepreneurs more interested in money than the welfare of their patients. Animal control agency personnel are visualized as insensitive slaugherhouse overseers of a place where animals are wantonly killed. The management of far too many humane organizations is considered idealistically impractical and largely unproductive.

Public relations programs necessarily must be predicated upon widely different critera which depend on the particular circumstances and opportunites present in a given situation. In the case of professional

Hugh Tebault is president of The Latham Foundation for the Promotion of Humane Education, in Alameda, Calif. He has been associated with the foundation since 1944 and was instrumental in the concept and development of this book.

human and animal care organizations, one of the most cost-effective, least recognized and underused public relations programs available is that involving the human/companion animal bond.

It is interesting that one of the least appreciated aspects of human/companion animal bond programs is the improvement such programs provide to an agency's or institution's public image. Though it is important that each program be one of sincere public service, one which considers the overall welfare of the persons and animals involved, well-conceived and implemented programs carry tremendous potential for helping an agency to improve its image within various publics and to publicize not only its existence, but also its concern for human and animal welfare and highlight its diversity of programming. Proper publicizing of the bond will boost the agency's relations with its public especially among the people who really count in a community by conveying its care and concern and also lead to an elevated employee morale as these publics come to understand what the organization is really about.

It should not be assumed, or course, that one program, or one publicity drive, will miraculously change an agency's image overnight. Nor should it be presumed that publicity can give substance if there's nothing to the organization to begin with. Public relations and publicity are professions requiring on-going attention and constant monitoring. But any agency interested in caring for and helping others—whether a non-profit organization desperately in need of donations, a tax-supported agency, or a profit-oriented group which needs to maintain its position in the marketplace—can and should, benefit from the advantages of a successful PR program which "bond" activities can provide.

What is public relations?

There is no one, uniform definition of public relations which fits all cases, though there have been a number of good working definitions put forth. In simple terms, public relations is a communication to the public via print or broadcast press of desired points of image at no charge. (Note: this is the difference between PR and advertising). A more detailed definition was proposed by Dr. Rex F. Harlow, former professor of education, social science and public relations at Stanford University, who wrote:

> "Public relations is a distinctive management function which helps establish and maintain lines of communication, understanding, acceptance and cooperation between an organization and its publics; involves the management of problems or issues; helps management to keep informed on and responsive to public

opinion; and emphasizes the responsibility of management to serve the public interest; helps management keep abreast of and effectively utilize change, serving as an early warning system to help anticipate trends; and uses research and sound and ethical communication techniques as its principal tools."

These descriptions embrace the elements of a successful PR program: confidence, respect, addressing the variety of publics involved, management-oriented thinking, a high value placed in two-way communications and publicity with a reliance on the news media.

Understanding the news media

Since the media are such an integral part of any publicity or PR effort, it behooves the agency to know what the media want, how they think and how to approach them. Media communications is a two-way street: just because an agency is conducting an unusual program is no automatic guarantee that radio and TV stations and newspapers will pick up the story. What seems important to the veterinarian, the social worker, the animal shelter official, the psychiatrist, or the nursing home administrator may or may not be of interest to general audiences. So, in order to obtain good publicity one must know what the media want and why.

The function of a newspaper, radio, or TV news operation is to inform the *general* public about *general* news of *general* interest to the *general* community. Specialized publications such as professional journals or in-house newsletter, may address a restricted, particular audience who are already closely familiar with the basics of an operation and its goals and a different type of writing appears in these media. For this chapter, we will talk about publicizing activities to the mass audience.

One definition of news is, "Anything that makes people say, 'Gee whiz!' " While your particular program may be the most interesting thing in your field right now, unless you can present it as being of major interest to many listeners, viewers and readers, you'll have a difficult time selling the story. As an example, local "bond" programs had been going on for many years with limited, local publicity; it was only after reports began to emerge that the therapeutic value of pets may include increasing survival rates after heart attacks and lowering blood pressure levels—news of widespread interest—that the major networks and wire services began publicizing the pet-facilitated therapy programs nation-wide.

Editors at news outlets are deluged daily with hundreds of valid requests from many worthwhile community agencies, each of which has a following and each of which honestly feels its particular program is the most exciting. To their credit, editors are usually extremely conscientious in balancing the needs of the Cancer Society, the Girl Scouts, the Humane Society, the City Council, the Highway Department and the Chamber of Commerce. It's practically a miracle, when you think about it, that in an age of "the information explosion" they can take all that information from local, state, national and international sources, put it together between the ball scores, the stock market quotations, the weather forecasts and the obituaries, package it in an attractive, accurate and informative format and present it on your doorstep every morning or on your TV screen every night at a ridiculously modest price. Needless to say, there's only room for so much news and not everything that is submitted is going to be covered. Editors must establish priorities, too. Assuming a story is newsworthy, of general interest and the medium has the staff to cover it, here are three decisions the editor must make:

1. *Time value:* How urgent is it that it run on the 5 o'clock news or in tomorrow's editions? Could it wait until the weekend when there's less competition from government-and business-based stories? Could it hold until a holiday weekend when everything shuts down and they're desperate for copy, particularly something heartwarming?

2. *Space value:* How much space in the newspaper or precious time on the air is it realistically worth? A brief story may fit in easier when there's not much room to play around with: it could make a nice "filler." However, a major feature may become the backbone around which the layout of a broadcast, a newspaper page, or a magazine may be based. A good photo opportunity with little "hard" news may realistically be worth only a dramatic photo with an accompanying, explanatory caption.

3. *Photographic value:* How much does this story lend itself to photographic illustration, which is a backbone for all layouts? (In the case of radio, photographs are replaced with "actualities", interviews with people in the story whose different voices give listeners a colorful variety from the same-old voices of the newscasters.

In the case of "bond" publicity, stories can fit nicely within these priorities and can even be a worried editor's dream, but only if the person offering them to the media knows how to present the opportunity for the story in a format the media can use. For example, a call for volunteers to assist a program is realistically worth only two or three paragraphs in a community affairs section in the newspaper; a 10- or 15 second public service announcement on the radio; and probably no mention at all on TV. However, the actual conducting of a "bond" program, particularly if it has vivid photographic possibilities with adorable or unusual animals and elderly or handicapped people, could easily be worth a full-page feature in the newspaper; a 30-second interview on radio; and a 45-second feature on the TV evening news.

Editors are like eveyone else: they're human. They want things given to them in as easy a format to follow as possible. The less work they have to do, the more likely they are to work with you. The more they have come to trust you over the years for honesty, credibility and reliability, the more likely they are to believe you when you tell them this is, in fact, a good story.

Editors aren't just trying to "sell newspapers": that's the job of the publisher. Editors want to go home every night (or in the wee hours of the morning) feeling that they've put out a good product today, artistically pleasant and factually accurate, comprehensive (considering their limitations), of widespread interest and including all the major news items that could be fit in to the limited space available, without missing a major story that their competition covered and responsibly balancing all the newsworthy activities that occured anywhere in the world that day.

People involved with "bond" programs have several important advantages on their side when they request media coverage:

• The news is usually local, involving community organizations which the media feel responsible to cover.

Public relations programs, such as these educational display boards for an animal control agency, can help change an image and create a new awareness of the organization's role and purpose in the community.

(Photo by Phil Arkow)

• The news is part of a national picture, with "bond" research and activities going on constantly, giving the local media a great opportunity to "localize" stories for a local angle on the information they receive over the wires.

• There are four things which readers and viewers love to see: kids, animals, sex and violence. Anything with a universal, emotional appeal is of great interest to their audiences. By convincing the editors that your story is what their readers, viewers and listeners want to see and hear, you stand a better chance of getting your activity covered.

Who to contact

Newspapers: The *publisher* owns the newspaper and has to balance the needs of editorial space against the advertising revenue and circulation figures; he or she is not as concerned with the actual content of each individual story as are the editors below. The *editor* determines the newspaper's policy and writes the editorials: again, unless you're caught in the middle of a community-wide controversy the editor usually doesn't have too much to do with you except, perhaps, write an innocuous editorial once a year supporting "Be Kind to Animals Week" or "National Nursing Home Week" or some other safe subject. The *managing editor* is a chief-of-staff and is closer to the editorial office but is more concerned with personnel matters and inter-department affairs. The editor you want to see and get to know personally, is the *city editor* (or the *metro editor* on larger newspapers) or the *features editor*. The city editor is responsible for assembling all the fast-breaking, day-to-day, "hard" news which occurs constantly, news which must run in this afternoon's edition or the next day's paper. Features editors are concerned with the longer, less timely news which lacks the immediacy of instant coverage and which can hold for a few days to give it more space. Most bond programs probably fit into the features or city news categories, but there can be exceptions: in larger cities there are special weekend editors who handle the longer, more detailed articles which can run in the Saturday and Sunday editions due to increased advertising. Or there may be a magazine editor for a home-grown Sunday magazine. Or your story may be of such a specialized nature that a specialized editor may be particularly interested: a bond program at a church or religious-based camp may be of interest to the religious editor; a research study may find itself on the science editor's desk; and equestrian special olympics might interest the sports editor, etc. Use your imagination: find the "peg" upon which an editor can hang a story. Be flexible. Put yourself in the newspaper's place and ask where this story can go for maximum impact.

TV and radio: Again, the middle-management editors are the best contact and personal rapport with them is vital so they can associate a face with your name. In most cases, it will be the *news editor* who decides what is going to be covered and the *assignments editor,* who schedules the reporters to make their daily rounds. Get to know these people, respect them for the difficult tasks and priorities which they face every day and convince them that your story is something of widespread interest to their listeners and viewers and will make them say "Gee Whiz!" Feature and special interest editors may be applicable here, particularly in larger markets.

How to write a news release

A news release is a brief statement given to the media that explains the "5 W's", the basics of the story you would like them to cover: Who, What, When, Where and Why (and sometimes How Much) *There is no substitute for personal contact:* the release dropped off in person is going to get much more coverage than the one anonymously dropped in the mail. Each news release is going to compete with the 50 or 100 other news releases the editor receives daily, many of which automatically end up in the wastebasket. (It's a lot harder for the editor to refuse you face-to-face: editors feel guilty, too!) A release must be competitive to be successful. A good release includes the following components:

1. A brief, concise "lead." The "lead" is the first sentence of the release, which may be the only sentence the busy editor may read. It has to jump out and make the editor want to skim at least two or three more sentences to decide whether it's worth giving it to a reporter. If this happens, the reporter may either rewrite it, in which case it will result in a three- or four-paragraph story, or follow up with an interview, to be developed into a longer story. If you lose the editor at the first impression, you've lost the story.

2. All the basic elements are included: *what's* happening, *who's* doing it, *when* and *where* it's happening and *why* it's going on.

3. A resource person who can be contacted for further information, with a telephone number where this individual can be reached during media working hours (which are rarely 8-to-5).

4. A clean, crisp writing style in the active tense, rather than passive. Use lots of action verbs and vibrant quotes, which can make even a dull rewrite sound exciting. And neatness still counts: the release must be double-spaced, typed on a clean typewriter, with lots of white space for editing notes. Start the first page in the middle of the sheet, to leave room for headline and other notations and have a heading at the top listing the

name, address and phone number of the organization and the date of release. Use company letterhead if possible. Try to keep it under 1½ pages; if anything longer than that is required, they'll want an interview. Keep the paragraphs short: usually one or two sentences. Pique interest, make sentences short and easy to read and repeat key points.

The value of photographs

Even in today's age of microinformation and home computers, a picture is still worth a thousand words. One of the most appealing facets of bond programs is the fact that people smile and cry. Heartwarming, human-interest photos of people and animals together win prizes, dress up a newspaper or TV layout and leave readers and viewers feeling happy. News media are not exclusively concerned with bad news (this idea fits along with the other misconceptions people have about nursing homes, veterinarians, shelters, etc.) Happy news has its place, too and photos enhance this concept.

There are a few important precautions one should be aware of if photographers are going to come out to observe a program:

1. *Rights:* If the participants are wards of the state, under governmental custody, or juveniles, it may be necessary to secure their written permission before they can be photographed. Most institutions where this is a problem already have a standard release form and a governing policy. For many agencies, this is not a problem. However, if you have a question, check before the crews arrive.

2. *Timing:* The reactions on the residents' faces as the puppies are brought in can be captured only once. TV crews in particular require a lot of set-up time and may have to bring a clumsy array of artificial lighting equipment indoors. Try to have the photographers in place early to set up before the animals arrive: the resulting pictures will be worth the extra wait.

3. *Submitting your own photographs:* In most cases, newspapers will not run anyone else's photos. They have their own photographers who are professionals and unless you happen to catch a photo of a plane falling out of the sky on your Instamatic they don't want your pre-shot pictures. However, newsletters may be somewhat less restrictive. Check with the photo editor, but don't be offended if rejected. Polaroid-type photos and 110 color snapshots do not reproduce well enough. Black-and-white, 35mm film, well-photographed and printed is called for.

4. *What pictures won't run:* There are certain types of photographs which, to an editor, "When you've see one you've seen them all." Consequently, many newspapers have a blanket policy and usually refuse

to run a "line-up" shot (where five people are lined up and smiling about whatever is happening), or a check-presentation shot (no matter how worthy the cause, there are only so many ways to photograph a person handing someone else a check), or a ground-breaking shot (where four famous people stand around and look ridiculous in hardhats while one of them turns the "first " spadeful of earth). Many TV stations refuse to do "talking head" shots, where someone is interviewed and for 30 boring seconds all you see is his or her head on camera. There may be exceptions to this, of course (like when it's the publisher holding the shovel or his wife with the check). In order to get stories of this type photographed, a gimmick is needed. A ribbon-cutting is only a ribbon-cutting, unless the kid with the scissors is obviously physically disabled; a hardhatted dog digging up the ground is more interesting than the officials; a 4′ x 8′ check painted on plywood and drawn in by a therapeutic horse is infinitely more interesting than one handed over by an officer of the board.

Again the key is to use imagination, "think pictures," and know what the editors want and how to give it to them in a way that inspires them.

Mechanics of the interview

Assuming a release catches the eye of the editor and assuming it's worth more than a simple rewrite or a photo-with-a-caption, you or the participants in the bond program may find yourself interviewed in person, This may involve a telephone call for some additional facts or a reporter accompanying you to the facility to observe the program first-hand and to talk to the participants involved. Here are some tips for a successful interview:

1. *Spokesperson:* One person should be designated as the official spokesperson for the activity. This gives the reporter a sense of continuity and the agency a means of control. Remember, PR is a management-based action. Staff can talk about their program, of course, but one person must coordinate all the publicity.

2. *Facts:* Have plenty of background information available and prepare handouts if necessary (particularly if there is a lot of statistical data). This gives the reporter something reliable to use if he or she has questions.

3. *Subject:* Know what you're going to be interviewed about and stick to that subject. If there's something else interesting going on, you might point it out as being worthy of future coverage, but in most cases the reporter will want to work on only one story at a time.

4. *Punctuality:* This still counts. Reporters are very busy. Be on time and ready. Know where the medium's office is, if your're going there and allow time for parking, etc. Be particularly punctual for TV appearances, such as talk shows, which may require pre-interviews, make-up etc.

5. *Compose yourself:* Don't be nervous. TV stars are just people. Very few reporters are after "hatchet jobs" and most have a genuine interest in what is going to be talked about.

6. *Watch what you say:* The rules of the game dictate that anything you say may be held against you. If a glib comment is made, make sure there's no chance it can be misconstrued or taken out of context. If you don't know the answer, simply say so. Don't say, "No comment": nothing drives a reporter more into looking for a controversy that may or may not be there than hearing an interviewee avoid an answer. If something must be said "off the record," make absolutely certain that the reporter agrees *before* it is said. If patients' confidentialities must be protected, make sure the reporter knows why and work out ways around the obstacles, such as pseudonyms, etc.

7. *Information they can use:* Remember who's interviewing you. Don't speak in scientific jargon if it's for a general audience. Give informative, authoritative material in good, simple basic descriptions. Skip fancy scientific lingo.

8. *Speak with enthusiasm:* Short, slow phrases with colorful words and a bright tone of voice give the reporter grist for the media mill. If the reporter is taking notes, give him or her time to copy down what is said. In the case of a radio interview or a newspaper reporter using a tape recorder, keep eye contact with the reporter—not the microphone—and speak distinctly, using vocal intonations to give the interview color and emphasis. Try to speak freely rather than with notes. Be informal, but not breezy. In the case of TV, talk to the audience through the camera as well.

9. *Be professional:* Dress according to the purpose of the interview and the program. Western wear may be appropriate for an equestrian therapy program, but not a nursing home. Avoid wearing white clothing for a TV interview (the bright white throws the camera off color balance). White shirts or blouses or accessories are permissible.

10. *"Think pictures":* If the photographers will be present use props, charts and especially animals to help illustrate your point. Conduct your program outdoors in natural light if possible.

11. *Be flexible:* If a plane falls out of the sky or someone fires a shot at the mayor, all news crews are going to be there and a scheduled interview will be canceled. Understand the media's priorities, get it rescheduled and don't take it personally.

Some final pointers

1. *Treat all the media fairly.* The newspapers, radio and TV stations in your town are highly competitive. If you consistently favor one paper over

the other, or TV over radio, you'll eventually regret it. Give one story to one paper as an exclusive, then alternate. Give your first interviews on one story to radio, then to TV next time. Build a reputation within the media community as being impartial and fair.

2. *Learn the format they want, down to the details.* Let's say, for example, the newspaper allows you to write a regular column. Find out what their stylebook says and follow it. (For example, do they use "Ms."? How are certain words abbreviated? Which words are capitalized?) The less work they have to do with your copy, the more they'll like to run it.

3. *Understand deadlines.* Editors have a daily (or weekly) product to put out. After many years they have developed a successful routine which works for them. Find out what time and which days are best for interviews and photo sessions, or what's the best time to call or visit them with ideas for articles. Does releasing a news story at a particular time unfairly restrict another medium's operations? You obviously can't always bend a program to fit the needs of the media, but the more you can accommodate them the more coverage will be realized.

4. *Public Service Announcements (PSA's).* Under the terms of recent deregulation by the Federal Communications Commission, radio and TV stations are not as likely to provide free PSA's to qualifying non-profit agencies as before. Community spirit is the secret : stations still have to serve community needs and they welcome good announcements for their license record. (Newspapers never had such obligations). PSA's may promote a specific event (an open house, a fundraising event, a call for volunteers) to benefit a bond program, or may be a generalized promotion of the organization's existence and activities. Observe the radio and TV station to learn what their formats are: do they flash quick announcements at the end of the weathercast or do they have 30-second announcements aired sporadically during the day? Are all public service obligations met by a 30-minute interview at 4 a.m. on Sunday? Do the disc jockeys read a quick announcement in the 10 seconds while a song is starting up? Find out what their format is and give the PSA to them in a style they can use.

5. *Radio talk shows.* Most cities now have at least one station featuring local or network call-in programs, where people can call in and hear themselves talk. If you can speak authoritatively on the human/animal bond, regarding the benefits of animals for people and people for animals, on the needs animals have and on your agency and your programs, you're a "natural" for this type of show. But don't expect callers' questions to be logical, rational, or even sane. Don't get into shouting matches. *Do* be polite, informative, interesting, colorful and perhaps even a little controversial. Be prepared for everything, from answering a hundred

diverse questions in an hour to talking for an hour straight because no one calls. Relax and don't be afraid of the microphone, or of the host, either.

6. *Where to go for help:* The media in your community want to offer good reliable, honest coverage and they want to help local agencies and organizations learn how to provide them with ideas quickly and easily. Check around: you may find that the newspaper has a community relations officer or ombudsman whose job is to explain to local groups how to submit articles for coverage. The press club may conduct a periodic seminar to teach groups like yours the mechanics of requesting a press conference or issue a directory of who to contact at each medium. There may be a public relations club or advertising federation in your town, or local chapters of the International Association of Business Communicators (IABC) or the Public Relations Society of America (PRSA). Ask some of the corporate PR and communications specialists at local factories, military installations, colleges, or large non-profit associations how they get publicity. Your state and national trade associations often conduct training seminars and offer guidebooks. You can organize a local cooperative association for media coverage: an association of nursing home activity directors can get more interest than can one individual and a local veterinary society can organize promotions and get publicity where the individual practitioner may be prohibited due to professional ethics restrictions. Your organization can consider hiring a part- or full full-time publicity director to coordinate all media and public relations activities: if so, look for an individual who is charismatic, with many contacts in the community, with a background in media or journalism. (It's a lot easier to learn the particulars of a specific program than it is to learn public relations.)

Suggested reading:

Public Relations Guidelines. In, *Operational Guide.* Denver, Colo.: American Humane Association, 1978.

19

Staffing Pet Facilitated Therapy Programs

Juana Lyon

"Volunteers are the heart of most PFT programs . . ."

Volunteers are the heart of most Pet Facilitated Therapy (PFT) programs. Even if the program has funds to employ salaried staff, most of the direct contact work with therapy recipients will probably be carried out by volunteers. In discussing personnel, the focus will be on volunteers. If paid personnel carry out the same functions, the components of a successful volunteer program, will in large measure apply to them as well.

The Companion Animal Association of Arizona, which I represent, is totally dependent on volunteer efforts. We carry the concept of PFT beyond the pet visitation to nursing homes and other care-giving facilities, which is one of our projects, to the interpretation that enabling elderly and handicapped persons to keep pets is a therapy-related service. Consequently, volunteer activities include pet-related supportive services such as obedience and behavioral training; in-home and foster care; transportation to veterinary and grooming services; provision of veterinary and grooming services; provision of emergency food and supplies; and counseling in the areas of pet loss, euthanasia and alternatives, and pet adoption.

No matter what activities are carried out by the volunteer staff, there are certain action steps and program components which must be included to ensure a successful program:

Juana Lyon is founder and past president of the Companion Animal Association of Arizona, a Phoenix-area group with more than 200 volunteers and 80 veterinarians statewide offering foster care, grooming, transportation and other therapeutic programs to needy pet owners. CAAA achieved major breakthroughs in obtaining legislation allowing elderly and handicapped residents of public housing to keep their pets. She has a Ph.D. in linguistic anthropology and served as program development manager for the Aging and Adult Administration of the Arizona Department of Economic Security.

- Recruitment
- Assessment (screening)
- Training and orientation
- Assignment
- Supervision (guidance, monitoring, evaluation)
- Record keeping
- Counseling (motivating, reassuring, sustaining)
- Recognition and appreciation.

RECRUITMENT — Volunteers are recruited through distribution of our brochure to veterinary offices, public libraries, pet lover and breeder organizations, and organizations servicing the target population (elderly and handicapped persons). Presentations are also utilized to community groups, college classes, and on radio and television. Personal recruitment by the volunteers has also been very effective.

ASSESSMENT (SCREENING) — The purpose of careful assessment of prospective volunteers is obviously to ensure that the assigned activity is carried out appropriately and effectively, that it benefits the recipients and, at the same time, that the organization is represented in an appropriate manner.

Factors taken into consideration during the screening of prospective volunteers include pertinent education and professional experience, paid or volunteer activities in a related field, personal interests, and reasons for volunteering.

The final test is observation of the volunteer, for example, while accompanying an experienced volunteer on a nursing home visit.

Our volunteer visitors take their own animals with them on visitations, and these pets must have passed an assessment of their own. They must have been certified as healthy and temperamentally suited by a veterinarian and, if necessary, by animal behavior specialists who are also volunteers.

It can happen that a prospective volunteer passes muster but his or her animal does not. Tactful prevention of hurt feelings can lead to that volunteer's assisting another volunteer who may have more than one animal to take visiting.

TRAINING AND ORIENTATION — Once volunteers have been selected, their training needs are also assessed, based on the activities they have volunteered for. A volunteer who will function in his or her area of professional expertise, such as a veterinarian, counselor, dog groomer or trainer, will require only a brief orientation as to what is expected. On the other hand, pet visitation volunteers will have to be thoroughly and carefully trained unless their professional experience includes prior exposure to care-giving facilities serving elderly, handicapped, or mentally impaired persons.

It is a good idea to have **written guidelines** for pet visitation volunteers which include the following points:

1. Pets must have been bathed and/or groomed (depending on the type of pet), and their nails must have been trimmed and filed smooth. (The skin of elderly persons is particularly sensitive.)
2. The volunteer should be appropriately dressed.
3. The volunteer should be prepared by bringing lap pads or towels, paper towels (for puppy "accidents"), treats to be given pets by the residents, pets' drinking water and container, and means to keep pets under control at all times.
4. The volunteer must control his or her personal reaction to sights and smells which are normally encountered in care-giving facilities. He or she must be prepared to face residents who are disoriented, have short attention spans, become emotional and tearful as they reminisce about pets they may have had, or who do not want to give up a pet placed on their lap or bed. Conversely, there will be residents who do not wish to be exposed to visiting pets; the volunteer should courteously respect their wishes. Residents in wheelchairs, or those who are blind or deaf, require special considerations.
5. Once a visitation schedule is established, the volunteer must not deviate from it without adequate notice to program coordinators and facility staff.
6. Any problems should be reported immediately to the facility's activity director or designated staff liaison person and to the volunteer program coordinator.
7. Establishment of cordial working relations with facility staff is crucial!

SUPERVISION — Effective supervision of volunteers includes continuous guidance, monitoring, and performance evaluation. In the case of volunteer staff, this calls for even more tact, diplomacy, and sensitivity than would be required with salaried personnel. The success of the program, after all, is dependent on the enthusiasm with which volunteers carry out their assignments and can offer no reward other than respect and appreciation!

Volunteers must have a clear understanding of what is expected of them. This is provided through such means as written guidelines or job descriptions, on-the-job orientation, and discussions with the assigned supervisor or coordinator. It has also been found useful to hold periodic meetings of pet visitation volunteers to relate experiences, pinpoint problems, exchange opinions and recommendations, and ensure uniform approaches and procedures.

Performance monitoring and evaluation must be handled with great sensitivity and tact. Feedback from facility staff is very useful and can be accomplished through telephone follow-up by the coordinator or by means of questionnaires. During the early stages of our pet visitation program, a written evaluation was obtained of each visit by having the activity director or designated staff person fill out a questionnaire designed to pinpoint both positive and negative aspects of the visit and the volunteer(s) conducting it. Now that the program and the capabilities of the volunteers have become established, the facility is furnished with a questionnaire to be completed and sent only in the event of problems or concerns. This does not, of course, prevent telephone contact between the coordinator and facility staff as necessary.

Problems or concerns reported to have been caused by the volunteer are tactfully discussed, and remedial action is suggested where indicated. Problems attributable to facility staff action (or inaction!) are discussed with the appropriate facility representative. If necessary, volunteers are reassigned or relieved of their assisgnment. Visits to a particular facility may be cancelled if findings indicate this to be appropriate.

Effective supervision also includes counseling the volunteer as needed, reassuring and motivating him or her, and sustaining interest in and enthusiasm for the volunteer activity. Sharing of complimentary letters and comments received from participating facilities or individual residents, photographs taken during pet visits, or newspaper articles reporting on a particular visit are always appreciated and help to sustain motivation. (Some facilities include the program's volunteers in their own appreciation activities.) The volunteers are also especially gratified by residents' interest in the pets they have brought to visit; they find it rewarding when their pet is admired and appreciated.

RECORD KEEPING is important for a number of reasons, including accountability to membership, recognition of outstanding volunteers, and to establish a "track record" for potential donors. The extent and nature of records to be kept should be based on the structure, scope, and purposes of the organization or program. As a minimum, have volunteers keep track of the time they donate to the projects.

Also, a monthly record of the number of pet visitations made, including the number of volunteers and animals involved. Another type of record to keep is the "Assistance Record" which reflects specific support services provided to individual elderly or handicapped pet owners; one sheet is completed per case.

RECOGNITION AND APPRECIATION — Motivation and enthusiasm are greatly enhanced through recognition and appreciation of volunteer efforts. A variety of means can be used for this purpose. The organization's financial status usually dictates the selection of the means employed.

If the organization has a newsletter, outstanding volunteers can be featured. Special events, such as luncheons and dinners at which volunteers are honored, involve the organization membership and guests in paying tribute. Certificates, plaques, desk sets, and other items with appreciative inscriptions can also be awarded on such occasions. One type of recognition being planned is to institute the awarding of heart-shaped "Companion Animal" tags to the animal volunteers. To their proud owners, this will probably mean more than personal recognition.

In any case, determination of the type of recognition to be given will be based on each organization's specific volunteer activities, assessment of what those volunteers would most enjoy and, of course, budget. The important thing is to express appreciation in some manner.

One subject which must be touched on here briefly is BURNOUT. Burnout is the combination of physical and mental exhaustion which can result from any activity which entails strong emotional involvement and exposure to stressful experiences. Burnout may result in reduced physical energy, waning interest and enthusiasm, and a general feeling of being overwhelmed by the demands of one's job or assignment. There are no pat answers to this problem; sometimes a change in assignment, or a vacation, can bring about renewed energy and enthusiasm.

Volunteers are the backbone of most PFT programs. Make sure that they know exactly what is expected of them and that their contribution is acknowledged and appreciated.

20

Motivating Others: Expanding the Possibilites

Carol Browning

"...helping create a world where the ultimate dignity of life is respected."

Developing successful charitable service organizations

Whether organizations pay people for their services or not, a few general principles apply to the recruitment of volunteers and paid staff. These concepts also apply to selecting board members who serve in either a volunteer or a paid capacity.

Often, organizations do not actively recruit volunteers or employees. Rather, they passively wait for interested citizens to contact them and for job hunters to apply. An active recruitment policy can be effective in bringing together a variety of people with diverse talents that can be directed toward a common cause. In recruiting volunteers and employees two areas should be clearly considered:

1. the organization - its purposes, goals and needs.
2. the individual - his or her integrity, needs, interests, skills and available time to participate.

The balance between organizational productivity and individual needs is critical. The organization will be more productive and effective if:

1. its purposes, goals and needs are clearly defined.

Carol Browning of Ogden, Utah, holds a Ph.D. in comparative education from Columbia University. A noted lecturer and educator, she serves on numerous local and national advisory committees. She is a consultant to the Ford Foundation and the U.S. Agency for International Development. She helped compile the Humane Education Projects Handbook for the Junior League of Ogden, serves on the Board of Directors for the Ogden-Weber County Humane Society, and has won numerous awards for humanitarian service and improving international relations.

2. the group needs and individual members' needs are interrelated.
3. if the individual members, whether volunteers or employees, understand and accept their roles.
4. if the individual members have mutual respect and trust for one another (i.e. between board and staff; between professional and volunteer organizations; between different interest groups).

The individual will be more productive and effective if:

1. his or her own needs and interests are satisfied by participation.
2. his or her skills are used so that the contribution as a unique individual is valued.
3. he or she feels comfortable working with the organization.
4. he or she is accepted by the board, staff and other members of the organization.

An employee or a volunteer is a precious resource. Once trained he or she should add a range of competence to the organization and bring "outside" diversity to help resolve common problems. He or she should be a source of advice and counsel, feeling free to ask critical questions and to offer suggestions, formulate strategies and participate in the organization. In a sense this person is a consultant to the organization which has actively asked him or her to serve either in a paid or voluntary capacity because of his or her skills, integrity, interests, enthusiasm and available time. In another sense, the volunteer or employee is a sounding board for ideas generated by the organization. Thus, the volunteer or employee recruited should be a strong self-confident individual.

Creating a meaningful experience

Shelves of books have been written about business management techniques, on training effective employees, on developing successful volunteers and boards for not-for-profit organizations, on group effectiveness and advocacy training. The attempt in this chapter is to discuss, in a general way, the importance of individual training and participation in order to enhance the effectiveness of the organization and the satisfaction of its members, for better Human/Companion Animal Bond programs.

Orientation sessions about the organization are a key to an effective volunteer or employee experience. Most people welcome orientation for it gives them a more complete understanding of the organization and makes them feel more secure in participating. An orientation session for new members might serve the following purposes:

1. give members an overview of goals, objectives, priorities and operating procedures.

2. help members become acquainted with one another and discover what unique qualities each has to offer.
3. provide an opportunity for members to meet the staff and board and learn to know them as individuals as well as specialists.
4. delineate more clearly the kinds of issues members are likely to confront and the areas they will not be expected to handle.
5. give new members a chance to develop a group feeling, to identify a method of operation before plunging into actual problem-solving.
6. make it clear what is expected of a member and emphasize the importance of his commitment.

Such orientation sessions should occur early in the appointment of the employee or volunteer.

Advocacy training is also helpful to new members. Advocacy is the art of persuading others to one's own (or an organization's) point of view. The skills learned are: identifying issues, gathering data, writing reports, building coalitions and partnerships, monitoring, public relations, intervening, negotiating and lobbying. It involves the following general steps:

1. Know your "product" or the point of view you are "selling" or representing. If you are offering a service, such as pet-facilitated therapy, or lobbying for legislation understand why that service or legislation, is unique and special.
2. Understand what you want from the people you are trying to convince. Be specific and work as a team with the other volunteers or employees.
3. Study the people you are trying to convince. .Know what their self-interests are. Analyze what they do and do not want. Use their language.
4. Plan your strategy ; that is, to whom should you speak, who should attend, where and when. Here are some strategy tips:
   a. Be clear about your purpose and straight-forward about your intentions. Prioritize your proposal so you can match your request with the needs of the others, if it does not distort your own purpose. State how long you expect the conversation to last.
   b. Ask questions about their goals, purposes, priorities. Listen to them. Notice if you have any common needs.
   c. Try to explain your purpose in terms of their needs. When a project or a philosophy can be approached as mutually beneficial, the advocacy skills are successful.
   d. You may not convince everyone, so focus on those who are undecided. Target your resources. If possible, have some converts

from the "inside" work with you in the advocating process.

e. Moral arguments or value judgments are not persuasive. Debating the "shoulds" of a commitment, a service, a point of view is not convincing, no matter how appropriate the value is that you are "selling." If you can match the "product" to the needs of the "buyer" the "sale" will happen without the moral pitch.

5. Close the "deal". Sum up the conversation as positively and fairly as possible, clarifying what the next step will be. If there were no "deals" made keep the door open for further contacts.
6. Deliver whatever was agreed upon as promptly as possible. Acknowledge the co-operation with appreciation. Be realistic in defining the goals, making commitments and setting a time frame. Know what you and your organization, committee or team can and cannot do before making your commitment.

In summary, successful projects are conducive to volunteer and employee satisfaction as well as organizational effectiveness. Orientation sessions and advocacy training are two basic services that encourage successful projects.

Leadership and participation are two important areas to touch upon here. Leadership can be described simply as the ability to motivate others. Since active participation of volunteers and employees is desired, a delicate balance must be found between the powers of the leader and those of the members. Effective groups work with an ultimate authority that does not dominate. If leadership responsibilities are shared members tend to become more concerned about contributing ideas, elaborating on and clarifying ideas of others, offering opinions, testing the feasibility of potential decisions, and participating in the decisions and thus the responsibilities of the group. If volunteers or employees are recruited as a resource they will be more effective as active participants who share in setting policy and making decisions.

Board, committee and staff relationships

The responsibilities of the board and those of the staff are distinguished in the following general manner:

Board	Staff
1. Ultimate accountability to owners (community, county); can grant certain authority to officers and others according to constitution, by-laws and applicable laws	1. Accountable to the board; may initiate action within the boundaries of authority granted by the board

2. Primarily concerned with "idea" decisions
3. Primarily concerned with organizational character
4. Responsible for decisions on over-all purpose, policies and goals
5. Responsible for decisions involving long-range commitment of resources including facilities, finances and manpower
6. Responsible for decisions related to the perpetuation of the institution/organization including assurance of succession of capable executive directors as well as orientation and training of other board members and selection of board chairs
7. Control over the executive director, long-range and substantial financial commitments and financial structure, public relations and performance related to over-all purpose, policies and goals

2. Primarily concerned with "action" decisions
3. Primarily concerned with organizational behavior
4. Responsible for decisions related to how purposes, policies and goals are to be attained
5. Responsible for decisions involving intermediate and short-range commitment of resources and the organization and control of these resources
6. Responsible for decisions related to the maintenance of professional competence of staff so as to provide the highest quality services within the guidelines set by the board
7. Control over operations, subordinate managers and employees, budgets and implementation of action programs within each key programs (result) area

The relationship between the board and the staff might be visualized as an hourglass. Each controls a vital part of the organizational operation. The frequent contact is normally between the board chair and the executive director. The board does not meddle in the daily affairs of the staff nor does the staff try to lobby the board. Negotiations funnel through the chair (who is selected by the board and responsible to the board) and the executive director (who is also selected by the board and responsible to it). The staff, however, is generally responsible to the executive director who has hiring and firing powers.

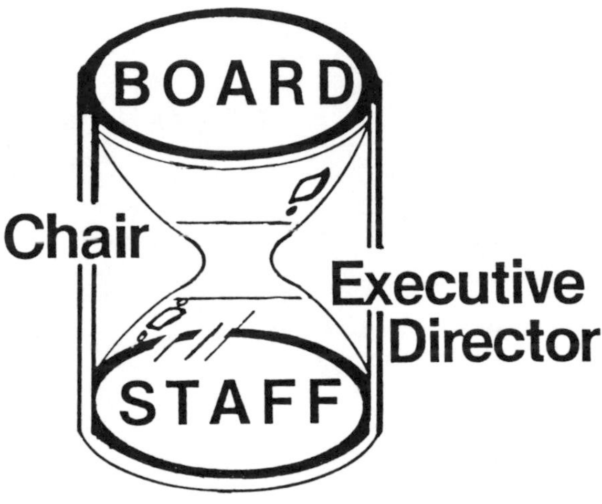

The skills of the board are generally more conceptual and those of the staff more technical.

Not-for-profit corporations vary greatly in their structures. Some have large paid staffs, some have only a paid executive director; some have non-working boards, some have boards with working ad hoc as well as standing committees. (Standing committees are those that the organization feels are necessary for the continuing effective operation of the institution. Ad hoc committees or task forces are those created to deal with particular problems or opportunities over a specific limited period of time.) The following are generally standing committees; executive, nomination, programs, finance and development. In some cases active committees exist even though the institution has a fully paid staff. In either case the committees are appointed by the board. They report through the committee chairs to the full board or the executive committee.

In summary, successful organizations have relationships between volunteers, board and staff clearly delineated. All individuals work effectively together in a spirit of cooperation rather than competition. By considering some of the above general guidelines and suggestions, more effective Human/companion animal bond projects can be developed by your organization.

Coalition building and networking

Humane Education programs, including H/CAB Work, whether expanded existing projects or new ones based on recent research, are more powerful if they are sponsored by several institutions. Working together from different perspectives or constituencies adds to the collective resources in terms of broader expertise and information; additional money; in-kind support and manpower; and increased credibility and entree into new sectors of the community. In these days of sharp federal cutbacks, pooled resources for common causes is the only way many projects survive.

Forming partnerships, building coalitions, networking, co-sponsoring and creating collaborations are some of the buzz words used by volunteer as well as professional organizations these days. The spirit behind all of these concepts is the same.

A *partnership* is a state of sharing in the action, the possession or the enjoyment of something. Partnership is a melding of what often are very dissimilar parts. To achieve a partnership you must first agree on who is going to do what, which requires compromise—giving up something to gain something. It implies sharing control and authority and increased accountability.

A *coalition* is an alliance of individuals, organizations, or institutions united for a common purpose. Coalitions are often mini-movements focused around an immediate issue. They are generally loosely organized and short term. The issue will dictate whether the coalition should be composed of all like groups, or unlike groups, or solely community leadership groups, i.e. elected officials, or a combination of any or all of the above. The coalition may be continuous, or it may be disbanded upon achieving its objectives, or it may form a new organization to continue further objectives. The difference between a task force and a coalition is that the task force studies an acknowledged problem and makes a recommendation about that problem. A coalition corrects an acknowledged problem.

A *network* is a set of points connected by lines; that is individuals or organized groups connected by continuing relationships or specific exchanges. Where lines from one individual or group intersect with lines from another, a linkage exists and an exchange or relationship is possible. Networking is an informal, non-policy-setting communication of ideas and concerns. There are no networking rules or forms. They can be made up of a handful of people or several organizations. What they seem to have in common is that they depend on informal personal contacts and the need to do something that is not or has not been handled very well by formal procedures or organized structures. Networking recognizes the power of shared resources and the value of mutual support, but does not work well where there are problems or situations that need a routine and sustained response, that require explicit or accountable actions, or that involve the management of budgets and other resources. Such tasks need standardization and specialization of roles and responsibilities, which are the bases of organizations.

A *co-sponsorship* is a state of working together with another sponsor or group of sponsors. It is a state of accepting responsibility for something together. Generally a specific event has already been decided upon and the co-sponsors lend their names, resources, support and promise to see that event to completion

A *collaboration* is a more formal commitment to work or labor together. It implies shared decision making, shared goal and objective setting, joint writing of the by-laws and shared responsibilites and liabilities.

Although an organization may give up independence, authority and ownership of its own projects, although it may be invading someone else's turf and in turn be invaded by others, although it may take a lot of negotiating time and communication effort—despite these potential negatives , partnerships, coalitions, networks, co-sponsorships and collaborations are essential to successful, powerful projects. To work in lofty isolation or with fanatic resolve is not an effective mode of operation in a participatory democracy. It is not possible to function in a vacuum if you want to change public attitudes and behavior. For example, if you are working with a Humane Education curriculum-integrated project you have a more solid foundation by including the local school board, the PTA, administrators; teachers and curriculum specialists than working alone as a local humane society or as an individual concerned citizen. If you are developing a Pet-Facilitated Therapy project the inclusion of an articulate local pastor, veterninarian and physician strenghthen your project.

An organization may ask itself, what will we lose if we cooperate with another group? What will we gain? What can we give? Make a list of the "trade-offs." Analyze the pros and cons. Clearly, not all partnerships or co-sponsorships are ideal. Seek out those organizations that hold a broad and objective view of community needs; that address issues analytically and impartially; that seek solutions which are balanced and fair to all. In so doing, you and your organization will break down traditional barriers (i.e., the lack of communication between humane societies and veterinarians or the local Junior League, and become exposed to a wealth of new ideas, new resources, new constituencies and new transferable skills.

There are certain basic principles inherent in forming partnerships, coalitions, networks, co-sponsorships and collaborations. All must be organized around a central, clearly defined target. The target will determine the constituency. Some considerations might be:

1. Determine whether the partnership is to be ongoing or temporary.
2. Separate out individual identity to form a coalition.
3. Be sure that all parties agree on the goals of the partnership. (It's all right to abstain if members of the group take stands on other issues with which you don't agree.)
4. Be sure all groups in the coalition have joined as equals.
5. Avoid taking an extreme position, one which the other members could not accept.
6. Language becomes important. Avoid the splits of "them" and "us."
7. Leadership should be shared or rotated. There is a greater sense of partnership when each group participates equally.

The major purpose of working together is to share the problem in order to create a more effective solution. By following the above steps, diverse interest groups—teenagers and retired people, volunteers and paid employees—can work successfuly to create a more humane world for all living things.

How to create a project

The first step in creating a project is to analyze the needs in your community and the interest and resources available to meet those needs. Appoint a task force or an ad hoc committee to do this research and analysis.

A task force is a group of persons, with various specialities and representing different interest groups, charged with investigating a particular problem and formulating proposals for its solution. It is frequently a part of a larger group dealing with a complex of related problems.

For example, if you are a humane society and you want to launch a Humane Education program in your local elementary schools, you might invite a teacher, a curriculum specialist, a principal, a PTA president, a school board member, a city council member, a pastor, a journalist and a businessman to belong to an elementary school curriculum task force, in addition to a few members of your humane organization. This task force will analyze the existing curriculum for humane ethics materials and resources; research available materials; discuss the pros and cons of integrating films, books and units into the existing curriculum in terms of educational issues, ethical considerations, the general public's responses, interest groups' concerns, etc.; develop a budget and identify funding sources for the project. The task force will develop a Management By Objective outline (see explanation below). In general, task forces are temporary appointments automatically terminated when the specific task or definite objective has been completed. The task force does not implement the project.

If you want to create a Pet-Facilitated Therapy project you would appoint a PFT task force. If you are interested in creating a project that focuses on legislation you would appoint a legislation task force. In this section the elementary school curriculum model is an example that can be applied to any project area.

Management By Objective process

The MBO process is a management tool. It is a system of organizing five basic resources (manpower, material, money, time and authority) in order to accomplish an objective, to check the progress and to assess the outcome. There are five basic steps to this process.

Step I -

Define the goals and objective of the Humane Education project. These are two different definitions:

Goal	a statement of intent or direction which is general, broad and unmeasureable.
Objective	a specific statement of achievement, or what is to be accomplished which defines and communicates; what will be different, by when, and how these results will be measured.

Step II -

Plan the primary and secondary strategies to accomplish the objective by analyzing the five basic resources.

Concept	a statement of how a plan will be achieved; a strategy which will cause the objective to happen.

Five Basic Resources:

Manpower	the number of people it will take to achieve the objective.
Materials	the goods necessary to achieve the objective.
Money	the dollars it will take to achieve the objective.
Time	the days, months, or years necessary to achieve the objective.
Authority	who has the ultimate power and responsibility for achieving the objective.
Alternate Plan	a secondary strategy which may be used to achieve the objective should circumstances disallow execution of the primary plan, again allocating the five basic resources. It is a back-up plan.

Step III -

Build into the original plan regular checks as assessments of the progress. Controls such as standards of performance, feedback from others and personal observation keep the project focused on the objective and warn of impending failure.

Standard of Performance	criterion set in order to detect variation and deviance.
Feedback	written or oral reports from each person assigned a responsibility regarding the progress in carrying out that responsibility. Cross-checks or reports from outside observers are also helpful.
Personal Observation	analysis of the authority or manager with the final responsibility for the project.

Step IV -

Execute the plan. Implement the strategies.

Step V

Appraise and evaluate the results. Was the objective achieved? This is the systematic analysis of the project results compared with the project objective, which is measurable. Analyze the following:

Results	measurable accomplishments.
Resources	results achieved compared with resources expended.
Management	results achieved compared with management efforts.

The last step of the MBO process, appraisal and evaluation, can lead to the redefinition of objectives and the reimplementation of the five MBO steps. Unless the project is terminated after step V, the MBO process is cyclical, theoretically producing more perfect results.

Although the MBO process may seem like a lot of theoretical planning and not much implementation or "actual doing," it is a management tool which creates efficiency, effectiveness and increasingly better projects. Volunteers as well as employees find it satisfying for they know what is expected of them, how long it will take, where they are during the process and what to do if a plan doesn't work. Evaluations are often enlightening and satisfying, creating a sense of self-worth in the volunteers or employees and a sense of well-being in the organization. Many major U.S. corporations use this management technique as do national volunteer organizations, such as the Association of Junior Leagues, Inc. and its 251 member Leagues.

Junior Leagues are always looking for community projects that meet the needs of the local community and fulfill the interests of League members. The Association of Junior Leagues encourages its 251 member Leagues to build coalitions and form partnerships with other local organizations. Thus, mutual needs can be satisfied with proper advocacy.

Many Leagues have adopted on-going projects related to pet-facilitated therapy as part of the *Humane Projects Handbook.* This handbook was compiled by the Junior League of Ogden in cooperation with the Junior Leagues of Boston and Champaign-Urbana and is a reference guide of successful projects developed by over 20 Leagues across the country. It is a "how-to" guide written in the Management By Objective format, focusing on 10 project areas:

1. Humane education in the schools
2. Legislation
3. Pet-facilitated therapy
4. Child abuse projects
5. Legislation
6. Aquarium projects
7. Nature center projects
8. Humane society projects
9. Public information
10. Additional projects

The purpose of the handbook is to serve as a detailed guide for organizations wanting to develop a project, at costs ranging from no-cost to $500,000. It is an effective model for planning, implementing and evaluating the projects. It is intended to stimulate creative thinking and project development and building coalitions with other organizations.

Each Junior League in the U.S. received a copy of the *Handbook* in 1982 as a permanent resource guide for their office. Other copies are available at the offices of NAAHE, the Humane Society of the United States, the American Humane Association, the Latham Foundation and the American Humane Education Society. Most large cities have a Junior League. In order to build a project together, contact your nearest Junior League and ask for the President. She can direct you to the appropriate committee chairman, probably the Community Research Committee, to study your proposed partnership or coalition and make a recommendation to the Executive Committee. If approved, the proposal will be voted upon by the full membership. Much research, voting and planning goes into League projects so be patient with the process. Once a League decides to co-sponsor a program the volunteer resources, energy, skills and commitment are outstanding.

The following is an example of a Junior League Pet-Facilitated Therapy project laid out in MBO format, taken from the Handbook:

HUMANE EDUCATION PROJECTS HANDBOOK	PROJECT: PET FACILITATED THERAPY
NAME OF JUNIOR LEAGUE	The Junior League of Boston, Inc.
ADDRESS OF JUNIOR LEAGUE	117 Newbury Street Boston, Massachusetts 02193
NAME AND ADDRESS OF CO-ORDINATOR OF HANDBOOK OF HUMANE EDUCATION PROJECT	Mrs. Henry Phillips Williams, III (Marilyn) 476 Concord Road Weston, Massachusetts 02193
HUMANE EDUCATION PROJECT TITLE	Pet Facilitated Therapy and Companionship Project for the Elderly, the Mentally Retarded and the Emotionally Disturbed
BRIEF DESCRIPTION OF PROJECT	A. Organizational structure of the project. This project was initiated under the auspices of the Junior League of Boston and established in conjunction with the Massachusetts Society for the Prevention of Cruelty to Animals (MSPCA),

the American Humane Education Society (AHES) and Angell Memorial Animal Hospital in May, 1976, AHES is the sister education affiliate to the MSPCA. The MSPCA owns and operates Angell Memorial Hospital. The same project is being undertaken in Springfield, Mass., by an MSPCA branch there and Rowley Memorial Hospital, also owned by the MSPCA. The project in Springfield is being supervised by the Junior League of Boston and it will soon be taken over by the Junior League of Springfield.

B. Definition of Pet Facilitated Therapy.

Pet Therapy is one form of rehabilitating individuals who are physically, mentally, or emotionally disabled through the introduction of animals into their environment. It is successful because of the natural affinity between man and animal. In the words of Dr. Boris Levinson, "A pet can provide a boundless measure of love, adoration, and unqualified approval. Many elderly and lonely individuals have discovered that pets satisfy their needs and enable them to hold on to the world of reality, of care... and of intense emotional relationship. Their self concept as worthwhile individuals is restored and even enhanced when thy find that the pet they have been caring for loves them in return." *The pet itself is the therapist.*

Pet Therapy is the natural giving of unconditional love and unqualified approval from a pet, a person receiving that love effortlessly and unconsciously and that person returning this love spontaneously. The spiritual and emotional therapy is the love and acceptance of the pet to the person and the person receiving and giving back this love. The physical therapy for the person results from the care this person gives the pet, which is the result of the outflow of his love for the pet and inseparable from it. Hence, the pet spontaneously elicits from people their love, concern and practical care in terms of feeding, walking and grooming.

Pet Therapy is predicated upon the establishment of an enduring, natural rapport between humans and animals, independent of other therapists, family, or friends. Pet Therapy is not only legitimate, it is crucial to the mental and physical health of isolated individuals because no therapist or human being of any relation can give to the lonely a total sense of dependency for his very existence. The very nature of a pet in its absolute need for humans makes it a therapist in its very essence because it gives humans a vital sense of usefulness and responsibility. Pet Therapy is a way of fulfilling a moral commitment to our fellow man by using God's creatures, who can love purely and unconditionally even when we cannot, either because we cannot physically be present with a fellow human being, or we just cannot always maintain a balance of projected love for one another.

C. Application of Pet Therapy.
The Junior League, in cooperation with the MSPCA, places animals from the MSPCA shelter (after they have been screened for their temperament by the shelter staff and their health qualifications by Angell Memorial) into homes. The animals are donated by the shelter and their first year's basic medical requirements are donated by Angell Memorial Hospital.

The Junior League volunteer acts as an

adoption agent for the placement of the animal, as well as undertaking a series of visits designed to assist in the adjustment of the animal. She seeks to educate the staff of a home concerning the value of animals as natural therapists and she stimulates and fosters a relationship between the residents and their animal. In the process, she forms her own friendships with staffs and residents of an institution.

EXPLANATION OF HOW TO SET UP AND IMPLEMENT PROJECT

Any Junior League should be interested in adopting a Pet Therapy Project because it is very helpful to forgotten groups in society. Even if certain people in a specific League do not have an affinity for isolated groups and/or animals, this project is very valuable to thc League because it is very low-budgeted and it commands a huge amount of positive, unsolicited publicity from newspapers and television stations. Local humane societies should be very anxious to help because they are utilizing homeless animals for therapeutic purposes rather than having to euthanize them. These humane societies will also receive an enormous amount of unsolicited publicity because the elderly and other unfortunate groups are very much in the public eye as is the enormous number of homeless pets all over the country. Pet Therapy is also receiving acclaim all over the country from medical doctors, who note changes in their more difficult patients who did not respond to more conventional therapy. The pet is viewed as a co-therapist, as a healing catalyst for the individual and a bonding catalyst between that individual and the doctor, other people and the outside world.

Concerning the legality of the project for each state, it is important for one

League person to have one good friend, who is extremely knowledgeable concerning state rules and regulations for long-term care facilities (nursing and rest homes). The advisor in Boston is the nursing home ombudsman for the entire state. He is a lawyer and the only legal advisor (only one is necessary to avoid confusion). The most important point in the legal area is that the legal advisor for the Boston League is not only knowledgeable, but sympathetic for the mission of Pet Therapy. Otherwise, a lawyer will give a fast and superficial answer, possibly incorrect, and not in favor of the project. Never call the state office for the elderly or any other group and talk to anyone who answers the phone. As the Massachusetts ombudsman stated, "For every call, you will get a different answer." This ombudsman has been with the Boston project from the days of research and he is still informed of progress. This is very important. Stay with the same good, sympathetic legal person, always take his or her advice to protect you.

See "Plan of Action - General Concepts" for a detailed explanation of how to set up and implement a Pet Therapy Project.

COMMUNITY RESPONSE TO PROJECT

The responses from the rest home administrators have indeed, been touching and gratifying. The media have responded with great interest and many radio and T.V. broadcasts have been done on this project.

M B O FORM

COMMITTEE:

Pet Facilitated Therapy and pet Companionships for the Elderly, the Mentally Retarded and the Emotionally Disturbed, Administrative Year 1982 - 1983.

GOAL:

To enrich the lives of the elderly, mentally retarded and emotionally disturbed by adding to their sense of purpose and fulfillment through the companionship of an animal. The greatest need of the human being is to love and to be loved.

OBJECTIVE:

To present the volunteer with both the opportunity and the responsibility of representing to the rest home industry, four service organizations (MSPCA, AHES, Angell Memorial Hospital and the JLB), whose combined interest is to promote an understanding of the potential impact of Pet Therapy on the lives of elderly people. To this end, a volunteer ultimately seeks to place an animal. She is the adoption agent between the MSPCA and the home adopting the pet. The volunteer also offers pet programs which are provided by the AHES to the homes. The volunteer is offering a service which has no definable limits or time constraints on the duration of the service. Herein lies the uniqueness of this project: it is predicated on potentially indeterminable therapeutic effect upon the life of a human being over an indefinite period of time.

PLAN OF ACTION:

GENERAL CONCEPTS:

1. To explain that Pet Therapy is a legitimate therapy because it fulfills vital needs to the human being. Therefore, even if only one or two residents come to mind who would benefit from having a pet, these residents should have that pet (because the pet fulfills vital needs) as long as the pet is not inflicting physical harm on other residents. This becomes a non-issue due to the controls of screening the pet.

2. The responsibility of the volunteer is to act as a Pet Therapy educator, and as an adoption agent for the pet placement. Included in the placement is a follow-up program consist-

ting of a series of visits designed to assist in the adjustment of the animal. Volunteers will have one training session with instruction in basic geriatrics, veterinary care, and animal training. The training session consists of the following:

(a) A lecture is given either by a rest home administrator who acknowledges the benefits of Pet Therapy due to the feeling of isolation, aloneness, and uselessness of the residents, or by an administrator who has a pet placed in his or her home.

(b) Volunteers, who are founders or veterans of the project, together with members of the American Humane Education Society explain how to introduce the subject of Pet Therapy to rest homes, how to discuss pets with residents of rest homes and how to introduce the pet itself to a rest home.

(c) Veterinarians and nurses discuss animal nutrition, medication and how to deal with emergencies.

(d) The Society for the Prevention of Cruelty to Animals shelter staff teach basic animal obedience.

3. The Pet Therapy Project procedure is as follows:

(a) The volunteer arranges an appointment with a rest home administrator. Never discuss the project in any detail over the phone. Simply make an appointment based on the fact that a *volunteer* (no money required) project is offered.

(b) During the time with the administrator, the volunteer discusses the concept of Pet Therapy and establishes a rapport with the rest home staff and residents.

(c) A Pet Program given by the American Humane Education Society is arranged by the volunteer. Live kittens and puppies are brought in so that administrators and staff can see how residents respond spontaneously to animals without having to ask the residents directly. To ask residents if they want a pet is self-defeating as the normal first reaction is to fear they would not be able to care for the pet because they are no longer caring for themselves. However, once the resident has a pet, care for the pet is natural and immediate.

(d) When the administrator has decided to adopt the Pet Therapy Project, the volunteer notifies the MSPCA. The Angell Memorial Hospital and MSPCA shelter staff screen the pet for health and temperament. This project deals basically with the adoption of dogs and cats because these pets elicit a maximum amount of feedback from the residents. (Goldfish and parakeets, for example, can be purchased by rest homes themselves and can provide "live entertainment" for residents without needing the volunteer follow-up program.) The most docile animal possible will be chosen by the staff of the MSPCA shelter. The dog or cat must be a minimum of a year old and house trained. A dog must be leash trained. After either a dog or cat has been carefully screened over a period of time for temperament, it is then examined by the Angell Memorial Hospital staff for its immediate and long-term health.

(e) Before placing an animal, the volunteer emphasizes to the rest home and its occupants that because the animal is a therapist in a very special sense and is providing a service, it is a privilege, not a right to have it. The volunteer is an adoption agent and should be just as discriminating in deciding whether or not the institution should have an animal as the institution is in deciding whether or not it desires one. The volunteer is offering a service and applying a proven theory. We are inspiring the responsibilities of ownership and the realization that these responsibilities are on-going. With the help of the MSPCA and the AHES, the volunteer will assist the institution in selecting an animal for its specific needs (dog or cat, temperament, size, age). The MSPCA donates the animals with a clean bill of health.

(f) The pet is actually placed by the volunteer. During this time, the volunteer discusses with the residents what to expect from the animal, where it should spend most of its time, where it will eat and sleep. The volunteer is a mediator between the residents and their pet and can assist in bathing the animal, teaching it basic obedience, tricks, or anything that is desired. It is both therapeutic and helpful for resident interaction to provide sign-up sheets for the sharing of the responsibilities of caring for the pet, i.e. walking, feeding, brushing, etc.

(g) The volunteer's responsibilities for the follow-up program include:

1) Visiting the rest home the day after placement.

2) Making a follow-up visit one week later.

3) Calling the rest home at the end

of the second week.
4) Re-visiting the rest home during the third week.
5) Making a monthly call or visit to the rest home for 6 months to a year thereafter.

6) The above are guidelines. For the reassurance of the rest home, the volunteer should make herself available at all times.
(h) The receiving institution will have ultimate legal and financial responsibility for the animal. The shelter ownership papers are sufficient to make this clear. No extra papers are needed.

ALLOCATION OF RESOURCES:

MANPOWER	MATERIALS	MONEY
Only 7-10 women are necessary as a core to start. Volunteers should work in pairs, or 3s, or even 4s. This is an ideal project for sustainers as they have an affinity for the mission of Pet Therapy because many of their parents are in homes.	Office expenses:	
	supplies	$10.00
	duplicating	20.00
	postage	20.00
	Training program:	
	supplies	30.00
	duplicating	100.00
	films	100.00
	honorarium	50.00
	Public relations:	
	special flyers	30.00
	new brochures	350.00
	current pictures	30.00
	Recommended reading:	
	Dr. Boris Levinson *Pets and Human Development*	None, borrow from the library
	Elizabeth Yates, *Skeezer, Dog With a Mission*	

TIME FRAMEWORK	AUTHORITY	ALTERNATE PLAN
Volunteer is expected	The shelter staff must have	Depending on

to give the combined equivalent of 12 half days in time. Uniqueness of project: No time constraints, runs all year and it is especially good for professional women who can make their own schedule to make follow-up visits to homes at night or on weekends.	the ultimate authority on the selection of the animal, not the volunteer. The hospital staff have the authority to turn down a pet for adoption after the pet has been passed by the shelter staff for the pet's temperament if the pet is not physically fit or if health problems are foreseeable in the future (i.e. hip trouble in larger dog in later life.) The chairperson of the project must have authority over the volunteers, who must report to her after every visit to a rest home.	the problem—work with another rest home or animal.

CONTROLS:

1. Training program for volunteers with precise standards of performance.
2. Follow-up program by dedicated volunteers who should always be available to homes in trouble or homes which simply need reassurance.
3. Temperament screening of animal by shelter staff; health screening of animal by hospital. More is known about these pets than any animal purchased by anyone at any pet store or fancy kennel.

APPRAISAL/EVALUATION:

The response from the rest homes. Evaluate energy and resources committed compared to results.

RECOMMENDATIONS:

The rest home industry is one of the most difficult businesses anyone can have. Problems of a critical nature (life and death, bill payment, etc.) arise daily. Administrators need to feel great empathy and respect from volunteers. Never discuss or even briefly describe the project over the phone. (If an administrator hears the word "pet" he or she is apt to think, "I am dealing with sick and dying people.

I do not have time to take care of anyone or anything new. I am in the business of people—not animals.") To give the project the best possible chance and the administrator and his or her home the best possible chance of having the best, fastest and least expensive therapy, simply state on the phone when making an appointment with an administrator that you wish to discuss a volunteer service project designed especially for them. Knowing that you are not selling anything and that your services are not purchasable, an administrator will see you because he or she is always looking for new ideas in an often frustrating industry.

Once administrators realize the controls involved in the project, which could never be fully explained over the phone, they will be open to trying it once they realize that if for any reason it does not work, the pet will be quietly returned to the shelter. But this project is not sold on the basis of a trial. There is no testing. An administrator should not attempt the project on the basis that a pet can be returned. An administrator must go into the project with a positive attitude, knowing the volunteer will do all in her power to make it work. If an administrator knows only one or two residents who would benefit from the adoption of a pet, a job is to be done. As long as the pet is not inflicting harm on other residents (whether they say they do or do not like animals becomes irrevelant), the pet must be there and its adoption is justified because it is providing therapy.

A resident is entitled to what he or she needs, and by definition, therapy is essential and necessary. This is not an entertainment program, which administrators can "take or leave." It is a vital rehabilitation program based on therapy provided by animals, which works when there hardly seems a glimmer of hope in giving back to the lonely and isolated a reason to keep on living to their fullest, simply due to the natural affinity between people and animals.

An overview of Humane Education

Humane Education is a broad umbrella-like term encompassing a variety of activities and relationships based upon the humane ethic—respect for all living things. The Human/Companion Animal Bond falls under this umbrella.

Humane Education is encouraging in the family; fostering in the school curriculum, nature centers, zoos, aquariums; teaching in the churches; improving the quality of life for the elderly; giving comfort to the neglected and abused; advocating through the media; lobbying in the city councils, school board rooms and state legislatures; recommending to community service, youth and correctional organizations the principles of kindness, good will and humanity toward all forms of life, plant, animal and human. Humane Education is based upon the premise that those who learn to extend kindness, sensitivity, respect and justice to lower forms of life will generally be more kind, sensitive, respectful and just with one another—in every way more valuable citizens.

Humane Education is not sentimentality, emotionalism, saving puppies and kittens. It is not anti-hunting, anti-abortion, pro-mercy killing, pro-abortion, pro-sterilization, pro-vegetarianism, nor is it a passing fad. It is a philosophy of life held by many great thinkers whose lives have inspired our civilization—St. Francis of Assisi, Charles Darwin, Henry David Thoreau, Dr. Albert Schweitzer, to mention a few. Simply stated, Humane Education is cultivating the natural tendency in human beings to be kind. It is developing and refining the human spirit to its highest and most civilized potential.

Why is Humane Education important?

Today we are living in precarious times, both domestically and internationally. Our traditional value system is changing. The family is being redefined in an age of relative values and ethics. As Los Angeles Chief of Police Daryl Gates stated, "We've lost a whole generation. Totally lost. No self-discipline. Total indulgence. Drugs. Lack of respect for the law. Lack of respect for values. A whole generation thumbed its nose at everything that was held sacred in this country. America has to take a look at its heart and its soul." Humane Education attempts to touch the heart and soul of all human beings and to bring out the good, the kind, the compassionate side of mankind.

Insensitivity, dispreSpect, abuse, cruelty and violence fester in our communities nationwide. Callousness flourishes. The curse of violent

"We share this planet with other living things....It is their world, too, a world that belongs to us and to future generations. We share this existence, we are interdependent, we must interact."

crime is rampant not just in depressed ghettos, where it always has been a malignant force, but also in suburbs and peaceful countrysides. According to the National Crime Survey, conducted in 1981 by the Census Bureau for the Justice Department, 30% of the nation's households were touched by crime in 1980 and 6% of the households experienced rape, robbery, or assault. Dr. Marvin E. Wolfgang, professor of sociology and law at the University of Pennsylvania, claims, "We're 2 to 10 times more violent than any country in Western Europe. And the comparison with Japan is even more dramatic." One analyst has calculated that a baby born and remaining in a large American city is more likely to die of murder than an American soldier in World War II was to die of combat. Some claim that Americans have become insensitive about violence and immune to kindness and caring for others due, in large part, to media reporting and programming. Whatever the reasons may be, clearly we live in a society in which significant sectors are largely motivated by brutality, cruelty, violence—the antithesis of the humane ethic.

Thus, Humane Education is important, critically important. The "American heart and soul" can be touched by the humane ethic. Humane Education is an effective response to these unfortunate circumstances, as well as a preventative measure. The application of its principles have broad ramifications. For example, a child who grows up being kind and considerate of all living things is less likely to become a child abuser as a parent. The unpleasant and often tragic duties carried out by correctional institutions, by animal shelters, by environmental and law enforcement agencies, by hospitals for the handicapped, by rest homes, etc., are inevitably made more pleasant when people live by the principles of justice, good will and humanity. The quality of daily life is enhanced by the humane ethic in extending kindness, sensitivity and consideration to all life, of understanding and appreciating the natural world we live in and share with other animals, plants and other human beings. It is urgent that we, as citizens in a democratic and participatory society, retrench and assess our values, our attitudes, our behavior. If we are offended by insensitivity, callousness, cruelty and violence it is critical that we participate in helping create a world where the ultimate dignity of life is respected.

In many communities nationwide, Humane Education programs exist. Some are sophisticated curriculum-integrated projects co-sponsored by the State Board of Education, the Governor's office, the PTA and local school boards. Some are well-managed pet-facilitated therapy programs co-sponsored by a local shelter, animal hospital and medical and veterinary medical associations. Others consist of haphazard one-time visits to schools or rest homes, by an untrained volunteer who has good intentions.

Whether Humane Education programs are conducted by professionals or volunteers, whether they are highly funded or barely funded, they can make a difference in our society on local, state and national levels. To alter inhumane values, to affect attitudes, to change destructive behavior is a long-range but feasible goal, which can be reached if many participate. Through coalition building, partnership, networking, Management By Objective organization and effective advocacy, powerful projects can be developed. By working together we can touch the "American heart and soul" and help create a better world for all living things. What could make a more significant contribution to the welfare of our children, our communities, our country, indeed, to the entire human race?

Humane education research

Although Humane Education may be critically important, how do we know that existing programs are accomplishing the results we desire? Is it worthwhile? Do we really know if we can alter inhumane values, affect attitudes or change destructive behavior in children or adults through Humane Education programs?

The answer is simple—no, we do not know this. We are making an assumption that teaching children to be kind is good; that respect for all living things is an important value for all humans to hold; that fostering in children and adults a sense of compassion is worthwhile. We are also assuming that by integrating the humane ethic into the school curriculum and by exposing children to Humane Education we can impact their attitudes and values, even change their behavior. We are acting on faith.

As Edward Vockell and Frank Hodal pointed out in 1977, there are no instruments developed which measure children's attitudes and values, particularly toward animal life. In addition, we do not know if exposure to Humane Education programs makes any difference at all. With a Humane Education integrated curriculum do children relate more humanely to animals? Are they more humane with other people? Is the classroom the most effective place for Humane Education to take place, are children the best target population and if so at what grade level do Humane Education programs have the highest impact?

In the past decade a variety of research has gone on that focuses upon these questions. A number of studies on empathy and altruism have indicated that exposure of humane values positively affects attitudes and behavior. Television programs have been shown to be capable of reinforcing positive behavior toward animals. An annotated bibliograpy of

Humane Education research is available through the National Association for the Advancement of Humane Education, Box 362, East Haddam, CT 06423.

The most comprehensive research to date is the Humane Education Evaluation Project conducted by the Wasatch Institute for Research and Evaluation. This three-year project is co-sponsored by NAAHE, a division of The Humane Society of the United States; the Utah State Office of Education; the Junior League of Ogden; and the Dodge Foundation.

Specifically, the purpose of the study is to determine whether *People and Animals: A Humane Education Curriculum Guide* brings about the following changes in K-6 grade children:

1. Increases their knowledge and understanding of animals and their humane treatment.
2. Develops more favorable attitudes towards animals and their humane treatment.
3. Leads children to behave more humanely in situations involving animals.
4. Leads children to behave more humanely in situations involving other children.
5. Results in a lower level of aggression and punitive behavior among children.
6. Improves pupil scores on standardized achievement tests in the areas around which the *Humane Education Curriculum Guides* are built: language arts, social studies, math, health/science.

The relationship between teacher and parent attitudes and pupil attitudes is also being measured.

The data should answer many questions, in addition to a range of other critical issues for humane educators. For example, do children learn English skills better through the humane ethic? Do they score lower in math because the subject matter of the problems they are solving is Humane Education? Does the concept or ethic interwoven throughout the curriculum have any impact at all on children's academic skills?

Clearly this research will have a major impact on Humane Education programs and projects and will help us spend our limited resources in the most effective way. In the meantime, we continue to believe in our assumption that those who learn to extend kindness, sensitivity, respect and justice to lower forms of life will generally be more kind, sensitive, respectful and just with one another—and that this is good for all living things: plants, animals and people.

The future of humane education and the human/animal bond

The Human/Companion Animal Bond has existed since man and animals have shared this planet we call Earth. It is a part of the broader concept defined in this chapter as Humane Education, which is part of the religious notion that all living things deserve respect because they are alive. In this day of potential nuclear holocaust such a notion seems most relevant.

Humane Education may be clumsy and redundant terminology. It would seem that those who are educated are by definition humane and those who are humane are by definition educated. Yet, as we read the headlines of our daily newspapers we have to ask ourselves, are we really an educated civilized society? Except for man, there is no other animal on the face of this earth that has the power to act as its own destroyer. And there is no other animal that systematically acts to destroy other animals except toward the end of sustaining its own life. Yet man, throughout history, has acted to destroy both himself and other life forms, often for reasons that have no bearing on his own necessity for survival. As the late Joseph Wood Krutch once said, "To be truly human has always meant to be compassionate."

We share this planet with other living things: with plant life, with other animals, with peoples who speak a different tongue and worship a different God. It is their world, too, a world that belongs to us and to future generations. We share this existence, we are interdependent, we must interact. And since man is the only creature endowed with the capacity for moral judgment, he must become educated and therefore humane.

We believe that man is basically good, that children are naturally compassionate. Even without the proof of quantitative research we believe that diverse groups working together with a positive attitude can help create a world that respects the dignity and worth of all life. The commitment to respond to community needs; to anticipate what the future will bring for our children, for our environment, for mankind; to respect and improve the quality of life for all living things is, indeed, a noble one. It is the essence of humaneness. As John Hoyt, President of the Humane Society of the United States, has said, "It is not, finally, survival that we seek, but a quality of life that gives meaning and purpose to our existence. Yet not for the sake of our life alone, but for the sake of all that lives."

Suggested reading:

Browning, Carol (ed.) *Humane Education Projects Handbook.* Junior League of

Ogden, 1982.

Whitlock, Eileen *Humane Education: An Overview.* Tulsa: National Association for the Advancement of Humane Education, 1975.

Savesky, Kathleen and Malcarne, Vanessa (Eds.) *People and Animals: Humane Education Curriculum Guide.* East Haddam, Conn.: National Association for the Advancement of Humane Education, 1981.

Crawford, Robert *In Art We Trust.* New York: FEDAPT, 1981.

Section VI - Reference Points

Appendix I: Resources

Resource Reading List

Human-Animal Bond: Overviews, Anthologies and Bibliographies

Allen, R. and Westbrook, W. (eds.) *The handbook of animal welfare: Biomedical, psychological and ecological aspects of pet problems and control.* New York: Garland STPM Press, 1979.

Anderson, R.S. (ed.) *Pet Animals and Society.* Baltimore: Williams and Wilkins, 1975.

"Animals Assiting in Therapy." Reprint. *Our animals.* San Francisco: San Francisco SPCA, 1983.

Arkow, Phil *"Pet Therapy": A study of the use of companion animals in selected therapies.* Colorado Springs, Colo.: Humane Society of the Pikes Peak Region, 1986.

Beal, Louisa and Hines, Linda *Annotated Bibliography of the People-Pet Partnership Resource Library.* Alameda, Calif.: The Latham Foundation.

Beck, Alan and Katcher, Aaron *Between Pets and People.* New York: Putnam's, 1983.

Carson, Gerald *Men, beasts and gods: a history of cruelty and kindness to animals.* New York: Charles Scribner's sons, 1972.

Clark, Kenneth *Animals and Men.* New York: William Morrow and Co., 1977.

Clark, Kenneth *Civilisation.*New York: William Morrow and Co., 1977.

Corson, Samuel and Corson, Elizabeth (eds.) *Ethology and Nonverbal Communication in Mental Health.* Elmsford, N.Y.: Pergamon Press, 1982.

Curtis, Patricia *Animal Partners: Training Animals to Help People.* New York: Lodestar/Dutton, 1982.

Fitzgerald, Thomas *Pet Facilitated Therapy: A Selected Annotated Bibliography.* Denver: American Humane Association, 1981.

Fogle, Bruce (ed.) *Interrelations Between People and Pets.* Springfield, Ill.: Charles C. Thomas, 1979.

Jones, Barbara *The Psychology of the Human/Companion Animal Bond: An Annotated Bibliography.* Philadelphia: University of Pennsylvania, 1981.

Kellert, Stephen and Felthous, Alan Childhood Cruelty Toward Animals Among Criminals and Noncriminals. *Archives of General*

Psychiatry (in press).

Levinson, Boris The Future of Research into Relationships Between People and Their Animal Companions. *International Journal for the Study of Animal Problems,* 3(4): 283-294, 1982.

Lorenz, Konrad *Man Meets Dog.* Baltimore: Penguin Books, 1965.

McCulloch, Michael Animal facilitated therapy: Overview and future direction. *California Veterinarian,* 36(8): 13-24, 1982.

Messent, Peter A Review of Recent Developments in Human-Companion Animal Studies. *California Veterinarian,* 37(5): 26-31, 1983.

Morris, Desmond *The Naked Ape.* New York: Dell Publishing Co., 1969, 177-197.

Petcare Information and Advisory Service *Pets As a Social Phenomenon: A Study of Man-Pet Interactions in Urban Communities.* Melbourne, Australia, 1976.

Randolph, Elizabeth Loving Bonds: Pets and People. *Family Circle,* 11/24/81, 18.

Salt, H. *Animal rights: considered in relation to social progress.* Clarks Summit, Pa.: Society for Animal Rights, 1980.

White, Betty with Watson, Thomas *Betty White's Pet Love: How Pets Take Care Of Us.* New York: William Morrow and Co., 1983.

Human-Animal Bond: Conferences and Proceedings

Proceedings of the National Conference on the Ecology of the Surplus Dog and Cat Problem. Denver: American Humane Association, May 21-23, 1974 (Chicago).

Proceedings of the National Conference on Dog and Cat Control. Denver: American Humane Association. Feb. 3-6, 1976 (Denver).

Yoxall, A. (ed.) *Proceedings of a meeting held at the University of Dundee.* Dundee, Scotland: University of Dundee, March, 1979.

The Inaugural Seminar of the Joint Advisory Committee On Pets In Society. Melbourne, Australia: Petcare Information and Advisory Service, Sept. 3, 1980.

Katcher, Aaron and Beck, Alan (eds.) *New Perspectives on our Lives with Animal Companions.* Philadelphia: University of Pennsylvania Press, 1983. (Proceedings of the International Conference on the Human/Companion Animal Bond, Philadelphia, Oct. 5-7, 1981).

Canadian Federation of Humane Societies and Canadian Veterinary Medical Association: *3rd Symposium: Pets in Society: The Social Importance of Pets in an Aging Society: Proceedings.* Toronto: Pet Food Manufacturers Association, April 28-30, 1982.

Anderson, Robert, Hart, Benjamin and Hart, Lynette (eds.) *The Pet Connection: Its Influence on our Health and Quality of Life.* South St.

Paul, Minn.: Globe Publishing Co., 1984. (Proceedings of the 1983 Conferences on the Human/Animal Bond, June 13-14, 1983, University of Minnesota and June 17-18, 1983, University of California-Irvine.)

Proceedings of the International Symposium on the Human-Pet Relationship. Renton, Wash.: Oct. 27-28, 1983 (Vienna).

Animals as therapeutic aids

Correctional institutions

Curtis, Patricia Animals are good for the handicapped, perhaps all of us. *Smithsonian,* July 1981, 48-57.

Hines, Linda Pets in Prison: A New Partnership. *California Veterinarian,* 37(5): 6-17, 1983.

"Hi Ya, Beautiful" (film) Alameda, Calif.: Latham Foundation

Levinson, Boris Household pets in residential schools. *Mental Hygiene,* 1968, *52,* 411-414.

Levinson, Boris Household pets in training schools serving delinquent children. *Psychological Reports,* 1971, *28,* 475-481.

Rosenblatt, Rae When Society's Strays—Men & Cats—Meet in Prison. *American Humane Magazine,* August 1976, 14-15.

Equestrian therapy

"Ability, Not Disability" (film) Alameda, Calif.: Latham Foundation

Davies, John *Reins of Life.* London: J.A. Allen & Co., 1967.

Haipertz, Wolfgang *Therapeutic Riding: Medicine, Education, Sports.* Ottawa: Canadian Equestrian Federation, 1982.

Hulsey, Robin *Horseback Riding for the Hearing Impaired.* Chesterfield, Mo.: Riding High, 1979.

McCowan, Lida *It Is Ability That Counts.* Olivet, Mich.: Olivet College Press, 1972.

Rosenfeld, Judith They've Finally Got an Edge! *American Education.* May 1979, 20-26.

Small, Mary And Alice Did the Walking. London: Oxford Unversity Press, 1978.

Williams, Corinne Horsemanship for the handicapped. *Western Horseman,* September 1971, 67-70.

Guide dogs

Coon, Nelson *A Brief History of Dog Guides for the Blind.* Morristown, N.J.: The Seeing Eye, Inc., 1959.

Curtis, Patricia *Cindy: The Story of A Hearing-Ear Dog.* New YorK: E.P. Dutton, 1981.

Curtis, Patricia *Greff: The Story of a Guide Dog.* New York: Lodestar/

Dutton, 1982.

Gibbs, Margaret *Leader Dogs for the Blind.* Fairfax, Va.: Denlinger's Publishers, Ltd., 1982.

Hartwell, Dickson *Dogs Against Darkness.* New York: Dodd Mead and Co., 1942.

Rappaport, Eva *"Banner, Forward!"* New York: E.P. Dutton, 1969.

Long-term care facilities

Brickel, Clark The therapeutic roles of cat mascots with a hospital-based geriatric population: A staff survey. *The Gerontologist,* 19(4):368-371, 1979.

Hines, Linda *The People-Pet Partnership Program.* Alameda, Calif.: Latham Foundation, 1980.

Lee, Ronnal, et al., *Guidelines: Animals in Nursing Homes.* Renton, Wash: Delta Society, 1987.

Levinson, Boris Nursing Home Pets: A Psychological Adventure for the Patient. *National Humane Review,* July-August and September-October, 1970.

McLeod, Cappy *Animals in the Nursing Home: Guide for Activity Directors.* Colorado Springs, Colo.: By the author, 1982.

Robb, Susanne and Miller, Ruth *Pilot Study of Pet-Dog Therapy for Elderly People in Long Term Care: Final Report.* Pittsburgh: VA Medical Center, 1982.

Robb, Susanne, et al. A wine bottle, plant and puppy: Catalysts for social behaviors. *Journal of Gerontological Nursing,* 1980, 6, 721-728.

Salmon, I.M. and Salmon, P.W. *A Dog in Residence: A Companion-Animal Study Undertaken in the Caulfield Geriatric Hospital.* Melbourne, Australia: Joint Advisory Committee on Pets In Society, 1982.

Psychotherapy

Clayton, Florence *Pet-Oriented Therapy: Rationale, Application, Implications.* San Gabriel, Calif.: Unpublished master's thesis, 1972.

Corson, Samuel and Corson, Elizabeth Pets as mediators of therapy. In Masserman, J.H. (ed.) *Current Psychiatric Therapies.* New York: Grune & Stratton, 1979, 195-205.

Harvey, Alice Pets Help Schizophrenics Respond to Outside World. *Clinical Psychiatry News,* May 1982, 19.

Levinson, Boris *Pet-Oriented Child Psychotherapy.* Springfield, Ill.: Charles C. Thomas, 1969.

Wolff, Ethel, *A Survey of the Use of Animals in Psychotherapy in the United States.* Denver: American Humane Association, 1970.

Yates, Elizabeth *Skeezer: Dog With a Mission.* Irvington-on-Hudson, N.Y.:

Harvey House, 1973.

Guidebooks, models and demonstration projects

Arkow, Phil *How to Start a "Pet Therapy" Program.* Colorado Springs, Colo.: Humane Society of the Pikes Peak Region, 1984.

Corson, Samuel and Corson, Elizabeth *Proposal for Research Project Designed to Facilitate Therapy of Adult and Adolescent Psychiatric and Psychosomatic Patients and Shorten Hospitalization Stay.* Columbus, Ohio: Ohio State University, 1973.

Hines, Linda *Establishing a People-Pet Partnership Program.* Alameda, Calif.: Latham Foundation, 1982.

Lee, Ronnal et al., *Guidelines: Animals in the Nursing Home.* Renton, Wash.: 1987.

Maryland Department of Health and Mental Hygiene *The Maryland Companion Pet Program, Demonstration Project.* Baltimore: Division of Veterinary Medicine, 201 W. Preston St., 1982.

McLeod, Cappy *Animals in the Nursing Home: Guide for Activity Directors.* Colorado Springs, Colo.: By the author, 1981.

Monterey County SPCA *Pet Visitation Program: Guidebook for volunteers.* Monterey, Calif., 1982.

PACT (People and Animals Coming Together) *PACT: Promoting Bonded Relationships Between People and Animals.* University Park, Pa.: College of Human Development, Pennsylvania State University, 1983.

Wolfle, Thomas *Outline for Proposed Guide for Companion Animal Programs.* Washington: National Institutes of Health, 1982.

Animal behavior, breeding, training and selection

American Kennel Club *The Complete Dog Book,* New York: Howell Book House, Inc., 1980.

Dunbar, Ian *Dog Behavior: Why Dogs Do What They Do.* Neptune, N.J.: TFH Publications, 1979.

Fox, Michael *Understanding Your Dog.* New York: Coward, McCann and Geoghegan, Inc., 1972.

Hart, Benjamin and Hart, Lynette Selecting the Best Companion Animal: Breed Specific Behavioral Profiles. In: Anderson, R.K., et al. (eds.), *The Pet Connection: Its Influence on our Health and Quality of Life.* South St. Paul, Minn.: Globe Publishing Co., 1984.

Lorenz, Konrad *Studies in Animal and Human Behavior.* Cambridge: Harvard University Press, 1970.

The Monks of New Skete *How to Be Your Dog's Best Friend.* Boston: Little, Brown & Co., 1978.

Randolph, Elizabeth *How to Be Your Cat's Best Friend.* Boston: Little,

Brown & Co., 1981.

Woodhouse, Barbara *No Bad Dogs: The Woodhouse Way.* New York: Summit Books, 1978.

Human health implications of pet ownership

Cooper, J. Pets in hospitals. British Medical Journal, 1976, 1, 698-700.

Friedmann, Erika *et al.* Animal companions and one-year survival of patients after discharge from a coronary care unit. *Public Health Reports,* 1980, *95*(4), 307-312.

Journal of the American Medical Association Patient progressing well? He may have a pet. Feb 2, 1979, *24* (5), 438.

Journal of the American Veterinary Medical Association. Pets by Prescription: A Novel Program of Minnesota Humane Society. Nov. 1, 1972, 971.

"Intimate Companions" (film) Garden City, N.Y.: Adelphi University, 1984.

Lynch, James *The Broken Heart—The Medical Consequences of Loneliness.* New York: Basic Books, 1977.

Katcher, Aaron and Friedmann, Erika Potential Health Value of Pet Ownership. *California Veterinarian* 36(7): 9-13, 1982.

Wille, Rosanne *Study of the relationship between pet ownership and health status.* New Brunswick, N.J.: Rutgers University, 1982.

Pet loss and grief

Grollman, E. *Explaining Death to Children.* Boston: Beacon Press, 1967.

Kubler-Ross, E. *Death, the Final State of Growth.* Englewood Cliffs, N.J.: Prentice-Hall, 1975.

Nieburg, Herbert and Fischer, Arlene *Pet Loss - A Thoughtful Guide for Adults and Children.* New York: Harper and Row, 1982.

Pet Loss and Human Emotion. Schaumburg, Ill.: American Veterinary Medical Association, 1984.

Pets and human/child development

Condoret, Ange For a Biology of Childhood Behavior: The Child's Relationships with Household Pets and Domestic Animals. *Bulletin of the French Veterinary Academy,* 1977, 50, 481-490.

Harris, Judy Dogs Contribute to Ego Strength: Highlights from an MA Thesis. *Latham Letter,* 3(1): 2, 1981-82.

Pets and the elderly

Bustad, Leo *Animals, Aging and the Aged.* Minneapolis: University of Minnesota Press, 1980.

Bustad, Leo and Hines, Linda Placement of animals with the elderly:

Benefits and strategies. *California Veterinarian* 36(8):37-44, 1982.

Cusack, Odean and Smith, Elaine *Pets and the Elderly: The Therapeutic Bond.* New York: The Haworth Press, 1984.

Kidd, Aline and Feldman, Bruce Pet ownership and self-perceptions of older people. *Psychological Reports,* 1981, *48,* 867-875.

Levinson, Boris Pets and old age. Mental Hygiene, 1969, *53* 364-368.

Robb, Susanne and Stegman, Charles Companion animals and elderly people: A challenge for evaluators of social support. *The Gerontologist,* 1983, *23,* 277-282.

Veterinarians and the bond

Harris, James A Study of Client Grief Responses to Death or Loss in a Companion Animal Veterinary Practice. *California Veterinarian,* 36(12): 17-19, 1982.

Journal of the American Veterinary Medical Association. AVMA Guidelines for Veterinarians: Animal-facilitated therapy programs. 184(2), 146-148, Jan. 15, 1984.

Katcher, Aaron and Rosenberg, Marc Euthanasia and the Management of the Client's Grief. *Compendium on Continuing Education,* 1(12): 887-890, 1979.

McCulloch, William and McCulloch, Michael The Practicing Veterinarian—Contributions to Comparative Medicine. *California Veterinarian,* 36(8): 26-30, 1982.

Resource organizations

Animal health and care

Animal Medical Center — (212) TE8-8100
510 E. 62nd St.
New York, N.Y. 10021

American Animal Hospital Association — (303) 279-2500
P.O. Box 15899
Denver, Colo. 80215

American Boarding Kennel Association — (303) 591-1113
4575 Galley Rd. #400-A
Colorado Springs, Colo. 80915

American Veterinary Medical Association — (312) 885-8070
930 N. Meacham Rd.
Schaumburg Ill. 60196

California Veterinary Medical Association — (916) 921-9300
655 University Ave. #115
Sacramento, CA 95825

International Association of Pet Cemeteries — (312) 231-1117
27 West 150 North Ave.
West Chicago, Ill. 60185

Animal information and publicity

Petcare Information and Advisory Service
117 Collins St.
Melbourne 3000, Australia

Pet Food Institute — (202) 847-1120
1101 Connecticut Ave. #700
Washington, D.C. 20001

Pet Food Manufacturers' Association of Canada — (416) 429-1074
1185 Eglinton Ave. East #101
Don Mills, Ont., Canada M3C 3C6

Pet Information Bureau
518 Fifth Ave.
New York, N.Y. 10036

Pets Are Wonderful Council — (312) 836-7145
500 N. Michigan Ave. #200

Chicago, Ill. 60611

Ralston-Purina Pet Adoption Services (314) 982-3974
Checkerboard Square
St. Louis, Mo. 63164

Animal welfare and control

American Humane Association (303) 695-0811
9725 E. Hampden Ave.
Denver, Colo. 80231

American Kennel Club (212) 481-9380
51 Madison Ave.
New York, N.Y. 10010

Humane Society of the Pikes Peak Region (303) 473-1741
633 S. 8th Street
Colorado Springs, Colo. 80901

Humane Society of the United States (202) 452-1100
2100 L St. N.W.
Washington, D.C. 20037

Latham Foundation (415) 521-0920
Latham Plaza Building
Clement and Schiller Streets
Alameda, Calif. 94501

Massachusetts Society for the Prevention of Cruelty to Animals/American Humane Education Society (617) 237-2310
P.O. Box 2314
Framingham, Mass. 01701

National Animal Control Association (206) 297-3293
P.O. Box 321
Indianola, Wash. 98342

National Association for the Advancement of Humane Education (203) 434-8666
P.O. Box 98
East Haddam, Conn. 06423

San Francisco Society for the Prevention of Cruelty to Animals (415) 621-1700
2500 16th Street
San Francisco, Calif. 94103

Society of Animal Welfare Administrators (612) 522-4325

845 Meadow Lane North
Minneapolis, Minn. 55422

Hospice programs

Love A Pet (LAP) Program (202) 337-0120
MacArthur Animal Hospital
4832 MacArthur Blvd.
Washington, D.C. 20007

St. Christophers Hospice 01-778-9252
51-53 Lawrie Park Rd.
Sydenham, England SE26-6DZ

St. Vincent's Hospital and Health Care Center (317) 871-2345
Hospice Program and Stress Center
2001 W. 86th Street
Indianapolis, Ind. 46260

Program certification and training

Canine Companions for Independence (707) 528-0830
P.O. Box 446
Santa Rosa, Calif. 95402

Hearing Dogs International (617) 829-9519
Bryant Hill Farm
76 Bryant Rd.
Jefferson, MA 01522

North American Riding for the Handicapped Association (312) 644-6610
111 E. Wacker Dr. #600
Chicago, IL 60601

Programs for long-term care facilities and the elderly

American Health Care Association (202) 833-2050
1200 15th Street
Washington, D.C. 20005

Companion Animal Association of Arizona (602) 258-3306
P.O. Box 13606
Phoenix, Ariz. 85002

National Association of Activity Professionals (213) 684-1100
P.O. Box 90130
Pasadena, Calif. 91109

Scientific and research organizations

Center for the Interaction of Animals and Society (215) 243-4695
3800 Spruce St.
University of Pennsylvania
Philadelphia, Pa. 19104

Center to Study Human-Animal Relationships and Environments (CENSHARE) (612) 373-8032
1-117 Health Sciences Unit A
515 Delaware St. S.E.
University of Minnesota
Minneapolis, Minn. 55455

Delta Society (206) 226-7357
321 Burnett Ave. South, #303
Renton, Wash. 98055

Human-Animal Relation Center (916) 752-1383
School of Veterinary Medicine,
University of California
Davis, Calif. 95616

People and Animals Coming Together (PACT) (814) 865-1717
S-110 Henderson Human Development Building
Pennsylvania State University, University Park, Pa. 16802

Tufts Center for Animals (617) 956-7603
203 Harrison Ave. School of Veterinary Medicine
Boston, MA 02111

Society for Companion Animal Studies 0-664-64117
Freeby Lane, Waltham-on-the-Wolds,
Melton Mowbray, Leicestershire, England

Training programs

See Chapters 8 and 9 for directories of Dog Guide Schools training dogs to help the blind, and training schools to train animals to help the handicapped and hearing-impaired

Other Resource Material

Films and audio-visual materials

Adelphi Productions "Intimate Companions"
Blodgett Studio, Adelphi University
Garden City, N.Y. 11530
(516) 294-8700 x7369

Source	Film
Canine Companions for Independence P.O. Box 446 Santa Rosa, Calif. 95402 (707) 528-0830	"Canine Companions for Independence"
Canine Consultants 600 Country Lane Cary, N.C. 27511	"I Thought You Said Your Dog Didn't Bite!"
FilmFair Communications 10900 Ventura Blvd. Studio City, Calif. 91604 (213) 985-0244	"A Special Friendship"
Filmmakers Library 133 E. 58th St. #703A New York, N.Y. 10022 (212) 355-6545	"Companions"
International Film Foundation 475 Fifth Ave. New York, N.Y. 10017 (212) 580-1111	"Bill, Peggy, Roy and Friends —London Horses"
ITC Entertainment 115 E. 57th Street New York, N.Y. 10022 (212) 371-6660	"Skeezer"
Kinetic Films 255 Delaware Ave. #340 Buffalo, N.Y. 14202 (716) 856-7631	"Who Cares, Anyway?"
Latham Foundation Latham Plaza Building Clement and Schiller Street Alameda, Calif., 94501 (415) 521-0920	Human/Companion Animal Bond "Just a Little Hope" "P.A.C.T. - People and Animals Coming Together" It's a Very Special Privilege" "Ability, Not Disability" "Hi Ya, Beautiful" "The Phenomenon of the Human/Companion Animal Bond" "Pet-Facilitated Therapy" "Institution Without Walls" "Canine Companions for Independence"

Organization	Titles
	Humane Education "Animal Control, Who Needs It?" "Cat Tale" "Doing a Good Job" "The Family Chooses a Pet" "Heel, Sit, Stay, Come" "How to Raise a Puppy and Live Happily Everafter" "To Care is to Love" "What is a Dog?" "What is a Cat?"
Leader Dogs for the Blind 1039 S. Rochester Rd Rochester, Mich. 48063 (313) 651-9011	
Learning Corporation of America 1350 Avenue of the Americas New York, N.Y. 10019 (212) 397-9330	
National Animal Control Association P.O. Box 187 Colorado Springs, Colo. 80901 (303) 473-1741	"Today's Animal Control" "Dog Tags—More Than Meets the Eye"
North American Riding for the Handicapped Association P.O. Box 100 Ashburn, Va. 22011	"Exceptional Equestrians" "The Right to Choose" "But I Can Ride a Pony"
Phoenix Films 470 Park Ave. New York, N.Y. 10016 (212) 684-5910	"Manimals"
Pyramid Films Box 1048 Santa Monica, Calif. 90406 (213) 828-7577	"Animals Can Bite"
Roycemore School 640 Lincoln St. Evanston, Ill. 60201 (312) 866-6055	"Pet Pals"

University of Minnesota - CENSHARE
1-117 Health Sciences Unit A
515 Delaware St. S.E.
Minneapolis, Minn. 55455
(612) 373-8032

"Three is Company... Not a Crowd"

University of Minnesota - Independent Study
55 Wesbrook Hall
77 Pleasant St. S.E.
Minneapolis, Minn. 55455

"Perspectives: Interrelationships of People and Animals in Society Today" (Independent study audio cassette course: 20 ½-hour programs)

Publications

Delta Society
321 Burnett Ave. South, #303
Renton, Wash. 98055
(206) 226-7357

Interactions Anthrozoos: The Journal of The Delta Society

Latham Foundation
Latham Plaza Building
Clement & Schiller Streets
Alameda, Calif. 94501
(415) 521-0920

The Latham Letter

Appendix II: Research Directory

A Guide to On-Going Research Activities and Human/Companion Animal Bond Studies

Animal behavior, breeding and selection

Borchelt, Peter (Animal Behavior Therapy Clinic, New York)
- Preventing behavior problems through breeding, socialization and training
- Separation and attachment to pets and the resulting animal behavior problems

Deitrich, Craig (Guide Dogs for the Blind, San Rafael, Calif.)
- Temperament evaluation in puppies used in guide dog selection

Dunbar, Ian (Psychology Department, University of California -Berkeley)
- Animal behavior and owners' expectations

Hart, Benjamin, and Hart, Lynette (School of Veterinary Medicine, University of California - Davis)
- Selecting the best companion animal: breed-specific behavioral profiles

Houpt, Katherine (College of Veterinary Medicine, Cornell University)
- Aggressive behavior in dogs as disrupting the H/CAB

Karsh, Eileen (Psychology Department, Temple University)
- Factors influencing the socialization of cats to people

Scott, John (Bowling Green State University)
- Manual on training of dogs and measurements

Anthropology and the bond

Fisher, Maxine (Queens College)
- Why people taboo as food those species they regard as pets

Lawrence, Elizabeth (Department of Environmental Studies, School of Veterinary Medicine, Tufts University)
- Human relationships with horses

Ruby, Jay (Anthropology Department, Temple University)
- Methodology of examining family photographs to determine pets'
- roles

Savishinsky, Joel (Department of Anthropology, Ithaca College)
- Anthropological study of companion animal program at a nursing home
- Variations in pet-keeping patterns in different cultures

Schwabe, Calvin (Department of Epidemiology and Preventive Medicine, School of Veterinary Medicine, University of California - Davis)
- Drinking cow's milk as the most intensive man-animal bond

Elderly people and pets

Burt, Marianna, et al. (Massachusetts SPCA, Framingham, Mass.)
- Case study in private pet ownership by the elderly

Bustad, Leo and Hines, Linda (College of Veterinary Medicine, Washington State University)
- Placement of animals with the elderly: benefits and strategies

Connell, Cathleen and Lago, Daniel (Department of Individual and Family Studies, College of Human Development, Pennsylvania State University)
- Favorable attitudes toward pets and happiness among the elderly

Karsh, Eileen (Psychology Department, Temple University)
- Two-year following study of psychological and physical benefits of elderly persons with cats

Lago, Daniel, Connell, Cathleen, and Knight, Barbara (Department of Individual and Family studies, College of Human Development, Pennsylvania State University)
- Community-based companion animal programs
- Rural-elderly persons' relationships with companion animals

McCulloch, Michael (Portland, Ore.)
- Pets in therapeutic programs for the aged

New, J.C. (University of Tennessee)
- Pet placement with community-based elderly receiving in-home services

Ory, Marcia and Goldberg, Evelyn (National Institutes on Aging and Department of Epidemiology, School of Hygiene and Public Health, Johns Hopkins University)
- Epidemiological study of pet ownership in the community
- Pet possession and life satisfaction in elderly women

Farm animals and bond programs

DePauw, Karen (Department of Physical Education, Washington State University)
- Therapeutic horseback riding in Europe and North America

Diesch, Stanley (CENSHARE, College of Veterinary Medicine, University of Minnesota)
- Human-animal bonds with farm animals

Dismuke, Ruth (Therapeutic Horsemanship of New Mexico, Sandia Park, N.M.)
- Rehabilitative horseback riding for children with language disorders

Kilgour, Ron (Hamilton, New Zealand)
- Role of human-animal bonds in farm animals and welfare issues

Ross, Samuel, et al. (Green Chimneys, Brewster, N.Y.)
- Effects of farm programming with emotionally handicapped children

Handicapped persons and pets

Bieber, Natalie (Southern Connecticut State College)
- Therapeutic equestrian programs for children with physical and multiple disabilities

DePauw, Karen (Department of Physical Education, Washington State University)
- Therapeutic horseback riding in Europe and North America

Zee, Alysia (School of Social Work, University of Pennsylvania)
- Social and psychological significance of guide dogs for the blind

History, culture and the bond

Bustad, Leo and Burt, Marianna (People-Pet Partnership Program, Washington State University)
- Impact of history, literature and art on teaching reverence for life

Bustad, Leo and Hines, Linda (People-Pet Partnership Program, Washington State University)
- Historical perspectives of the human-animal bond

Levinson, Boris (Yeshiva University)
- Future of research into relationships between people and their animal companions

McCulloch, William (College of Veterinary Medicine, Texas A & M University)
- Historical overviews of the human/animal bond

ten Bensel, Robert (CENSHARE, University of Minnesota)
- Historical perspectives of human values for animals and vulnerable people

Human health implications

Anderson, Robert (CENSHARE, School of Public Health, University of Minnesota)
- A description of the responsibilities of veterinarians as they relate to human health

Atlas, Jerry et al. (Long Island University)
- Potential physiological and psychological benefits of pet-facilitated therapy

Baun, Mara, et al. (College of Nursing, University of Nebraska)
- Physiological effects of petting dogs: influences of attachment

Friedmann, Erika, et al. (Center for the Interaction of Animals and Society, School of Veterinary Medicine, University of Pennsylvania)
- Animal companions and one-year survival of patients after discharge from a coronary care unit.
- Significance of companion animals during hospitalization

Katcher, Aaron, et al. (Center for the Interaction of Animals and Society, School of Veterinary Medicine, University of Pennsylvania)
- Talking, looking and blood pressure: physiological consequences of interaction with the living environment
- Contemplation of an aquarium for the reduction of anxiety

Wille, Rosanne (College of Nursing, Rutgers University)
- Relationships between pet companionship and health status

Institutions and animals

Hines, Linda (People-Pet Partnership Program, Washington State University)
- Pets in prison: a new partnership

Levinson, Boris (Graduate School of Humanities and Social Sciences, Yeshiva University)
- Household pets in training schools serving delinquent children

Long-term care facilities

Anderson, Robert and Quigley, Joseph (CENSHARE, School of Public Health, University of Minnesota)
- Analysis of laws and regulations restricting companion animals in nursing homes

Andrysco, Robert (Ohio State University)
- Pet-facilitated therapy in a retirement nursing care community

Blake, Dorothy Sewell (Columbia University)
-Introduction of pets to institutionalized elderly

Brickel, Clark (Department of Psychology, University of Southern

California)
- Depression in the nursing home: pilot study using pet-facilitated psychotherapy
- Pet-facilitated psychotherapy: a theoretical explanation via attention shifts
- Therapeutic roles of cat mascots with a hospital-based geriatric population: a staff survey

Corson, Samuel and Corson, Elizabeth (Psychiatry Department, Ohio State University)
- Companion animals as bonding catalysts in geriatric institutions

Francis, Gloria (School of Nursing, Virginia Commonwealth University)
- Impact of domestic animal visits on nursing home populations

Hendy, Helen (Psychology Department, Pennsylvania State University)
- Effects of pets on the sociability and health activities of nursing home residents

Jendro, Connie, et al. (VA Medical Center, St. Cloud, Minn.)
- Effects of pets on the chronically-ill elderly

Olsen, Geary, et al. (CENSHARE, University of Minnesota)
- Guidelines for planning, implementing and evaluating nursing home pet-facilitated therapy programs
- Study of the utilization of pet-facilitated therapy in Minnesota health care facilities

Robb, Susanne (VA Medical Center, Pittsburgh, Pa.)
- Pets as catalysts for social behavior

Robb, Susanne and Miller, Ruth (VA Medical Center, Pittsburgh, Pa.)
Pilot study of pet dog therapy for elderly people in long-term care

Salmon, I.M. and Salmon, P.W. (JACOPIS, Melbourne, Australia)
- "Dog in residence" - Companion animal study at Caulfield Geriatric Hospital

Thompson, Mary (VA Medical Center, Coatesville, Pa.)
- Behavior changes in psychiatric patients with pets and establishing guidelines for pet-facilitated therapy in institutions

Torrence, Mary (Charleston, W.Va.)
- Veterinarians' roles in pet-facilitated therapy in nursing homes

Wilson, Cindy (University of Tennessee)
- Measuring the effects of companion animal intervention on the health of elderly populations at senior citizen homes through functional assessment inventory

Loss of a pet and grief management

Katcher, Aaron and Rosenberg, Marc (Center for the Interaction of

Animals and Society, School of Veterinary Medicine, University of Pennsylvania)
- Euthanasia and the management of the client's grief

Quackenbush, James (Center for the Interaction of Animals and Society, School of Veterinary Medicine, University of Pennsylvania)
- Pet bereavement in older owners

Stewart, Mary (Veterinary Hospital, University of Glasgow)
- Comparative study of bereavement with loss of a pet and loss of a person

Pets and human behavior

Adell-Bath, M., et al. (School of Social Sciences, University of Gothenburg)
- Do we need dogs? Study of dogs' social significance to man

Brown, Donna (Psychology Department, Duke University)
- Personality and gender influences on human relationships with horses and dogs

Cain, Ann (School of Nursing, University of Maryland)
- Dimensions of attachment between people and their animals
- Study of pets in the family system

Friedmann, Erika, et al. (Department of Health Science, Brooklyn College)
- Pet ownership and psychological status

Katcher, Aaron, et al. (Center for the Interaction of Animals and Society, School of Veterinary Medicine, University of Pennsylvannia)
- Men, women and dogs: sex-based degrees of attachment

Kellert, Stephen (School of Forestry and Environmental Studies, Yale University)
- Typology of nine attitudes towards animals with social and demographic variables

Kellert, Stephen and Felthous, Alan (School of Forestry and Environmental Studies, Yale University and Menninger Memorial Hospital, Topeka, Kans.)
- Childhood cruelty toward animals among criminals and noncriminals

Kidd, Aline, et al. (Psychology Department, Mills College)
- Personality characteristics of horse, turtle, snake and bird owners
- Pet ownership and self-perceptions of older people

Lockwood, Randall (State University of New York - Stony Brook)
- Influence of animals on social perception

Ludwig, Edward and Larson, David (Department of Sociology, State University of New York - Fredonia)
- Inverse relationship between participation in sports and importance attached to pets

- Social correlates of pet ownership

Messent, Peter (Animal Studies Center, Waltham-on-the-Wolds, England)
- Social facilitation of contacts with other people by pet dogs

Okoniewski, Lisa (Philadelphia, Pa.)
- Comparison of human-human and human-animal relationships

Salk, Lee (Cornell University Medical Center)
- Emotional and educational benefits of pet ownership

Salmon, Peter (Victoria, Australia)
- Psychological research into the human-pet bond in Australia

Sanders, Robert (University of Toronto)
- Relationship between cruelty to animals in children and later anti-social activities

Serpell, James (University of Cambridge)
- Personalities of dogs and their owners

Signorielli, Nancy (Annenberg School of Communications, University of Pennsylvania)
- Protocol to examine television programming of animals and how it affects attitudes and expectations

Simon, Leonard (New York, N.Y.)
- Negative effects of pet ownership on families and individuals: the "pet trap"

Smith, Sharon (Center for the Interaction of Animals and Society, School of Veterinary Medicine, University of Pennsylvania)
- Interactions between pet dogs and family members

ten Bensel, Robert, et al. (CENSHARE, School of Public Health and Department of Sociology, University of Minnesota)
- Attitudes of violent criminals toward animals

Vogel, Lyle, et al. (School of Public Health, University of Minnesota)
- Study of perceptions and attitudes towards pet ownership

Pets and human development

Condoret, Ange (Bordeaux, France)
- A biology of childhood behavior: child's relationships with household pets and domestic animals
- Speech and companion animals: experience with normal and disturbed nursery school children

Gislason, Less, et al. (Department of Psychiatry, University of California - Irvine)
- The human-animal bond in children with attention deficit disorder

Hutton, J.S. (Hitchin Herts., England)
- Animal abuse as a diagnostic approach in social work

Kellert, Stephen (School of Forestry and Environmental Studies, Yale University)
- Attitudes towards animals: age-related development among children

Robin, Michael, et al. (CENSHARE, University of Minnesota)
- Abused children and their pets
- Study of the relationship between childhood pet animals and the psycho-social development of adolescents

Psychotherapy

Corson, Samuel and Corson, Elizabeth, et al., Psychiatry Department, Ohio State University)
- Ethology and nonverbal communication in mental health
- Pets as mediators of therapy
- Pet-facilitated psychotherapy
- Pet dogs as nonverbal communication links in hospital psychiatry

McCulloch, Michael (Portland, Ore.)
- The pet as prosthesis: defining criteria for the adjunctive use of companion animals in the treatment of mentally ill, depressed outpatients

Van de Castle, Robert (School of Medicine, University of Virginia)
- Animal figures in dreams: age, sex and cultural differences

Wallin, Pauline (School of Public Health, University of Minnesota)
- Psychological factors in pet ownership

Public health implications

Arkow, Philip (Humane Society of the Pikes Peak Region, Colorado Springs, Colo.)
- The ties which do not bind: human-companion animal bonds which fail

Beck, Alan et al. (Center for the Interaction of Animals and Society, School of Veterinary Medicine, University of Pennsylvania)
- Companion animals in society—legal, ecological and public health aspects
- Pre-disposing factors in severe or fatal dog bites

Catanzaro, Thomas (U.S. Army Health Services Command, Ft. Sam Houston, Tex.)
- The human-animal bond in military communities

DeGroot, Alice (Animal Care and Education Center, Rancho Santa Fe, Calif.)
- Characteristics of animals surrendered to a shelter

Jones, Barbara and Beck, Alan (Center for the Interaction of Animals and Society, School of Veterinary Medicine, University of Pennsylvania)

- Development of human-animal bond curricula for school children
- Unreported dog bites and attitudes towards dogs

Neil, David (Department of Animal Care, Colorado State University)
- Research into canine-human urban ecology

Ory, Marcia and Goldberg, Evelyn (National Institute on Aging and Department of Epidemiology, School of Hygiene and Public Health, Johns Hopkins University)
- Epidemiological study of pet ownership in the community

Research methodologies

Olsen, Geary et al. (CENSHARE, Division of Epidemiology, School of Public Health, University of Minnesota)
-Evaluating pet-facilitated therapy in long-term care facilities

Robb, Susanne (VA Medical Center, Pittsburgh, Pa.)
-The challenge of research and research-based solutions

Veterinarians and the bond

Anderson, Robert (CENSHARE, University of Minnesota)
- Description of the responsibilities of veterinarians as they relate to human health

Beaver, Bonnie (College of Veterinary Medicine, Texas A & M University)
- Veterinarian's role in prescribing pets

Bustad, Leo (The Delta Society, Renton, Washington)
- The veterinarian and animal-facilitated therapy

DeGroot, Alice (Animal Care and Education Center, Rancho Santa Fe, Calif.)
- Veterinarians' ability to cope with the stress of euthanasia

Hopkins, Alton (Dallas, Tex.)
- Ethical implications in issues and decisions in companion animal medicine

Katcher, Aaron and Rosenberg, Marc (Center for the Interaction of Animals and Society, School of Veterinary Medicine, University of Pennsylvania)
- Euthanasia and the management of client's grief

McCulloch, Michael (Portland Ore.)
-Veterinary contributions to mental health

McCulloch, William and McCulloch, Michael (College of Veterinary Medicine, Texas A & M University)
- The human-companion animal bond in veterinary education
- The veterinarian and the human-companion animal bond

McLeod, James (College of Veterinary Medicine, University of Minnesota)

- Guidelines for veterinarians in companion animal programs

Quackenbush, James (Center for the Interaction of Animals and Society, School of Veterinary Medicine, University of Pennsylvania)

- Pets, owners, problems and the veterinarian: applied social work in a veterinary teaching hospital

Schwabe, Calvin (Department of Epidemiology and Preventive Medicine, School of Veterinary Medicine, University of California - Davis)

- Veterinary medicine and human health

Torrence, Mary (Charleston, W.Va.)

- Veterinarian's role in pet-facilitated therapy in nursing homes

Miscellaneous

Hines, Linda (Renton, Wash.)

- Basic references on human-animal interactions

Pitcoff, Paul, et al. (Communications Department, Adelphi University)

- Films on potential of pet-facilitated therapy and visual role model on how to start a pet-facilitated therapy program

Smith, Betsy (School of Public Affairs and Services, Florida International University)

-Using dolphins to elicit communications from an autistic child

THE LATHAM FOUNDATION HOPES THAT YOU HAVE FOUND THIS BOOK ENJOYABLE, STIMULATING AND BENEFICIALLY THOUGHT-PROVOKING. FOR OVER 65 YEARS THE LATHAM FOUNDATION HAS UTILIZED ITS MODEST RESOURCES AND EFFORTS TOWARDS THE ENRICHMENT OF ALL LIFE THAT SHARES THIS PLANET, EARTH. EARNESTLY PROMOTING THE PUBLIC'S RECOGNITION OF THE BENEFITS OF "THE LOVING BOND" IS YET ANOTHER WAY OF HELPING TO ACHIEVE THE FOUNDATION'S GOAL. OTHER MAJOR ACTIVITIES AND SERVICES INCLUDE THE PRODUCTION OF EDUCATIONAL FILMS, VIDEOTAPES, PERIODICALS, SYMPOSIUMS AND EDUCATIONAL PRESENTATIONS AND BIBLIOGRAPHIC MATERIAL FOR THE EXTENDED STUDY OF THE HUMAN/COMPANION ANIMAL BOND. DURING THE PAST 30 YEARS THE FOUNDATION HAS PRODUCED AND DISTRIBUTED YOUTH-ORIENTED TELEVISION PROGRAMS, NATIONALLY AND INTERNATIONALLY.

YOUR COMMENTS ABOUT THIS BOOK, LATHAM'S PURPOSES AND PUBLIC SERVICES WOULD BE WELCOMED—AS WOULD YOUR NEEDED FINANCIAL SUPPORT.

Please Send Me:

☐ Information about The Latham Foundation

☐ Latham's Television Programs

☐ Latham's Educational Film Catalog

☐ Educational Film and Videocassette Catalog

☐ Complimentary Copy of "The Latham Letter"

☐ List of Available Bibliography Materials

The Latham Foundation, Latham Plaza Building, Clement & Schiller Streets, Alameda, Calif. 94501 • (415) 521-0920.